CLINICAL ENCOUNTERS IN SEXUALITY

D1002869

The collection is very rich and raises the debate over the place of psychoanalysis in contemporary sexualities to a new level. The book is a must-read for anyone interested in psychoanalysis — clinicians and theorists alike."
— **Russell Grigg**, Psychoanalyst in Melbourne, Australia, author of *Lacan, Language, and Philosophy,* and co-editor of *Female Sexuality: The Early Psychoanalytic Controversies.*

"The relationship between psychoanalysis and sexuality has long been in need of a shake up. This remarkable collection of essays re-draws the lines of this encounter, offering provocative, exciting challenges to both its contributing authors and its readers. In a series of deft and insightful moves, Giffney and Watson have created a project that dares to speak to complexity by weaving together voices that utter the unexpected and harness experience to theory and practice. The result is often breathtaking, offering a compendium of personal, clinical and critical reflection that is both charged and compelling. The reader is invited in to grapple with the queer imperatives of the volume, so that the tapestry becomes ever more intricate. This is an important, passionate book, one that, by turns, tantalises and assuages as it interrogates the messy intimacies of multiple desire."
— **Caroline Bainbridge**, University of Roehampton, author of *A Feminine Cinematics* and *The Cinema of Lars von Trier,* and Film Editor of *The International Journal of Psychoanalysis.*

"Given the centrality of sexuality to theories of psychoanalysis, it is striking how little it is actually taught in institutes. This unique and creatively organized book seeks to remedy this lack, by creating a layered dialogue between academics writing queer and sexuality theories, practicing clinicians, and psychoanalytic theorists. The chapters pull the reader into an exciting liminal space where cultural, societal, and clinical discourses intermingle, creating embodied experiences of gender, sexualities, and sex. As editors, Giffney and Watson curate an encounter between queer theorists, clinicians and psychoanalytic theorists. But the experience of the encounter includes the reader, who has the invaluable opportunity to be a fly on the wall as these cross-disciplinary conversations unfold chapter by chapter. Reading this book is not a passive experience but one requiring active participation in an examination of the ways cultural discourses of sexuality shape transferences and clinical engagement. Most exciting was the historical register, where established theorists glance back to their own individual romances with psycho-analysis, sharing their initial hopes for the radical potentials of clinical theory and practice to transform our experiences. This radical potential of psychoanalysis is rekindled through the layered dialogues and passionate encounters captured in *Clinical Encounters in Sexuality*."

— **Katie Gentile**, Director, Gender Studies Program, John Jay College of Criminal Justice, CUNY and co-editor of the journal *Studies in Gender & Sexuality*.

"This great collection of essays fills an important gap in the often contested relationship between psychoanalysis and queer theory. Clinical cases presented here illustrate how people struggle with questions about their sexual identity and how troubles related to desire, drive, and *jouissance* attest that there is something inherently queer in human sexuality as such. For the first time we have a volume which opens a dialogue between different psychoanalytic schools and its perceptions of sexual identity. This book is essential reading for anyone who is dealing with the riddle of sexual difference. And who isn't!"

— **Renata Salecl**, Professor of Psychology and Psychoanalysis at Birkbeck, University of London, and Senior Researcher in Criminology in the Faculty of Law at the University of Ljubljana, Slovenia. Her books include *(Per)versions of Love and Hate*, *On Anxiety*, and *Tyranny of Choice*.

"'Rightly,' writes one of the psychoanalysts in this volume, 'Queer Theory has not always been respectful of psychoanalysis, and it is laudable that a serious attempt to engage with psychoanalysis has been promoted.' This book arises from the recognition that each 'partner' to this engagement is itself based on encoun-

ters — the two-way event of the clinic and the multiple events of queer desire. It goes beyond both the couch and the bed. In its three sections, queer theorists present key concepts; clinicians respond; and 'leading thinkers' take an overview. The result is a fascinating patchwork of ideas which places reading upon reading. Tones of voice, levels of sympathy and understanding vary — this may be "a provocatively uneasy intimacy" — but in the main this volume is indeed, as a third contributor notes, 'a rich repertoire of possibilities for getting creative with the differences that divide and connect us."'
— **Naomi Segal**, Birkbeck, University of London, author of *Consensuality: Didier Anzieu, Gender and the Sense of Touch* and translator of Didier Anzieu's *The Skin Ego*.

"Psychoanalysis and queer theory have a special interest in sexuality but usually follow diverging paths in framing its importance for human subjectivity. This volume brings together key scholars from both disciplines and engenders a fruitful encounter, with clinical and theoretical papers, as well as reflective essays. Enthusiasts of queer theory or psychoanalysis will find advanced papers relating to their interest, and will also be drawn to explore up-to-date viewpoints in each discipline. Students and advanced scholars alike will appreciate these subtle discussions."
— **Stijn Vanheule**, psychoanalyst, clinical psychologist, Professor of Psychoanalysis at Ghent University, Belgium, and author of *Psychiatric Diagnosis Revisited: From* DSM *to Clinical Case Formulation, Diagnosis and the* DSM: *A Critical Review* and *The Subject of Psychosis: A Lacanian Perspective.*

Fig. 1. Hieronymus Bosch, *Ship of Fools* (1490–1500)

First published in 2017 by punctum books, Earth, Milky Way.
www.punctumbooks.com

ISBN-13: 978-0-9985318-5-4
ISBN-10: 0-9985318-5-5
Library of Congress Cataloging Data is available from the Library of Congress

Book design: Vincent W.J. van Gerven Oei
Cover Image: Karla Black, *There Can Be No Arguments,* 2011. Polythene, plaster powder, paint, thread. 240 × 270 × 59 cm. Photo by Ruth Clark. Courtesy Galerie Gisela Capitain, Cologne.

CLINICAL ENCOUNTERS
in SEXUALITY

Psychoanalytic Practice & Queer Theory

edited by
Noreen Giffney & Eve Watson

For Nicole, three words: I love you

For Deirdre, you are, quite simply, the best

TABLE OF CONTENTS

Section 2 — Psychoanalytic Responses

ACKNOWLEDGMENTS

We would like to thank Eileen A. Joy, Vincent W.J. van Gerven Oei, and their colleagues at punctum books for their warm welcome, their enthusiasm for this book and their careful attention to the work. We particularly appreciate Eileen's vision, energy, intellectual courage and commitment to knowledge for its own sake. Rare gifts, which we recognize and value. This book took a long time to be published, due to its structure and content. We are grateful to the contributors who have shown great patience during this process. We are excited that you will finally get to meet all of your many different voices gathered together in one place. We extend our sincere thanks to Karla Black, Ruth Clark, and Galerie Gisela Capitain in Cologne for permission to use Ruth's image of Karla's sculpture, *There Can Be No Arguments,* on the front cover, and to Vincent van Gerven Oei for designing the cover. The cover image is the reader's first encounter with a book, and it has been so important to us to find an image that invites the reader into an experience, while at the same time not defining in advance what that experience might look like. We appreciate Robert Levy and Ona Nierenberg in New York for their help when we were initially trying to track down permissions for the cover image. Vincent has designed both the cover and the text. We admire his sense of style and feel fortunate that he has shared it with us and our book. We are also indebted to colleagues for their generous endorsement of the collection: Caroline Bainbridge, Lauren Berlant, Katie Gentile, Russell Grigg, Renata Salecl, Naomi Segal, and Stijn Vanheule. As those of us who publish know very well, we rely on the kindness of our colleagues who give their time freely to support and promote work in the fields in which we all write. And we would not be able to do the work that we do without the encouragement, guidance and friendship of colleagues in Ireland and beyond.

— Noreen Giffney and Eve Watson

Nicole Murray, you are my most important collaborator. No idea makes it into print without me first thinking it through with you. Eve Watson, you've been a trusted friend and supportive colleague in the psychoanalytic community in Dublin. What an experience this particular editing-encounter has been. Michael O'Rourke, we've been friends for over twenty years. I remember with deep fondness the creativity, vibrancy and hopefulness of our early meetings in the LGS, as we hammered out our wild ideas on the computer keyboard. Many people have welcomed me into the psychoanalytic community in Ireland in different ways and at different times: Margaret Boyle Spelman, Fran Burns, Olga Cox Cameron, Fionán Coyle, Sheena Eustace, Joanna Fortune, Mary Logue, Ian Miller, Liz Monahan, Ann Murphy, Berna O'Brien, Toni O'Brien Johnson, Pauline O'Callaghan, Anne O'Leary, Carol Owens, Mary Pyle, Silvia Roncalli, Medb Ruane, Michelle Sludds-Hickey, Caríosa Walsh, Marie Walshe, and Rob Weatherill.

— Noreen Giffney

Noreen Giffney, co-editor, fellow psychoanalytic practitioner, and good friend, without whom this book would not have been possible, and with whom it has been a joy to work. Noreen and Michael O'Rourke, who together established queer theory in Ireland, for their warm welcome, creativity and boundless spirit of openness, cooperation, and interdisciplinarity. It laid the groundwork for this book. Olga Cox Cameron in Dublin, perspicacious interlocutor, and Ian Parker in Manchester: psychoanalytic practitioners and exceptional interdisciplinarians, for their unflagging encouragement. Pauline O'Callaghan, Ona Nierenberg, and Annie Rogers, for generous parlaying and spirit lifting. Carol Owens, for publishing support over the years. All of my psychoanalytic and academic colleagues, whose support and collegiality is deeply treasured. Most importantly, Deirdre Kiely, for her inexhaustible love and encouragement. The encounters go on.

— Eve Watson

Clinical Encounters in Sexuality: Psychoanalytic Practice and Queer Theory[1]

Noreen Giffney

Clinical Encounters in Sexuality makes an intervention into the fields of clinical psychoanalysis and sexuality studies, in an effort to think about a range of issues relating to sexuality[2] from a clinical psychoanalytic perspective. This book concentrates on a number of concepts, namely identity, desire, pleasure, perversion, ethics, and discourse. Eve Watson and I have chosen queer theory, a sub-field of sexuality studies, as an interlocutor for the clinical contributors, because it is at the forefront of theoretical considerations of sexuality, as well as being both reliant upon and suspicious of psychoanalysis as a clinical practice and discourse. The book brings together a number of psychoanalytic

1   I am grateful to Eve Watson and Nicole Murray for extensive discussions about the themes discussed in this Introduction, and for their feedback on earlier drafts. An early version of this Introduction was discussed at a meeting of the Psychoanalysis Working Group at Birkbeck, University of London. My thanks to members of the Group for their comments and questions, which helped me to extend and develop my original points.

2   A note on terminology: When I use the term sexuality, I understand it to be a broad umbrella term which encompasses sexual identities; sex acts; sexual thoughts, desires and pleasures; sexual fantasies and daydreams; and phantasies that do not make it to consciousness, yet have an effect on the life of the person. Eadie (2004) edited an expansive glossary of terms relating to sexuality.

schools of thought and clinical approaches, which are sometimes at odds with one another and thus tend not to engage in dialogue about divisive theoretical concepts and matters of clinical technique. Traditions represented here include: Freudian, Kleinian, Independent, Lacanian, Jungian, and Relational. We also stage, for the first time, a sustained clinical psychoanalytic engagement with queer theory. By virtue of its editorial design, this book aims to foster a self-reflective attitude in readers about sexuality which historically has tended toward reification, particularly in clinical practice. The central questions we present to readers to think about are:

- What are the discourses of sexuality underpinning psychoanalysis, and how do they impact on clinical practice?
- In what ways does sexuality get played out for and between the psychoanalytic practitioner and the patient?
- How do social, cultural and historical attitudes towards sexuality impact on the transference and countertransference, consciously and unconsciously?
- Why is sexuality so prone to reification?

Divided into three sections, *Clinical Encounters in Sexuality* begins with six chapters on prominent themes in queer theory: identity, desire, pleasure, perversion, ethics, and discourse. The authors in section one are academic writers, based in the humanities and specializing in theories of gender and sexuality, particularly queer theory: Alice Kuzniar, Lara Farina, Kathryn Bond Stockton, Lisa Downing, Michael D. Snediker, and Will Stockton. When inviting the authors, we asked them to write on a particular theme and with the express aim of directing their writing towards a clinical audience, who may not be familiar with queer theory. We asked them to reflect upon the influence of psychoanalytic thinking in the development of queer theory, and to consider their own investment in both discourses. We did not ask them to draw on any specific psychoanalytic tradition in their chapters. The authors in section one are at the forefront of research in the field of queer theory, and so their chapters also display their own particular research expertise.

Section two includes fourteen responses to the chapters in section one by practicing psychoanalysts and psychoanalytic psychotherapists from a number of traditions. They work with adults and/or children and adolescents: Robert D. Hinshelwood, Abe Geldhof, Paul Verhaeghe, Ann Murphy, Ian Parker, Claudette Kulkarni, Carol Owens, Aranye Fradenburg, Olga Cox Cameron, Katrine Zeuthen, Judy Gammelgaard, Ken Corbett, Rob Weatherill, Dany Nobus, Ami Kaplan, and Patricia Gherovici. The authors in section two were invited by us to reflect on their encounters with the chapters in section one, and to consider whether queer theory might be useful for them in thinking about clinical work. The chapters in section two attest to the particularity of each individual's encounter and their different approaches and styles when writing of those encounters. Section two includes a variety of responses, based on the respondent's clinical experience, the psychoanalytic tradition within which they were schooled, the setting in which they work, and their own subjective position. While some writers make direct reference to the chapters in section one, others do not. In this, contributors address specific themes, ideas, or phrases presented in the chapters they have read. In order to explore their engagement with the material in section one, some authors present a clinical case study or discuss a clinical vignette, others use cultural texts to address their concerns, while a number of contributors reflect on how the chapters have prompted them to think about their positioning *vis-à-vis* clinical psychoanalytic theory. Some respondents reflect on the encounter itself and the unease generated by it. Whatever their approach to the invitation to "respond," all display a clinical sensibility to the task at hand.

Section three features seven short commentaries on the nature of the encounters enacted by the book, by leading thinkers whose own clinical practice and/or theoretical work engages directly with both discourses: psychoanalytic and queer. In section three, the seven contributors are as well versed in psychoanalysis as they are in theories of sexuality: Stephen Frosh, Jacqueline Rose, Tim Dean, Noreen O'Connor, Mark J. Blechner, Susan Stryker, and Ona Nierenberg. We invited them to comment briefly on the encounters they witnessed in the book, as well as their impression of the book's overall setup. They were not asked to respond to particular chapters.[3] Most have responded in a brief and broad way to the chapters in sections one and two, and their chapters tend to focus on identifying themes or problematics they witnessed, before adding their own thoughts about the conceptual encounter between the two discourses. Some people have also chosen to take examples from some of the chapters to illustrate their points (some to applaud them, others to critique them). While authors rarely reflect explicitly on their own encounters with sections one and two, their encounters are nonetheless present in their pieces. Thus, the chapters in section three add a further temporal dimension to the book, in so far as the authors are writing about a series of encounters that have already taken place, while doing so from the perspective of their current preoccupations.

The cover image for the book is artist Karla Black's sculpture, *There Can Be No Arguments,* photographed by fine art photographer Ruth Clark. Medb Ruane, a clinical psychoanalytic practitioner and one of Ireland's leading writers on contemporary art, has contributed a piece to the book on the significance of the cover image within the context of the work presented here in *Clinical Encounters in Sexuality.* I first encountered Black's work in her exhibition at the Irish Museum of Modern Art (IMMA) in Dublin in 2015. While enthralled by the delicacy of her sculptures, I was also excited to learn that she is interested in, and informed by, the work of Melanie Klein (IMMA 2015; Archer 2008), particularly as I trained and work clinically in the Kleinian psychoanalytic tradition. For the purpose of this book, one of the things that makes Black's (2011b) work so interesting is her insistence on leaving a space open for an encounter with

---

3   One author, Susan Stryker, was invited to respond to the chapters that dealt with or mentioned issues relating to trans people.

the art work, seeing "art in general as a place, a place to behave. I think of it as a [...] sort of boxed off little bit of civilised society where permission is given for us to sort of freely behave like the animals we are." There is an emphasis on the experience itself, outside of and apart from language; a space where preverbal, non-verbal, and unverbalizable aspects of experience can emerge. In an interview about her work showing at the fifty-fourth Venice Biennale, Black (2011a) says:

> My work doesn't point outside of itself to [...] metaphor or to the symbolic [...] to language, to meaning. Often people say what is the meaning of this sculpture? I can't understand that question. I don't know what *that* means, and I'm not remotely interested. I think that rather than it having a meaning, it has a function [...] rather than it having this sort of ephemeral sort of relationship to language outside of itself, it exists as a physical reality in the world. So, rather than say what is the meaning of this sculpture?, I would prefer to ask what are the consequences of this sculpture? How does it function? How does it operate in the world? What does it do?

The term "meaning" — which I interpret here as the result of a premature move towards intellectualization or rationalization — can function as a defensive action, which can become a barrier to experiencing or getting in touch with the experience an encounter might provoke. This is particularly relevant for *Clinical Encounters in Sexuality,* as our endeavor has been to keep a space open for the reader's experience, but the reader has to be willing to meet us halfway in that.

Clinical Encounters in Sexuality is edited by two psychoanalytic practitioners who work in clinical practice — one Kleinian, one Freudian–Lacanian — who also have research expertise in sexuality studies. I have written the Introduction in an effort to provide a rationale for the book and to open up a space for the reader to enter into an engagement with the text. Eve Watson has written the Afterword to reflect on the encounter between clinical psychoanalysis and queer theory within the context of the material contained in this book, as well as to highlight the clinical and theoretical contributions the book makes to the two fields.

I have deliberately avoided summarizing the chapters, as I think including my interpretations of the chapters would have the potential to close down the reader's own engagement with the text. In place of this, this Introduction offers readers a broad overview of each section, keeping the focus on the rationale for the book. My aim has been to encourage people to interact with the different discourses in whatever way feels right to them, and to bring awareness to the ways in which they are reacting to the various contributors and their ideas about sexuality.

Psychoanalysis and Sexuality

Psychoanalysis is a clinical practice and a theoretical tool for considering how the internal and external worlds of individuals and groups meet, diverge, and play out, as well as the unconscious underpinnings of occurrences and their representations in societal and cultural contexts. Since Sigmund Freud founded psychoanalysis as a therapeutic treatment in the late-nineteenth and early-twentieth centuries, it has also evolved into a field of theoretical knowledge, which influences diverse disciplines, such as literature, psychiatry, music, neuroscience, art, psychology, mathematics, medicine, philosophy, nursing, classics, social work, film, theater, and so on. Freud's insights about the mind have become significant reference points for talking about our feelings, thoughts and behaviors, especially those aspects of ourselves which we cannot change or understand. Psychoanalysis has continued to develop over the decades into a number of traditions, which take Freud's work as their grounding and inspiration but have different clinical and theoretical foci. There are nonetheless important points of overlap between them, such as the unconscious, free association, transference, symbolization, relationality, and desire. The fundamental tenet of all traditions is a belief in the unconscious, which is situated at the core of the psyche. While inaccessible to our conscious minds, the unconscious is dynamic and exerts a formidable influence over how we feel, think and behave. Psychoanalysts understand the persistent influence of the unconscious in the life of the person, and how unconscious elements can become manifest in sexuality.

Sexuality is crucial to Freud's formulation of psychoanalysis as a clinical field and to his theorization of the unconscious. Whatever he is writing about — the uncanny, hysteria, dreams, the death drive, transference, psychosis, the Oedipus complex, fetishism, melancholia, jokes, to name but a few — he is attendant to aspects of the sexuality of the person that may be being sublimated, protected against or acted out. In the preface to the fourth edition of his "Three Essays on the Theory of Sexuality" (1905), for example, he writes of his book's "insistence on the importance of sexuality in all human achievements and the attempt that it makes at enlarging the concept of sexuality" (134). He critiques assumptions that sexuality is a natural process, uninfluenced by the societal or cultural context within which an individual lives. He advocates that it is complex, particular to each individual and a source of conflict. For Freud, there is no *one* pre-established sexual object or aim. Instead he understands sexuality as being on a continuum — from the polymorphous perversity of childhood to the variances of adult sexuality — which result from the individual's attempts to constrain the drives. So-called "normal" sexuality is as much a construct as "perversion": "even in the most normal sexual process we may detect rudiments which, if they had developed, would have led to the deviations described as 'perversions'" (149).

Freud, being a man of his time, nonetheless struggled to give all forms of sexuality an equal footing in his writing. His deep ambivalence is evident in his instantiation of a sexual norm while at the same time challenging the very notion of a normative conception of sexuality. While employing terms such as "normal person" (137), "even the most normal person" (149), "normal development" (231), "normal sexuality" (231), "healthy people" (160), and "final, normal shape" (207), he sets out that it is his task to investigate "what is assumed to be normal" when it comes to sexuality:

> Let us call the person from whom sexual attraction proceeds the sexual object and the act towards which the instinct tends the sexual aim. Scientifically sifted observation, then, shows that numerous deviations occur in respect of both of these — the sexual object and the sexual aim. The relation between these deviations and what is assumed to be normal requires thorough investigation. (136–137)

This appears alongside a more normative, developmentally-oriented path towards reproductive heterosexuality:

> The final outcome of sexual development lies in what is known as the normal sexual life of the adult, in which the pursuit of pleasure comes under the sway of the reproductive function and in which the component instincts, under the primacy of a single erotogenic zone, form a firm organization directed towards a sexual aim attached to some extraneous sexual object. (197)

This split in Freud's thinking, which lays bare his conflicted attitude towards sexual life, has been taken up, interpreted, critiqued and acted out in a number of ways by psychoanalysts over the years. Psychoanalytic theories of sexuality have arisen from clinicians interpreting aspects of Freud's own discordant approach to sexuality, as well as experiences drawn from their clinical work.[4] This is further complicated by the understanding

---

4   For a small sample of the extensive work that has been done on sexuality by psychoanalytic practitioners, see Birksted-Breen (1993, 2016); White and Schwartz (2007); Irigaray (1985); McDougall (1995); Lichtenberg (2008); Ettinger (2006); Benjamin (1998); Caldwell (2005); Orbach (2000); Blechner (2009); Corbett (2009); Grigg et al (1999); Watson (2009); Fonagy et al (2006); Chodorow (2012); O'Connor and Ryan (2003); Kulkarni (1997); Gammelgaard and Zeuthen (2010); Welldon (1988); Stoller (1986); Nitsun (2006); Gherovici (2010); Quindeau (2013); Mitchell (1974), Mann (1999);

that individual psychoanalytic practitioners possess about the relation and disjunctions between sexuality, gender and sex. All of this has resulted in a disparate set of theories: from the tentative to the unequivocal; and from those expounding an expansive continuum of sexual possibilities to those that prescribe a sharp differentiation between the normal and the pathological. In the latter case, curiosity gives way to societal normativity and symbolic thinking to concretization. The sexuality of the individual is no longer something to be wondered about, because the psychoanalytic practitioner already knows the answer, projecting their own assumptions about sexuality onto the patient and judging the patient against such projections. Theory and/ or social prejudice trumps what is going on in the room, and in the more extreme cases, the patient becomes someone with a sexuality to be altered to fit some narrow definition of sexual maturity.

Charles Socarides (1962, 1968), a psychiatrist and psychoanalyst who spent much of his clinical career studying homosexuality, co-founded the National Association for Research and Therapy of Homosexuality (NARTH) in 1992, which proposes reparative therapy for homosexuals wishing to change their sexual orientation. Reparative therapy, according to NARTH co-founder Joseph Nicolosi (2014), uses a number of "interventions" which "will result in reducing, and sometimes eliminating, sexual or romantic attractions toward individuals of the same sex." Homosexuality is perceived as a psychopathological symptom here, resulting from an environmental trauma or an internal disturbance. In a review of the psychoanalytic treatment of bisexuality, Esther Rapoport (2009) found that it is "often relegated to the realm of fantasy" (286). She argues that psychoanalysts are operating from various "grossly outdated theoretical assumptions,"

Dimen (2003); Harris (2009); Celenza (2011, 2014); Green (2008); Gyler (2010); Giffney (2015); Lemma and Lynch (2015); Benvenuto (2016); Corbett (2014); Gabbard (2016). See also the international, peer-reviewed journal *Studies in Gender and Sexuality* (2000-), which publishes psychosocially-informed psychoanalytic work that bridges the clinical, social and cultural spheres.

resting on a number of factors, including the inaccurate view that "biological sex, gender and object choice imply each other and are virtually synonymous" (292). In this case, adherence to theoretical doctrine interferes with the clinician's capacity to remain open to their experience with their patients. Elsewhere, Shana T. (2014) writes that "The failures of psychoanalysis with respect to transgender people are somewhat — and sadly — familiar" (169), while Patricia Elliot (2014) remarks that "The history of the relationship of psychoanalysis to transsexuals is one that is exceedingly fraught, and trans persons have good reason to be sceptical about the potential for reconciliation" (165). In certain instances, transsexuals are considered to be unsuitable for psychoanalysis because they have sought a solution through the body. In this instance psychoanalysis is a method in which theory has become more important than clinical experience; the patient an inconvenient add-on to theoretical conventions.

Clinical practices like the aforementioned, as well as psychoanalytic attitudes towards homosexuality as a "developmental arrest" (Segal 1990, 253), bisexuality as an immature regression to fantasy (Rapoport 2009) and transsexuality as a marker of a psychotic structure (Millott 1990), have resulted in uneasy and suspicious reactions from those involved in sexuality studies (Dean and Lane 2001). Beliefs that some psychoanalytic training institutes only accept heterosexuals for clinical training (Ratigan 2012, 99; British Psychoanalytic Council 2011) have provoked complaints that homosexuals, bisexuals, and transsexuals are good enough to be patients but not colleagues. Criticism has been leveled at psychoanalysis as a discipline, and the unconscious motives of psychoanalysts who espouse perceived-to-be homophobic, biphobic, or transphobic attitudes have come in for scrutiny. For just one example, Stephen Frosh (2006) writes:

The ferocity of psychoanalysis' attacks on homosexuality suggests a deep anxiety, present in individuals and institutions alike — perhaps the anxiety of a profession fearing that its interest in sexuality and disturbance will make it an outcast from the society out of which it makes its living. By struggling to be acceptable in a conservative environment, embarrassed perhaps by the subversiveness of their own discoveries and by the secrets to which they are privy, and trying to establish their "professional" credentials, psychoanalysts have (as a breed and with exceptions, of course) too uncritically enacted the homophobia of the dominant culture. (245)

This fraught atmosphere between sexuality studies and psychoanalysis has been particularly evident in queer theory, where theorists are drawn to and make use of psychoanalytic theories while being wary of the clinicians who formulate them.[5]

Queer Theory and Sexuality

Queer theory is an umbrella term used to describe a variety of approaches to sexual norms, identities, desires, and pleasures. It is also attendant to sexuality's relation to other identitarian regimes governing gender, race, class, and so on (Giffney 2009, 2013). Queer theory is not a unified discourse and the singularity of its name belies the many different perspectives and conflicts present within the field. It is a highly politicized discourse, concerned with uncovering, critiquing, and flouting moral imperatives underpinning representations of sexuality in societal and cultural contexts. Theorists working within the field are meticulous in their unpicking of biased attitudes which present themselves as neutral while serving unspoken motives. They are uncompromising in their rejection of such attitudes. According to David Halperin (1995),

---

5   For example, see Dean and Lane (2001); Butler (1990, 1993); Bersani (2009, 1995); Kosofsky Sedgwick (1990, 1993); Dean (2000, 2009); Eng (2001); de Lauretis (1994); Frosh (1994); Rose (1986, 2016); Fuss (1995); Thomas (1996, 2000); Berlant (2012); Edelman (2004); Mulvey (2009); L. Segal (1994); N. Segal (2009); Bainbridge (2008); Grosz (1995); Pollock (1988); Probyn (1996); Gallop (1982); Silverman (1988); Salamon (2010); Copjec (1994); Johnson (2015); Elliot (2010); Freccero (2006); Campbell (2000); Salecl (1994), Wiegman (2012). This list is by no means exhaustive.

> "queer" does not name some natural kind or refer to some determinate object; it acquires its meaning from its oppositional relation to the norm. Queer is by definition whatever is at odds with the normal, the legitimate, the dominant. There is nothing in particular to which it necessarily refers. (62)

Writers engage critically and in a provocative way with normative or morally prescriptive thinking relating to sexuality, whether it is heteronormative or homonormative. In other words, thinking that favors either heterosexuality or homosexuality. Theorists enact a confrontational style of engagement, which aims to challenge what is societally deemed to be respectable, permissible and intelligible. The term "queer" resists conventions based particularly upon a heterosexual bias and the privileging of certain sex acts, gender performances, sexual identities, and relationship styles, while pathologizing others as unnatural, abnormal or psychologically underdeveloped.

Queer theorists believe that there is no "normal" teleology of sexual development, and insist that desire and pleasure are both fluid and historically contingent. They argue that people cling to socially constructed identity categories, rather than accepting the destabilizing and potentially unbearable effects of their own desires and pleasures. Proclamations that heterosexuality is the one and only endpoint of healthy sexual development are understood as a denial of the reality of "the radical impersonality of desire" (Dean 2000, 17) and the fact that "desire is essentially perverse" (Penney 2006, 1). In Guy Hocquenghem's (1972) words, "Properly speaking, desire is no more homosexual than heterosexual. Desire emerges in a multiple form, whose components are only divisable *a posteriori,* according to how we manipulate it" (49). Attempts to set up a "charmed circle" (Rubin 1984) or hierarchy of sexual desires, pleasures, acts, and identities are perceived as superegoic efforts to keep the sexual realm good by splitting off the messiness of the sexual as bad; to reduce difference to sameness. Theorists argue that queer facilitates a less limiting relationship to desire, pleasure, and the choices available to the subject, by unsettling habits and conventions relating to sexuality and gender, on the one hand, while promoting people's capacity for self-reflection, on the other. While the descriptor "queer" functions as an identity category for some, most theorists approach the notion of identity with caution, with an understanding that while the taking up of identity categories is a necessary precondition for societal recognition, identities can also constrain and imprison a person, while excluding those who feel they do not fit in (Butler 1991). A strong desire exists in queer theory to be recognized for oneself with all the messiness and incongruity that entails, rather than being reduced to the orderliness and neatness of a category that can never fully represent one's desires, because they are un-representable and ultimately unknowable to the conscious mind.

Queer theory developed as an academic discipline out of poststructuralist feminism and lesbian, gay, bisexual, and transgender studies (Haggerty and McGarry 2007), as well as being heavily influenced by the work of the philosopher Michel Foucault (Spargo 1999). It is an interdisciplinary field, including researchers from across the humanities and the social, natural, and medical sciences (Giffney and Hird 2008; Giffney and O'Rourke 2009). The academic component has an activist underpinning, coming into being as it did alongside queer activist groups, such as Queer Nation, OutRage!, the Lesbian Avengers, and the AIDS Coalition to Unleash Power (ACT UP), who sported slogans such as "Queers Bash Back," "We Recruit," "We're Here, We're Queer, Get Used to It" and "Silence = Death" (Blasius and Phelan 1997). These direct-action groups harnessed the rage of individuals against government agencies in reaction to governmental failures to help gay people during the early years of HIV/AIDS, or the perceived refusal to censure the perpetrators of homophobic beatings (Crimp 2002). Queer theory also arose from bisexual and transgender criticisms of the exclusionary politics of lesbian and gay communities, who while claiming to be excluded by the heterosexual norm, excluded bisexuals and transgender people in turn (Hemmings 2002; Stryker 2004). Queer theory is an attempt by theorists and activists to think about sexuality outside of identity-based movements, by operating on the basis of inclusivity rather than exclusivity. The aim is to work towards common goals rather than those based merely on the identity one professes. Work in the field is characterized by a jubilant disregard for propriety and a deep suspicion of all claims to truth or naturalness.

The development of queer theory as an intellectual mode of enquiry has been heavily influenced by psychoanalysis, particularly the works of Sigmund Freud, Luce Irigaray, Jacques Lacan, Jean Laplanche, Julia Kristeva, Jessica Benjamin, and, to a lesser extent, Melanie Klein. Theorists use psychoanalytic concepts to help them to think about a variety of topics, for example, practices of reading (Sedgwick 2007); gender identity (Butler 1991); the death drive (Edelman 2004); transgender embodiment (Salamon 2010); heterosexuality (Thomas 2000); trauma and lesbian public cultures (Cvetkovich 2003); affective relations between humans and their dogs (Kuzniar 2006); and sexual practices (Bersani 1995; Dean 2009). Psychoanalysis is used to explore the psychic life of subjects, sometimes together with a Foucauldian[6] approach to the environmental discourses that shape contemporary attitudes towards sexuality. This approach can be more properly described as psychosocial, which is concerned with the interrelation between internal and external worlds. In the words of Stephen Frosh and Lisa Baraitser (2008),

> the concern of psychosocial studies with the interplay between what are conventionally thought of as "external" social and "internal" psychic formations has resulted in a turn to psychoanalysis as the discipline that might offer convincing explanations of how the "out-there" gets "in-here" and vice versa. (347)

Within the field of queer theory, psychoanalytic concepts are often chosen for their use value — how they can be applied to enact change — for conscious outcomes. There is a concerted ef-

---

6   Foucauldian refers to the work of Michel Foucault. See, for example, Foucault (1998, 2002, 1992, 1990).

fort made to take psychoanalysis outside of the clinical setting and adopt it for political purposes. Queer theorists focus on the latent, normative underpinnings of discourse. These latent underpinnings might be consciously put there by the subject or the person may be unaware of what they are saying, due to their being so immersed in normativity. The focus for queer theorists is to uncover and discredit the latent inferences contained within the manifest material.[7]

While some queer theorists are rigorous in their close reading of psychoanalytic material, there is an inclination in the field to read the works of writers, like Judith Butler, Leo Bersani, Eve Kosofsky Sedgwick, or Tim Dean,[8] and rely on their interpretations of psychoanalytic texts rather than reading what the psychoanalysts have to say for themselves. In spite of claims of an expansive inclusivity, the focus on a critique of normativity tends to produce a split between heteronormativity/heterosexuality as bad and everything else as good (Wiegman and Wilson 2015; Halberstam 2015). Writers have a propensity towards idealizing acts or positions that are deemed to be radical, while denigrating those that are considered to be conservative. The always-in-opposition to the norm stance of many queer theorists is sometimes accompanied by a self-righteous attitude, and lofty claims as to what queer theory can achieve. In cases such as the aforementioned, certainty gives way to wondering, and the word "queer" becomes another concrete object to protect against the difficulty of experiencing uncertainty. Grandiose fantasies of the power of queer theory might arguably serve to

---

7   This is quite different from psychoanalytic understandings of, for example, "unconscious phantasy," "reverie," "dreaming the session" or clinical practitioners' attendance to experiences of "projective identification" in their countertransference. There is insufficient space to discuss these concepts here, except to say that clinical practitioners will find scant consideration of the aforementioned in queer theoretical writings. Those wishing to learn more about the aforementioned four concepts might start with Grotstein (2009, 143–54); Ogden (1999); Levine (2016); Spillius and O'Shaughnessy (2012).

8   See, for example, Butler (1990, 1993); Bersani (1995, 2009); Kosofsky Sedgwick (1990, 1993); Dean (2000, 2009).

split off feelings of vulnerability and powerlessness, and the potentially painful reality that these exciting thought experiments are unlikely to produce the kind of social change theorists might hope for.

In spite of their many differences and points of conflict, queer theory and psychoanalysis both have important things to say about sexuality, independently and to each other, and ultimately together.

Psychoanalytic Practice and Queer Theory

This Introduction functions as a frame for the encounters to follow. In psychoanalytic treatment, the frame is the setting or holding environment for the work (Eichler 2010, 29–34): the practical arrangements for the session, including the physical environment within which the treatment takes place (Schinaia 2016), the frequency of the sessions, the fees, and the analyst's maintaining of a space free, as much as possible, from intrusions or interruptions, including in their own mind. Without the frame, there would be no space within which to conduct analytic work. Without the analyst, there would be no frame. As Dana Birksted-Breen (2010–2011) explains:

The setting is more than a reference to the physical layout and the practical arrangements. The analyst's attitude is part of the setting. This attitude includes an openness to the patient and whatever the patient is bringing, refraining from action, judgment and retaliation, a desire to understand the patient's point of view, actions and phantasies within the context of what that person has experienced and the ways in which the patient has had to deal with those experiences, as well as the recognition that all emotions, however abhorrent, exist in all of us, including the psychoanalyst. (56)[9]

---

9 Various contributors refer to the person who comes for treatment as the "patient," "client" or "analysand," and identify themselves using the terms "psychoanalyst," "psychoanalytic psychotherapist" or "psychoanalytic prac-

The frame represents the reality principle, in incorporating the beginning and ending of sessions, the fees, the analyst's breaks and so on. It is a reminder to the patient that they do not control the setting; it exists independently of their wishes or demands (Lemma 2003). The setting, while sometimes perceived as persecutory by patients who find the boundary difficult, also provides holding and containment.[10] This is because the consistency and regularity of the analytic environment, together with the analytic attitude and behavior of the analyst, keep a space open for the unexpected to emerge in the analytic work itself.

Clinical Encounters in Sexuality is framed around the notion of "encounter." Eve Watson and I used the phrase "in sexuality" in the book's title rather than "on" or "with" or "about." This is because we wanted to situate the encounters within the messiness of sexuality, to configure the term as a space for thinking, but not an easy space that reduces complexities, differences, or tensions. The subtitle employs the terms "psychoanalytic practice" and "queer theory." We thought through a number of different configurations and whether to use "psychoanalysis," "psychoanalytic practice" or "practices," "psychoanalytic theory" or "theories," "queer," "queer theory" or "theories," or "queer practice" or "practices," and whether to make them equivalent, e.g., "psychoanalytic practice and queer practice" or "psychoanalytic theory and queer theory." We settled on "psychoanalytic practice and queer theory," because the two fields are not equivalent. They are very different in how and where they operate. This is not to say that psychoanalytic clinical practitioners are not theorists and queer theorists are not practitioners. It is rather to emphasize the different functions they perform in this book and to highlight, however open we hope the space we have provided

titioner." These are discursive terms that have a long and fraught history, being the site of fierce border wars on some occasions and used interchangeably at other times. See, for example, Eisold (2005); Kächele (2010); Blass (2010); Busch (2010); Widlöcher (2010).

10 Holding and containment are clinical concepts introduced by the psychoanalysts Donald Winnicott and Wilfred Bion respectively. On the former, see Boyle Spelman (2013, 13–28) and on the latter, see Britton (1992).

contributors is, that our positioning of the book is firmly within the discursive space of the clinical practice of psychoanalysis. This is because a book like this — focusing squarely on psychoanalytic practitioners' views about sexuality and their impact on practice — is sorely needed in clinical training and further professional development training. It is our belief that the book will find a warm welcome among queer theorists and within sexuality studies more broadly, but that its content might prove more challenging within clinical circles.

We became involved in *Clinical Encounters in Sexuality* because we saw it as an opportunity to explore the transferences to sexuality that circulate between individuals and among groups, and how such transferences become intermingled with cultural and societal discourses, before ending up embedded in clinical practice. We presented contributors with "sexuality" — a frame, an object, a signifier — and left them to interact with it, in the process inviting them into an experience with the concept and their own transferences and countertransferences to the material before them. While opening up a space for thinking about sexuality through the establishment of a theoretical frame, we have given minimal direction to authors as to how they might use that space or how they might approach the discursive objects they encounter. One set of contributions leads on to the next but no contributor gets to respond to those who responded to their writing.[11] So, we have not given anyone a "right of reply," because the book is set up as a series of encounters in which contributors engage with discourses they have read, rather than it being a dialogue between the contributors. This is deliberate. We have worked very hard to keep a space open, so that one discourse is not used to cancel out another discourse. Thus, the

---

11 There are also a series of missed encounters in this book: The ten people, whom we invited, accepted our invitation and withdrew from the project at a later date, without contributing a written piece. One person withdrew after submitting a piece. This has also had the effect that there are more Lacanian voices present in section two. We will leave it to readers to think about how the over-representation of one particular psychoanalytic discourse impacts on their reading experience.

book brings together a number of psychoanalytic and queer discourses and facilitates them being able to speak together without one or other of them silencing the others.

This is a book about psychoanalytic technique as much as a meditation on sexuality. Queer theory facilitates an encounter between different traditions of psychoanalysis, not to get them to agree but to encourage them to address common themes alongside one another. It is unusual for so many different psychoanalytic traditions to be brought together in one volume. This book illustrates similarities and differences between the various approaches, which coexist here, not in harmony but in difference. Our primary aim in this book has been to keep a space open for different views existing alongside one another, even when contributors have been unable to do so in their individual contributions. The idea of encounter provides space for new creative ideas and critical points of engagement to emerge. Every encounter has many levels: practical, professional, personal, and political. It encompasses both a conscious and an unconscious engagement; one that is arrived at through, in spite of, and apart from the words on the page. The concept of encounter is crucial to psychoanalytic practitioners because it is the clinical condition that facilitates the emergence of things that cannot be known in advance in an analysis.

Structured as it is around a series of encounters, *Clinical Encounters in Sexuality* points to the fact that all writing-encounters are temporal — moments that are contingent, provisional, and dependent upon the context within which the person is writing. Each chapter in the book also constitutes an experience in reading. As readers we engage with texts relative to our past experiences and our current preoccupations. The text points to a number of impasses, and why it is neither possible nor desirable to have agreement. *Clinical Encounters in Sexuality* brings psychoanalytic and queer discourses together to see what happens, nothing more. It is readers' task to complete the meaning-making process by deciding, for themselves, why the encounters do or do not play out in ways they might expect, wish or need. This is a book of "and" rather than "either/or." It is not demanded of readers that they choose psychoanalysis over queer theory or vice versa, or one psychoanalytic tradition over another, though they might choose to do so. We remind the reader that the framing of the book does place other demands on readers, in asking people who read this book to reflect on their encounters with each of the chapters and to think about why they might be reacting to authors and ideas in particular ways. The book is, above all, an opportunity for readers to engage in an experience with their own views on sexuality and how they might be bringing pre-determined beliefs into the consulting room unbeknownst to themselves, if they work in clinical practice. So, while we as editors can open up a space between two discourses, each reader must find their own way among the chapters.

Works Cited

Archer, Michael. "Michael Archer on Karla Black." *Artforum International* 46.7 (2008): 342–44.

Bainbridge, Caroline. *A Feminine Cinematics: Luce Irigaray, Women and Film*. Basingstoke and New York: Palgrave Macmillan, 2008.

Benjamin, Jessica. *Shadow of the Other: Intersubjectivity and Gender in Psychoanalysis*. New York and London: Routledge, 1998.

Benvenuto, Sergio. *What Are the Perversions? Sexuality, Ethics, Psychoanalysis*. London: Karnac, 2016.

Berlant, Lauren. *Desire/Love*. Brooklyn: punctum books, 2012.

Bersani, Leo. *Homos*. Cambridge and London: Harvard University Press, 1995).

———. *Is the Rectum a Grave? and Other Essays.* Chicago: University of Chicago Press, 2009.

Birksted-Breen, Dana, ed. *The Gender Conundrum: Contemporary Psychoanalytic Perspectives on Femininity and Masculinity*. London and New York: Routledge, 1993.

Birksted-Breen, Dana. "The Psychoanalytic Setting." In *Psychoanalysis: The Unconscious in Everyday Life,* eds. Caterina Albano, Liz Allison, and Nicola Abel-Hirsch, 53–58. London: The Institute of Psychoanalysis and Artakt, 2010–2011.

———. *The Work of Psychoanalysis: Sexuality, Time and the Psychoanalytic Mind*. London and New York: Routledge, 2016.

Black, Karla. "Karla Black talks about her exhibition at the 54th Venice Biennale." YouTube video uploaded by Fruit Market Gallery, June 6, 2011a. http://www.youtube.com/watch?v=omaPSIkhosM.

———. "Turner Prize Shortlist 2011: Karla Black." YouTube video uploaded by Channel 4, October 19, 2011b. Dir. Jared Schiller. http://www.youtube.com/watch?v=SBtoVYLCLE4.

Blasius, Mark, and Shane Phelan, eds. *We Are Everywhere: A Historical Sourcebook of Gay and Lesbian Politics*. London and New York: Routledge, 1997.

Blass, Rachel B. "An Introduction to 'Distinguishing Psychoanalysis from Psychotherapy.'" *The International Journal of Psychoanalysis* 91, no. 1 (2010): 15–21.

Blechner, Mark J. *Sex Changes: Transformations in Society and Psychoanalysis*. London and New York: Routledge, 2009.

Boyle Spelman, Margaret. *Winnicott's Babies and Winnicott's Patients: Psychoanalysis as Transitional Space*. London: Karnac, 2013.

British Psychoanalytic Council. "6.2 Statement on Homosexuality." http://www.bpc.org.uk/sites/psychoanalyticcouncil. org/files/6.2%20Position% 20statement%20on%20homo-sexuality.pdf.

Britton, Ronald. "Keeping Things in Mind." In *Clinical Lectures on Klein and Bion,* ed. Robin Anderson, 102–13. London and New York: Routledge, 1992.

Busch, Fred. "Distinguishing Psychoanalysis from Psychotherapy." *The International Journal of Psychoanalysis* 91, no. 1 (2010): 23–34.

Butler, Judith. *Gender Trouble: Feminism and the Subversion of Identity*. London and New York: Routledge, 1990.

———. "Imitation and Gender Insubordination." In *The Judith Butler Reader,* ed. Sara Salih, 119–37. 1991; rpt. Oxford: Blackwell, 2004.

———. *Bodies that Matter: On the Discursive Limits of "Sex."* London and New York: Routledge, 1993.

Caldwell, Lesley, ed. *Sex and Sexuality: Winnicottian Perspectives*. London: Karnac, 2005.

Campbell, Jan. *Arguing with the Phallus: Feminist, Queer and Postcolonial Theory — A Psychoanalytic Contribution*. London: Zed Books, 2000.

Carlson, Shana T. "Psychoanalytic." *TSQ: Transgender Studies Quarterly* 1, nos. 1–2 (2014): 169–71.

Celenza, Andrea. *Sexual Boundary Violations: Therapeutic, Supervisory, and Academic Contexts*. Plymouth: Jason Aronson, 2011.

———. *Erotic Revelations: Clinical Applications and Perverse Scenarios*. East London and New York: Routledge, 2014.

Chodorow, Nancy. *Individualizing Gender and Sexuality: Theory and Practice.* London and New York: Routledge, 2012.

Copjec, Joan. *Read My Desire: Lacan against the Historicists.* Cambridge: MIT Press, 1994.

Corbett, Alan. *Disabling Perversions: Forensic Psychotherapy with People with Intellectual Disabilities.* London: Karnac, 2014.

Corbett, Ken. *Boyhoods: Rethinking Masculinities.* New Haven and London: Yale University Press, 2009.

Crimp, Douglas. *Melancholia and Moralism: Essays on AIDS and Queer Politics.* Cambridge: MIT Press, 2002.

Cvetkovich, Ann. *An Archive of Feelings: Trauma, Sexuality, and Lesbian Public Cultures.* Durham and London: Duke University Press, 2003.

De Lauretis, Teresa. *The Practice of Love: Lesbian Sexuality and Perverse Desire.* Bloomington: Indiana University Press, 1994.

Dean, Tim. *Beyond Sexuality.* Chicago and London: University of Chicago Press, 2000.

———. *Unlimited Intimacy: Reflections on the Subculture of Barebacking.* Chicago and London: University of Chicago Press, 2009.

——— and Christopher Lane, eds. *Homosexuality & Psychoanalysis.* Chicago and London: University of Chicago Press, 2001.

Dimen, Muriel. *Sexuality, Intimacy, Power.* Hillsdale: The Analytic Press, 2003.

Eadie, Jo, ed. *Sexuality: The Essential Glossary.* London: Arnold, 2004.

Edelman, Lee. *No Future: Queer Theory and the Death Drive.* Durham and London: Duke University Press, 2004.

Eichler, Seth. *Beginnings in Psychotherapy.* London: Karnac, 2010.

Eisold, Kenneth. "Psychoanalysis and Psychotherapy: A Long and Troubled Relationship." *The International Journal of Psychoanalysis* 86, no. 4 (2005): 1175–95.

Elliot, Patricia. *Debates in Transgender, Queer, and Feminist Theory: Contested Sites.* Aldershot: Ashgate, 2010.

———. "Psychoanalysis." *TSQ: Transgender Studies Quarterly* 1, nos. 1–2 (2014): 165–68.

Eng, David. *Racial Castration: Managing Masculinity in Asian America.* Durham: Duke University Press, 2001.

Ettinger, Bracha L. *The Matrixial Borderspace,* ed. Brian Massumi. Minneapolis and London: University of Minnesota Press, 2006.

Fonagy, Peter, Rainer Krause, and Marianne Leuzinger-Bohleber, eds. *Identity, Gender, and Sexuality: 150 Years after Freud.* London: Karnac, 2006.

Foucault, Michel. *The Archaeology of Knowledge,* trans. A.M. Sheridan Smith. London and New York: Routledge, 2002; orig. in French 1969.

———. *The History of Sexuality, Vol. 1: The Will to Knowledge,* trans. Robert Hurley London: Penguin, 1998 (1976).

———. *The History of Sexuality, Vol. 2: The Use of Pleasure,* trans. Robert Hurley. London: Penguin, 1992 (1984).

———. *The History of Sexuality, Vol. 3: The Care of the Self,* trans. Robert Hurley. London: Penguin, 1990 (1984).

Freccero, Carla. *Queer/Early/Modern.* Durham: Duke University Press, 2006.

Freud, Sigmund. "Three Essays on the Theory of Sexuality" (1905) in *The Standard Psychological Works of Sigmund Freud,* vol. 7, trans. James Strachey in collaboration with Anna Freud and assisted by Alix Strachey and Alan Tyson, 123–245. 1953; rpt. London: Vintage 2001.

Frosh, Stephen. *Sexual Difference: Masculinity and Psychoanalysis.* London and New York: Routledge, 1994.

———. *For and Against Psychoanalysis.* 2nd ed. London and New York: Routledge, 2006 (1997).

——— and Lisa Baraitser. "Psychoanalysis and Psychosocial Studies." *Psychoanalysis, Culture & Society* 13, no. 4 (2008): 346–65.

Fuss, Diana. *Identification Papers: Readings on Psychoanalysis, Sexuality, and Culture.* London and New York: Routledge, 1995.

Gabbard, Glen O. *Boundaries and Boundary Violations in Psychoanalysis.* 1995; rpt. Arlington: American Psychiatric Publishing, 2016.

Gallop, Jane. *Feminism and Psychoanalysis: The Daughter's Seduction.* London and Basingstoke: Macmillan, 1982.

Gherovici, Patricia. *Please Select Your Gender: From the Invention of Hysteria to the Democratizing of Transgenderism.* London and New York: Routledge, 2010.

Giffney, Noreen. "The 'q' Word." In *The Ashgate Research Companion to Queer Theory,* eds. Noreen Giffney and Michael O'Rourke, 1–13. Aldershot: Ashgate, 2009.

———. "Quare Theory." In *Theory on the Edge: Irish Studies and the Politics of Sexual Difference,* eds. Noreen Giffney and Margrit Shildrick, 241–57. New York and London: Palgrave Macmillan, 2013.

———. "Sex as Evacuation." *Studies in Gender and Sexuality* 16, no. 2 (2015): 103–9.

——— and Myra J. Hird, eds. *Queering the Non/Human.* Aldershot: Ashgate, 2008.

——— and Michael O'Rourke, eds. *The Ashgate Research Companion to Queer Theory.* Aldershot: Ashgate, 2009.

Green, André. *The Chains of Eros: The Sexual in Psychoanalysis,* trans. Luke Thurston. London: Karnac, 2008; orig. in French, 1997.

Grigg, Russell, Dominique Hecq, and Craig Smith, eds. *Female Sexuality: The Early Psychoanalytic Controversies.* London: Rebus Press, 1999.

Grosz, Elizabeth. *Space, Time and Perversion: Essays on the Politics of Bodies.* London and New York: Routledge, 1995.

Grotstein, James S. *"…but at the same time and on another level…": Psychoanalytic Theory and Technique in the Kleinian/Bionian Mode.* Vol. 1. London: Karnac, 2009.

Gyler, Louise. *The Gendered Unconscious: Can Gender Discourse Subvert Psychoanalysis?* London and New York: Routledge, 2010.

Haggerty, George E., and Molly McGarry, eds. *A Companion to Lesbian, Gay, Bisexual, Transgender, and Queer Studies.* Oxford: Blackwell, 2007.

Halberstam, Jack. "Straight Eye for the Queer Theorist — A Review of 'Queer Theory without Antinormativity.'" *Bully Bloggers.* September 12, 2015. https://bullybloggers.wordpress.com/2015/09/12/straight-eye-for-the-queer-theorist-a-review-of-queer-theory-without-antinormativity-by-jack-halberstam/.

Halperin, David M. *Saint Foucault: Towards a Gay Hagiography.* New York: Oxford University Press, 1995.

Harris, Adrienne. *Gender as Soft Assembly.* 2004; rpt. London and New York: Routledge, 2009.

Hemmings, Clare. *Bisexual Spaces: A Geography of Sexuality and Gender.* London and New York: Routledge, 2002.

Hocquenghem, Guy. *Homosexual Desire,* trans. D. Dangoor. Durham: Duke University Press, 1993; orig. in French, 1972.

IMMA. *Karla Black Exhibition Guide.* Dublin: Irish Museum of Modern Art, 2015.

Irigaray, Luce. *Speculum of the Other Woman,* trans. Gillian G. Gill. Ithaca, New York: Cornell University Press, 1985; orig. in French, 1974.

Johnson, Katherine. *Sexuality: A Psychosocial Manifesto.* Cambridge and Malden: Polity, 2015.

Kächele, Horst. "Distinguishing Psychoanalysis from Psychotherapy." *The International Journal of Psychoanalysis* 91, no. 1 (2010): 35–43.

Kosofsky Sedgwick, Eve. *Epistemology of the Closet.* Berkeley: University of California Press, 1990.

———. *Tendencies.* Durham: Duke University Press, 1993.

———. "Melanie Klein and the Difference Affect Makes." *The South Atlantic Quarterly* 106, no. 3 (2007): 625–42.

Kulkarni, Claudette. *Lesbians & Lesbianisms: A Post-Jungian Perspective.* London and New York: Routledge, 1997.

Kuzniar, Alice A. *Melancholia's Dog: Reflections on Our Animal Kinship.* Chicago and London: University of Chicago Press, 2006.

Lemma, Alessandra. *Introduction to the Practice of Psychoanalytic Psychotherapy.* Chichester: Wiley, 2003.

_____ and Paul Lynch, eds. *Sexualities: Contemporary Psychoanalytic Perspectives.* London and New York: Routledge, 2015.

Levine, Howard B. "Dreaming into Being." In *The W.R. Bion Tradition,* eds. Howard B. Levine and Giuseppe Civitarese, 285–90. London: Karnac, 2016.

Lichtenberg, Joseph D. *Sensuality and Sexuality across the Divide of Shame.* New York and London: The Analytic Press/Taylor and Francis Group, 2008.

McDougall, Joyce. *The Many Faces of Eros: A Psychoanalytic Exploration of Human Sexuality.* London: Free Association Books, 1995.

Mann, David, ed. *Erotic Transference and Countertransference: Clinical Practice in Psychotherapy.* London and New York: Routledge, 1999.

Millot, Catherine. *Horsexe: Essay on Transsexuality,* trans. Kenneth Hylton. New York: Autonomedia, 1990.

Mitchell, Juliet. *Psychoanalysis and Feminism.* 1974; rpt. New York: Basics Books, 2000.

Mulvey, Laura. *Visual and Other Pleasures,* 2nd Ed. Basingstoke and New York: Palgrave Macmillan, 2009 (1974).

Nicolosi, Joseph. "What Is Reparative Therapy? Examining the Controversy." 2014. http://www.narth.com/main-issues/what-do-clinical-studies-say/#!important-updates/c19sp.

Nitsun, Morris. *The Group as an Object of Desire: Exploring Sexuality in Group Therapy.* London and New York: Routledge, 2006.

Ogden, Thomas H. *Reverie and Interpretation: Sensing Something Human.* 1997; rpt. London: Karnac, 1999.

O'Connor, Noreen, and Joanna Ryan. *Wild Desires and Mistaken Identities: Lesbianism and Psychoanalysis.* 1993; rpt. London: Karnac, 2003.

Orbach, Susie. *The Impossibility of Sex: Stories of the Intimate Relationship between Therapist and Patient.* London and New York: Touchstone/Simon & Schuster, 2000.

Penney, James. *The World of Perversion: Psychoanalysis and the Impossible Absolute of Desire.* Albany: State University of New York Press, 2006.

Pollock, Griselda. *Vision and Difference: Femininity, Feminism and the Histories of Art.* London and New York: Routledge, 1988.

Probyn, Elspeth. *Outside Belongings: Disciplines, Nations and the Place of Sex.* London and New York: Routledge, 1996.

Quindeau, Ilka. *Seduction and Desire: The Psychoanalytic Theory of Sexuality since Freud,* trans. John Bendix. London: Karnac, 2013.

Rapoport, Esther. "Bisexuality in Psychoanalytic Theory: Interpreting the Resistance." *Journal of Bisexuality* 9, nos. 3–4 (2009): 279–95.

Ratigan, Bernard. "Letter to the Editor." *Psychoanalytic Psychotherapy* 26, no. 2 (2012): 99–101.

Rose, Jacqueline. *Sexuality in the Field of Vision.* London and New York: Verso, 1986.

Rose, Jacqueline. "Who Do You Think You Are?" *London Review of Books* 38, no. 9 (2016): 3–13. http://www.lrb.co.uk/v38/n09/jacqueline-rose/who-do-you-think-you-are.

Rubin, Gayle. "Thinking Sex: Notes for a Radical Theory of the Politics of Sexuality." In *The Lesbian and Gay Studies Reader,* eds. Henry Abelove, Michèle Aina Barale, and David M. Halperin, 3–44. New York and London: Routledge 1993 (1984).

Salamon, Gayle. *Assuming a Body: Transgender and Rhetorics of Materiality.* New York: Columbia University Press, 2010.

Salecl, Renata. *The Spoils of Freedom: Psychoanalysis, Feminism and Ideology after the Fall of Socialism.* London and New York: Routledge, 1994.

Schinaia, Cosimo. *Psychoanalysis and Architecture: The Inside and the Outside.* London: Karnac, 2016.

Segal, Hanna. "Hanna Segal interviewed by Jacqueline Rose."
In *Hanna Segal, Yesterday, Today and Tomorrow,* 237–57.
1990; rpt. London and New York: Routledge, 2007.

Segal, Lynne. *Straight Sex: Rethinking the Politics of Pleasure.*
Berkeley: University of California Press, 1994.

Segal, Naomi. *Consensuality: Didier Anzieu, Gender and the
Sense of Touch.* Amsterdam: Rodopi, 2009.

Silverman, Kaja. *The Acoustic Mirror: The Feminine Voice in
Psychoanalysis and Cinema.* Bloomington: Indiana University Press, 1988.

Socarides, Charles W. "Theoretical and Clinical Aspects of
Overt Female Homosexuality." *Journal of the American
Psychoanalytical Association* 10 (1962): 579–92.

———. "A Provisional Theory of Aetiology in Male Homosexuality — A Case of Preoedipal Origin." *The International
Journal of Psychoanalysis* 49 (1968): 27–37.

Spargo, Tamsin. *Foucault and Queer Theory.* Cambridge: Icon
Books and New York: Totem Books, 1999.

Spillius, Elizabeth, and Edna O'Shaughnessy, eds. *Projective
Identification: The Fate of a Concept.* London and New York:
Routledge, 2012.

Stoller, Robert. *Sexual Excitement: Dynamics of Sexual Life.*
1979; rpt. London: Karnac, 1986.

Stryker, Susan. "Transgender Studies: Queer Theory's Evil
Twin." *GLQ: A Journal of Lesbian and Gay Studies* 10, no. 2
(2004): 212–15.

Studies in Gender and Sexuality, eds. Lisa Baraitser, Katie
Gentile, Stephen Hartman and Eyal Rozmarin. London and
New York: Routledge, 2000–.

Thomas, Calvin. *Male Matters: Masculinity, Anxiety, and the
Male Body on the Line.* Urbana and Chicago: University of
Illinois Press, 1996.

———, ed. *Straight with a Twist: Queer Theory and the Subject
of Heterosexuality.* Urbana and Chicago: University of Illinois Press, 2000.

Watson, Eve. "Queering Psychoanalysis/Psychoanalysing Queer." *Annual Review of Critical Psychology* 7 (2009): 114–39, http://www.discourseunit.com/arcp/7.htm.

Welldon, Estela V. *Mother, Madonna, Whore: The Idealization and Denigration of Motherhood.* London: Karnac, 1988.

White, Kate, and Joseph Schwartz, eds. *Sexuality and Attachment in Clinical Practice.* London: Karnac, 2007.

Widlöcher, Daniel. "Distinguishing Psychoanalysis from Psychotherapy." *The International Journal of Psychoanalysis* 91, no. 1 (2010): 45–50.

Wiegman, Robyn. *Object Lessons.* Durham: Duke University Press, 2012.

———— and Elizabeth A. Wilson. "Introduction: Anti-normativity's Queer Conventions." *differences: A Journal of Feminist Cultural Studies* 26, no. 1. (2015): 1–25.

Zeuthen, Katrine, and Judy Gammelgaard. "Infantile Sexuality — The Concept, Its History and Place in Contemporary Psychoanalysis." *The Scandinavian Psychoanalytic Review* 33, no. 1. (2010): 3–12.

SECTION 1

QUEER THEORIES

Precarious Sexualities: Queer Challenges to Psychoanalytic and Social Identity Categorization

Alice A. Kuzniar

In the essay "The Theory of Seduction and the Problem of the Other" (1997), Jean Laplanche writes of a concept that attractively resonates with the term queer, insofar as queer sexuality is quintessentially defined by its inexplicability, incoherence, volatility, and contingency in contradistinction to a sexuality whose owner would claim is stable, fixed, and identifiable as an integral part of the self. Destabilizing claims to an abiding, undisturbed notion of the self, Laplanche speaks of *das Andere* — the other-thing in us, the otherness of our unconscious — that all attempts at psychoanalytic interpretation cannot master. Laplanche posits that sexuality is an enigma, both for the child confronted with the riddle of sexuality that the adult represents and for the adult who can never master the uncanny as first encountered in childhood. The parent in turn unconsciously transmits an aura of sexual mystery to the child, perpetuating and completing the cycle. *Das Andere* is hence the internal otherness that we perpetually carry within us and that de-centers us, but that is founded by contact with an external otherness. //

"Queer is by definition whatever is at odds with the normal, the legitimate, the dominant. *There is nothing in particular to which it necessarily refers*. It is an identity without an essence"

(Halperin 1995, 62). As David Halperin here suggests, queer is "*das Andere*" and, as such, resists the very labeling that society demands. Indeed, queer theorists have time and again insisted on the necessity of rewriting "queer" anew so as to prevent it from becoming an identity marker that would become yet another category of the sort it opposes. As Judith Butler (1993) has written, "[i]f the term 'queer' is to be a site of collective contestation, the point of departure for a set of historical reflections and futural imaginings, it will have to remain that which is, in the present, never fully owned, but always and only redeployed, twisted, queered from a prior usage and in the direction of urgent and expanding political purposes" (19). Or, as Eve Kosofsky Sedgwick (1993) has famously put it, "queer" is "a continuing moment, movement, motive — recurrent, eddying, *troublant*"; ideally it represents an "immemorial current" (xii). I want to propose in this chapter that the qualities of oddity, hybridity, and transgression that "queer" has captured can be reframed, recalled, and revitalized through reference to Laplanche and other similar accounts of psychic life that underscore the precariousness of any attempt to decipher oneself and to label one's sexual identity. Such an approach refuses to ignore the insistence of *das Andere* in erotic magnetism. Insofar as "queer" can encapsulate or sum up the unfinishedness and perpetual enigma of sexuality that Laplanche speaks of — that sense of an internal otherness that we always carry within us and that comes as a gift from others — it promises to offer a unique approach to psychoanalytic inquiry. In conclusion, I want to push the envelope further to pursue how *das Andere* can even be embodied in the household companions whom we love — those whose strangeness comes from being of another species. The cost to psychoanalysis of seeing our erotic attractions as unidentifiable and perpetually enigmatic would be the abandonment of its classic attempt to narrativize psycho-sexual life. In other words, the analyst could venture neither to reconstruct the etiology of psychic development nor to offer closure to the narrative by assigning an identifiable label (for instance, heterosexual or homosexual) that would purport to erase the troubling, ongoing riddle of sexuality. Or to put it yet another way, traditionally psychoanalysis has been quick to accept the pathologizing identity label of "homosexual" only to search for the developmental factors leading to that result. How, then, if at all, can we instrumentalize psychoanalysis to do the opposite?

Laplanche's (1997) argument runs as follows: in the bodily care of the child, the parent transmits to the child various sensuous signals or messages (*Botschaften*) that the child cannot decipher. These pure perceptual indices (*Wahrnehmungszeichen*) are destined to remain ambiguous, leaving the child open and vulnerable to the Other. The origin of fantasy resides in the child's trying to make sense of such perceptions, indeed to create a story around them. Meanwhile, the adult's relation to his or her own sexual unconscious continues to be baffling. In fact, it is this mystery that is transmitted as a message or oracle, causing the child to sense that the parent addresses it: the parent is "the other who 'wants' something of me" (661). Laplanche thus speaks of the "[i]nternal alien-ness 'held in place' by external alien-ness; external alien-ness, in turn, held in place by the enigmatic relation of the other to his own internal alien" (661). It follows that all identity, seen as an attempt at self-centering, will necessarily be destabilized by the unconscious and the arcanum that sexuality always represents. Laplanche wishes to preserve this openness, this "relation of address to the other and of vulnerability to the inspiration of the other" (665) precisely because it can serve as the source of creativity in individuals.

There are three moments in this description that I wish to draw out with the purpose of aligning it with the anti-identitarian thrust of queer theory. First, Laplanche never specifies the gender of either parents or child, moving his discussion away from the gendered Oedipal scenario that dominates psychoanalytic discourse. He thus deliberately leaves open to gender variation the fantasies that arise in the child's imagination in response to the enigma. What this absence suggests is that Laplanche discounts the possibility of the development of a concrete, fixed sexual orientation in the individual or that the sexuality of the parents would predetermine the eventual sexual orientation of the child, since, regardless, sexuality is inherently an enigma. Secondly, Laplanche further queers sexual self-identity by stressing that the "adult's relation to his own unconscious, by unconscious sexual fantasies" (661) is not transparent. Moreover, this lack of intelligibility is why the child senses that it is addressed to begin with. Laplanche thus can be aligned with queer theorists such as Eve Kosofsky Sedgwick who wish to break away from a minoritizing view of homosexuality, which is to say, from it as a category restricted to a sexual minority. Although he does not say so explicitly, Laplanche implies that for all individuals, at the very least in their fantasy, there resides the potential for same-sex attraction or erotic excitability. The queerness of these fantasies — above all, the fantasy of seduction that the child harbors — is precisely why sexuality remains perplexing to the adult. Queer, in this case, cannot be limited to homosexuality or bisexuality but, in Ellis Hanson's (1993) words, is "wonderfully suggestive of a whole range of sexual possibilities (deemed perverse or deviant in classical psychoanalysis) that challenge the familiar distinctions between normal and pathological, straight and gay" (137–38). Or, as Alexander Doty (1995) has put it, queer "marks a flexible space for the expression of all aspects of non (anti-, contra-) straight production and reception. As such, this cultural 'queer space' recognizes the possibility that various and fluctuating queer positions might be occupied [...] within the nonqueer" (73). Thirdly and finally, Laplanche's essay stresses the importance of the Other in the seduction of the child, moving the focus away from a settled sexual identity unique to the individual; in fact, by virtue of this preeminence of the Other, his theory could be said to be anti-identitarian at its very base. In other words, Laplanche reminds us that it is something off, oblique, ambiguous, or "*verquer*" — *das Andere* in the Other that is at the source of the child's attraction. What seduces the child is a certain queerness.

A few years before queer theory hit the academic scene in the early 1990s, as a scholar in German and comparative literature I had become enamored with psychoanalysis. It tantalizingly investigated those "deviant" and "perverse" possibilities that Hanson later referred to as "queer." Above all, I found in psychoanalysis the appealing exploration of the inherently pathological dimensions to the normative heterosexual family romance with which I could not begin to identify. But in the years since queer theory's genesis, although there have been challenges to the traditional psychoanalytic explanation of homosexuality as failed Oedipal development (as I shall rehearse later in reference to the writings of Martin Frommer, Noreen O'Connor, Joanna Ryan, and Teresa de Lauretis), these criticisms have not come from a self-consciously queer theoretical camp. Queer theory's most momentous work has been that of Judith Butler's (1990, 1993, 1997) Freudian-inspired challenge to heterosexual ego formation. But there are very few psychoanalytically-informed theories of queer sexuality, indicating that queer theory has not explored the full potential psychoanalysis has to offer it, such as Laplanche's recognition of the incoherence, inexplicability, and precariousness in sexuality. Nor has psychoanalysis benefited from the potential insights offered by definitions of queer as a sexuality deviating from a simplistic homosexual-heterosexual binary. I want to discuss other recent models (put forward by Leo Bersani, Tim Dean, and Lisa Diamond) that rethink sexuality outside of identity labels, followed by a consideration of pet love. But first I want to review briefly how psychoanalysis has classically examined the "homosexual" as an object of study in the very terms of "identity" that queer has called into question. /

Psychoanalytic Identifications

The Oedipal structure of psychosexual development presumes as its telos a stable, fixed identity of personhood that rests solidly within a unitary gender role and unwavering sexual object choice based on the opposite of one's own gender. At the heart of the problem with the Oedipal narrative of identity formation — together with its pathologized deviations for homosexuals as well as for women in general — is that it assumes closure: In the end the individual has arrived at a fixed sexual identity in accordance with a categorizable gender identity. It is inconceivable that developmental models of psychoanalysis, given their mission of archeologically excavating and reconstructing psychic *Bildung,* would even approach sexuality as queerly incoherent — unless from the outset, as with Laplanche, sexuality is conceived as being mystifying and unexplainable. The classic, prescriptive course of maturation (parenthetically aside let it be noted that belief in this prescription is widely adopted by society despite its general scorn for Freudian concepts) calls for the child to identify with the parent of the same gender, with this identification then facilitating or grounding the desire for the opposite sex (see Fuss 1995). Identification and desire are thus 1) set up as binary, mutually exclusive opposites from each other and 2) seen to be determined exclusively by genital anatomy. In homosexuals, so the argument goes, the proper identifications are not lined up, resulting in a botched or counterfeit man or woman. Homosexuality thus becomes pathologized as a deviation from this identity formation and is considered to be a type of arrested development resulting in sexual immaturity. But when a failed Oedipal trajectory is claimed to be at the root of pathological resistance to heterosexuality, what is not recognized is that this trajectory itself is highly problematic. As Nancy Chodorow (1992) has pointed out, heterosexuality itself is a compromise formation. She suggests that psychoanalysts treat "all sexuality as problematic and to be accounted for" (104), not just homosexuality. All erotic passions, involving such characteristics as compulsiveness, addictiveness, humiliation, and so forth, apply to both sexual orientations. Moreover, she asks the striking question: "How do we reconcile a complex and varied view of the multiplicity of sexualities and of the problematic nature of conceptions of normality and abnormality with a dichotomous, unreflected upon, traditional view of gender and gender role or an appeal to an undefined 'masculinity' and 'femininity'?" (97).

I want to single out two challenges that have been mounted to the simplistic binary juxtaposition of identification and desire and what its implications have been for gay and lesbian life — by Noreen O'Connor and Joanna Ryan in their book with the telling title *Wild Desires and Mistaken Identities* (1993) and by Martin Steven Frommer in his essay "Offending Gender Being and Wanting in Male Same-Sex Desire" (2000). Frommer criticizes the binary because of the stereotypes it creates about homosexuality as well as heterosexuality. The heterosexist normative assumption about love is that opposites attract (masculine men desire feminine women), with the correlative supposition being that gay male desire, which is to say the desire for likeness, must be aberrant and narcissistic. Frommer argues that "identity categories impose commonality and coherence by ignoring the actual diversity and ambiguity of lived life" (192). He intends to complicate these identity categories by adopting a "postmodern perspective regarding gender and sexuality which challenges the heterosexual–homosexual binary and the resulting discourse that has been used to define two different kinds of men: those who are straight and those who are gay" (192). He observes that the pursuit of likeness *and* difference are common to gays and straights and that the pull toward difference is not invariably benign or natural, for it can be an expression of defensive, rigid complementarity that reifies one's narcissism. To give an example of how the latter works, he refers to an article by J. Hansell who suggests that underlying male heterosexuality is the anxiety of being too much like women, a fear that can be allayed by underscoring the *gender* difference by having *sex* with them instead. In other words, any feminine identification or homosexual feelings must be disavowed via reconsolidation of one's biological gender, facilitated by espousing desire exclusively for the opposite sex. Women can be the object of sexual desire provided they are considered to be inferior and hence nonthreatening to masculinity. Frommer then gives an equivalent example of a gay male patient who sought out sexual relations with men he could regard as inferior to himself, in other words, by reifying difference: "Since with these men he most often played the role of the top sexually, he maintained a sense of himself that was protected from feelings of humiliation. Stuart's ability to objectify hustlers allowed him to fend off anxiety and humiliation. He could ask for what he wanted sexually without fearing that he would be thought of as 'a little girl'" (200). In other words, anxiety about being identified with women could be equally present in both gay and straight men — as well as the capacity to pursue difference to shore up one's narcissism.

What Frommer does not address in this essay is that psychoanalysis itself has traditionally propagated the notion that gay men are feminized — a stereotype that Stuart himself fears and that likewise fuels straight male homophobia, as Hansell indicates. Frommer points out only one negative implication for gay men of the identification-desire or being-wanting dyad, namely that to desire someone of the same sex (with whom you identify) means you must be narcissistic. The converse model is to say that to desire someone of the same sex, you must therefore identify with the opposite sex: lesbians are masculinized women, while gays are feminized men. Same-sex object choice hereby becomes tethered to the overriding binaries of masculinity and femininity as well as activity and passivity. As Stephen Frosh (2006) summarizes in *For and Against Psychoanalysis*: "This line of thought, that sexual object choice is an aspect of gender identity, has been swallowed by most post-Freudian analysts, despite the obvious category confusions it involves and the everyday evidence that there is no necessary connection between object choice and gender identity" (236).

Successive generations of psychoanalysts (Karen Horney, Ernest Jones, Jeanne Lampl de Groot, Joan Rivière, and Joyce McDougall) have generated competing narratives about psychosexual development in order to invent explanations for this cross-gender identity. In fact, in so doing they hark back to gender inversion theories put forward by such pre-Freudian German sexologists as Karl Heinrich Ulrichs, Carl Westphal, and Magnus Hirschfeld, who in the latter half of the nineteenth century and into the twentieth century described and classified various sexual and gender orientations. Westphal, in fact, coined the word "homosexuality" in 1869, whereas Hirschfeld can be called the first homosexual rights activist (see Bland and Doan 1998). Previously I referred to Frommer's clinical investigation of gay men; now I would like to turn to studies by Noreen O'Connor/Joanna Ryan and Teresa de Lauretis for their trenchant criticism of these post-Freudian psychoanalytic hypotheses regarding gender inversion that purport to structure lesbian identity.

In her influential study on the castration complex in female homosexuality, Karen Horney (1924) surmises that, on having to abandon the father as love-object, the young girl substitutes the object-relation to him with identification instead, replacing the earlier bond with the mother. To play the father's part consequently means to desire the mother (in a strange reversal of the notion that what prompted her desire for him and to have a child by him in the first place was envy of the mother). Similarly, Lampl de Groot in 1928 sees the young girl as going through the Oedipal renunciation of the mother in loving the father. Only when she is rejected by him does she regress to her previous love for the mother: female homosexuality is thus seen as a regression to an earlier state. Ernest Jones's contribution in 1927 to this masculinity complex thesis is his explicit phallocentricism: lesbians have "penis identification," while their "interest in women is a vicarious way of enjoying femininity; they merely employ other women to exhibit it for them" (cited in O'Connor and Ryan 1993, 52–53).

In their review of the psychoanalytic literature on homosexuality, O'Connor and Ryan report on how pervasive this theory of conflicted gender identity has been. Even as late as 1979, more than one hundred years after Ulrichs began writing on gender inversion, Joyce McDougall (1989) writes that the homosexual version of the Oedipal complex involves "*having* exclusive possession of the same-sex parent and […] *being* the parent of the opposite sex" (206). O'Connor and Ryan (1993) trenchantly criticize the inflexibility and persistence of this gender bifurcation:

[…] there is no other alternative, no other way in which difficulties with femininity can be seen, except as a recourse to masculinity. Furthermore, to be like a man in these respects means that desire will inevitably be for a woman, if only unconsciously; there is no possibility of desiring a man from this position, or of desiring a woman from a "feminine" identification. The homosexual position is cast as an inevitably masculine one, involving a repudiation of femininity. (51)

Highly suspicious of the problematic concept of "gender identity" they observe that this formulation of "deviant" identity "blocks the exploration of what it means to desire another woman from the position of being a woman, what the nature of this desire could be" (120). Moreover it ignores the "huge range and diversity of conflicts that lesbian patients may have in relation to themselves as women, or about their bodies […] [which] do not invariably amount to serious gender identity conflicts, and […] are not necessarily specific to lesbians; they may also be experienced in various ways by some heterosexual women" (124).

Both O'Connor/Ryan and Teresa de Lauretis find more congenial the work by Helene Deutsch for her move away from the masculinity complex as well as her rejection of the notion that masculine and feminine roles govern lesbian relations. Equally troubling for them, however, is the centrality of motherhood in Deutsch's (1933) focus on the mother/child dyad. They do perceive, though, a note that points beyond infantile oral attachments: Deutsch observes in mature interactions of one of her patients "no sign of a 'masculine-feminine' opposition of roles," but a vivacious oscillation between active and passive antitheses in her sexual relationships: "One received the impression that what made the situation so happy was precisely the possibility of playing *both* parts" (40). Deutsch here hints at a flexible adoption and reversal of mother-child re-enactments, a playful taking on of various roles that suggest that ego formation is not a matter of simplistic identification with one, immovable gendered position. De Lauretis (1994) also finds suggestive in Deutsch the notion of "consent to activity" offered by the mother/female partner: "encouragement given by a partner's physical participation in the sexual activity itself would then provide a knowledge of the body," contributing "to the effective reorganization of the drives" (75). In the rest of *The Practice of Love,* de Lauretis goes on to argue that what is required are a proliferation of visual, verbal and gestural representations and fantasies that "may serve as an authorizing social force" for lesbian sexual practices (76). To summarize O'Connor/Ryan and de Lauretis, then: what they seek is a move away from the constricting, Oedipally determined, dual-gendered identity configurations that have defined much psychoanalytic thought on homosexuality and that see it as re-enacting primitive or infantile attachments. Instead they envision a discovery of a variety and coexistence of positive identifications that would explore shifting erotic desires and fantasies.

The Need for Dis-identification

It is this line of reasoning that I wish to develop in the remainder of this chapter. What other ways do we have of conceiving identity formation for GLBTIQA+[1] persons outside of traditional psychoanalytic Oedipal accounts? And what models does psychoanalysis provide in order to think through these alternative imaginaries? As we have seen, queer thought resists the notion of a predictable narrative of psychogenesis that can be generalized to fit all homosexuals. But it cannot, of course, abandon the psychoanalytic notion of ego formation in the process. This being the case, is it not possible to loosen the constraining, self-assertive demands of the ego in order to respond more spontaneously — more queerly — to *das Andere*? Judith Butler (1993) has adopted Freudian tenets to outline the melancholic heterosexual ego formation, establishing how normative identity arises out of the reiteration or what she terms performativity of societal gender norms. However much she complicates and adds to the Oedipal trajectory toward heterosexuality, though, it could be argued that she also maps out a predictable path of development based on disavowal of love for the same-sex parent (71–72). Would it not be possible, by contrast, to wish a utopically queer ego formation for purported heterosexuals as well

Utopic?

---

1   GLBTIQA+ is an acronym that stands for gay–lesbian–bisexual–transgender–intersex–queer–asexual and allies. Plus (+) indicates adding such sexual orientations as pansexual or polysexual.

as for queers? Is there evidence of a queer potential in hetero-sexuality, so as to recognize how all intense, passionate sexual experiences and fantasies transcend ego boundaries that cling to social norms? Is not all sexuality, to speak with Laplanche, an ongoing enigma? Without denying in the least the social stig-matization of homosexuality and the lack of entitlement that queers face that straights can take for granted, can it not be said that the process of ego formation is a difficult, compromised journey for all?

In today's society, identity functions to provide coherence to the subject for the purpose of self-presentation to others. In consumerist culture, identity serves the purpose of controlling, commodifying, and marketing the subject; it is assumed like a menu of options chosen in a Facebook profile. In being, as they must, adopted and acquired through imitation, all identities will fail to satisfy and will be constituted by loss, hallmarked by their fragility, and segregate the individual into discrete categories. As Jacqueline Rose (1986) poignantly observes:

> The unconscious constantly reveals the "failure" of identity. Because there is no continuity of psychic life, so there is no stability of sexual identity, no position for women (or for men) which is ever simply achieved. Nor does psycho-anal-ysis see such "failure" as a special-case inability or an indi-vidual deviancy from the norm. "Failure" is not a moment to be regretted in a process of adaptation, or development into normality [...] "failure" is something endlessly repeated and relived moment by moment throughout our individual his-tories [...] there is a resistance to identity at the very heart of psychic life. (90–91)

Yet, despite such inevitable "failure," is it not possible to speak positively of identification and identity formation as adapta-tion — as harboring the potential for a productive resistance to the very norms that determine restrictive ego boundaries? For if our identities are the repository of abandoned ego cathexes, it does mean that various *Ichideale* can be introjected and assimilated over time, and that these must be welcomed and they will be multiple and contradictory. To give an example, to do so would be to take up Teresa de Lauretis's encouragement to artists to produce counter-hegemonic images of lesbian identity that will deviate from those that circulate in mass media and thereby provide alternative imaginaries for women. Identity in this case could mean the embrace of forms of difference rather than similarity and sameness. Yet, also, insofar as such images can never overlap with the self and will be rejected and abandoned, so too will they leave behind traces of loss and mourning.

What models do we have, then, of identification based on desire and love that are open to ambiguity and change — that take into account unpredictability and incoherence? Could it be that the queerly self-identified individual has less defensive ego boundaries open to such possibilities? To return to Laplanche's notion of enigmatic sexuality: sensitivity alone to this enigma means the recognition of an irreparable misfit. Dis-identification from heterosexuality and the constraints it imposes is important because it entails retaining a sense of openness to *das Andere*. Thus, rather than seeing, in the classical psychoanalytic interpretation, the homosexual as someone who has failed to adopt a heterosexual identity, I would argue that s/he productively dis-identifies with heterosexuality and the coerciveness and predictability of the Oedipal ego formation, all while acknowledging the pain it produces. This dis-identification would pave the way for more gender-variable identifications and introjections that occur queerly or *verquert* across any clear dividing line between homosexuality and heterosexuality or female and male. Openness to the incomprehensibility and enigma of sexuality is, to recall Laplanche, the source of creativity.

Judith Butler (1997) has theorized the repudiation of identification with homosexuality, followed by overcompensation by a masquerading of gender-normative behavior (132–66). Clearly, *queer* dis-identification likewise cannot arise as well without ambivalence and defensiveness, the anguish of having to forfeit and not be able to assimilate standardized, heteronormative identities. One needs to stress here that insofar as psychoanalysis forthrightly acknowledges the pain resulting from the abandonment of former ego cathexes— as Rose puts it the "failure" of identity— it challenges those theories by Gilles Deleuze, Rosi Braidotti, Donna Haraway, and Elizabeth Grosz that celebrate the volatile, deterritorialized, nomadic subject whose mobility occurs largely without the trace of trauma, loss, and resistance. At the root of this ambivalence is the contradictory coexistence of diverse identifications within the ego. Yet it is this multiplicity, incoherence, transitoriness, and impossibility that make the term "queer" helpful for those individuals trying to find a language to reflect their disjointedness. The task of current psychoanalysis would be not simply to acknowledge the failure of previous conceptual psychic models but to adopt or develop hypotheses such as Laplanche's that would help articulate why one feels queer. Here it is crucial to keep in mind the uniqueness of every individual's circuitous path, which resists generalization into a theorem. As Eve Sedgwick (1993) notes: "'Queer' seems to hinge much more radically and explicitly on a person's undertaking particular, performative acts of experimental self-perception and filiation […] there are important senses in which 'queer' can signify only *when attached to the first person*" (9). I want to examine now a few recent forays that take as their starting point queer resistance to identity labels and to the impervious ego that clings to them. They then offer models for rethinking desire. In conclusion I want to contribute my own response to what these models imply, namely a queerly theorized pet love.

A Singular Love

In his contributions to *Intimacies*, co-written with Adam Phillips, Leo Bersani (2008) formulates what he calls "virtual being," a part of ourselves that is psychically anterior to "the quotidian manifestations of our individual egos" and that is "unmappable as a distinct entity" (86). He claims that it is this virtual being that is in ourselves that responds in love to the same quality in others. This love replies to the "universal singularity" in the beloved ("and not his psychological particularities, his personal difference"), as a potentiality of his own being (86). The emblematic advocate of such a love is Socrates. The sameness to which the lover reacts designates not a narcissistic love that bolsters the ego's boundaries and would be "driven by the need to appropriate the other's desire." (29) Instead it signifies "the experience of belonging to a family of singularity without national, ethnic, racial, or gendered bodies" (86) or, as Bersani and Ulysse Dutoit (1999) state elsewhere, "a perceived solidarity of being in the universe" (80). What is crucial about Bersani's formulations in terms of my previous discussion is his effort to frame this love for another person not based on particularities that would comprise his/her identity. He redefines this different sort of subjecthood as "a hypothetical subjectivity," in other words not a self that would be defined, constrained in terms of its identity, desires, or its acts (2008, 29). The words "hypothetical," "virtual," and "unmappable" indicate that this love is unmoored from both gender and sexual identity. At the same time, they also resonate with the "enigma" that Laplanche sees the Other representing. Love can be defined as the open, nondefensive, vulnerable response to this enigma, to *das Andere*, or, cast differently, to the ideal possibility that another person in their very being represents. And, likewise importantly, despite its resistance to identity labels, Bersani's "virtual being" characterizes what is quintessentially singular and unique in each and every individual, a point to which I want to return in discussing the work of Lisa Diamond.

One of the most articulate scholars forging new paths in the area of queer theory via psychoanalysis has been Tim Dean (2000). His research is significant because, via reference to Jacques Lacan, he more directly than Bersani casts desire as largely unbound by the gender of one's object choice. Because he dares to conclude that desire can be neither homosexual nor heterosexual—that it is "beyond sexuality," as the title of his book indicates—his work has been highly controversial especially among gay scholars. He writes: "By describing sexuality in terms of unconscious desire, I wish to separate sexual orientation from questions of identity and of gender roles, practices, and performances, since it is by conceiving sexuality outside the terms of gender _and_ identity that we can most thoroughly de-heterosexualize desire" (222). As this excerpt indicates, desire would be fundamentally anti-identitarian and anti-normative, rendering, to quote Jacques Lacan (2001), the "'normality' of the genital relation" is "delusional" (187). The Lacanian psycho-analytic categories that Dean (2000) finds productive for un-derstanding desire outside socially rigid identitarian categories are the "real" and "_objet a._" As "a conceptual category intended to designate everything that _resists_ adaptation" (230), the real moves our understanding of sexuality outside the framework of the imaginary and symbolic, hence outside the realm of "im-ages and discourses that construct sex, sexuality, and desirabil-ity in our culture" (231). In a passage that echoes Laplanche on the child's sexual incomprehension, Dean explains how the real arises and why it is linked to an enigmatic sexuality:

> Freud's claims on behalf of infantile sexuality entail recogniz-ing that sex comes before one is ready for it — either physi-cally or psychically. In the case of children it seems relatively clear what being physically unprepared for sex means: psy-chically it means that the human infant encounters sexual impulses — its own as well as other people's — as alien, un-masterable, unassimilable to its fledgling ego, and hence ultimately traumatic. As a consequence of this capacity to disorganize the ego or coherent self, sexuality becomes part of the unconscious; and it is owing to this subjectively trau-matic origin that Lacan aligns sex with the order of the real. The real — like trauma — is what resists assimilation to any imaginary or symbolic universe. [...] [H]uman sexuality is constituted as irremediably perverse. (232)

Following the same reasoning, Dean (2001) concludes that "in the unconscious heterosexuality does not exist" (138) and that "[o]ur identities, including sexual identity, invariably conflict with our unconscious" (133).

Dean (2000) then finds in Lacan's notion of the "*objet a*" a means to articulate how this unconscious, enigmatic desire finds representation. *Objet a* is "a term intended to designate the remainder or excess that keeps self-identity forever out of reach, thus maintaining desire" (250). It is associated with various, multiple erogenous zones on the surface of the body that displace and substitute for the original erogenous focus on the mouth. In the very multiplicity, excess, or polymorphous perversity that it comes to signify, *objet a* becomes decoupled from any gender bias or organization and thus is instrumental for a queer, anti-heteronormative reassessment of sexuality. But it also queers any domestication of homosexuality. Dean summarizes thus: "what psychoanalysis considers essential to desire is precisely that it obtains no essential object: *desire's objects remain essentially contingent*" (239).

Dean's statement is both confirmed and challenged by a fascinating study outside the arena of psychoanalysis that nonetheless has strong repercussions for its clinical practice — Lisa Diamond's (2008) book *Sexual Fluidity: Understanding Women's Love and Desire*. A professor of psychology and gender studies, Diamond interviewed numerous women belonging to a sexual minority (lesbian, bisexual, and nonspecific) and found that the persons to whom they were attracted depended on circumstance and varied over time: in other words, their objects of desire were radically contingent. They were also largely independent of gender. But these desires were not so conditional as to be independent of specific persons, suggesting that Dean's (2000) conclusion on the "impersonality of desire" (240) is male-oriented and untrue to women's experiences. Nonetheless, Diamond's research on female sexual fluidity has vast implications for a queer theorization of desire and substantiates the anti-identitarian, queer academic scholarship of Bersani and Dean.

If queer theory has been accused of erasing and marginalizing female specificity, for instance, in its focus on "camp, traditionally a gay men's paradigm" (Wilton 1995, 7), then Diamond rewrites a queer component back into women's sexuality, albeit exclusively cis-gender women. She deliberately maintains how female sexuality differs from male sexuality, with the implicit critique that female same-sex desire has been cast according to a male-centered model that strictly divides same-sex from opposite-sex orientation. She also notes how the label queer feels comfortable for many women who wish to eschew sexual identity labels and to better account for the fluidity of their desires. But the terms Diamond (2008) uses herself are quite unique and specific to her study. Her findings are nothing short of astonishing: after interviewing over the course of ten years close to ninety women belonging to a sexual minority (along with a smaller heterosexual comparison group), she discovered that more than two thirds had changed their identity labels from the time of the first interview (65). Diamond prefers her term "nonexclusivity" to bisexual to characterize this fluctuation in attraction to or relationships with both sexes, because the bisexual label presumes a significant, steady, and equal degree of interest in both men and women rather than the openness to the option or prospect of a relationship with someone of either sex. Not only did the women she interviewed acknowledge this flexibility but they also "underwent identity changes (such as adopting bisexual or unlabeled identities) specifically to accommodate such possibilities" (83). The heterosexual comparison group also demonstrated similar results: "fluidity appears to manifest itself similarly in both heterosexual and sexual-minority respondents, the primary difference being that heterosexual women take the gap between their physical and emotional attractions more seriously than do sexual-minority women: in their estimation, if their attractions to women are exclusively emotional, then they are probably not gay" (79). Indeed, Diamond later notes, physiological studies done on women's sexual arousibility indicate that women regardless of their acknowledged orientation unconsciously respond to erotic images of both men and women.

Diamond's study is fascinating for its other results as well. First, she found that early experiences do not predict later ones: being in a heterosexual or homosexual relationship earlier in life is no guarantee of gender attraction at a different stage in life, nor can either be regarded as a transient phase towards a more stable sexual orientation. Though not random, a woman's sexual desires remained fluid over her lifetime. Although she could not intentionally change her orientation, her desires would be sensitive to situation and context. Secondly, Diamond came to the conclusion that the majority of her interviewees were attracted to a person independent of that person's gender. In fact, she proposes that "the capacity for person-based attractions might actually be an independent form of sexual orientation" (186) or adopted as an additional aspect of sexual variability.

How, then, do these findings line up with the various queer psychoanalytic theories discussed previously? Diamond's deduction that women fall in love with the person rather than gender contradicts Dean's claim about the "impersonality of desire," indicating that his Lacanian model might not be adequate for describing female desire. One can conceivably attribute this difference to how men and women are socialized: women are taught to be more attentive to others and consequently less inclined to claim the prerogative of the impersonal. Be that as it may, Diamond's theories do align with Lacan's (1975[1972–73]) notion that "*quand on aime il ne s'agit pas de sexe*" (27) in both meanings of the term "*sexe*"; the phrase could be translated as either "when one loves it's not about having sex" or "when one loves, the sex of the person one loves is immaterial." Furthermore, Diamond's work confirms Dean's emphasis on the contingency of desire. She also substantiates Bersani's notion that one falls in love with another person for the possibility, virtuality, and singularity that he or she represents regardless of and in the face of the particularities of that person's identity, whether these are related to gender, sexuality, nationality, and so on. Diamond's claim that women's sexuality and arousability are variable, unpredictable, and gender-indeterminate likewise overlaps with various aspects to the enigma of sexuality that Laplanche addresses. Above all, women's preference for de-labelling along with the realization that to assume a sexual identity would be to compromise a sense of self-integrity ring true to the anti-identitarian tenets of queer theory.

Other questions arise, however, for practicing psychoanalytic clinicians on the basis of Diamond's work. What new vocabulary does psychoanalysis need to adopt to adequately help either cisgender or transgender individuals organize fluid sexual desires? How would one, for instance, begin to reconstruct an etiology of a patient's variable desire given that there is no obvious developmental path to chart? If a woman can switch affections at any point in her life and this fluidity is regarded as normal and pervasive, to what extent are foundationalist narratives of psychosexual life, especially the Freudian or Lacanian psychogenesis of hysteria, misleading if not downright harmful? Butler, too, has formulated a hegemonic, normalizing narrative for the development of gender and sexual identity: how would her narrative of ego formation accommodate Diamond's findings? Or would Diamond corroborate Butler's (1993) finding that the ego can be an ongoing, volatile, fragile composite, especially across gender boundaries? Butler moreover has similarly challenged the notion of lesbian sexuality as "an impossible monolith" (85). Finally, to what extent would Diamond concur with Helene Deutsch's study of one female patient that indicated she derived pleasure from adopting various role-playing with her lovers, in other words, that she found happiness is escaping the pre-patterning of identity strictures? Diamond seems to indicate that risking the incoherence of identity is liberating for the women she interviewed, insofar as they are involved in an ongoing process of acknowledging and affirming their fluctuating desires. Her findings indicate that queer love is actually the norm of sexuality for sexual-minority women — even possibly for those with a heterosexual orientation. "Queer," "person-based attraction," and "nonexclusivity" as anti-identitarian categories offer these women the possibility for better grasping the intricacies and vitalism of their psychic life. Would individuals who self-identify as asexual then also find such anti-identitarian categories attractive and appropriate? Why or why not? The larger issue at stake here is that, if psychoanalytic theory and practice cannot offer GLBTIQA+ individuals flexible, enriching

support, simplifying identitarian categories will step in to normalize, regulate, supervise, and police.

Beyond Sexual Identification: Pet Love

In concluding I briefly want to draw out the queer implications
of Bersani's, Dean's, and Diamond's work but move in a different
direction; I want to propose that one's sensual and emotional life
is non-exclusionary in other ways that dualistic identity categories do not grasp. In thinking over the last several years about
how my life has been enriched by my canine companions, I have
frequently wondered about the queer consequences of that attachment. To queerly embrace dog love means exploring a sensuality, pleasure, comfort, and commitment consciously outside
the norms of heterosexual cohabitation. Put differently, dog love
has the potential of continuing and furthering the work of queer
studies that interrogates the binaries — you are either masculine
or feminine, gay or straight — that arise from inflexible gender
and sexual identity categories. Our life with its fluctuating sensual needs, devotions, and obsessions can be complex and in-
consistent in ways that call into question self-definitions based
primarily on sexual preference. When the object of affection is a
pet, male–female or hetero–homosexual binaries used to define
one's intimate self become less relevant. In other words, to admit
that one's object choice might not always be human diminishes
the power of sexual identity categories that socially regulate the
individual. As Kathryn Bond Stockton has written, "[t]he family
pet swerves around the Freudian Oedipus in order to offer an
interval of animal and thus a figure of sideways growth" (113).

To cast the matter in another light, perhaps the reassurance
and calm a canine companion brings arise precisely because
transspecial love rises above the constrictions that gender and
sexuality place upon the human body. Pet devotion has the potential to question the regulating strictures and categories by
which we define sexuality, eroticism, family, and love, though
not in the banal sense that it offers different forms of genital
stimulation, indeed quite the opposite. Dog love corroborates

Lacan's dictum: "*quand on aime, il ne s'agit pas de sexe.*" Those who have an ardor for dogs know that their passion is unavailable and inaccessible elsewhere. Being independent of gender and sexuality, which is to say freed from either loving or being loved in terms of identity, this affection is cathartic. Because in one's emotional life the dog plays out various "roles"—friend, parent, child, lover, sibling (think pack member)—it cannot be restricted to any one of these. Hence the companion species is more than just a substitute, for it transcends these very categorizations. Even over the course of a day, the role the human being assumes in the relationship varies and mutates. Moreover, for the pet devotee the singularity or uniqueness of that one specific animal is what constitutes the bond as one of love, recalling Diamond's theory that attraction is individual-based not gender-based. Yet despite such particularity, insofar as this love betokens a profound kinship between species, in Bersani's words, it is founded on the consciousness of shared being in the world.

"O Lord, let me be the person my dog thinks I am." This popular bumper sticker expresses the unconditional nature of the dog's affection for its human companion. In other words, the dog loves us apart from our identity—whether this is defined by gender, race, class, or age. To be so loved also means we are loved, in Bersani's terms, for our virtual, ideal self that the dog perceives, responds to, indeed creates in us, freeing us from arbitrary social identities. Pet love can also be liberating because it redefines what we usually understand by the term "intimacy." Clearly, to love one's dog means to enjoy the sensuality of stroking and petting it. But this closeness means something far more profound. By virtue of its companionship, the pet offers nearness to one's very self, a certain calmness or equilibrium. This private, quiet, deep-seated familiarity and co-situatedness indicate a type of "intimacy." Synonyms for intimate include not only "close" and "dear" but also "innermost" and "intrinsic." Intimacy allows the bond with the animal to be affirmed. It entails a self-exploration whereby one opens oneself to life with a wholly different species. Not only is this other species ultimately foreign to us, but the *connection,* however quotidian, is mysteri-

72

ous too insofar as it miraculously arises between species. It is an intimacy that is also an "extimacy" (Lacan 1999[1959–60], 139), an openness to *das Andere.*

I have deliberately used the word "pet" here as opposed to the rather ungainly term "companion species." "Pet" evokes the gentleness and soft sensation of stroking fur, but more importantly it is a term of endearment and affection. We often give the people we love pet names, and frequently these will be those of smaller animals, such as "mouse." Paradoxically, pet names seem somehow to signal the singularity of the beloved one, more so even than his or her personal name. They represent the attempt to get away from social regulations and the constraining roles that stifle the expression of feeling. Pet names thus raise the question of whether people can have pet love for each other! Could it be that human relations are happiest when people reach the stage of viewing each other as beloved animals? An example of such intimacy would be when one does things together without feeling the need to converse.[2] Whatever form, then, "pet" love assumes, be it for a human or nonhuman being, and as long as the term "pet" does not imply a structure of domination and control, it has the potential of freeing one from identity strictures.

Although one of the most beautiful and sensitive dog stories, *Topsy,* was written by Marie Bonaparte (1940) and translated into German by Sigmund and Anna Freud while they were awaiting their exit visas to England, not one of these psychoanalysts delved in any great detail into the theoretical implications of their love for chows. Although animals have famously played a role in Freud's case studies of the Wolfman and the Rat Man, psychoanalysis has been oddly quiet on the topic of pet love. A queer perspective, however, offers an illuminating angle from which to consider the psychic complexities of pet love, above all its capacity to loosen the "regulatory regime" of identity categorizations (although one must avoid reducing this love to something therapeutic).

---

2   I wish to thank Maria de Guzman for these reflections.

Works Cited

Bersani, Leo, and Ulysse Dutoit. *Caravaggio*. London: BFI
Institute, 1999.

——— and Adam Phillips. *Intimacies*. Chicago: University of
Chicago Press, 2008.

Bland, Lucy and Laura Doan, eds. *Sexuality Uncensored: The
Documents of Sexual Science*. Chicago: University of Chicago Press, 1998.

Bonaparte, Marie. "Topsy." In *The Story of a Golden-Haired
Chow,* trans. Princess Eugenie of Greece. London: Pushkin,
1940.

Butler, Judith. *The Psychic Life of Power: Theories in Subjection*.
Stanford: Stanford University Press, 1997.

———. *Bodies that Matter: On the Discursive Limits of "Sex."*
New York and London: Routledge, 1993.

———. *Gender Trouble: Feminism and the Subversion of Identity*. New York and London: Routledge, 1990.

Chodorow, Nancy J. "Heterosexuality as a Compromise Formation: Reflections on the Psychoanalytic Theory of Sexual
Development." *Psychoanalysis and Contemporary Thought* 15
(1992): 267–304.

Dean, Tim. "Homosexuality and the Problem of Otherness."
In *Homosexuality and Psychoanalysis,* eds. Tim Dean and
Christopher Lane, 120–43. Chicago: University of Chicago
Press, 2001.

———. *Beyond Sexuality*. Chicago: University of Chicago
Press, 2000.

De Lauretis, Teresa. *The Practice of Love: Lesbian Sexuality and
Perverse Desire*. Bloomington: Indiana University Press,
1994.

Deutsch, Helene. "Homosexuality in Women." *International
Journal of Psycho-Analysis* 14 (1933): 34–56.

Diamond, Lisa M. *Sexual Fluidity: Understanding Women's
Love and Desire*. Cambridge: Harvard University Press,
2008.

Doty, Alexander. "There's Something Queer Here." In *Out in Culture: Gay, Lesbian, and Queer Essays in Popular Culture,* eds. Corey Creekmur and Alexander Doty, 71-90. Durham: Duke University Press, 1995.

Frommer, Martin. "Offending Gender: Being and Wanting in Male Same-Sex Desire." *Studies in Gender and Sexuality* 1, no. 2 (2000): 191–206.

Frosh, Stephen. *For and Against Psychoanalysis,* 2nd ed. London and New York: Routledge, 2006.

Fuss, Diana. *Identification Papers.* New York and London: Routledge, 1995.

Halperin, David M. *Saint Foucault: Towards a Gay Hagiography.* Oxford: Oxford University Press, 1995.

Hanson, Ellis. "Technology, Paranoia, and the Queer Voice." *Screen* 34, no. 2 (1993): 137–61.

Lacan, Jacques. *Book VII: The Ethics of Psychoanalysis,* ed. Jacques-Alain Miller, trans. Dennis Porter. London and New York: Routledge, 1999 (1959–60).

———. *Écrits: A Selection,* trans. Alan Sheridan. 1982; rpt. London and New York: Routledge, 2001.

———. *Livre XX: Encore. Séminaire de Jacques Lacan.* Paris: Seuil, 1975 (1972–73).

Laplanche, Jean. "The Theory of Seduction and the Problem of the Other." *International Journal of Psycho-Analysis* 78 (1997): 653–66.

McDougall, Joyce. "The Dead Father: On Early Psychic Trauma and its Relation to Disturbance in Sexual Identity and in Creative Activity." *International Journal of Psycho-Analysis* 70 (1989): 205–19.

O'Connor, Noreen, and Joanna Ryan. *Wild Desires and Mistaken Identities: Lesbianism and Psychoanalysis.* New York: Columbia University Press, 1993.

Rose, Jacqueline. *Sexuality in the Field of Vision.* London: Verso, 1986.

Sedgwick, Eve Kosofsky. *Tendencies.* Durham: Duke University Press, 1993.

Stockton, Kathryn Bond. *The Queer Child, or Growing Sideways in the Twentieth Century.* Durham: Duke University Press, 2009.

Wilton, Tamsin, ed. *Immortal, Invisible: Lesbians and the Moving Image.* London and New York: Routledge, 1995.

Missing Something?
Queer Desire

Lara Farina

Given that a particular configuration of sexual desire is the central emphasis of terms like "queer," "homosexual," "heterosexual," "lesbian," and "gay," it is a somewhat odd fact that theorization of non-normative desire(s) has been outpaced by scholarly work on sexual identity. In the humanities, the overwhelming interest in identity has been furthered by two important influences. The first is the work of Michel Foucault, whose multivolume *History of Sexuality* (1990, 1990, 1988) argued for the historical variability of identity-categories and, in doing so, shaped a field of study devoted to understanding the various configurations of sexual identity in particular historical moments and locations. The second is the challenge to lesbian and gay studies posed by scholars of race, class, and ethnicity, who have rightfully drawn attention to the varying intersections of identity previously obscured by analysis that assumes but does not acknowledge its own white, middle-class perspective. Still, even the most identity-focused work either presupposes or points to models of desire, and analysis of these models is necessary not just for understanding the sexual self but for thinking about the affective communities available to that self.

A "queer" take on desire may mean several things. We could, for instance, attempt to describe, theorize, or trace the effects of the desire *of queers,* where we understand "queer" to be a sexually non-normative self, and thus a kind of identity. Such work, however, has the effect of inscribing and normalizing a queer sexual identity and, consequently, limits the radical potential of "queer" as a method of critique. This critical potential is more available if we take our task to be the queering *of desire,* for there the dismantling of sexual norms, rather than their mere extension to include homosexuality, is the aim. Yet this tactic, which is indebted to the methods and politics of deconstruction, can leave us bereft of alternative models. As Margrit Shildrick (2007) writes of her own queer/crip critique of psychoanalytic theory, "although the value of investigating normative [sexual] anxiety [...] is undeniable, it scarcely yields a positive account for those who wish to celebrate sexuality and sexual expression" (237). The choice of approach to queer desire is not merely a matter of deciding which is most logical or productive, it is, as Shildrick's sentiment makes clear, also a matter of critical ethics. The value of each approach is to a large degree dependent on who it serves and to what ends.

The prevailing Western theories of desire, psychoanalytic theory included, have not served many of us well. Although many queer critics have now revisited Freud's hypotheses about homosexuality, the post-Freudian institutionalization of psychiatry has a history of isolating and denigrating non-normative desire, representing it as a disease to be confronted and cured. The account of desire that I will give here attempts to resist the medical model of homosexuality and perversion (which aims at a cure/normalization). I concur with Tim Dean and Christopher Lane's (2001) sentiment that "the problem is not homosexuality but social attitudes toward it [...] homophobia, rather than homosexuality, makes people ill" (4). Accordingly, I will revisit some historically influential narratives of desire together with the work of several queer theorists in the interests of suggesting models of desire that do not frame non-normative sexual desires as uniquely pathological, regressive, under-developed, or incomplete. The task, that is, is to think about the desires that have been excluded from sexual norms but to do so without understanding them as defined by lack (i.e., their "missing some-thing" that a normate sexual subjectivity supposedly possesses). Doing this, I argue, requires that we think about the very long-standing place of lack itself in theories of desire.

In the Beginning, There Was a Void

The analysis of desire always finds its stories, from Oedipus and Narcissus to the narratives of Genesis. Though Oedipus may have claimed the starring role on the psychoanalytic stage, I will begin with another classical text just as profound for its setting a template for desire in Western thought, and one that has had an important place in histories of sexuality (See Halperin 1990; Boswell 1992, 163–164).

Plato's *Symposium* (1999) is both story and theory in uneasy embrace, a multi-layered meditation on the nature and habits of desire. Here Plato, the philosopher who would ban poets from the ideal Republic, indulges in some fiction-making of his own in the form of a framed narrative. The text opens by eavesdrop-ping on a conversation between one Apollodorus and an un-named interlocutor, in which the anonymous character begs Apollodorus to recount the speeches delivered at the hippest dinner party in memory. This legendary gathering was a tribute to *eros* attended by the leading lights of Athens, including, of course, Plato's beloved Socrates. The discussion at this all-male affair was devoted largely to love between men and, in particu-lar, to the proper place of sexual desire in the pederastic system for educating the male youth of Athens. The *Symposium* would thus seem an ideal text to look for a theorization of same-sex de-sire, and, consequently, to hold some promise for a queer injec-tion of past narratives into present ones (especially into modern pathologizing discourses). Ironically however, the *Symposium*'s legacy has largely functioned to naturalize an implicitly hetero-sexist understanding of desire.[1]

---

1   "Heterosexism," broadly defined, refers to any practice that privileges an idealized heterosexuality, making it a standard by which other sexual prac-

Plato's text repeatedly represents desire as rooted in lack. The role of lack is of crucial importance in the defense of the man/boy relationships of the pederastic system. Early in the *Symposium*, the character Pausanias argues that the desire of older man and younger boy for one another relies on their complementarity: the young boy has beauty but lacks and wants wisdom; the older man has wisdom but lacks and wants beauty. Significantly, desire for Pausanias is a matter of ethics rather than ontology; educative pederasty is normalized as the most socially beneficial form for sexual desire to take, not as the most instinctual. But the two speeches following his give the principle of complementarity first an anatomical basis then a mytho-ontological one. Eryximachus, the doctor, argues that the body's desires are best understood in terms of "filling and emptying" (19) and that, when properly ordered, are desires for the meeting/balancing of opposites, the redressing of any perceived deficiency. Aristophanes the comedian, in the most narrative speech, imagines the human species, divided into three types, as instinctively desirous of a previous wholeness, one that has been missing ever since the gods split originally four-legged, two-faced humans in half. Our sexual desires, Aristophanes states, are for our missing "other halves" and reside in a kind of Unconscious where they evade self-understanding: "It's clear that each [half] has some wish in his mind that he can't articulate; instead, like an oracle, he half grasps what he wants and obscurely hints at it" (25). Although Aristophanes's three types (male homosexuals, heterosexuals, and female homosexuals) promise to diversify the possible configuration of desire depending on object-choice, his narrative actually elides the challenge that same-sex desire might pose to the principle of complementarity. Male and female homosexuals, rather than wanting a person like themselves, are represented as wanting a missing piece, their physi-

---

tices are judged, usually to the disadvantage of those who deviate from the imagined ideal. Few people perfectly match a normative idea of heterosexuality; consequently, heterosexism is also damaging to many who identify as "straight."

cally *opposite* half, and in this way, their desire is structurally no different than heterosexual desire.

The idea that lack is the essential precondition for desire receives its most authoritative endorsement in the *Symposium* from none other than Socrates, who makes the point a foundation for his further discourse on love, beauty, and wisdom. His argument responds to a prior speech made by Agathon, the popular young tragedian of the group. Agathon's reflections on *eros* are markedly different than those in the other speeches. Rather than argue that erotic desire has as its aim the coming together of opposites, Agathon fashions an enamored portrait of the God of Love, who he portrays as an idealized version of himself: young, beautiful, and sensitive. Agathon's speech both understands desire's operation as a form of self-copying and is itself an exercise in narcissism, as the other members of the party clearly understand: "there were shouts of admiration from everyone present, because the young man had spoken in a way that reflected well on himself and the god" (32). Socrates, however, quickly demolishes Agathon's poetic fantasy, arguing first that love must be love *of* something, then that love must be of something the lover needs. Since we do not need what we already have, desire must always be directed at what we lack: "so this and every other case of desire is desire for what isn't available and actually there" (35). As Leo Bersani (2001) notes, this is the only argument that Socrates himself makes in the *Symposium*; the rest of the philosopher's contributions are ostensibly his repetition of arguments made to him by the visionary Diotima, though those are characteristically Platonic in their focus on Ideal Forms (1999, 360). That desire is always desire for "what isn't available and actually there," leads Socrates/Diotima to outline a progression to the ultimate form of love in which we, mere material mortals, know that what we really love/need is our opposite, the perfect, eternal Form of Beauty.

The principle of opposition outlined by Socrates and his fellow discussants has some important consequences for understanding the place of gender in models of desire. Although the subject of the *Symposium* is men's love for other men (and then men's love of the Ideal through loving other men), the principle of opposition requires that partners embody different gender roles. The lovers of young boys are the active partners, whose masculinity is established in their higher status, older age, and developed intellect. The young boys themselves are the pursued, socially unformed, passive partners, lacking everything except for youth and beauty. Their reduction to a pleasing corporeality locates them in a feminine position, if we recall the understanding of gender that Plato himself develops in his *Timaeus*. There, the masculine force of "heat" creates new beings by acting upon feminine "matter," which is passive and lacking its own generative vitality (1977, 69). The young boys are not women: they will not forever be passive bodies to be shaped by the attentions of older men. But it is their femininity in their youth that makes them appropriate partners for masculine citizens. Once they themselves become masculine adults, they must switch to the opposite role in coupling. The desire among the *Symposium*'s participants to maintain this gender binary is evident in the consternation caused by the example of Achilles and Patroclus, where the idea that the younger and more beautiful Achilles might be the active lover is dismissed as "nonsense" (1999, 30). This dismissal is, in effect, an attempt to "straighten" the more queer representations of the literary tradition inherited by the *Symposium*'s Athenians.

What may have given rise to a theory of queer desire, i.e., a conversation in which men discuss their love for one another, largely stresses the need for gender opposition that also grounds claims that heterosexuality is natural, instinctive, and proper. Now, the text of the *Symposium* may be read differently, as Bersani has done (and to which I'll return below), but the legacy of Plato's story, which largely resides in the arguments I've outlined above, matters as much as the work itself for understanding, and intervening in, Western models of desire. The understanding of desire as springing from lack, and specifically from lack of a complementary other, has had pride of place in Western theory and representation.

The Persistence of Absence

Neither Sigmund Freud nor his major post-structuralist inter-preter, Jacques Lacan, work extensively with Platonic philoso-phy, and at least one recent reading of Lacan argues that his thought is "anti-Platonic" and more in keeping with the writings of the Pre-Socratics (Badiou 2006). Nonetheless, their referenc-es to Plato are provocative. Lacan on more than one occasion compares the psychoanalyst to Socrates (2006[1966], 310), and Freud (1905) prefaced "Three Essays on the Theory of Sexual-ity" with a nod to the *Symposium*'s author, writing in his work's fourth edition, "anyone who looks down with contempt upon psycho-analysis from a superior vantage-point should remem-ber how closely the enlarged sexuality of psycho-analysis coin-cides with the Eros of the divine Plato" (xix). Plato thus provides an intellectual heritage and authority for the psychoanalytic sci-ence of desire.

It is odd, however, that Freud should see in Plato's *eros* an "enlarged sexuality," given his rather disingenuous allusion to the *Symposium* itself at the beginning of the "Sexual Aber-rations" section of "Three Essays" (22). Freud rewrites Aris-tophanes's myth so that gender coincides more neatly with sex difference, giving us a story exclusively focused on an original heterosexuality. Although Aristophanes does maintain the mas-culine/feminine binary in the love couple, in his account the op-positional structure is manifest in three possible arrangements: man/boy, man/woman, and (the barely discussed) woman/woman. Freud's claim that readers may find it a "great surprise" that there should be a "very considerable" number of cases of same-sex desire, belies his expectation of an audience already familiar with Plato, and seems aimed, rather, at holders of the "popular opinion" against whom he argues for his theory of in-fantile sexuality (21).

Freud argues for the prevalence, even the normality, of same-sex desire in "Three Essays," and in doing so, he re-presents what he perhaps thought to be the true Platonic *eros* against its popular heterosexualization (64). Nonetheless, Plato's principle legacy in Freud's writing is an account of human development in which desire is seen to result from the lack of an opposite, principally in the domain of gender. The Oedipus complex, of course, locates this account in the triadic familial arrangement of father/mother/child rather than in the dyad of man/boy. Sexual desire, conceived largely as experienced by a male child, is born of the trauma of losing the mother's body, under the threat of the father's competition for it. The mother is further not only the forbidden/missing object of desire but is the signifier of absence itself because of her lack of a penis/phallus. The mother, famously, is perceived as castrated, lacking, when the child comes to realize she has no penis. The child's forced separation from the mother and recognition of her as lacking brings about a subsequent identification with the father, instituting what Carla Freccero (2006) terms "the hegemonic heterosexual matrix (whereby gender, desire, and sex are imaginarily unified according to the desire/identification split)" (22). The child comes to identify with his proper gender (via the father) and to distinguish himself, and thereby come to desire, the "opposite" gender (via the mother); indeed, the Oedipus complex, which Freud sees as a foundational structure of modern Western society, produces the opposition of gender and the experience of desire as lack.

Of course, perverts (homosexuals, fetishists, pedophiles, and others) and women of all kinds don't fit neatly into the most simple formulation of Oedipus, but Freud largely tries to account for the "considerable" numbers of these while keeping the oppositional structure of desire intact. Women get the Electra complex, which tries, rather unconvincingly, to explain why a female child would not also desire the mother's nurturing body and regard the father as competition for it — why, that is, women should "normally" come to desire men. The answer is again that desire is for what one does not have, in this case, the phallus/penis; if a woman cannot have the phallus, she can at least try to be the phallus for a man (hence her narcissistic self-absorption in her own body) (Freud 1914, 1931). Male homosexuals also pose a problem, and, as Tim Dean (2001) notes, "though

Freud rarely stops talking about homosexuality, he never actually theorizes it as a distinctly psychoanalytic idea" (121). Nonetheless, Freud does not take the prevalence of homosexuality to indicate that the universal experience of Oedipus may not be so universal, but, rather, that the male homosexual accedes to Oedipus in a different way. Rather than take psychic measures to prevent castration, the homosexual boy accepts castration in advance of the fact, identifying with the feminine mother and mimicking her desire for the masculine father. Why this should happen is unclear, but Freud (1910) suggests that the work of Oedipus in creating a socially acceptable heterosexual becomes undone by competing desires to return to a pre-Oedipal state (100). Homosexual desires, while common, are regressive, "an atavism, in which the child gets stuck — fixated — at some more primitive stage of psychic evolution, whether it be narcissistic, oral, or anal" (Robinson 2001, 92). Fetishists, too, dabble in the pre-Oedipal, for their object attachments are substitutes for the mother's lost penis. Although they are aware of the mother's castration, their fetishes allow for a disavowal of her lack and a return to the phantasmic perception of the pre-Oedipal mother as "phallic" (1927).

Lacan's parsing of Freudian desire is notoriously complex. Suffice it to say here that Lacanian psychoanalysis preserves and even magnifies the role of lack in desire. Lacan sees the crucial moment in identity-formation as that in which a child realizes a distinction between self and other, thereby forming a notion of the self based on a visual (specular) body image rather than on its earlier, unbounded physical sensation. This process allows the child entrance to the realm of the Symbolic, organized by language, which Lacan understands as operating on the principle of difference (words convey that something is this and not that). Riven by difference, the Symbolic is haunted by the "Other," and the Other, is, in turn, the site of lack, since the endless chain of difference that structures language will never find the completion that the child experienced early in its life when it did not distinguish itself from anything else. Desire is motivated by this lack, as the subject strives (unsuccessfully) to fill the void with an endless series of objects. If this lack were to be satisfied, which it cannot be, desire would cease, as presumably would our participation in the Symbolic. If we are to maintain our participation in the realm of language then, ultimately what we must desire is to keep desiring (see Lacan 2006[1966], 3–9, 31–106).

Whether Lacanian theory just as powerfully re-inscribes the importance of gender complementarity as it does the place of lack is the subject of some debate. Tim Dean (2001) has argued that Lacan enables us to think about the relation of self and other without automatically conflating this psychic development with the recognition of sex difference: "Lacan sees in Freud's theory of narcissism the possibility of a relation to otherness before any relation to difference" (126). More typically, however, queer and feminist theorists have found in Lacan, as in Freud, an unpalatable reliance on the opposition of masculine/feminine and the equation of the feminine with the negation of a privileged masculine (see Grosz 1995, 177). The relation between lack and the feminine is established in Lacan's writing, as it is in Freud's, in the representation of the inaccessible body of the Mother, which Lacan (1992[1959–60]) terms "the absolute Other of the subject" or "*das Ding*" (the Thing) beyond signification (70). Though the Other is what motivates desire, the mother cannot be a positive locus of a Platonic Ideal such as the Good or the Beautiful because the subject is barred from enjoying her, thereby contaminating the Good with the taboo. An example of the deformation of the feminine can be seen in Lacan's reading of courtly love lyrics as paradigmatic of "the madness of love." The central feature of the troubadour lyrics cited by him is their idealization of the beloved Lady by her male lover and their sharp contrast in gender attributes: he is hot, active, and passionate; she is cold, passive, and unfeeling. She is a path toward the Ideal but with a distinctly Lacanian twist, for as the psychoanalyst perceives, "In this poetic field, the feminine is emptied of all real substance" and, as the carrier of lack, becomes a "terrifying, an inhuman partner" (149–50).

As might be expected, any contact with this terrifying, inhuman Other, with, that is, the true focus of desire, threatens to annihilate the masculine subject. Lacan notes that the best that the courtly lover could hope for would be a mere signal, a vague salutation emanating from the Other's position (152). Anything more might well obliterate the ego. Lacan's yoking together of desire and death is indebted, of course, to the Freudian death drive, but it also borrows from the work of Lacan's friend and fellow theorist of desire, Georges Bataille, who doubtless influenced Lacan's reading of the troubadour lyric (Holsinger 2005). Bataille's (1986) work has many continuities with Lacan's, and its central thesis is that eroticism, which is independent of the social imperative to reproduce, always aims at the "continuity of being" (13) to be found in death. Bataille sees in sexual reproduction not an extension of the self but a reminder that we are isolated beings: children may be similar to their parents, but parent and child are not one. Eroticism, though linked to sexual reproduction, is in fact a refusal of its imposition of discontinuity. It is a radical urge to break down the "established patterns" that define us as separate individuals (18). Such ego-dissolving practices as poetry, religious mysticism, and "primitive sacrifice" are for Bataille paradigmatically erotic. Bataille's theory of *eros* as the pursuit of interpersonal "continuity" might seem to hold promise for thinking about queer desire, since a shattering of ego-stabilizing patterns would presumably make gender identity irrelevant. However, passages like the following set us back within oppositional gender roles: "When I come to religious eroticism which is concerned with a fusion of beings with a world beyond everyday reality I shall return to the significance of sacrifice. Here and now, however, I must emphasize that the female partner in eroticism was seen as the victim, the male as the sacrificer, both during the consummation losing themselves in the continuity established by the first destructive act" (18).

If the feminine role is to be a sacrificial victim, and masculine desire is a desire to be continuous with the sacrificed, we might understand why Lacan thought that the masculine subject must content himself with a mere nod from the Other. For in Bataille's account, the consummation of true desire demands one's death.

Queer Interventions

So what can queer theories of desire take from psychoanalysis and related inquiries into *eros*? The writing of desire as masculine desire for the feminine Other, and the equation of, on the one hand, desire with lack, and on the other, the feminine Other with lack and death seems nearly unworkable for empowering models of same-sex eroticism. While some queer theorists trace out a radical vision of embracing the death drive (Edelman 2004), it is hardly surprising that others feel only frustration with the continued status of psychoanalysis in critical narratives on the subject: "given that for most contemporary readers the idea that a woman is either castrated, or that her clitoris is really an atrophied and inferior penis is unbelievable, then why, one could ask, does this 'myth' continue to play such a central role in psychoanalytic accounts of sexual difference and so-called sexual perversions?" (Sullivan 2003, 181). Quite apart from a more careful working out of the relation between penis and phallus, we might answer the above question thus: because theorizing desire without lack is hard to do. Western philosophy has been re-writing the story of desire as lack for at least 2,500 years, and Freud re-positioned it into the realm of the domestic privileged by twentieth-century culture. Therein lies the power of psychoanalytic narratives. Further, the perception of a gender binary in which masculine and feminine are opposed and complementary is so entrenched that it is prevalent in not only the "straight" world but in lesbian and gay cultures as well. Top versus bottom, butch versus femme, daddy versus twink, dom versus slave (see Hogan and Hudson 1999) are all iterations of this arrangement of gender and are often so normative that a person identified as one of these types may feel the need to write to advice columns for assurance that it is not pathological to be attracted to one of her own kind (to be, for example, a butch who is attracted to other butches).

This does not mean, however, that no other stories have been told or that even the iconic stories may not be read differently. The literature of "courtly love," for example, when viewed more broadly than the canonical texts with which Lacan was familiar (and this canon was itself of twentieth-century making), contains a diversity of gender representations and desiring subjects. The troubadour lyrics themselves can be easily read as more about the masculine subject's desire for other (masculine) men than they are about heterosexual *eros,* given the prevalence of the "senhal," or dedication to another man, at the end of poems. When the poet Peire Vidal, for example, laments the pain of his love for the lady "Vierna," he does so by addressing his fair lord (*bel senher*) Raymond V of Toulouse, who he nicknames "Castiat." The poem's conclusion, including the senhal "Vierna, I walk bright in loving you/ lacking only the sight of Castiat, my lord," leaves open the question of who provides the poet greater "joy," lady or lord or even perhaps the two together (Proenza 1978).

In her work, *Queer/Early/Modern,* Carla Freccero (2006) takes up precisely the task of reading the canonical love lyric differently. Using the example of Petrarch's *Canzioniere,* a classic of Western poetry, she argues that the love lyric is shot through with "the trace of something queer," noting that the poet's depiction of his love for the inaccessible Laura actually portrays a relation of both desire for and identification with the beloved Lady. This collapsing of desire and identification is further apparent in the love poems of the Renaissance writer Louise Labé, who "articulates the predicament of occupying both sides of the subject/object split but only one side of the sexual difference divide." (22) Labé's desiring female subject is her own object, she receives the wound of love from her own projection/voicing of desire: "Those shafts of mine those same eyes of mine undid." (23) Freccero reads this self-circling love as a demystification of "the blatant pretext" that the love lyric's traditionally masculine subject addresses a feminine other when in fact he is the origin of both male lover and beloved Lady.

We might describe this desire, though Freccero does not, as narcissistic. And, indeed, queer theorists are revisiting the con-

cept of narcissism, from both within and without psychoanalytic paradigms (the myth of Narcissus far predates Freud). In
his attempts to take up Michel Foucault's challenge of theorizing "new ways of being together," Leo Bersani (2001) returns to
Plato's *Symposium*, "the founding text of desire as lack" (359), to
offer a different reading than the one I outline above. Arguing
that "Socrates' coercive move" against Agathon's poetic speech is
enabled by "a logical confusion that makes us glimpse the possibility of love, or desire, as including within itself its object"
(360), he notes that the philosopher's logic performs something
different than it ostensibly describes. While Socrates's argument
is for desire as lack, the examples he uses actually suggest that:
"Presence is always relational; desire would be the affective recognition of something like our debt to all those forms of being
that relationally define and activate our being. Desire mobilizes
correspondences of being" (361).

This understanding of desire as productive, rather than the
result of negation, is further supported by Diotima's teaching
(as repeated by Socrates) that what desire wants is not a lacking Ideal like Beauty or Goodness, but rather "reproduction in
birth and beauty," whereby the subject more or less becomes a
channel for Beauty or Goodness by authoring/birthing beautiful
things — art, poetry, and philosophy among them. Thus, Bersani argues that the important thing about Platonic *eros* in the
Symposium is its "replicative structure," whereby the self both
longs for and produces its copies. While this may sound like
a re-valorization of biological reproduction (and the heterosex needed for it), begetting children, which is associated with
women, ranks rather low in Socrates/Diotima's vision of desire
as cultural project. Bersani argues that "the philosophical lesson
of the fable is that we relate to difference by recognizing and
longing for sameness. All love is, in a sense, homoerotic" (365).
As per Socrates's emphasis on beautiful discourses, the replicative structures Bersani emphasizes largely occur in the domain
of the aesthetic, and here we should recall the uncharacteristi-
cally literary form of the *Symposium*, with its frames, multiple
and overlapping points of view, and interest in re-presenting

its characters for future generations. Indeed, we might wonder whether Agathon's narcissistic paean to the God of Love might not, after all, be exactly what Diotima's vision ultimately validates: an embodiment of Beauty (Agathon) desiring and creating a beautiful copy of itself in language.

Of course, the endorsement of a model of *eros* based on narcissism raises some troubling ethical questions. To say that a loving relation must be based on a recognition of sameness outside of the self risks promoting a kind of affective clannishness, and homosexual communities are hardly immune to an ethically dubious policing of the boundaries of the self-same, as Jasbir Puar (2007) has demonstrated in her recent work on "homonationalism." Returning to the text of the *Symposium,* it is impossible not to note that its network of loving relations still extends only to the masculine citizenry of Athens. Foreigners, slaves, and women are pointedly excluded from the party. If, following Bersani's reading, we do not see desire as originating in a ghastly, feminized lack, what we witness is instead the rendering of women as unnecessary for civilization, which can erotically reproduce itself in Beauty better without them.

Both Bersani and Tim Dean have tried to confront narcissism's ethical dilemma by working on a concept of "impersonal narcissism." While in his article on the Symposium, "Genital Chastity" (2001), Bersani dismisses psychoanalytic discourse as unhelpful in thinking about "new ways of being together," he returns to a dialogue with psychoanalysis (via his co-author, the analyst Adam Phillips) in his more recent work, *Intimacies* (2008). There, Bersani and Phillips return to another Platonic text, *Phaedrus,* to suggest ways in which desire might have as its object a, its object cause, the recognition of one's *potential* being *in* others. Such an expansive form of narcissism, which does not need to solidify the self as it is, but rather postulates new forms of being, would be non-appropriative, eschewing the *acquisition* or mastery of one's object of desire. Working more firmly within psychoanalytic theory, specifically with Lacan's version of it, Dean (2001) has also argued for "an ethics of sexuality that does not reduce Otherness to personhood or [sex] difference"

(128). Lacan places the subject's navigation around the Other in the unconscious, Dean notes, arguing that doing so allows us to confront the Other's "inhuman strangeness" in a venue that precedes gender. Thus Dean's work in *Beyond Sexuality* attempts to envision a desire for the Other disentangled from object-choice or even personhood altogether.

Still, as Dean himself acknowledges, the conflation of the Other with the recognition of sex difference is hard to avoid in Lacanian theory (137), and, ultimately, it may be impossible or undesirable to use psychoanalysis to theorize female sexuality independently of masculine desire. In her work on lesbian desire, Elizabeth Grosz (1995) comes to the same conclusion (via a critique of Teresa de Lauretis [1994]), and she suggests another tactic entirely for understanding the work of *eros* in same-sex relations. Grosz notes that de Lauretis's thorough-going attempt to modify psychoanalytic theory to better account for lesbian desire still leaves intact its central postulate about desire as lack. Moreover, Grosz questions the ethics and politics of arriving at a unified theory of lesbian desire, one that leaves little room for the variety of relations clumped together under the term "lesbian" or for historical and cultural specificity. Her response is to dispense with the *ontology* of desire. Drawing inspiration from the philosophy of Friedrich Nietzsche and the "anti-Oedipal" theory of Gilles Deleuze and Félix Guattari, Grosz writes: "I don't want to discuss lesbian desire in terms of a psychical depth or interiority, in terms of a genesis, development or process of constitution, history, or etiology. I am much less interested in where lesbian desire comes from, how it emerges, and the way in which it develops, than where it is going, its possibilities, its future" (174).

Grosz's approach, which privileges the analysis of "becoming" over the understanding of "being," does for desire what Judith Butler's work (1990, 1993), with its argument that difference is "performative," does for gender. It does not deny that persons come to adopt identities, or that gay and lesbian collectivities may need to embrace such identities for political reasons, but it tries to decouple desire from identity in order to envision desire as *productive* rather than reactive.

In looking at *eros* as essentially creative, Grosz's work has continuities with Bersani's. However, her eschewing of psychic interiority and focus on the desiring body is more explicit. She proposes we think about desire "as a mode of surface contact" in which bodily regions become covetous of the intensity and excitation of other, adjacent bodily regions. The erotic is a manifestation of an excessive materiality, of "libidinal zones [that are] continually in the process of being produced, renewed, transformed, though experimentation, practices, innovations, the accidents or contingencies of life itself" (199). This is not just an argument against the privileging of genital sexuality over the pleasures sought by other bodily locations. It is also a way of thinking about desire in which the body (which is not reducible to a singular body-image) comes first, leading the "self" along with it as a current of "continuous excitation" constantly remakes it. Grosz portrays desire not as lack, but as an exuberant, expansive fullness in perpetual movement and transformation. One might well observe that Grosz, whose ostensible subject is lesbian desire, offers a model of *eros* without any specific ties to lesbian or even same-sex sexuality. By disaggregating the self in the focus on the shifting contact between bodily zones, Grosz portrays the operation of desire as having little to do with gendered object-relations. But her aim is to offer not a diagnosis of same-sex desire so much as an account that can be of service to lesbians, among others, via its refusal to repeat and thereby authorize a gender binary in which the feminine can only shadow the masculine.

Beyond Sobriety, a Queer Intoxication with Desire

> *We are drunk with love and intoxicated and cannot be still.*
> — Jalal al-din Rumi, Lyric 141, 1968, 118

Socrates is the only participant in the symposium who remains sober. His nearly inhuman capacity to remain level-headed amidst all sorts of chaos — Bacchic frenzies, war, political witch hunts — is legendary and attested to in the *Symposium* by his soused admirer Alcibiades. But the rest of the party's members are drunk, very drunk. Their intoxicated movements around the couches at Agathon's house, getting up to be close to new arrivals, shifting places as desiring relations must be re-negotiated (Who gets to be closer to Socrates? To Agathon? Where should Alcibiades go? Who should occupy the speaker's place?) echo Grosz's portrait of the repositioning of the body by the continuous productions of desire. The bodies at the symposium, in restless motion, are drunk with love. Socrates the sober one, however, does not want this. Responding to Agathon's invitation to share his seat, the philosopher sarcastically replies "How splendid it would be, Agathon, if wisdom could flow from the fuller to the emptier of us when we touch, like water, which flows through a piece of wool from a fuller cup to an emptier one. If wisdom is really like that, I regard it as a great privilege to share your couch" (1999, 7). Socrates does not want to be moved by those proximate to him; his remark distances himself from the amorous Agathon and insists that his desire, which is for wisdom, cannot just "flow" into the other, into the site of lack. There will be no easy equalization of subject and object. Sobriety wants fixity; it wants boundaries; it wants to maintain the purity of the Truth. I mentioned earlier that we might perhaps think of Agathon's narcissistic speech as an example of precisely the "giving birth in Beauty" that Socrates appears to endorse. But Socrates himself does not respond to it this way, because the speech, though beautiful, is not *true*; "I was so naïve, I thought you should tell the truth about the subject of the eulogy," he carps. Party pooper. Asserting the truth, in contra-distinction from mere poetic eloquence, allows Socrates to dismiss Agathon as intellectually inferior and to put everybody else in their proper place as well.

What are the risks of tipsy perspectives on desire? I ask this, in part, because psychoanalysis itself is often given the role of policing giddiness in queer theory. Even in the alternative-seeking work of Bersani and Grosz, Freudian/Lacanian psychoanalysis, with its emphasis on the original trauma of subjectivity (forced detachment, castration, loss of the Other), is hailed as a necessary agent of sobriety (Grosz 1995, 242, n. 1). Bersani (2008), for his part, writes that the "greatness" of Lacanian theory "may lie in its insistence on a human destructiveness resistant to any therapeutic endeavors whatsoever" (60). Why is it so necessary to be sober, even pessimistic, when thinking about queer desire? Why is it "great" that we theorize aggression as inevitable for *jouissance*?

We return here to the ethics and politics of queer theory, and to Margrit Shildrick's (2007) opinion that queer-as-critique (as opposed to queer-as-identity) can be depressingly "gloomy." Shildrick herself ultimately finds Lacanian theory unsalvageable for theorizing the desire of "disabled" bodies, an affective collectivity from whom queer theory has much to learn. Bersani and Grosz both caution against "Utopian" narratives, and the former argues that adherence to these allows us to overlook or even validate contemporary political atrocities. Perhaps it is just my perspective, here in West Virginia, with its endemic poverty, ravaged environment, and ingrained (but historically justified) mistrust of collective enterprise, but Utopian thinking hardly seems to be the greatest liability for counter-hegemonic politics. Frustration, depression, and inertia seem far more powerful obstacles. So it is not surprising that I find Grosz and Bersani most inspiring when they are least sober. When Bersani writes about the pleasurable multiplication of potential selves in art or when Grosz's own language for describing desire vaults from metaphor to metaphor, these writers make room for their reader's experience of affect, an improper pleasure in the conversation about eros. The theoretical Truth about desire becomes contaminated with a little poetry. The philosopher is a little besotted with *eros*.

A popular legend about Socrates's philosophic predecessor, Thales, depicted the logician falling into a ditch, after being so taken up in the contemplation of philosophy that, not heeding where he is going, he bumbles and reels around, eventually toppling over.² Interestingly, Socrates applies the story of Thales to himself in the dialogue *Theaetetus,* stating "that same gibe [about Thales] will do for everyone who spends his life in philosophy." (1973, 51) Rather than mere anti-intellectual mockery, then, this figuration of the reeling philosopher perhaps reveals the further implications of the *Symposium's* associations between love, philosophy, and intoxication. Socrates desires wisdom; to experience desire is to be drunk on love; therefore Socrates is drunk on love. Talking about *eros* is participating in *eros,* even if that talk aims at knowledge. So perhaps what "queer" theorization of desire needs is not to remain sober, or to retain the pessimism of Freudian/Lacanian psychoanalysis, but to allow for ways in which the analyst, too, can be drunk on love rather than remain at a remove from the erotic object of analysis. How splendid it would be to rejoin the party, sitting at the side of beauty, among all the others.

Works Cited

Badiou, Alain. "Lacan and the Pre-Socratics." In *Lacan: The Silent Partners,* ed. Slavoj Žižek, 7–16. London: Verso, 2006.

Bataille, Georges. *Erotism: Death and Sensuality,* trans. Mary Dalwood. San Francisco: City Lights, 1986.

Bersani, Leo. "Genital Chastity." In *Homosexuality and Psychoanalysis,* eds. Tim Dean and Christopher Lane, 351–86. Chicago and London: Chicago University Press, 2001.

———. *Homos.* Cambridge and London: Harvard University Press, 1995.

——— and Adam Phillips. *Intimacies.* Chicago and London: University of Chicago Press, 2008.

Boswell, John. "Categories, Experience, and Sexuality." In *Forms of Desire: Sexual Orientation and the Social Construc-*

---

2 I am grateful to Jessica Rosenfeld for drawing my attention to the figure of Thales and the connection with *eros.* See her discussion of the tale in *Ethics and Enjoyment in Late Medieval Poetry* (2011, 108–10).

tionist Controversy, ed. Edward Stein, 133–73. New York and London: Routledge, 1992.

Butler, Judith. *Bodies That Matter: On the Discursive Limits of "Sex."* New York and London: Routledge, 1993.

———. *Gender Trouble: Feminism and the Subversion of Identity.* New York and London: Routledge, 1990.

Dean, Tim. *Beyond Sexuality.* Chicago and London: University of Chicago Press, 2000.

———. "Homosexuality and the Problem of Otherness." In *Homosexuality and Psychoanalysis,* eds. Tim Dean and Christopher Lane, 120–43. Chicago and London: Chicago University Press, 2001.

——— and Christopher Lane, eds. *Homosexuality and Psychoanalysis.* Chicago and London: University of Chicago Press, 2001.

De Lauretis, Theresa. *The Practice of Love: Lesbian Sexuality and Perverse Desire.* Bloomington and Indianapolis: Indiana University Press, 1994.

Edelman, Lee. *No Future: Queer Theory and the Death Drive.* Durham and London: Duke University Press, 2004.

Foucault, Michel. *The History of Sexuality, Vol. 1: An Introduction,* trans. Robert Hurley. New York: Vintage, 1990 (1976).

———. *The History of Sexuality, Vol. 2: The Use of Pleasure,* translated by Robert Hurley. New York: Vintage, 1990 (1984).

———. *The History of Sexuality, Vol. 3: The Care of the Self,* translated by Robert Hurley. New York: Vintage, 1988 (1984).

Freccero, Carla. *Queer/Early/Modern.* Durham and London: Duke University Press, 2006.

Freud, Sigmund. "Female Sexuality" (1931). In *The Standard Edition of the Complete Psychological Works of Sigmund Freud,* vol. 21, trans. James Strachey in collaboration with Anna Freud and assisted by Alix Strachey and Alan Tyson, 225–43. 1961; rpt. London: Vintage 2001.

———. "Fetishism" (1927). In *The Standard Edition of the Complete Psychological Works of Sigmund Freud,* vol. 21, trans. James Strachey in collaboration with Anna Freud and assisted by Alix Strachey and Alan Tyson, 149–57. 1961; rpt. London: Vintage, 2001.

———. "On Narcissism: An Introduction" (1914). In *The Standard Edition of the Complete Psychological Works of Sigmund Freud,* vol. 14, trans. James Strachey in collaboration with Anna Freud and assisted by Alix Strachey and Alan Tyson, 69–102. 1957; rpt. London: Vintage, 2001.

———. "Leonardo da Vinci and a Memory of His Childhood" (1910). In *The Standard Edition of the Complete Psychological Works of Sigmund Freud,* vol. 11, trans. James Strachey in collaboration with Anna Freud and assisted by Alix Strachey and Alan Tyson, 57–137. 1957; rpt. London: Vintage, 2001.

———. "Three Essays on the Theory of Sexuality" (1905). In *The Standard Edition of the Complete Psychological Works of Sigmund Freud,* vol. 7, trans. James Strachey in collaboration with Anna Freud and assisted by Alix Strachey and Alan Tyson, 123–245. 1953; rpt. London: Vintage, 2001.

Grosz, Elizabeth. *Space, Time, and Perversion: Essays on the Politics of Bodies.* New York and London: Routledge, 1995.

Halperin, David M. *One Hundred Years of Homosexuality and Other Essays on Greek Love.* New York and London: Routledge, 1990.

Hogan, Steve, and Lee Hudson, eds. *Completely Queer: The Gay and Lesbian Encyclopedia.* New York: Holt Paperbacks, 1999.

Holsinger, Bruce. *The Premodern Condition: Medievalism and the Making of Theory.* Chicago and London: University of Chicago Press, 2005.

Lacan, Jacques. *Ecrits,* trans. Bruce Fink. New York and London: W.W. Norton, 2006 (1966).

———. *Book VII: The Ethics of Psychoanalysis,* ed. Jacques-Alain Miller, trans. Dennis Porter. New York and London: W.W. Norton, 1992 (1959–60).

Plato. *The Symposium,* trans. Christopher Gill. New York: Penguin, 1999.

———. *Theaetetus,* trans. John McDowell. Oxford: Clarendon, 1973.

———. *Timaeus and Critias,* trans. Desmond Lee. New York: Penguin, 1977.

Proensa: An Anthology of Troubadour Poetry, ed. George Economou, trans. Paul Blackburn. Berkeley: University of California Press, 1978.

Puar, Jasbir. *Terrorist Assemblages: Homonationalism in Queer Times.* Durham and London: Duke University Press, 2007.

Robinson, Paul. "Freud and Homosexuality." In *Homosexuality and Psychoanalysis,* eds. Tim Dean and Christopher Lane, 91–97. Chicago and London: University of Chicago Press.

Rosenfeld, Jessica. *Ethics and Enjoyment in Late Medieval Poetry, Love after Aristotle.* Cambridge and New York: Cambridge University Press, 2011.

Rumi, Jalal al-din. *Mystical Poems of Rumi,* trans. A.J. Arberry. Chicago and London: University of Chicago Press, 1968.

Shildrick, Margrit. "Dangerous Discourses: Anxiety, Desire, and Disability." *Studies in Gender and Sexuality* 8, no. 3 (2007): 221–44.

Sullivan, Nikki. *A Critical Introduction to Queer Theory.* New York: New York University Press, 2003.

3 | PLEASURE

Jouissance,
the Gash of Bliss

Kathryn Bond Stockton[1]

> … that moment when my body pursues its own ideas — for
> my body does not have the same ideas I do […] I need to
> distinguish euphoria, fulfillment […] from shock, distur-
> bance, even loss, which are proper to ecstasy, to bliss.
> — Barthes 1975, 17, 19.

> It is the same as for Saint Theresa — you only have to go and
> look at Bernini's statue in Rome to understand immediately
> that she's coming […]. And what is her *jouissance,* her com-
> ing, from? It is clear that the essential testimony of the mystics
> is that they are experiencing it but know nothing about it.
> — Lacan 1985, 147.

Jouissance is the strangest glistening, a dark glamour of rapture and disruption. It shines and cuts and leaves its bearer not
knowing what to make of herself — or her pleasure. She is left
beside herself, feeling ecstatically severed from herself, seized
by subtleties, strange to say, even though bliss is an overwhelm-

---

1 I gratefully acknowledge Stanford University Press and Duke University
   Press for kindly permitting me to draw some materials for this chapter from
   my books (2009, 2006, 1994).

ing force. ("Spiritual joy," says *American Heritage*; "paradise," "seventh heaven," "cloud nine," adds *Roget's*.) Bliss is a word for impossibilities, *felt* and *grasped* as such. Something (im)possible coursing through the body, bending the mind. Then, on a dime: rapid, luminous deteriorations.

If per chance it didn't exist, queers would invent it. Along with irony, bliss is a quintessential queer accouterment. It's hedonistic and wedded to pain. It's clearly buoyant, yet it is dark. It's provocatively sexy, intimate, scandalous, and bodily, while it's evasive of capture and speech. Beyond the reach of words, it's both spiritual and material — spiritual materialist — a materiality that is ineffable and escapes norms. It's the perversion everyone shares, no one knows, and, with its shadows and ties to loss, society denies in favor of "pleasure."

The psychoanalysis, then, that jibes with queer theory's thought and brio — its scandalous eruptions — sees *jouissance* as a means of naming explosive, infinite, unsolvable desire (not the imagined serenity of plenitude), which requires us to reconceive relationships around such oddities as caressing lack, embracing shame, and flirting with the cutting force of beauty (Bernini's Saint Theresa). Psychoanalysis, for this reason, benefits from having bliss (as a concept) go on tour, swerve toward queer theoretical contemplations, which themselves have been shot through with psychoanalytical suggestions and perspectives. When it comes to *jouissance*, one can't always tell one body of thought from the other, as it happens. One can only say that if there are writings sacred to queer theoretical minds on the gash of bliss, they are Roland Barthes's *The Pleasure of the Text* (1975), Georges Bataille's *Visions of Excess* (1985), Leo Bersani's "Is the Rectum a Grave?" (1987), Jacques Lacan's *Écrits* (1977), and Luce Irigaray's spectacular *Speculum of the Other Woman* (1985a) and its companion, *This Sex Which is Not One* (1985b).

And there are myriad texts momentarily capturing bliss in singular ways, queer aesthetic ways, conveying the shock and disturbance of joy that is bound up with unwilled insight. Bliss in the fiction of Jean Genet (1974) is a buggered sailor thinking for the first time he is a "faggot" and finding this "quite de-

pressing thought" sending "up his spine [a] [...] series of vibra-
tions which quickly spread out over the [...] surface of his black
shoulders and covered them with a shawl woven out of shivers"
(88). Bliss in Charlotte Brontë (1979) is finding that one can't kill
desire, can't make quiet violent longings; that even if you drove
an iron stake through them, "they did not die but [...] turn[ed]
on the nail with a rebellious wrench"; "then did the temples
bleed and the brain thrill to its core" (176). Bliss in Toni Morrison (1973) is liquid, hypnotic, and mysterious, tied to the climax
a woman rides to thoughts of death, where sex becomes her way
of feeling sorrow, hollowing a space in which she "leap[s] from
the edge into soundlessness and [goes] down howling, howling
in a stinging awareness of the endings of things" (123), which
has communal, even political, value for her. Bliss as awareness?
What can it know? That all ecstasy lies adrift in a sea of emotions
that surrounds and colors it, joins with it, abrades it. Roland
Barthes explores this drift.

The Drift of Bliss

> We are scientific because we lack subtlety [...] (that the
> voice, that writing, be as fresh, supple, lubricated, deli-
> cately granular and vibrant as an animal's muzzle).
> — Barthes 1975, 61, 67

To Barthes's way of thinking, subtlety and vibrancy signal awareness and emerge with bliss — which itself results from the in-
eluctable erotics of *reading*. Strange, you might think, that queer
theory should so fetishize the thoughts of a writer describing
how we read. But might the goal of psychoanalysis be to produce Barthes's kind of reader, his anti-hero, who snubs the prat-
tle of logical consistency for the liquid subtleties, the flash force
of dreams?

Richard Howard's (1975) foreword to *The Pleasure of the Text*
(his set-up of Barthes as writer and reader) beats Barthes to
noting the intrigue of words: the word *jouissance*, in particular,
which makes "pleasure" inert and disappointing:

The French have a distinguishing advantage which Roland Barthes [...] has exploited in his new book [...]. In English, we have either the coarse or the clinical [...] so that if we wish to speak of the kind of pleasure we take — the supreme pleasure, say, associated with sexuality at its most abrupt and ruthless pitch — we lack the terms acknowledged and allowed in polite French utterance; we lack *jouissance* and *jouir,* as Barthes uses them [...]. The nomenclature of active pleasure fails us [...]. The Bible [...] calls it "knowing" while the Stuarts called it "dying," the Victorians called it "spending," and we call it "coming" [...]. Roland Barthes, in any case, calls it *jouissance.* (v–vi)

Indeed, this drift from "pleasure" to "bliss" (the translator's term for Barthes's *jouissance*) indicates queer theoretical values and investments. Awash in words, we read for bliss, for "pulsional incidents," "language lined with flesh" (66), "the cohabitation of languages working side by side" (4), leading to a "layering of significance" (12). This tiered building of word upon word, to the point of bliss, culminates not in clarity or meaning in some sharp sense. At best, it *senses* subtleties — fine distinctions, fleeting and slight, but no less alluring for their evasions. And, paradoxically, no less smiting or forceful for their fineness. No wonder Barthes terms this kind of layering — characteristic also of analysis? — a "vertical din" (12), "a sanctioned Babel" (4), productive of "the site of a loss" (7) because it makes use of the seams between one word and the other words needed to define it, making meaning a set of gaps, a blissful grasp of this set of seams (like those occurring between latent and manifest content in the work of dreams).

Why bliss here? "Is not the most erotic portion of a body," Barthes analogizes, "*where a garment gapes*?" (9). "It is intermittence," he submits, "as psychoanalysis has so rightly stated, which is erotic: the intermittence of skin flashing between two articles of clothing (trousers and sweater), between two edges (the open-necked shirt, the glove and the sleeve); it is this flash itself which seduces" (10). And so this flash-based-on-loss is what we read for ("I am interested in language because it wounds or seduces me" [38]), and "it produces, in me," says Barthes, "the best pleasure if it manages to make itself heard indirectly" (24). We read a text of bliss "the way a fly buzzes around a room: with sudden, deceptively decisive turns, fervent and futile" (31). Moreover, "you cannot speak 'on' such a text, you can only speak 'in' it, in its fashion, enter into a desperate plagiarism, hysterically affirm the void of bliss" (22). Jacques Lacan apparently agrees: "What one must bear in mind is that bliss is forbidden to the speaker, as such, or else that it cannot be spoken except between the lines" (quoted in Barthes, 21).

Later, we'll return to the bliss of speaking and relating in-between and to the analysts, Lacan and his challenger, Luce Irigaray, who have queerly shaped it. But there's a strand of queer *jouissance* that conveys forcefully the power of loss and the dependence of bliss upon disruption — and destruction. This line of thought can be traced to Georges Bataille.

Bliss as Blast

Georges Bataille's visions of excess are gnarled contemplations and gnostic provocations on the topics of violence and debasement. Someone seen as perverse by surrealists, someone deemed an "excremental philosopher" by André Breton (the chief surrealist in the 1920s and 1930s when Bataille is writing; Breton 1969, 184), and someone who writes a novel entitled *W.C.* (with its heroine Dirty), Bataille is known for attacking dignity. Therefore, his essays, with their cryptic titles — "Mouth" (1985[1930]), "The Solar Anus" (1985[1931]), "The Big Toe" (1985[1929]), "Rotten Sun" (1985[1930]); with their crazed analogies — "an abandoned shoe, a rotten tooth, a snub nose, the cook spitting in the soup of his masters are to love what a battle flag is to nationality" (1985[1931], 6); with their yoking of physical explosions and political rebellions, comparing a volcano, which he deems an anus, to the "scandalous eruption" of erotic movements *and* of workers fighting their masters; with Bataille's fixation on a monkey's bottom: those "filthy protuberances, dazzlingly colored excremental skulls, sometimes dappled, going from shocking pink to an extraordinarily horrible […] violet" ("The Jesuve" 1985[1970], 75); with this kind of ferment, these essays seem removed from what we know as joy.

Or…not at all. In "The Big Toe," Bataille (1985[1923]) reminds us of the 'sacrilegious charm" (23), the dirty ecstasy, as it were, of touching something as revered as the queen's foot: "Here one submits to a seduction radically opposed to that caused by light and ideal beauty; the two orders of seduction are often confused because a person *constantly moves from one to the other,* and […] seduction is all the more acute when the movement is more brutal" (23; my emphasis). One specific rendering of this brutal, blissful movement is central to Bataille. It is a myth one often learns in childhood, largely in Anglo-American schooling. The myth of Icarus and his father, Daedalus. To craft their escape from the island of Crete, Daedalus designed for them feathery wings held together by wax. And though he warned his child not to fly too close to the sun, lest the sun melt the wax, Icarus, filled with the joy of flying, flew too close and fell from the sky.

Presumably, we are told this myth about a youth, especially in our youth, so as to cultivate a sense of moderation. (Listen to your parents: don't fly high). Predictably, Bataille, in *Visions of Excess,* sees a different point. In Bataille's (1985[1930]) way of thinking, ideal joys are "rotten sun" (57). They contain the doubleness of an elevation we blissfully seek (in Icarean flights) and the guarantee of a violent fall (courtesy of the ideal itself). As Bataille words it: "The myth of Icarus is particularly expressive from this point of view: it clearly splits the sun," our most joyful and elevated concept, into "two — the one that was shining at the moment of Icarus's elevation, and the one that melted the wax, causing failure and a screaming fall when Icarus got too close" (58). Human life, as Bataille conceives it, is about watching our flights fall to earth, dropping down in real time. Nothing is more violent than the gash of bliss.

Given his propensity to praise destructive flight, we are not surprised that, famously, Bataille ([1985]1933), in "The Notion of Expenditure," speaks to what he calls "the insufficiency of the principle of classical utility" (116), a principle he is unhappy to find upheld by Sigmund Freud. By "utility," Bataille means the goal, which he doesn't like at all, of taking one's "pleasure" in "moderate form," while one aims at the "acquisition," "conservation," and "reproduction" of goods and life. And though this moderation forms the basis of the "struggle against [human] pain" (116), Bataille proceeds to say that "personal experience" proves the falseness of this view. "Human society," Bataille goes on to claim, has "an *interest* in considerable losses, in catastrophes that, *while conforming to well-defined needs,* provoke tumultuous depressions, cries of dread, and, in the final analysis, a certain orgiastic state" (117; emphasis in original). Here, loss and orgasm are companion states. And perhaps thinking once again of Icarus, Bataille produces a father/son example: "the father may provide the son with lodging, clothes, food, and, when absolutely necessary, a little harmless recreation"; "but the son does not even have the right to speak about what really gives him a fever"; "humanity recognizes the right to acquire, to conserve, and to consume rationally, but it excludes in principle *nonproductive expenditure*" (117; emphasis in original).

What, exactly, is this nonproductivity, this kind of "spending," that Bataille embraces? Any outlay (Bataille in no way minds the word "wasting") of money or energy or even life — outlays that (happily) do not serve production. These would be wastings such as "luxury," "mourning," "competitive games," "artistic productions," and "perverse sexual activity (i.e., deflected from genital finality)" (118). For Bataille, the ultimate question thus becomes: who has this power to lose and destroy, ecstatically, defiantly? With undeniable Marxist strains running through his thoughts, Bataille scorns forms of "conspicuous consumption" (xvi). As his translator, Allan Stoekl, tells us: "'Conspicuous consumption' for Bataille is not a pernicious remnant of feudalism that must be replaced by total utility; instead, it is the perversion of man's 'need to destroy.' The noble, and even more hypocritically the bourgeois, use this 'destruction' not to destroy completely, but simply to reaffirm their place in the hierarchy" (xvi).

What Bataille affirms as the blast of bliss is the wish to create so as to destroy — and to lose anyone who would lose loss.

The Most Debased Bliss

Loss may plausibly tie to *jouissance* because one must descend from bliss eventually, even rapidly. And one "loses" oneself in joy, as is often said. But bliss as shame, *emerging* from debasement, or constituting a joyful destruction? Are these views excessive? Bataille hopes they are.

Leo Bersani, avowedly thinking through Bataille, writing out of the depths of theory in its psychoanalytic and deconstructive forms, and also out of the bowels of public animus against "homosexuals," supremely embraces debasement in his essay "Is the Rectum a Grave?" To put it more specifically, Bersani embraces debased and debasing, violent joy. That is to say, the aim of his piece, from 1987, written during the height of AIDS for (white) gay men, appears to be two-fold. First, Bersani's essay explores a malignant aversion to gay male sexuality — and thus he explores a shaming of gay men and their pleasures — in public discourse when he is writing. Second, he explores the debasement and violence that are *fundamental* to sexual pleasure, anyone's pleasure-unto-climax, odd as that may seem.

On the first score, Bersani explains that public discourse, with denigration as its purpose, closely associates gay men with women by associating gay men with anal penetration — and thus with feminine sexual passivity, since "to be […] penetrated," even going back to the days of the Greeks, is presumably "to abdicate power" (212), according to Michel Foucault. More precisely, public discourse about gay men, in the 1980s' age of AIDS, resembles public depictions of prostitutes in the nineteenth century, conceiving of them as contaminated vessels of sexual disease and sexual pleasure, thus as the sign of "an unquenchable appetite for destruction" (211).

Rather than counter these prejudicial views, which make the rectum a literal grave, Bersani finds a more extraordinary aversion — to sex itself — in this invective. And this aversion, this unwillingness to embrace debasement, we might say, is something Bersani discovers in various kinds of thinkers, along the spectrum of homophobic moralists to radical theorists of sexuality. Never mind the homophobes, the problem with the sexuality theorists (from Catherine MacKinnon and Andrea Dworkin to Michel Foucault — unlikely bedfellows, as he notes) is that they all seek "to alleviate" "the problem" of the passive role in sex as "demeaning" (though in quite different ways, to say the least). Bersani, by contrast, wants to affirm the so-called passive and therefore demeaning aspects of sex, to stop denying the "equally strong appeal of powerlessness [...] in both men and women," and to recognize the "self-debasement" fundamental to sexual "ecstasy" — what he deems a "*jouissance* of exploded limits [...] the ecstatic suffering into which the human organism momentarily plunges when it is 'pressed' beyond a certain threshold of endurance" (213; 217). In other words, the act of sexual pleasure (for either penetrator or penetrated — or, presumably, someone reaching climax by other means) is a "self-shattering," "a kind of [...] self-debasement," "a radical disintegration and humiliation of the self," in which "the sexual itself [is] the risk of self-dismissal," since "the self" is psychically overwhelmed at climax (217).

Bersani explains, drawing on both Bataille and a somewhat reluctant Freud:

For there is finally, beyond the fantasies of bodily power and subordination [...] a transgressing of that very polarity which, as Georges Bataille has proposed, may be the profound sense of both certain mystical experiences and of human sexuality. In making this suggestion I'm also thinking of Freud's somewhat reluctant speculation, especially in the *Three Essays on the Theory of Sexuality,* that sexual pleasure occurs whenever a certain threshold of intensity is reached, when the organization of the self is momentarily disturbed by sensations or affective processes somehow "beyond" those connected with psychic organization. (217)

This intriguing link between the mystical and the sexual will appear again in Jacques Lacan and Luce Irigaray — and appear full-blown, as opposed to Bersani's quick and glancing mention of it. Here, that is, the sexual trumps the mystical as a point of focus. And "reluctant" Freud gets more attention than Bataille. What Bersani takes as Freud's reluctance has to do with Freud's frequent emphasis on the relational, genital, normative coupling of men and women: the "post-Oedipal, genitally centered desire for someone of the opposite sex" (217). Against this Freud, Bersani posits a different Freud, a radical Freud, for whom the thing called *jouissance*, "sexual pleasure," shatters the very self that would relate. Men, more than women, are apt to deny these effects of *jouissance*, according to Bersani, to misrecognize sexual climax as self-inflating pleasure, as a "phallicizing of the ego," though "neither sex has exclusive rights to the [mistaken] practice of sex as self-hyperbole" (218). And, most importantly, "it is perhaps primarily *the degeneration of the sexual into a relationship that condemns sexuality to becoming a struggle for power*" (his emphasis).

This explanation of sexual pleasure fascinates for a few key reasons. First, it makes climax — sexual bliss — a pleasurable debasement that is largely willingly pursued and widely practiced. Secondly, Bersani never clearly tells us whether this *jouissance* causes or simply reveals self-dismissal. I suspect he means the latter: that sex is a kind of intensification or a mode of revelation of an already-shattering self. Thirdly, because the self is shattered, says Bersani, so, also, the supposed relationality or community of the couple (which depends upon selfhood) is undone. Sex, in this way, Bersani claims, keeps one free from the "violence" of relationships and so should be seen as an odd "ascetic" practice, a sexual instead of a religious self-denial (222) — and one that "male homosexuality," in his view, helpfully "advertises," since "it never stops re-presenting the internalized phallic male as an infinitely loved object of sacrifice" (222).

But the *measure* of this sacrifice and of destruction remains elusive in both Bersani and Bataille, for all their talk of one's destructions. How does one embrace their view of bliss and still survive so as to live through loss? Can bliss amount to one's close shave, grazing but missing full-on destruction so that one can continue to approach it? Might analysis help us to learn to shave our loss? Irigaray, writing against Lacan, envisions relations of blissful losing.

Shaving Loss, Finding Bliss

> Woman "touches herself" all the time, and moreover no one can forbid her to do so, for her genitals are formed of two lips in continuous contact. Thus, within herself, she is already two — but not divisible into one(s) — that caress each other [...] Woman derives pleasure from what is so near that she cannot have it, nor have herself [...] And she never ceases to look upon his nakedness [...] upon the gashes in his virgin flesh.
> — Irigaray 1985b, 24; 1985a, 31

Lacanian theory lies at the heart of much queer thought. Especially where desire and pleasure are conceptualized, Jacques Lacan's analytic pronouncements are likely to be cited. With his semiotic grasp of Freud, stressing the role of signification over (or deeply entwined with) biology, and his emphasis on the unconscious as that psychic structure that splits us ("I think of what I am where I do not think to think" [1977, 166]), Lacan lends lines of thought to queer thinkers who contest arguments based on naturalness, reproductive logic, or self-fulfillment through self-realization and romantic coupling. For queer theorists, sex is queer — riddling, elusive, excessive, and estranging — for anyone, for everyone.

Still, it may surprise us to learn that Lacan's take on bliss is bound to mysticism (which is riddling, elusive, excessive...), as is that of his feminist critic, Luce Irigaray, who is an analyst, philosopher, and linguist, nurtured at the breast of Lacanian analysis before being jettisoned from Lacan's school when her book was published. In fact, these analysts, Lacan and Irigaray, make a queer couple as they deem "the sexual relation" — Lacan's phrase for hetero-coupling — lacking on the front of desire, strange to say. Stranger still, an unexpected, even peculiar image and metaphor of genital lips figures for Irigaray her own vision of sexual relations. This is a vision that turns the slit of loss — two lips touching *because* they are slit, because they cannot fuse — into an erotics of fracture-as-bliss. To track these moves, we must enter into arguments between Lacan and Irigaray as they circle around two terms, "man" and "woman," that many queers would now regard as absurdly blocky, even totalizing, in their absence of further and finer specifications, never mind blurrings and bleedings between them. Nonetheless, for each of them, Lacan and Irigaray, these two positions, as we might term them, are distinct orientations toward desire. "Man" designates a drive toward fulfillment and satiating pleasure (as Bersani lamented). "Woman" is the word for an entrance into *jouissance* as a separation-from-oneself-unto-joy ("so near that she cannot have it, nor have herself" [Irigaray 1985b, 31]). In what *looks like* a lesbian tryst, Irigaray envisions a person positioned as a "woman" approaching another person so positioned, thus crafting erotic exchanges around the crack of desire between them. Whatever their given or even chosen "sex," and whatever their play of genders might be (at the level of dress, mannerisms, sex acts), the crucial factor in this exchange is stance on loss. Do they make forms of incompletion (non-possession, loneliness, separateness, sorrow, pain, debasement) and impossibility (non-knowledge, non-closure, non-fusion) central to their bliss and to their sexual nearness to each other? Do they caress desire-as-lack as the force shaping their sexual burn, as the very spacing that makes approach possible? Crucially, *jouissance* arises in-between.

Lacan to a great extent agrees. But you might not know it — Irigaray proceeds by decidedly not knowing it — given the tone he strikes on desire. Lacan's tragic tone is now familiar. "The subject is split and the object is lost," says Juliet Mitchell (1985, 25), recapping Lacan in a motto or maxim. Fracture and loss stand as twin pillars of Lacanian tragedy. They shade the infant's development from birth, when the subject who is sexed by the outside world is sent down the path of a split destiny, seeking its lost "other half" it will find only in the glaze of romance. Suited up in the armor of its "outsides"—the mirror image it mistakenly takes for its bodily identity, and the language by which it is gendered and ushered into culture—the subject, separated from its first beloved (the body that mothered it), seeks satisfaction in substitutions, in a range of people and objects that might satisfy. Desire is the lack that propels the subject along the track of these substitutions, according to Lacan, never to arrive at a destination that solves its sense of "original misery" (Ragland-Sullivan 1986, 22)

Appropriating this sorrow for sex, Irigaray converts lack into loss-productive-of-bliss. As if healing the subject's splits by caressing the slit between her lips, Irigaray nurtures self-parting for pleasure. As if disdaining Lacan's tragic tone, contemptuous of his confidence that lack must spell tragedy, Irigaray cradles the lack that Lacan deems original misery. Irigaray, we may say, "shaves" his desire: approaches his lack to graze it in passing; makes small cuts at the surface of his theory; buys desire at reduced rates (against his law); eludes Lacan's tragedy by a narrow margin.

For Lacan, the sexual relation is the lover's dodge of desire, as I've stated, since this relation purports to solve it. Lacan strictly states that nothing will satisfy insatiable longing—especially not sex or love. Taunting those who would make sex suffice, Lacan (1985) broadly questions, "For what is love other than banging one's head against a wall, since there is no sexual relation?" (170) Lacan insists that we cannot "disguise this gap" (81) with love's fantasy of two-become-one, substituting finite objects for the infinite object of desire.

In "God and the *Jouissance* of ~~The~~ Woman" (1985), followed by "A Love Letter" (1985), Lacan ridicules "man's" fantasy that makes "woman" be God for "man." Seeking to give his lack the slip, "man" (em)beds in "woman" his Other: whatever escapes him about himself, whatever might stroke and hold his self-truth, which he then thinks he confronts and conquers in the sexual relation. Seeking to rupture this kind of fantasy ("it is here that severance is still needed" [154]), Lacan must address himself to "the good old God of all times" (140), whose face "woman" is required to wear. "God has not made his exit," says Lacan, since "woman" is still made to bear his place, for "when one is a man, one sees in one's partner what can serve, narcissistically, to act as one's own support" (154, 157). What "man" seems to finger in "woman," what she is a "symptom" of, and why he tries to finesse what he feels with the "good old God," is his own hole, his impossible conquest of a lost complement. It is the Symbolic — Lacan's name for language, law, and culture — that poses this impassable barrier to completion, as if, by means of the cultural garments the Symbolic requires people to wear (indeed, by making them wear "man" and "woman"), they cannot get naked.

This far into his essay, Lacan plays his role as cynic, exposing what snares human subjects into fantasy. Rounding the bend of critique, however, he tumbles into the lap of the mystics. Startling his reader by a sudden shift in tone, he now affirms the mystics' caress of something along the lines of material opacity. The mystics suggest themselves to Lacan as those who "sense that there must be a *jouissance* which goes beyond," for "that is what we call a mystic" (147). Beginning with a joke, Lacan slides into what unfolds as his serious appreciation of mysticism:

Naturally we ended up in Christianity by inventing a God such that it is he who comes! All the same there is a bit of a link when you read certain genuine people who might just happen to be women [...] The mystical is by no means that which is not political. It is something serious, which a few people teach us about, and most often women or highly gifted people like Saint John of the Cross — since, when you are male, you don't have to put yourself on the side of [all]. You can also put yourself on the side of not-all. There are men who are just as good as women. It does happen. And who therefore feel just as good. Despite, I won't say their phallus, despite what encumbers them on that score, they get the idea, they sense that there must be a *jouissance* which goes beyond. That is what we call a mystic ...It is the same as for

Saint Theresa — you only have to go and look at Bernini's statue in Rome to understand immediately that she's coming, there is no doubt about it. And what is her *jouissance*, her coming from? It is clear that the essential testimony of the mystics is that they are experiencing it but know nothing about it. (146–47)

The mystics, male and female, lining up "on the side of not-all," allow themselves to be shaken and split by a lack-turned-opacity, obscure pleasure that refuses translucence. Lacan concludes with a joke that again returns him to God. Not the "good old God," but a "God" who courts "woman's" *jouissance* as "woman's" material complaint against her culturally-constructed, gendered place in the so-called straight relation:

These mystical ejaculations are neither idle gossip nor mere verbiage, in fact they are the best thing you can read — note right at the bottom of the page, *Add the* Écrits *of Jacques Lacan,* which is of the same order. Given which, naturally you are all going to be convinced that I believe in God. I believe in the *jouissance* of the woman in so far as it is something more [...] Might not this *jouissance* which one experiences and knows nothing of, be that which puts us on the path of ex-istence? And why not interpret one face of the Other, the God face, as supported by feminine *jouissance*? (147)

Lacan's jocular gambit is clever. Men can be mystics and so can Jacques Lacan. His passage, however, exceeds his cleverness. Read generously, it may bespeak his desire to depart from phallocentrism and the binding anguish of its conventions. At the very least, Lacan seems eager not to be abandoned by "woman" and mystics who go (and come) beyond. Here is "woman," then, "woman" along with her mystic partners, who are on her "side," teaching men (and women, for that matter) to find bliss in lack. This is to read Jacques Lacan straight-faced, to grant him his "ejaculation" not his joke.

As is her way, Irigaray (1985b) complains most against Lacan when she most follows him. Thus she makes her displeasure
known at Lacan's assigning pleasure to a statue: "In Rome? So
far away? To look? At a statue? Of a saint? Sculpted by a man?
What pleasure are we talking about? Whose pleasure? For where
the pleasure of the Theresa in question is concerned, her own
writings are perhaps more telling" (91). Along the axis of access,
Irigaray splits from Lacan. She reads him straight-faced when
he is joking, mocks him when she most repeats him. Irigaray
generally castigates Lacan, as if he were a sly gynecologist: hand-
in-glove with "man's" symbolic fantasies that Lacan would say
require rupture. Lacan, says Irigaray, even "silences" (as if he has
slipped his hands over) "woman's" *jouissance* in the act of posing
its "discovery." Irigaray on Lacan on "woman": "Pleasure without pleasure: the shock of a remainder of 'silent' body-matter
that shakes her at intervals, in the interstices, but of which she
remains ignorant. 'Saying' nothing of this pleasure after all, thus
not enjoying it" (96).

Though it might appear that Irigaray also rails against Lacan
for assigning an opacity to "woman's" bliss, she is really provoked by something subtler: that he takes in stride the limit that
he hits. Lacan is not shaken by his inability to locate "woman's"
active pleasure. There is no reason, no way, he would say, to pursue this limit (a *jouissance* that goes beyond) beyond the limits
of discourse as we know it. This impossible status of "woman"
and "woman's" bliss — the good news, something of her "escapes," the bad news, "she" does not fully know it nor does "she"
exist — provides the limit to Lacanian theory at the same time
that it sketches a fix. In its role as limit, the concept of this *jouissance* touches upon what Lacan calls the Real: the unapproach-
able, ungraspable, algebraic x. Since a difference in *urgency*
cracks her congruence with Lacan, Irigaray urgently desires to
pursue beyond the limit of not speaking — to listen to Theresa,
her writings, her thoughts, even to conduct us to what we might
feel beyond the fall of words.

Irigaray listens, ironically, by writing. She composes a mystical, critical, poetical essay, mimicking female mystic concerns

so as to reveal their analytic insights and her own conceptual schemes. Thus, in her lyrical "*La Mysterique*" she imagines "God" between "woman's" lips, using the "God" term under erasure to mark the mystic's lover. "God," she writes, "knows women so well that he never touches them directly, but always in that fleeting stealth of a fantasy that evades all representation: between two unities who thus imperceptibly take pleasure in each other" (1985a, 236). This declaration implies "God's" touch between the autoerotic lips. Given that this touch is not direct but involves a "fleeting stealth," and given that the lips only touch by means of a crucial apartness, "God," by this logic, *becomes spacing*. "God" is the space between (two) lovers. "God" is the gap, at the gap, in the gap. "God" is also the gap of "woman's" pleasure between the lips, "opening up a crack in the cave […] so that she may penetrate herself once more" (192).

Irigaray's mystical interests, then, are strongly staked to lack: who wears it, who suffers for it, and who envisions economies based upon it. For Irigaray plays with jubilation upon the mystic's holiness, celebrating "God's" holes that tell "woman" glorious things about "her" own:

And that one man, at least, has understood her so well that he died in the most awful suffering […] And she never ceases to look upon his nakedness, open for all to see, upon the gashes in his virgin flesh […] Could it be true that not every wound need remain secret, that not every laceration was shameful? Could a sore be *holy*? Ecstasy is there in that glorious slit where she curls up as if in her nest, where she rests as if she had found her home — and He is also in her […] In this way, you see me and I see you, finally I see myself seeing you in this fathomless wound which is the source of our wondering comprehension and exhilaration. And to know myself I scarcely need a "soul," I have only to gaze upon the gaping space in your loving body. (199–200)

This is Irigaray making the Christian tradition give back what Christ on the cross has borrowed from "woman": a "gaping space" in the body worth gazing upon. "Woman's" "slit," here pronounced "glorious," mirrors Christ's "fathomless wound." The wound itself acts as a mirror, enabling "woman" to reflect upon her folds. Irigaray takes on castration, then, to its most extreme degree, complete with Freud's fatal look upon nakedness that reveals the "shameful" "secret" of the "gaping space" — a secret and a sacred lack that "woman" shares with Christ, reminiscent of the mystics' stigmata that function as speaking wounds. Irigaray takes castration to the crypt, where she makes castration convert into autoerotic confessions. And "He" bleeds into "you" bleeds into "her" bleeds into "me."

We are back to Irigaray's shaving of desire. Irigaray's trick is to steal Lacan's desire: she shaves it and thus puts a new face on it. The new face she puts on desire is bliss. The way she does this, as we have seen, is by focusing on an image of female genitalia. At the lips, that is, Irigaray figures a touch that constitutes a mirroring touch: an identification that enjoys its own splitting, a failure to fuse that enjoys impossibility: "Thus, within herself, she is already two — but not divisible into one(s) — that caress each other" (1985b, 24). The mirrored images of genital lips reconceptualize the mathematics of division. Clear accounts escape calculation, and all because of a division that does not divide clearly. If Lacan's version of desire is a division and a lack — and one that "costs" the subject — then Irigaray shaves desire in that other sense of "shave" as well: "to lower (a price, etc.) by a slight margin"; "to purchase (a note, draft, etc.) at a discount greater than the legal or customary rate of interest." Irigaray has cut the cost of desire against the Lacanian law of tragedy. Irigaray's desire, in this respect, is not a wholly other desire, but a different orientation to lack that makes desire its own kind of bliss. This desire, as Irigaray fashions it, is desire with a different valence and a different tension. It is a lacking that is a having. In this sense, this desire *is jouissance* — a restless pleasure that is not limited to a single object or a single organ. Perhaps, most importantly, and quite differently than Bersani, Irigaray imagines this pleasuring (around the crack of desire) as a lacking *shared between* desiring bodies. By virtue of this move — a relocation of lack and holes to the space between bodies — "woman" ceases to be a lack or "hole-envelope": "With you, I don't have any ['holes']. We are not lacks, voids awaiting sustenance, plenitude, fulfillment from the other" (209).

"God," in Irigaray's theories, plays a vital role in this regard. "God," as we have seen, is figured as the material resistance of bodies to the cultural constructions that have barred their pleasure. More daring yet, because Irigaray locates this material resistance (this opacity) in "woman's" hole (where she is said to lack), "God," not "woman," is a crack, a gap — the fracture we need for conceiving new pleasures. In this respect, "God" is the wound of our relations but also the only hope for the lack that, fracturing us, allows us to touch ourselves.

But "God" is more than divine lack or an elegant figure for material opacities. In Irigaray's rendering, "God" also figures the body of a lover who, while coming close to "woman," nurtures the fracture that keeps "him" from possessing "her": "Thus 'God' will [...] have been her best lover since he separates her from herself only by the space of her *jouissance* where she finds Him/herself. To infinity perhaps, but in the serenity of the spacing that is thus projected by/in her pleasure" (1985a, 201). What looks like Irigaray's vision of lovers reveals her potent fracture of dyads (mother/child, husband/wife, two genders, two lovers). Irigaray, I suggest, splinters dyads and their unities into excess when she slips "God," and thus "infinity," between one and two. Here the necessity of conceiving two mirrors dramatically appears. Positioned, culturally, as a mirror (specifically, familiarly, and largely to men), "woman," when turned upon herself or her other, figures the turning of mirror upon mirror. Here, between mirrors, images are split from themselves to infinity. There are many bodies between these mirrors, in the gap of (her) desire. If she infinitely approaches her other, she comes nearer — as if she is always dividing the remaining distance between them — infinitely approaching, never reaching, becoming asymptotitc (asymptote: "tangent to a curve at infinity").

Sex, then, is fracture. Sex, understood as bodies at a brink, demands the attempt to keep closing the gap while nurturing the lack. This contradiction, lying at the heart of sex, stimulates ill-conceived attempts to close the space that shapes its burn — a movement which, if two could perform it, would annihilate otherness, make sex void. Irigaray's erotics of fracture, conversely, counsels embrace of this space that makes the sexual relation (im)possible: "The sky isn't up there: it's between us" (1985b, 213). She seeks to cure the sexual relation by putting divine *obstacles* to it. She affirms the obstacle and deems it "God," so that the obstacle is a fracture is a lover who spreads for "woman" "his" own gash.

Cleaving (to) the glassed surface of mirrors, Irigaray writes with incandescence a seemingly heterosexual embrace modeled on an erotics of fracture. For if Irigaray preserves "God" as "he," she does so only by conceiving the pleasures of the sexual relation as a queer, lesbian-seeming, erotic, hetero–homo inflation soaked in loss: "Her" (auto)-eroticism swells to recognition by touching "his" body that mirrors "her" wounds:

> Thus (re)assured of the complicity of this all-powerful partner, they/she play(s) at courtship, kneeling in self-abasement at one moment, adorning themselves with gold and diamonds the next, touching, smelling, listening, seeing, embrac(s)ing each other, devouring, penetrating, entering, consuming, melting each other. She is trusting as a dove, arrogant as a queen, proud in her nakedness, bursting with the joy of such exchanges. Her divine companion never tires of praising her and encouraging her (auto)eroticism that has so miraculously been rediscovered. (1985a, 201–2)

Subtleties and vibrancy abound in this bliss. Who wouldn't prefer to desire this desire over the staid nature of pleasure?

Perhaps it's the task of the analytic scene to venture this question.

Works Cited

Barthes, Roland. *The Pleasure of the Text,* trans. Richard Miller. New York: Hill and Wang, 1975.

Bataille, Georges. *Visions of Excess: Selected Writings, 1927–1939,* ed. and trans. Allan Stoekl. Minneapolis: University of Minnesota Press, 1985.

Bersani, Leo. "Is the Rectum a Grave?" In *AIDS: Cultural Analysis, Cultural Activism,* ed. Douglas Crimp, 197–222. Cambridge: MIT Press, 1987.

Breton, André. *Manifestoes of Surrealism,* trans. Richard Seaver and Helen R. Lane. Ann Arbor: University of Michigan Press, 1969.

Brontë, Charlotte. *Villette.* New York: Penguin, 1979.

Genet, Jean. *Querelle,* trans. Anselm Hollo. New York: Grove, 1974.

Irigaray, Luce. *Speculum of the Other Woman,* trans. Gillian C. Gill. Ithaca: Cornell University Press, 1985a.

———. *This Sex Which Is Not One,* trans. Catherine Porter. Ithaca: Cornell University Press, 1985b.

Lacan, Jacques. *Feminine Sexuality,* eds. Juliet Mitchell and Jacqueline Rose, trans. Jacqueline Rose. New York: Norton, 1985.

———. *Écrits: A Selection,* trans. Alan Sheridan. New York: Norton, 1977.

Mitchell, Juliet. "Introduction-I." In *Feminine Sexuality,* eds. Juliet Mitchell and Jacqueline Rose, trans. Jacqueline Rose, 1–26. New York: Norton, 1985.

Morrison, Toni. *Sula.* New York: Plume, 1973.

Ragland-Sullivan, Ellie. *Jacques Lacan and the Philosophy of Psychoanalysis.* Champaign: University of Illinois Press, 1986.

Stockton, Kathryn Bond. *The Queer Child, or Growing Sideways in the Twentieth Century.* Durham: Duke University Press, 2009.

———. *Beautiful Bottom, Beautiful Shame: Where "Black" Meets "Queer."* Durham: Duke University Press, 2006.

————. *God Between Their Lips: Desire between Women in Irigaray, Brontë, and Eliot.* Palo Alto: Stanford University Press, 1994.

Perversion and the Problem
of Fluidity and Fixity

Lisa Downing

It is a commonplace to state that the problem of sexuality is central to the endeavors of both psychoanalysis and queer theory. Whereas for psychoanalysis, traditionally at least, sexuality has an etiological status as the nexus of f/phantasies underlying an analysand's symptoms and behaviors, for queer theorists, especially following Michel Foucault, sexuality is a constructed epistemological category that functions to normalize the behaviors and bodies of social subjects. In the former, it is a source of truth to be tapped; in the latter it is a pervasive and power-laden lie to be exposed. Whereas psychoanalysis relies on a developmental model of sexuality (Sigmund Freud, Melanie Klein and so on) or a structural one (for example, Jacques Lacan), "queer" takes the theory of performativity as its explicatory model to account for the ways in which subjects learn to "do" their genders and sexualities. Moreover, the category of "perversion" has central import for theorizations of sexuality within both psychoanalysis and queer theory. For clinical psychoanalysts, perversion is sexuality gone awry; the failure of the subject to attain adult genitality. For queer theorists, on the other hand, perversion may be construed as a defiant performance of excess that shows up the constructedness and arbitrariness of the category of the "normal," and it is centrally implicated in queer's rejection of the meaning of identity in favor of the politics of practice. In what follows, however, I will focus on a pair of concepts that are central to both psychoanalytic and queer thinking on sexuality and its perverse forms — namely *fixity* and *fluidity* — in order to trouble certain orthodoxies within both bodies of thought. In this way, I will neither pathologize queer in the name of psychoanalysis, nor accuse psychoanalysis of reactionary politics in the name of queer. Rather I shall highlight — and challenge — a logic that is surprisingly shared by both systems.

In particular, this will involve examining how the theory of performativity has been used to privilege the status of the idea of fluidity in queer studies. I shall critique this as a deficiency within the body of thought, after Brad Epps (2001) who has pointed out, in an essay that uses a concept borrowed from psychoanalysis to critique "queer," that fluidity can be thought of as the "fetish" of queer theory. Privileging the ideal of fluidity leads to a concomitant stigmatization of the idea of fixity, establishing an unhelpful binary (fluidity or fixity) in a body of thought that usually attempts to deconstruct such dualities. The maintenance of this binary also perpetuates some of the most damning and pathologizing ideas that run through the history of knowledge about sexuality, featuring prominently in the very authority disciplines that queer exists to call into question — for example, sexology, some forms of psychoanalysis, and psychiatry. I argue that this imposes on queer thought a programmatic tyranny that runs counter to the epistemological and political aims of queer theory — in Michael Warner's (1993) words, to "oppose [...] the *idea* of normal behaviour" (xxvii). I want not only to show how this undesirable programmatic agenda works, but also to try to suggest some ways of overcoming this, of thinking outside of the paradigms that are becoming established.

Performativity

It may be productive to begin by thinking about the concept of performativity and its specific meanings for, and function within, queer theory. The term "performativity" is associated primarily with the work of English philosopher of language, J.L. Austin, whose *How to Do Things with Words* (published 1975, based on lectures given in the 1950s) influentially argued that some acts of language, called "speech acts," do not simply describe things but rather *do* things. They are performatives. Examples Austin gives are: "I pronounce you man and wife" and "I name this ship the *Queen Elizabeth*," These acts of speech alter something in the world — after the pronouncement, the couple is legally married, the ship officially named — so long as the context is "appropriate" and the person doing the speaking is imbued with legitimacy. Austin writes: "in these examples it seems clear that to utter the sentence, in, of course, the appropriate circumstances, is not to describe [...] it is to *do* it" (8).

The work of deconstructionist feminist and queer theorist Judith Butler has adapted, via Michel Foucault and Jacques Derrida, the idea of a "performative" in Austin's sense, to describe the workings of both speech about sexuality and gender, and the workings of gender and sexuality themselves. In *Excitable Speech: A Politics of the Performative* (1997), she looks at the function of hate speech as a type of performative, constituting subjects as injured parties. Terms such as "slut," "cripple," "queer" and so on, hurled as injurious insults, bear the "hey, you!" function of Althusserian interpellation — they construct specific types of social subjects from a position of oppressive authority. However, as a thinker interested in the flexibility of the power of resistance, Butler explores the capacity within political discourse for recuperative uses of hate speech — for what she calls "resignification." The most obvious example of such resignification is "queer," a homophobic slur turned radical political slogan during the 1980s AIDS crisis by groups such as ACT UP and Queer Nation. More recently, along the same lines, the academy has seen the adoption of the term "crip" by disability studies scholars such as Robert McRuer. For Butler, resignification rather than repression or censorship are the most politically expedient responses to acts of hate speech.

Excitable Speech comes relatively late in Butler's corpus. It is for *Gender Trouble: Feminism and the Subversion of Identity,* first published in 1990, and *Bodies that Matter: On the Discursive Limits of "Sex"* (1993) that she is perhaps best known, particularly in queer theory circles. In these two books, and in her essays and lectures on gender and sex, Butler has argued that, like performative language, the gestures and roles of gender we perform daily are what constitute us as gendered subjects. Rather than *reflecting* a feminine or masculine essence, behavior that is encoded as masculine or feminine *creates* what Derrida would call a trace, the inscription into the social world of something that appears to have already been there, waiting to be represented. Gender is a series of *citations* that reinforce the impression of the natural pre-existence of a binary order of sex. In *Gender Trouble* (1990), Butler writes: "the presumption of a binary gender system implicitly retains the belief in a mimetic relation of gender to sex" (10). In good postmodernist mode, she seeks to dismantle this mimetic fallacy. If gender performances are imitations, then they are imitations for which there is no original referent; citations that accrue meaning — and shore up their "truth" value — via the simple means of their being repeated *ad infinitum*. What they are definitely *not* for Butler are neutral, natural or inevitable extensions of biological or genetic facts about a person's gender, sex and sexuality. They do not convey our subject positions, but rather construct them. Carefully dissociating performance from performativity (a distinction that is often elided in postmodern criticism), Butler opines in an interview from 1993: "It is important to distinguish performance from performativity: the former presumes a subject, but the latter contests the very notion of the subject" (Osborne and Segal 1994, 36). In performativity then, the subject *appears* as the effect of the performance rather than the subject being a fixed agent who — consciously or otherwise — performs a given act. Or, as Butler (1990) puts it in *Gender Trouble,* "gender is always a doing, but not a doing by a subject who might be said to pre-exist the deed" (33). To put it another way, then, gender is certainly not ontology; but nor do we only "do" it. Rather, it "does" us.

Crucially for Butler — and lending political weight to the assertion that gender is performative, since gender and for

that matter sexuality are a series of performances that habitually *do us* — we can turn around and do them back. When we
understand that gender is a matter of doing rather than *being*,
we can also *transform* the meaning of gender, by performing
it self-consciously, playfully and with self-awareness — rather
than unconsciously and in ways that shore up the idea that gender emanates naturally from an essentially sexed subject. This
conscious gender performativity is termed "drag."[1] However, the
capacity of self-conscious gender performativity to transform
meaning must not be understood via the idea of straightforward "choice" in the neo-liberal sense. Butler explains: "One of
the interpretations that has been made of *Gender Trouble* is that
there is no sex, there is only gender, and gender is performative.
People then go on to think that if gender is performative it must
be radically free [...]. It is important to understand performativity — which is distinct from performance — through the
more limited notion of resignification (subversive repetition)"
(Osborne and Segal 1993, 32). This adoption of performativity
theory for queer allows both for an analysis of the normalizing
effects of regimes of knowledge about sex and gender and for a
limited strategy of resistance. Using a model of power relations
borrowed primarily from Foucault, in which power is a force
field of relations surrounding us, and in which we are always
implicated, rather than a uni-directional operation of oppressive force from the top downwards, Butler demonstrates that
gender performativity — literalized in her idea of "drag" — has

---

1   "Drag" in Butler's sense is any putting on of the gestures, clothing and ac-
    cessories attributed to one or the other gender by a person of either — or
    any — sex. Thus, it constitutes the performance of femininity by a biologi-
    cal, cisgendered woman as well as what would traditionally be thought of as
    "cross-dressing." Re-defining drag in this way entails a rejection of the no-
    tion that particular forms of gendered presentation correctly or inevitably
    "belong to" biologically binary sexed bodies. Understood in this light, drag
    also suggests the possibility for parodic repetitions of gender as the self-
    conscious subversion of gender norms. See Butler 1999, 174–80.

an inbuilt mechanism of *resistance* to normative meanings, by means of a parodic resignification.[2]

Although Butler has stated that she sees herself primarily as a feminist and a gender theorist, rather than as a queer theorist, her work has been constitutive within that field of thinking in the 1990s. One of Butler's key contributions to queer theory is to shift the focus from sexuality (so prominent in the analyses of Foucault and in many post-Foucaldian theorists) onto gender. She makes the claim, echoed by other feminist queer theorists, such as Marie-Hélène Bourcier in France, that Foucault's work —and much queer theory—sidelines questions of gender in its focus on the constructed nature of sexuality.[3] Butler states: "insofar as some people in queer theory want to claim that the analysis of sexuality can be radically separated from the analysis of gender, I'm very much opposed to them" (32). While considering this an important point, I want to consider how Butler's oft-discussed theory of gender performativity might intersect with the project of deconstructing both sexual identity categories and diagnoses of sexual abnormality, and how this move helps us get to grips with the role played by ideas of fluidity and

2   In *The Will to Knowledge*, Foucault (1990) writes of power: "In short, it is a question of orienting ourselves to a conception of power which replaces the privilege of the law with the viewpoint of the objective, the privilege of prohibition with the viewpoint of tactical efficacy, the privilege of sovereignty with the analysis of a multiple and mobile field of force relations, wherein far-reaching, but never completely stable, effects of domination are produced" (102). For more on Foucault's notion of power, see Downing 2008, esp. 86–117.

3   Bourcier (2006) writes: "Foucault isn't interested in undoing gender—or gender-fucking. That is to say in a political and parodic game with the signs of masculinity aiming to critique the sexual and social roles attributed to the masculine and the feminine. This avoidance of gender is, moreover, one of the problematic limits of Foucault's thought. Everything happens as if, for him, there were only one gender—homoerotic masculinity" (my translation). ["Foucault ne s'intéresse pas à la dé-genrisation—ou *gender fucking*—c'est-à-dire à un jeu parodique et politique avec les signes de la masculinité, valant pour critique des rôles sexuels et sociaux impartis au masculin et au féminin. Cet évitement des genres est d'ailleurs l'une des limites problématiques de la pensée de Foucault. Tout se passe comme si, pour lui, il n'y avait qu'un genre, le masculin homoérotique ..." (80–1)].

fixity in relation to "perversion" and queer. Butler wishes primarily to destabilize notions that the ways we perform gender reveal the truth of our sexual identity and/or orientation. (One thinks of historically ingrained clichés such as the lesbian who is inevitably butch in appearance or the effeminate man whose mannerisms reveal the secret of his homosexuality). Rather, for Butler (1993): "there are no direct expressive or causal links between sex, gender, gender presentation, sexual practice, fantasy and sexuality. None of these terms captures or determines the rest" (315). This idea of a series of interrelating, resignifying performative lines running between gender and sexuality deliberately highlights elements of play, fluidity and interchangeability at work in sexual behavior and sexual orientation. Butler's use of performativity, then, as we have seen, relies on an implicit logic of fluidity — but not of choice — as its central tool of resistance.

As Brad Epps (2001) argues in his psychoanalytically-informed essay, "The Fetish of Fluidity," to which I referred in the introductory section above, "Queer theory tends to place great stock in movement, especially when it is movement against, beyond, or away from rules and regulations, norms and conventions, borders and limits." He goes on to state that it "presents movement, fluid movement, as the liberational undoing of regulatory disciplinarity." In short, "It makes fluidity a fetish" (413). While Butler — after Foucault — has cautioned against the association of fluidity with a too-simple idea of free will, and while both are, in fact, famously suspicious of the discourse of liberation that Epps rather unfairly ascribes to them, Butler nevertheless reinforces the idea that it is via a movement away from expected chains of signification towards motile ambiguity, that queer theory offers an alternative to normalization. Eve Kosofsky Sedgwick (1993) echoes this idea of queer as perpetually and essentially in movement: "Queer is a continuing moment, movement, motive — recurrent, eddying, *troublant*. The word 'queer' itself means 'across' — it comes from the Indo-European root — *twerkw*, which also yields the German *quer* (transverse), Latin *torquere* (to twist), English *athwart*" (xii; cited in Epps 2001, 425). Brad Epps's argument against the "fetish of fluidity" in queer is that it ushers in a "degaying and delesbianising agen-da" (417). The movement against identity in queer — its strategic non-identitarian agenda — does indeed risk (more than risk; it *courts*) this de-specification of sexual identity labels. And this has to be understood as a deliberate response to, and rejection of, the *"specification of individuals"* that Foucault (1990) de-scribes in 1976 as an effect of the technologies of *scientia sexu-alis* that began to name the "inverts" and "perverts" in the mid-nineteenth century (42–43; italics in original).

A parallel concern to Epps's cry against the "degaying" of queer comes from feminist writer, Biddy Martin (1997). She worries about "defining queerness as mobile and fluid in rela-tion to what then gets construed as stagnant and ensnaring, and as associated with a maternal, anachronistic, and putatively pu-ritanical feminism" (110). Epps and Martin isolate as a problem of queer theory the very anti-identitarian energies which feed it. Indeed, queer texts often express concern that as soon as an identification is taken up, that identification stagnates into rec-ognizable meaning. This idea is found in work of proto-queer thinker *par excellence,* Foucault. In an interview conducted in 1982, which first appeared in 1984, for example, Foucault opined: "[T]he relationships we have to have with ourselves are not ones of identity, rather, they must be relationships of differentiation, of creation, of innovation. To be the same is really boring. We must not exclude identity if people find their pleasure through this identity, but we must not think of this identity as an ethi-cal universal rule" (2000, 166). In "Friendship as a Way of Life" (2000), he writes along the same lines: "another thing to distrust is the tendency to relate the question of homosexuality to the problem of 'Who am I?' and 'What is the secret of my desire?'" (135). For Foucault, then, operating before the establishment of queer (if such a deliberately unstable body of thought as queer can be said to have been established), the temptation to see one's sexual desire as the path to the secret of the truth of identity is a lie of modernity; one of the grand narratives of post-enlight-enment scientific thinking about the subject. Seeing identity as a truth about the self was a trap, as it fixed one's sense of self in pre-existing — and often unsympathetic, pathologizing or derogatory meanings.

My own concern with the rejection of fixity in queer theory has much less to do with Epps's and Martin's worries about the potential loss of an identity label to rally around (whether gay, lesbian, bi, feminist, or whatever else it may be) that is entailed by a deconstructive, anti-identitarian epistemology. For, as Butler contends convincingly, there is no reason why one cannot provisionally rally around an identity that is threatened or attacked, even while questioning the universality or singularity of the meaning of that label. She writes in "Imitation and Gender Insubordination" (1991): "This is not to say that I will not appear at political occasions under the sign of lesbian, but that I would like to have it permanently unclear what precisely that sign signifies" (308). Rather, my worry about queer's rejection of fixity and embrace of fluidity directly concerns the question of what this means for the status of non-normative erotic practices or — to put it in Foucault's (1990) language — "bodies and pleasures," which he proposes as the utopian alternative to the psychoanalytic logic of "sex-desire" (157). Queer theory has always had an ambivalent relationship with what — in a different discourse — would be called the perversions or paraphilias, and it is in respect to these that the fetishization of fluidity and the scapegoating of fixity risk being most damning. In some ways, non-normative bodily practices (what I do), rather than identities (how I define myself in terms of gender or sexuality) and orientations (whom I desire; my sexual object choice), are the very stuff of queer, the launchpad for its non-normalizing energetic trajectories that confound conservative discourses about sexuality as reproductive, productive, life-affirming, functional, and socially useful for maintaining the status quo.[4] Foucault

4   Such critiques of the (re)productive, utilitarian connotations of "sexuality" are found especially in those queer texts associated with the "anti-social" turn in queer theory. Lee Edelman's *No Future: Queer Theory and the Death Drive* (2004), which presents, using a Lacanian theoretical framework, an indictment of the ideology of "reproductive futurity" has been particularly influential in this regard. More recently, Tim Dean's *Unlimited Intimacy*

chose largely not to talk about being a homosexual but rather to talk about the bodily practices and new forms of erotic relationality that he espied in subcultural communities, such as the San Francisco SM scene and which he harnessed as "the rallying point for the counterattack against the deployment of sexuality" (157). Other writers, however, such as Elizabeth Grosz (1994), have worried about the extent to which "perversions" should be included under the term "queer" since, she argues, it would be wrong to see — for example — heterosexual "sadists" benefiting from the same depathologizing energies as lesbians and gay men — the "properly" oppressed (in a rather un-queer gesture of hierarchy-of-oppression-building).[5]

Tim Dean's *Beyond Sexuality* (2000), which attempts not only to write queer psychoanalytic theory, but to substantiate the claim that psychoanalysis *is* a queer theory, tries to move away from such binaristic — and covertly identitarian — ways of thinking about forms of desire that we see in Grosz. Here it is argued that within Lacanian theory, desire — that errant, dissident, anarchic force — is always perverse rather than identitarian. He stresses how, for Lacan, diversity is all: "there is no privileged sexual activity or erotic narrative to which we should all aspire, no viable sexual norm for everybody, because desire's origins are multiple and its ambition no more specific than satisfaction" (196). The aim of Dean's work is to conceptualize an impersonal account of desire by marrying Lacan's insistence

---

(2009) considers "barebacking" subcultures and their practices of voluntary HIV transmission as an alternative model of queer kinship, "breeding" bugs rather than children.

5   Grosz (1994) writes: "'Queer' is capable of accommodating and will no doubt provide a political rationale and coverage in the near future for many of the most blatant and extreme forms of heterosexual and patriarchal power games. They too are, in a certain sense, queer, persecuted, ostracized. Heterosexual sadists, pederasts, fetishists, pornographers, pimps, voyeurs, suffer from social sanctions: in a certain sense they too can be regarded as oppressed. But to claim an oppression of the order of lesbian and gay, women's or racial oppression is to ignore the very real complicity and phallic rewards of what might be called 'deviant sexualities' within patriarchal and heterocentric power relations" (154).

that in the unconscious there is no gender and no "proper" object of desire, with the Foucauldian ambition to "shift beyond sexuality as the primary register in which we make sense of ourselves" (88).

It is this enlarged sense of queer that Tamsin Spargo (1990) celebrates — in contradistinction to the worries expressed by Grosz — when she writes:

[A]s Foucault's history had shown, [...] object choice had not always constituted the basis for an identity and, as many dissenting voices suggested, it was not inevitably the crucial factor in everyone's perception of their sexuality. This model effectively made bisexuals seem to have a less secure or developed identity (rather as essentialist models of gender make transsexuals incomplete subjects), and excluded groups that defined their sexuality through activities and pleasures rather than gender preferences, such as sadomasochists. (33–34)

Perverse bodily practices, then, seem to be close to the heart of queer's concerns, yet — as I shall explain — they are one of the subjects it treats most problematically, often unwittingly imitating rather than countering the language and terms in which perversion has been historically conceptualized in the discourses of sexology, psychiatry and psychoanalysis.

Perversion

Sexologists of the late-nineteenth century, most famously Richard von Krafft-Ebing whose *Psychopathia sexualis* of 1886 is commonly seen as the bible of sexology, first posed the perversions — conditions of being responsive to non-normative stimuli or unusual sexual practices — as a social problem. Perverse sexuality was seen as the symptom of a morally corrupt state, in keeping with the sexually, ethnically, and nationalistically normative dominant discourse of the period: the threat of degeneration.[6] In the first of the "Three Essays on the Theory of Sexuality," Freud (1905) "worked hard to de-couple perversion from degeneration by introducing a developmental and unconscious model of sexuality.[7] He argued that perversion was one outcome of a failed Oedipal resolution, not the symptom of inherited degeneracy or a corrupt environment. What is more, with his model of infantile sexuality, primary bisexuality, and polymorphous perversity, Freud argued that all of us, at some time in our lives have desired perversely, enabling queer theorist Jonathan Dollimore (1991) to quip that, for Freud, "one does not become a pervert, but remains one" (176).

It is in this *remaining* that the trouble lurks from the point of view of the present argument. Freudian theory describes two models of perversion. First, it describes the free-floating, multivalent, polymorphous pleasure of infancy (that is lost forever after the trauma of Oedipus and the un-innocent "forgetting" of the latency period). Secondly, it describes adult perversion, defined according to the mechanism of what is, for Freud, the archetypical perversion of fetishism: namely, a mechanism of fixation. Freud comments that if we take as "perverse" any act that is not heterosexual intercourse — such as kissing, caressing and so on, then hardly anyone shall fail to avoid making an addition to their sexual life that may be called perverse. However, an adult is only to be clinically diagnosed as a pervert if their non-normative sexual practice is carried out to the exclusion of all others. In the first of his "Three Essays" he writes: "if […] a perversion has the characteristic of exclusiveness and fixation — then we shall usually be justified in regarding it as a path-

---

6   For more on Krafft-Ebing's sexological method, see Oosterhuis 2000. For more on Degeneration theory, and its application to theories of sexed and racial bodies, see Pick 1989. For more on nineteenth-century sexology's foundational contribution to "perversion theory," see Bristow 1997, 1–61; Hekma 1991; Nobus 2006, 3–18.

7   Even arch detractor of psychoanalytic method, Foucault (1990), acknowledged that Freud, unlike the sexologists he came after, "rigorously opposed the political and institutional effects of the perversion-heredity-degeneration system" (119).

ological symptom" (161). The irony of the logic will not be lost on us: the quality of fixity is both the definition of the desired norm (the "healthy" adult pursues only heterosexual genital intercourse rather than bisexual plural polymorphous pleasures) and yet it is also the definition of aberration (if the adult were to practice several perverse acts alongside genital intercourse — if he were to be more *fluidly* perverted — he would, for Freud, escape pathologization). Let us bear in mind that fixity, then, appears to be the aim of *both* the normalizing social order that would fix adult sexuality in genitality *and* the single-minded pervert, whom we might call the most creative of Freud's cast of characters by dint of his writing a more alluring alternative to the dull Oedipal "truth" of sexual difference.[8] It is by bearing this in mind that we begin to understand how the latter can have been collapsed onto the former, such that fixity appears as always already conservative and normative.

Most psychoanalytic thinkers and clinicians, following Freud's own description and understanding of perversion in 1905, draw a distinction between perverse elements of behavior or fantasy that may occur in any subject alongside more "normal" or socially acceptable sexual behaviors on the one hand, and a perverse *structure,* implying a sclerotic rigidity of psychical organization on the other. Authors of canonical studies of perversion, Robert Stoller and M. Masud R. Khan, writing in the 1970s, and Janine Chasseguet-Smirgel in the 1980s, have argued, respectively, that elements of hatred, aggression and intimacy-inhibiting alienation underlie the fixated perverse structure, leading the "pervert" to find difficulty in many aspects of social life and relationship-formation, not only those directly associated with their sexual life. The "being" of "being a pervert"

---

8   The idea that perversion is close to creativity and may be the foundation of political utopia is discussed in some works of psychoanalytically-informed theory, such as Whitebook 1995. Published clinical work, on the other hand, tends to be much less laudatory of perversion's creative potential. One study, Chasseguet-Smirgel 1985 takes account of this idea, but still pathologizes perversion and perverts. For more on these two strands of psychoanalytic work on perversion, see Downing 2006, 149–63.

in psychoanalytic ontology — or at least diagnostics — signifies beyond what is done by that person in bed and describes a typology of character, as much as of behavior. For Robert Stoller (1986), for example, the pervert is a deceptive, deluded figure, split against himself in his attempt to keep believing in the perverse script which he has written as a result of having "connived, pandered and dissimulated" (95). In classic psychoanalytic theory, moreover, the pervert is inevitably male, given that perversion in its archetypical form of fetishism can only be attained by a very particular male response to the Oedipus complex.⁹ It is against this mapping of both sexed and character-based essence onto practice that queer theory after Foucault has insisted on the importance of dissociating *what I do* from *who I am*. Right up to the present day, then, persistent practitioners of non-normative bodily practices are pathologized by psychoanalysts as suffering from broader mental disorders particularly, or uniquely, where they present as fixated upon those practices. Generalizations about personality are adduced from facts of sexual behavior.

In contemporary Anglo-American sexology and psychiatry, the term "perversion" has been replaced by "paraphilia" (literally: that which lies alongside love) after a suggestion made by Wilhelm Stekel in 1909, with the rationale that the latter term is less judgmental than "perversion," whose roots lie in religious moral discourse and which signifies a turning away from the "right" path. Moreover, the assumption that a paraphiliac will be of the male sex is not a given in the logic of this nosology. However, the notion that fixity defines perversion — or paraphilia — and determines what is unhealthy about it persists in the psychiatric model. The previous edition of the American Psychiatric Association's *Diagnostic and Statistical Manual of Mental Disorders* (*DSM-IV-TR*), asserts that "fantasies, behaviours, or objects are paraphiliac only when they [...] are obliga-

---

9   Some psychoanalysts and psychoanalytically influenced cultural critics
     have challenged and nuanced the Freudian notion that the fetishist in par-
     ticular and the pervert in general is always already male. See, for example,
     Kaplan 1991; Apter 1991.

tory" (*DSM-IV-TR*, 525), while the most recent edition, the *DSM* 5, published in 2013, which introduces a distinction between "paraphilias" which may be "discerned" in clinical practice and "paraphilic disorders" which are to be "diagnosed" as mental disorders, describes paraphilias as a "persistent sexual interest other than sexual interest in genital stimulation or preparatory fondling with phenotypically normal, consenting adult human partners" (*DSM 5th ed.*, 285).[10] Thus, the notion that variety makes sexual behavior and identity acceptable is consistent in mental health discourse from the early-twentieth- to the twenty-first centuries. Worryingly, however, it is also — implicitly — a tenet of queer theory (even if psychoanalysis and psychiatry require that the "variety" include heterosexual penetration, while queer theory obviously does not).

For example, queer theorist Moe Meyer (1994) defines queer as an "ontological challenge" to concepts of sexual subjectivity that are "unique, abiding and continuous," favoring instead sexualities that are "performative, improvisational, discontinuous" (2–3). This rhetorical privileging of discontinuity suggests that, for Meyer, those who are fixated in their practices are in thrall to a bourgeois and reactionary ideology of selfhood, to ontological staleness. Even in Tim Dean's (2000) ambitious work which valorizes perversion as the very stuff of dissident desire, the language of fixity and exclusivity borrowed from medicine disturbingly haunts the rhetoric: "the process of normalization itself is what is pathological, since normalization 'fixes' desire and generates the exclusiveness of sexual orientation as its symptom" (237). It is the polymorphousness of infantile perversion persisting in the unformed, unconscious model of desire — not the adult's fixated narrative of perversion — that is valorized by Dean here as being sexually radical. Thus, this bold attempt to write against the psychoanalytic orthodoxy (by pathologizing

---

10 For a discussion of the ways in which the move from "paraphilia" to "paraphilic disorders" is not quite so radical a depathologization of non-normative sexuality as the American Psychiatric Association (APA) has claimed, see Downing 2015.

the social imperative to reach hetero-genitality rather than by pathologizing perversion) risks taking the *structure* of fixity or "exclusiveness," rather than the *political content* of the imperative of compulsive heterosexuality, as the target of its attack.

In a similar vein, Butler ascribes to any exclusive sexual practice the status of normativity: "It's not just the norm of heterosexuality that is tenuous. It's all sexual norms. [...] If you say 'I can only desire x,' what you have immediately done in rendering desire exclusively, is created a whole set of positions which are unthinkable from the standpoint of your identity" (Osborne and Segal 1994, 34). According to Butler, self-subversion is essential for avoiding this identitarian trap, and it can be achieved by "occupying a position that you have just announced to be unthinkable" (34). Butler goes on:

> I think that crafting a sexual position, or reciting a sexual position, always involves becoming haunted by what's excluded. And the more rigid the position, the greater the ghost, and the more threatening in some way. I don't know if that's a Foucauldian point. It's probably a psychoanalytical point, but that's not finally important to me. (34)

This logic — proposed by one of the most influential voices in "queer" — is indeed a Freudian point. It is the logic of pure Freudian pathological perversion. The archetypical pervert, the fetishist, is haunted by the loss of his belief in mother's phallus that he displaces onto his fetish object or act, and thereby gets to keep in another form: the high-heeled shoe; the shine on the nose and so on. Queer theory repeats wholesale here the psychoanalytic rhetoric which holds that the fixated perverse structure is inferior to more "discontinuous" forms of sexuality. As a theoretical prescription about how our desire should work, how we are supposed to conduct our bodily practices, and how we should construe the idea of "fixated singularity" philosophically — as always-already normalizing — this is itself a strikingly normative directive.

Moreover, it becomes a discourse in which the ghost of what it disavows — normalization — returns surreptitiously in the prescription to desire appropriately plurally, fluidly and openly. The embalmed object of fixity haunts the queer position behind the shiny fetish of fluidity that it promotes. It is extremely problematic that queer should ape epistemologically the model of disavowal (based on a logical rigidity) that it scapegoats in its rejection of the figure of fixity. For this suggests a residual fear of, and belief in, an origin, rather than a defiant demonstration of the lack of origin beneath our performativity. If "queer" and "crip" are recuperable labels, how strange that being "fixated"; a "pervert'" a "'proper' pervert" — enjoying the same bodily practice time and again, however queer that practise may be in its anti-heteronormative energies — should be seen to lie so entirely beyond the pale. Queer theory would do well to harness its celebrated energies of motility and resignification in the service of re-inscribing fixated desire differently. This would be a more creative agenda than the construction, and reification through the repetition of discourse, of an unhelpful binary, which risks appearing as an archaic and originary truth: fixity is always a problem; fluidity is its "cure" (whether the antidote is political or clinical).

Instead of constructing its own type of exemplary plural subject, performing the right number of appropriately dissident and different sexual practices, in the correctly plural and queer relationship configuration, then, queer theory might do better to concentrate on challenging the meaning of such paradigms. It would be in keeping with Warner's description of queer as opposing "the *idea* of normal," with which I began, if queer theory were carefully to avoid the tyranny of all prescriptions and norms. This would include an avoidance of imputing normativity to the repetition of the same in the sphere of sexuality, where the same is a perverse practice enjoyed, not in the service of shoring up an identity, but simply in the service of enjoyment — useless, excessive enjoyment that is not recuperable for its utilitarian value or its meaning.[11] Radical theories of sexuality, then, might avoid echoing canonical psychoanalytic perspectives by giving up the commonplace assertion that fixity is somehow pathological or inferior to plurality — that fixity "means" anything very specific *at all* — and work to legitimize both plurality and singularity, not in a dialectical configuration, but as infinitely equal and different.

I hope to have shown that, while polemically valid and rhetorically empowering in places, the queer strategy of valorizing fluidity through its association with the transformative powers of performativity nevertheless falls into serious logical and ideological traps when applied to the problems and pleasures of perversion. I would go further and opine that a queer theory that does not embrace the energies of the "perverse" is missing a trick in failing to celebrate the "twistedness," the "athwart-ness" of which perverts have long been accused and which, as Eve Kosofsky Sedgwick has reminded us, are etymologically enshrined in the very notion of "queer" itself. Finally, I would suggest that psychoanalysts ask themselves whether historically ingrained orthodoxies about the meanings of fixated behavior are really

---

11 The notion that sexuality has a "function" (reproduction) is an inheritance of biological (as well, arguably, of theological) discourses that influenced nineteenth-century sexological and medical accounts of perversion. The idea that the human sex instinct is identical with an instinct for reproduction can be found in the work of Pierre Cabanis (1757–1808) and Paul Moreau de Tours (1844–1908), as well as in Krafft-Ebing's famous *Psychopathia sexualis*. See Nobus 2006, 6; Davidson 2001). The understanding of sexual desire as identical with the desire for reproduction is a logic that underpins the history of modern scientific thinking about sexuality. Queer's attempts to render sexuality as doing something other than serving a utilitarian biological and social aim are in direct response to such discourses. Foucault and Lacan, as Tim Dean has shown in *Beyond Sexuality* (2000), both characterize desire as useless, as refusing to serve the aims of the social imperative. Another important twentieth-century philosophical name in this debate is Georges Bataille, whose notion of sexuality as a limit-experience — as allied to death and dissolution rather than life, selfhood and continuity — has been underused by critics of utilitarian ideas of sex since Foucault's essay of 1963. This is regrettable as he is, in many ways, a natural ally to queer agendas. See Bataille 1962; Foucault 2000.

capable of accounting for the multiplicity of types of fixation that clinical practice yields, and — even more urgently — what investments are really at stake in making a symptom out of a pleasure.

Works Cited

Althusser, Louis. "Ideology and Ideological State Apparatuses." In *Lenin and Philosophy and Other Essays,* trans. Ben Brewster, 121–76. New York and London: Monthly Review Press, 1971 (1969).

American Psychiatric Association. *Diagnostic and Statistical Manual of Mental Disorders (DSM-IV-TR).* Washington, DC: American Psychiatric, Publishing, 2000.

———. *Diagnostic and Statistical Manual of Mental Disorders.* 5th ed. Washington, DC: American Psychiatric, Publishing, 2013.

Apter, Emily. *Feminizing the Fetish: Psychoanalysis and Narrative Obsession in Turn-of-the-Century France.* Ithaca: Cornell University Press, 1991.

Austin, J.L. *How to Do Things with Words,* eds. J.O. Urmson and Marina Sibsa. 2nd ed. Oxford: Clarendon Press, 1975.

Bataille, Georges. *Eroticism,* trans. Mary Dalwood. London: Marion Boyes, 1962 (1957).

Bourcier, Marie-Hélène. *Queer Zones: Politiques des identités sexuelles et des savoirs.* Paris: Éditions Amsterdam, 2006.

Bristow, Joseph. *Sexuality.* London and New York: Routledge, 1997.

Butler, Judith. *Gender Trouble: Feminism and the Subversion of Identity.* 1990; rpt: New York and London: Routledge, 1999.

———. "Imitation and Gender Insubordination." In *The Lesbian and Gay Studies Reader,* eds. Henry Abelove, Michele Aina Barale and David Halperin, 307–20. New York and London: Routledge, 1993 (1991).

———. *Bodies That Matter: On the Discursive Limits of "Sex."* 1993; rpt. New York and London: Routledge, 1996.

————. *Excitable Speech: A Politics of the Performative*. New York and London: Routledge, 1997.

Chasseguet-Smirgel, Janine. *Creativity and Perversion*. London: Free Association Books, 1985.

Davidson, Arnold. "How to Do the History of Psychoanalysis: A Reading of Freud's Three Essays on the Theory of Sexuality." In *The Emergence of Sexuality: Historical Epistemology and the Formation of Concepts*, 66–92. Cambridge: Harvard University Press, 2001 (1987).

Dean, Tim. *Beyond Sexuality*. Chicago: Chicago University Press, 2000.

————. *Unlimited Intimacy: Reflections on the Subculture of Barebacking*. Chicago: Chicago University Press, 2009.

Dollimore, Jonathan. *Sexual Dissidence: Augustine to Wilde, Freud to Foucault*. Oxford: Oxford University Press, 1991.

Downing, Lisa. "Perversion, Historicity, Ethics." In *Perversion: Psychoanalytic Perspectives/ Perspectives of Psychoanalysis*, eds. Dany Nobus and Lisa Downing, 149–63. London and New York: Karnac Books, 2006.

————. *The Cambridge Introduction to Michel Foucault*. Cambridge: Cambridge University Press, 2008.

————. "Heteronormativity and Repronormativity in Sexological 'Perversion Theory' and the DSM-5's 'Paraphilic Disorder' Diagnoses." *Archives of Sexual Behavior* 44, no. 4 (2015): 1139–45.

Edelman, Lee. *No Future: Queer Theory and the Death Drive*. Durham and London: Duke University Press, 2004.

Epps, Brad. "The Fetish of Fluidity." In *Homosexuality and Psychoanalysis*, eds. Tim Dean and Christopher Lane, 412–31. Chicago: University of Chicago Press, 2001.

Foucault, Michel. "Sex, Power, and the Politics of Identity." In *Essential Works of Foucault 1954–1984, vol. 1: Ethics*, ed. Paul Rabinow, 163–73. Harmondsworth: Penguin, 2000 (1984).

————. "Friendship as a Way of Life." In *Essential Works of Foucault 1954–1984, vol. 1: Ethics*, ed. Paul Rabinow, 135–40. Harmondsworth: Penguin, 2000 (1981).

———. "A Preface to Transgression." In *Essential Works of Foucault 1954–1984, vol. 2: Aesthetics,* ed. James D. Faubion, 69–87. Harmondsworth: Penguin, 2000 (1963).

———. *The History of Sexuality, vol. 1: The Will to Knowledge,* trans. Robert Hurley. Harmondsworth: Penguin, 1990 (1976).

Freud, Sigmund. "Three Essays on the Theory of Sexuality" (1905). In *the Standard Edition of the Complete Psychological Works,* vol. 7, ed. and trans. James Strachey in collaboration with Anna Freud and assisted by Alix Strachey and Alan Tyson, 123–245. 1953; rpt. London, Vintage, 2001.

Grosz, Elizabeth. "Experimental Desire: Rethinking Queer Subjectivity." In *Supposing the Subject,* ed. Joan Copjec, 133–58. New York: Verso, 1994.

Hekma, Gert. "A History of Sexology: Social and Historical Aspects of Sexuality." In *From Sappho to de Sade: Moments in the History of Sexuality,* ed. Jan Bremmer, 173–93. New York and London: Routledge, 1991.

Kahn, M. Masud R. *Alienation in Perversions.* London: Hogarth Press, 1979.

Kaplan, Louise. *Female Perversions.* 1991; rpt. Harmondsworth: Penguin, 1993 (1991).

Krafft-Ebing, Richard von. *Psychopathia sexualis: Eine Klinisch-forensische Studie.* Stuttgart: Ferdinand Enke, 1886.

McRuer, Robert. *Crip Theory: Cultural Signs of Queerness and Disability.* New York: New York University Press, 2006.

Martin, Biddy. "Extraordinary Homosexuals and the Fear of Being Ordinary." In *Feminism Meets Queer Theory,* eds. Naomi Schor and Elizabeth Weed, 109–35. Bloomington: Indiana University Press, 1997.

Meyer, Moe. "Introduction." In *The Politics and Poetics of Camp,* ed. Moe Meyer. New York and London: Routledge, 1994.

Nobus, Dany. "Locating Perversion, Dislocating Psychoanalysis." In *Perversion: Psychoanalytic Perspectives/ Perspectives of Psychoanalysis,* eds. Dany Nobus and Lisa Downing, 3–18. London and New York: Karnac Books, 2006.

Oosterhuis, Harry. *Stepchildren of Nature: Krafft-Ebing, Psychiatry and the Making of Sexual Identity.* Chicago: University of Chicago Press, 2000.

Osborne, Peter, and Lynne Segal. "Gender as Performance: An Interview with Judith Butler." *Radical Philosophy* 67 (1994): 32–39.

Pick, Daniel. *Faces of Degeneration: A European Disorder.* Cambridge: Cambridge University Press, 1989.

Sedgwick, Eve Kosofsky. *Tendencies.* Durham: Duke University Press, 1993.

Spargo, Tamsin. *Foucault and Queer Theory.* Cambridge: Icon Books, 1999.

Stoller, Robert. *Perversion: The Erotic Form of Hatred.* 1975; rpt. London: Karnac, 1986 (1975).

Warner, Michael. *Fear of a Queer Planet: Queer Politics and Social Theory.* Minneapolis: University of Minnesota Press, 1993.

Whitebook, Joel. *Perversion and Utopia: A Study of Psychoanalysis and Critical Theory.* Cambridge: MIT Press, 1995.

Out of Line, On Hold: D.W. Winnicott's Queer Sensibilities

Michael Snediker[1]

Ethics beyond Reciprocity

This chapter situates its discussion of ethics in the work of the mid-twentieth century British psychoanalyst, D.W. Winnicott. Winnicott's theorization of transitional objects and good-enough mothers has inspired the scholarship of thinkers such as Mary Jacobus (2005) and Adam Phillips (1989); at the same time, Winnicott's output figures, in Deleuzian terms, as a minor literature in the larger psychoanalytic landscape. The sympatico of Winnicott's work with many recent queer-theoretical investigations of intersubjectivity alone necessitates our continued reappraisal of what he may teach us. Unlike that of Jacques Lacan, who devoted a seminar to the ethics of psychoanalysis, Winni-

---

1   I wrote most of this essay five years ago or so. Life is full of entropy (even without the bedragglement of degenerative chronic pain) and had there been world enough and time, I would have revised it from start to finish. As it stands, however, the present version is a testimony to an earlier moment in my thinking. I accept responsibility for its faults (including its penchant for over-writing) and only hope my decision to publish it, as is, is more useful than not. For a revision of these pages, see my forthcoming book, *Contingent Figure: Aesthetic Duress from Ralph Waldo Emerson to Eve Kosofsky Sedgwick*.

cott's contribution to psychoanalytic ethics must be trawled in pieces, and culled without prior sense of what that ethics might eventually resemble. In this sense, the very practice of returning to Winnicott resembles the non-paranoid reading position of Eve Kosofsky Sedgwick, a queer theorist who taught, more than anyone I can think of, the inseparability of ethics from the surprise of not knowing in advance where desire might converge with rigor, gauziness, creativity, and or delight. To read Winnicott alongside Sedgwick is to aspire toward for an ethics freed from the normatively non-contingent, but no less predicated on the contingencies of availing dislocation.

"Let us treat the men and women well; treat them as if they were real; perhaps they are" (Emerson 1983, 479). Ralph Emerson's exhortation surfaces near the mid-point of his essay, "Experience," a sustained meditation on the grief of not only having lost his son to scarlet fever, two years prior, but of what he describes as the grief that he cannot grieve. Emerson's formulation laconically introduces some of the terms that inform my understanding of ethics as it bears on queer theory's relation to psychoanalysis. In its echo of analogously stated scenes of exhortation in the poems of Catullus and Herbert, the wishful élan of the opening two-word rejoinder illuminates one's wish for ethics to provide some version of clearing, of collectivity capable of moving between thought and action. Not unrelated, ethics takes as its object less the fact of relation than some relational hypothesis of care: not only how we *ought* to treat each other but how we might. The temporally indefinite processes of analytic treatment take as foundational that our "actual" — constative, physical, etc. — position in the world is at best a small percentage of all the equally incontrovertible forces by which we are constituted: contra conventional (e.g., non-psychoanalytic) standards, these latter, psychoanalysis has shown, are often one's most resistant, least remediable elements. A person's realness, by Emerson's formulation, isn't what justifies or necessitates one's care for them. The latter arises in the generative, literally creative space between what could be real and what "is." We find here a productive syncope between ethical treatment and the latter's implicit ontological grounds. That the former might arise in the temporary suspension rather than demand of the actual opens onto queer theory's own pre-occupations with the question rather than fact of the real as it might open onto rather than oppose the unreal, and by extension, the ways in which the literalness of our selves (our lives and their relations, centrifugal and centripetal alike) opens onto rather than opposes the figurative.

How have we moved so quickly from ethics to this notion of the figurative? For one, I think of the incessantly indeterminate relation between analogy and simile, and the ways that the action if not being of both categories explicitly depends on a precipice or imaginative leap internal to each. The leap — the willingness of what it is to recognize itself (if only reductively) in what isn't as a capacity for hypothesized being — lodges in the little auxiliary idiom of "as if." To return our attention to Emerson, however, it's not that creative believing is in service or otherwise subordinate to fact, but that the inhabiting of possibility suggests an indefinite, un-ending end in itself. Somewhat differently put (and in ways both informed and illuminated by Winnicott and Sedgwick alike), the queer psychoanalytic ethics imagined in these pages takes as its own point of departure that believing in something isn't inferior or prior to the fact of it, but a form of being unto itself: unwavering, as though we might treat the men and women well in a *perhaps* whose virtue lies in its ultimate non-equivalence to its nominal object.

The difference, then, between a belief and a fact wouldn't only be that *one* is whereas the *other* might be, or even that one exists in the orbit of abstraction whereas the other exists as a thing in the world, but that one is still becoming or, more simply, is becoming. When I call this becoming figurative, I therefore wish to invoke figurative as an affective, and affectively vital, motion. To be figurative is not only not to be less real but maybe, more so. This account of queer theory's resistance to the facticity of being isn't meant to displace earlier accounts of queer theory's differently calibrated identitarian investments, or the fact if not of bodies or gender than that of the realness of desire itself. For one, I think of the flexible spaciousness of the former in many

ways as a quiescence of displacement as such; and in this regard, I understand the queer modality of possibility ("perhaps")
along the lines of Roland Barthes's meditation on the Neutral, a
porous category of resistance (such as it's possible) to resistance
qua resistance. At least among more recent generations of queer
persons in certain cosmopolitan spaces, we've come a long-ish
way since the euphemistic language of gays interpellated less in
terms of their lives than their lifestyles. At the same time, this
leaning of "life" into "style" anticipates some of the ways that
queer theory explores living as it opens onto what Foucault
(1997), in "On the Genealogy of Ethics: A Work in Progress,"
calls "an esthetics of existence." Such a project is inseparable
from the ways both homosexual persons and acts — "acts," a euphemism to which we shall return, as we further consider the
impactions and instabilities of action qua category — have until
recently (and as often, to this day) been subject to omission, degrees of censorship, compunctions of translation and mistrans-
lation. In this respect, a certain strain of queer ethics begins not
in the fact but the belief that the survival of such failed efforts
at performative extermination depends first on a commitment
to the unmistakeable life of persons so unremittingly denied the
rights of the living. This is to say that queer theory's contribution to ethical thinking involves an expansion of the vocabulary by which we locate and articulate queer phenomena *as* real,
visible, conversible. Counterveiling such an enterprise has been
queer theory's wish to differently reclaim the slippery potency
of queer volatility, and in so doing, complicate any person's wish
to seem real.

It bears reminding that there is no more a single, monolithic
queer theory than there is a monolithic psychoanalysis; queer
theory, as a moniker for a constellation of disparate thinking,
invariably only sometimes barely does justice to the important
self-contradictions and auto-corrections it contains. Still, queer
theory, as cultivated, taught, and practiced for the past decades,
is remarkable for its simultaneous claims toward realness and a
politically informed wariness of it. The wariness arises from a
suspicion of realness as inextricable from ideological pulsions

that will always jettison some form of personness as its sacrifice. For instance, in the work of Lee Edelman (2004), the dubiousness of realness blooms into suspicion of a desire *for* realness: "a refusal — the appropriately perverse refusal that characterizes queer theory — of every substantialization of identity, which is always oppositionally defined" (4). Ethics, for Edelman, requires the eschewal of humanness as we know it, an uncompromising accession to the inhuman, which Edelman aligns with Lacan's account of the death drive: "the death drive refuses identity or the absolute privilege of any goal" (22). Set alongside an understanding of ethics as a care for "substantialization[s]," Edelman's work puts us in a bind of either/or. Either we avow identity, or we disavow it. This present chapter wishes differently to think about ethics in terms of the equivocation between avowal and disavowal; even as equivocation, for my purposes, mischaracterizes an interpersonal regimen that more precisely renarrates the relation between ethical and aesthetic contemplation. Aesthetic vitality, here, resonates with what the queer theorist, Judith Butler (2005), has described as "an experiment in living otherwise": "What might it mean to undergo violation, to insist upon *not* resolving grief and staunching vulnerability too quickly through a turn to violence, and to practice, as an experiment in living otherwise, nonviolence in an emphatically nonreciprocal response? What would it mean, in the face of violence, to refuse to return it?" (100).

Catherine Mills (2007) challenges Butler's aspiration toward such an ethics of non-violence in part because a passage such as the above "stands in tension, if not contradiction, with other aspects of her theorization of normativity and subjectivity" (134). Succinctly, even reductively, Mills calls attention to queer theory's own earlier and extant understanding of itself not only as a kind of violence, but as a certain necessary response *to violence.* What Mills in part wishes, reductively speaking, is for Butler's ethics not so quickly to give up on an Edelmanian aggressivity willing to eschew even antagonism (the returning of violence) for a sedulous white noise extrinsic to a normativity dictating from outset the terms not just of its own call but of our limited sense of responses to it.

Can ethics be separated from norms, and can norms be separated from the latter's withering repertoire of abusiveness? In the words of a magic 8 ball, answers would seem to point to "no," to the extent to which our psychoanalytic or queer-theoretical purview is a Lacanian one. If ethical choreography is a feat of the Symbolic, then it goes nearly without saying a constitutive normative violence, as Mills writes, would be irreducible (155). An ethical turn to D.W. Winnicott, on the other hand, salutarily moves us from the grounds of the inexorable to a stage of improvisation no less instructive for its extemporaneousness. If ethics for some time has subsisted on a sense (earned or otherwise) of what it is or is not doing, Winnicottian ethics might well inhabit the space of not knowing if one is being or not, acting or not — of non-anxiogenically not knowing, and learning to undo the sequestering spaces of ontology and action.

Ethics beyond Action

Queer theory, like psychoanalysis, optimally illuminates the modes in which we relate to other persons and ourselves. Neither field ultimately is able or willing to describe any given modality in advance as erotic or non-erotic, as kind or unkind. The difficulties of legibility, for psychoanalysis, arise most saliently in the intractable and wily "fact" of an unconscious. The difficulties of legibility, in queer theory, sometimes arise in the wiliness of an unconscious (to the extent that so much of queer theory, including the work of Leo Bersani (1986), Judith Butler (1997, 1999, 2002, 2005), Tim Dean (2000), and others is indebted to psychoanalytic thinking), and sometimes in the wiliness of ideology — an apparatus, through dramas of internalization, itself only sometimes distinguishable from the Symbolic, itself only sometimes distinguishable from an unconscious. Queer theory, like psychoanalysis, optimally affords new vocabularies for ruminating instabilities of affect and epistemology as feeling and thinking negotiate and jostle the ossifications and eidolons by

which they've been displaced. I betray my own thinking's instabilities, here, in conjuring a sort of psychoanalytic macaronic
to which practitioners of a given school rightfully might balk.
Ditto a queer-theoretical macaronic that potentially whiplash-
es from the hyperbolic to the synecdochal. The investigation
at hand lays out these fields as such for the sake of a terrain's
outlines, but my own argument will hew to a vocabulary increasingly less promiscuous. For instance, I admit great interest — as a reader of both queer theory and psychoanalysis — in
those moments when it seems unclear as to whether sex is a
literalization of a certain acuity of interpersonal joy and travail,
or a metaphor for differently recognizable and unrecognizable
modes of joy and travail. As both literalization of relation and
figure for it, sex potentially rewrites ethical pause not merely
as a question of getting fucked or fucked over (or conversely, a
wish to fuck with others), but more specifically as a question of
how one crosses metaphorical and literal lines. Winnicott seems
especially luminous in helping us to think about ethics in terms
of linear surprise and conundra.

Sex, at its most banal, imputes the possibility of being one
with another. Sex, on a differently banal register, assumes an
anonymous aggressivity played out between bodies. But if sex
is both literalization and metaphoricity, where elsewhere might
considerations of interpersonality lead? In terms of queer-theoretical ethics, the dangerousness of sex — as either Freudian
aggressivity or Lacanian *jouissance* — arises in the drama of internalization, by which we become our own worst nightmare
which we act out on others. If subjectivity is read, following
Michel Foucault and Leo Bersani, as the fruition of normativity,
then subjectivity is the problem that sex brings to a head, and
which sex has the potential to dismantle (Bersani 1986; Foucault
1997). This is to say that one of the ways ethics surfaces in queer
theory is in the problematic of being a person but not wanting to
be a person. Abdication of a subjectivity to which one is more or
less is attached. What follows doesn't extend a counterargument
so much as ask what is differently queer in interpersonality: all

the more so, when an ensuing ethics honors the difficulty, in Winnicott, of that prefixial "inter."

It behooves us to begin with Jacques Lacan, before Winnicott, for several reasons. For one, Lacan has written more on ethics, titularly speaking, than most psychoanalysts. Second, Lacan not only has energized much queer theory, but in many ways has provided the grounds from which to distinguish queer theory from queer studies. If the latter takes seriously the sympathetic responsibility of reading the empirical, the former presumes the hermeneutic difficulty of approaching the empirical. Hence Lacan's subtle distinction between action and the measure of action: if action is presumed as lost to the immanent thresholds of the signified, we might well less compunctiously trust our grasp of action's measurement, belated signifier of action, but at least in belatedness less of a mirage. To begin, that is, with Lacan, is perhaps to wish for a different beginning, which we might then find in Winnicott. Even as ethics, more generally, might describe the wish for both different beginnings and different ends.

Jacques Lacan (1992) writes, "If there is an ethics of psychoanalysis — the question is an open one — it is to the extent that analysis in some way or other, no matter how minimally, offers something that is presented as a measure of our action — or at least it claims to" (311). Following Lacan's reservations, we might well consider what this "something" is, or how this "something" is offered, how it is presented. The measurement of action — of the ways in which a person participates in or withdraws from the world — presumes, as Lacan nearly implies, that action itself might be intelligible enough for calibration if not valuation. While ethical involvement presumes some degree of purposive vocation, it remains unclear in Lacan's treatment of ethics how we might know action when we see it, or when we ourselves are acting. Already we find ourselves in the vicinity of ethical theatrics, as action slips despite itself into acting, which slips into the form of action without necessarily its consequence (even as ethics would conventionally insist on some assertion of consequentiality).

As queer theorists, including Judith Butler (2002) and Lee Edelman (2004, 102–11), have noted, Lacan's figure for psycho-analytic courage is Antigone, who — unlike Oedipus, who acts on misprision — acts in principle. In terms of ethics as it relates and does not relate to theatrics, it's worth noting that Lacan turns to a Sophocles character, turns inaugurally to theater. This is a move differently made by Winnicott, although as we shall see, when Winnicott turns to the theatrics of tragedy, he acknowl-edges the medium, the apparatus of genre, rather than eliding distinctions between persons and characters. This is an elision made by Lacan, which we need not, reading Lacan, repeat. Anti-gone, as figure, arises for Lacan and others as an instantiation of a theory — of her own theory — as much as she enables theories (of activism, feminism, kinship, politics) that follow. Needless to say, to speak of instantiations of figures too quickly glosses the "measure" of this instantiation, not to mention the theoretically vast (and ethically fecund) differences between being a charac-ter and being a person.

Ethics, following the example of Antigone, traces a circular movement from theory to action and back again. In the circu-larity, the distinctions blur not only between thinking and do-ing, but between activity, passivity, being, and feeling. Perhaps this blur in part explains why Lacan speaks of the measure-ment of action rather than of action qua action. Returning to Lacan's quotation, in "offer[ing] something that is presented as a measure of our action [...] or at least it claims to," we are at least thrice-removed from the domain of action itself, as though analysis could at best only approach, in the manner of Zeno's paradox, what otherwise might be most at hand. Again, how Antigone acts or doesn't act mustn't overshadow that she is scripted, that her actions have been repeated, one production after another.

It is in the drama of drama (to risk tautology) that psycho-analytically-informed ethics finds itself in the domain of queer theory, specifically, in the domain of dubious ontologies. Is An-tigone merely an example from which persons might learn, or is she a character played by an actor, from whose staged actions we might learn. The degree to which her actions are her own or already scripted returns us obliquely to questions of normativity and nonviolence, as invoked by Judith Butler. In Winnicott, however, doing and being differently solicit queer theoretical attention, since the distinction between the two is itself a gendered one. The blur of being and doing likewise describes some of Judith Butler's most influential work on gender performativity. *Doing's* floundering, flamboyant confusability with *being* is its own gender trouble — to recall the title of Butler's early work. Or as Winnicott (1992[1966]) appositely writes two decades earlier, "The male element *does* while the female element (in males and females) *is*" (178).

These confusions of the ontological and the aesthetic inform nearly all of Winnicott's contributions to psychoanalytic thought and practice. Furthermore, these confusions suggest that ethics (how one acts, as illuminated by what one thinks) and queer theory, via Winnicott, already are structurally analogous. I would be inclined to think of Winnicott, in this context, as the father of queer theory, were he not so under-estimated and under-invoked in queer-theoretical enterprises, and were the bestowal of paternity so variously, ideologically fraught. If not the father of queer theory, then to use Winnicott's (1992[1964]) own self-identification, in the context of a clinical session: "I am still being used as a brother-mother." (340) As brother-mother of queer theory, Winnicott teaches us that subjectivity is as much a fiction as it is an aspiration, that creativity is far more psychical necessity than filibuster of the empirical. The dubiousness of self-identificatory credulity — evident in ruminations as different as Butler's (1999) accounts of performativity as destabilization of gender; Edelman's (1994, 3–31) study of metonymic slippage as a rhetorical heroism against the oppressive identity politics implied in the essentialisms of metaphor; Bersani's (1986) innovation suggestion of masochism as Darwinian solution to the world's barrage of instability (Bersani) — can be found, with great intelligence and compassion, in Winnicott's work (see, in particular, 1971).

Reading Lines

Winnicott's interest in the variousness of dubiousness matches, I think, that of Eve Kosofsky Sedgwick, denominated the mother of queer theory, to whose work we shall turn in the next section. Although in the spirit of Winnicott's own identifications, perhaps Sedgwick might no less be imagined as *sister-father.* Alongside Winnicott's clinical cross-identifications, transferential ebullience arises in Winnicott's thoughts on William Shakespeare, which perhaps only now can be felt and understood as the radical, enabling tentativeness that they are. Earlier in his *Ethics of Psychoanalysis,* Lacan (1992[1959–60]) opines that "*Hamlet* is by no means a drama of the importance of thought in the face of action" (251). Lacan perhaps unsurprisingly turns to *Hamlet* in the context of ethics — "Hamlet's apathy belongs to the sphere of action itself" (251). Winnicott, anticipating Sedgwick, turns to Hamlet for the ways epistemological contretemps dovetail with an insolubly inadequate gender-system, itself the convoluted return of, if not materialization, of a certain Cartesian breakdown. Winnicott's (1992[1966]) Hamlet isn't inert on account of too much thinking, but rather on account of his inability to think sufficiently, deeply, enough: "It would be rewarding to hear an actor play Hamlet with this in mind. This actor would have a special way of delivering the first line of the famous soliloquy: 'To be, or not to be....' He would say, as if trying to get to the bottom of something that cannot be fathomed, 'To be, ...or...' and then he would pause, because in fact the character Hamlet does not know the alternative. At last he would come in with the rather banal alternative '...or not to be'; and then he would be well away on a journey that can lead nowhere" (179). Winnicott's account of what I shall call Hamlet's queerness accrues to the factitiousness of reasoning as placeholder for a more satisfying sense of veracity:

> Hamlet is depicted at this stage as searching for an alternative to the idea "To be." He was searching for a way to state the dissociation that had taken place between his male and

female elements, elements which had up to the time of the
death of his father lived together in harmony, being but aspects of his richly endowed person. Yes, inevitably, I write as
if writing of a person, not a stage character. (181)

How quickly we move from Hamlet's endowments to Winnicott's treatment of Hamlet as though he were a person. How
quickly, that is, we move from a rift between "male and female
elements" to a rift between ontology ("a person") and aesthetics
("a stage character"). It likely is more accurate to note that Hamlet's queerness — as the simultaneous volatility and recalcitrance
of gendered pulsion — is inseparable from the "awful dilemma"
of existing in and out of the aesthetic, of being and not being a
person at all. *Hamlet's* exploration of ethics cleaves to Hamlet's
own exploration of ethics, which might no less be described as
Hamlet's queerness or Hamlet's aesthetic predicament. Of less
interest, for Winnicott, than Hamlet's relation to his father,
Gertrude, Claudius, or even himself, is Hamlet's queer relation
to *Hamlet*. Winnicott is self-conscious of *Hamlet* as both text
and production ("it would be rewarding to hear an actor play
Hamlet with this in mind…"), as Lacan similarly is attuned to
the textuality of *Antigone*. Unlike Lacan's readings of tragedy,
however, Winnicott can't help but conjure the counterfactual of
Hamlet's own awareness of himself as text. In Lacan's vocabulary, Hamlet's queerness may reside in the near-recognition of
oneself as one's own *object petit a* — an asymptote brushing up
alongside the Symbolic, but more than anything else arising as
the stuttering unavailability of the very signifier one most, in
the moment, needs. Winnicott more straightforwardly offers
the following — again, as though aesthetic traversal were ineluctably coextensive with problematics of gender.

In this way it is the play (if Hamlet could have read it, or
seen it acted) that could have shown him the nature of his
dilemma. The play within the play failed to do this. It could
be found that the same dilemma in Shakespeare provides the
problem behind the content of the sonnets. But this is to ig-

nore or even insult the main feature of the sonnets, namely, the poetry. Indeed, as Professor L.C. Knights (1946) specifically insists, it is only too easy to forget the poetry of the plays in writing of the *dramatis personae* as if they were historical persons. (1992[1982], 182)

The ease with which we (or Lacan, or Winnicott) might confuse *dramatis personae* with historical persons is countered by the difficulty of *dramatis personae* actually learning from their *mise-en-scène* as though simultaneously inhabiting and estranged from it. How to be historical and aesthetic at once? How to weather not only the aesthetic architecture by which one is surrounded, but the aesthetic quiddity one is? Hamlet's only possible means of insight — the search for an alternative to being more persuasive than not being — resides in the impossibility of reading one's own aesthetic inevitability. Hamlet's problem, to return to Lacan, is less about action versus thinking, than the queer misfortune of being aesthetic but misrecognizing how such a circumstance might be mobilized. Winnicott invokes the pathos of performativity decades before queer theory imagines performativity as activism.[2] Pathos, insofar as Hamlet's particular performativity luxuriates, dolorously, in its own bristling ennui.

Winnicott's interest extends not only to literary characters perceived and misperceived as persons, but also to persons, in clinical practice, oppositely unable to *feel* real. If doing and being signal a psyche's choreography of gender, the sense of one's inauthenticity or self-depletion signals a psyche's queer stumbling. Winnicott's psychoanalytic work thus ballasts a form of queer theory predicated on aesthetics rather than desire. Or, on

---

2   Queer theory's understanding of performativity is indebted to J.L. Austin's sense, in *How to Do Things with Words* (1962), of performative utterances, i.e., words that are able to perform actions as potently as they are imagined to describe them. Words *are* actions. The paradigmatic performative utterance is the conjugal "I do," in which saying those words renders one, in certain particular situations, married. See Butler (1997); Kosofsky Sedgwick (2003).

the simultaneous attractions to and fears of desiring one's own aesthetic status. A sense of being in the world but not of it is not unto itself innovative, but Winnicott's engagement of self-distancing, through the duration of his career, is jarring for both its ubiquity and its particular psychoanalytic context.

If, as Lacan notes, the unconscious is structured like a language, then a psychoanalytic ethics might well be imagined not only as the presentation of a measure of action, but as the incessantly difficult project of staging a dialogue with one's self, the nurturing of untethered soliloquy into interlocution. As M. Masud R. Khan (1994[1986]) suggests, in his introduction to Winnicott's *Holding and Interpretation,* Winnicott found himself in Hamlet's non-feasible hypothetical vantage as much as did his patients. "Like the patient," Khan writes, "[Winnicott] too became partially an observer of the clinical process" (15), · which is to say that clinical practice for Winnicott afforded, if only obliquely, better and for worse, a form of Hamlet reading *Hamlet.*

The collusion of queerness and self-perceived fictiveness informs at outset the experience of the patient whose analysis fills *Holding and Interpretation's* pages. "In the first phase, he came in a state of depression with a strong homosexual colouring, but without manifest homosexuality. He was in a bemused state and rather unreal" (Winnicott 1994[1986], 19). Said patient "admitted into an institution himself because of unreal feelings" (19). Once again, we find queerness "colour[ed]" by the weather of non-reality. Feeling unreal, versus bearing "unreal feelings." Contra various homophobic narratives of homosexuality's genetic realness or non-realness, Winnicott's practice takes homosexuality as a problematic of incredulousness; a hermeneutics of suspicion turned psychically inward. Again, it merits repeating that homosexuality, in Winnicott's studies, accrues as much to questions of ontology as such, as it does to normative conceptions of erotic attachment. Survival of distance, for Winnicott, describes a fundamental impediment and requisite of subjectivity. Distance, for Winnicott, collects most movingly, around the balletically strenuous hocus pocus between mother and infant.

As often, however, distance describes the aesthetic disjunct of auto-affection. He writes, "The excitement in relation to me had only been indicated and had not appeared" (29). Or as the same patient offers, from the same analysis, "I feel that you are introducing a big problem. I never became human. I have missed it" (84).

Clinically, it isn't entirely reasonable to suppose Winnicottian practice as the therapeutic catalyzing translation of experiential fraudulence into ontological veracity—such an account underestimates Winnicott's non-pathologizing interest in phenomena of fraudulence; and too quickly presumes that an experience of veracity would could as fraudulence's "cure." Such a misprision falls under what Leo Bersani has in several instances denominated the normative pastoral impulse of unrigorous deformations of Freudian and Lacanian therapy. More precisely, Winnicottian practice delineates a constellation of fraudulence, as much as the conundrum of veracities by which the former are adumbrated. Speculatively, Bersani's myriad accounts of the intractability of aggression (Bersani and Dutoit 2004, 124–25), keep their distance from Winnicott's own theory of aggression for similar reasons, the extent to which Winnicottian aggression would seem either banal or falsifyingly roseate (see Winnicott 1971, 89–90). Bersani's career-long investigation of aggression in no way amounts to simple advocacy of aggression; aggression's recalcitrance and often capricious materializations compel Bersani's more recent work on forms if not of "solving" aggression, than circumnavigating it. Winnicott (1971), with wonderful counter-intuitive verve, insists on aggression as an act of love:

> A new feature thus arrives in the theory of object-relating. The subject says to the object: "I destroyed you" and the object is there to receive the communication. From now on the subject says: "Hullo object!" "I destroyed you." "I love you." "You have value for me because of your survival of my destruction of you." While I am loving you I am all the time destroying you in (unconscious) *fantasy*. (120–21; emphasis in original)

Such an account of aggression neither circumnavigates nor solves a Freudian or Lacanian embeddedness of aggressivity, so much as dispense with its vexing permanence altogether, a needle in a balloon. At the same time, Winnicott's theory of aggression arises only after an infant has discovered his separateness from the world (which is to say, his mother). Before this initial estrangement, the mother and child are bound in what Christopher Bollas (1987), following Winnicott, describes as the infant's first aesthetic situation (32). This is to say that aesthetic being, in Winnicott, precedes all other forms of being. Any sense of being real is subsequent to the largesse of shared fictiveness. Such a scenario both resonates with and complicates Bersani's (2008) and my own recent work on aesthetic subjectivity and aesthetic personhood, respectively. We might, in the anteriority not of violence or aggression but of aesthetics, think of an ethics predicated on the latter.

Arts of Losing: Winnicott with Sedgwick

This primal aesthetic moment, unlike, for instance, a Freudian primal scene, is predicated on the non-distance between subject and object: more radically, on the non-distinguishability of subject and object. We may call, for present purposes, our subject the infant. The infant has desires and needs that he is altogether unable to satisfy. In this limited sense, the infant is purely female, pure being without the capacity to *do*, in the Winnicottian sense of "a male element." The infant, however, has no sense of this incapacity, and no sense of a difference between being and doing, because the mother — specifically, what Winnicott calls the good-enough mother — supplements the infant's purely ontological and non-transitive vacancy with action choreographed as the infant's own. The infant is hungry and before the recognition of hunger, the mother nurses him. The infant wishes to be placed in a different position and before the registration of discomfiture settles, the mother repositions him. I am reminded here, of the distinction between being real and feeling real, in the above clinical study.

I am reminded of simultaneously immense and minimal distance between veracity and non-veracity; or less cynically posed, of the possible irrelevance of the distinction in a subject whose first memory — were the memory ever accessible, which it is not — would be of this exceedingly subtle drama without roles. Beyond the infant's incapability of so early a recollection, it seems plausible that there would in fact be nothing to remember, insofar as the materfilial economy's success is the semblance of having exchanged nothing. One remembers what no longer is there, but there was, on many registers, nothing there to lose. Never loved, never lost, the paradigm that structures Judith Butler's account of Freudian melancholy, has no place in Winnicott's version of never loved/never lost, if only because the success of the good-enough mother will have assured the infant that there was never a mother, per se, to have lost in the first place. Recognition *of* the mother, and concomitantly love of the mother, only would occur in the first pang of unsatisfied infant need. Prior to this, even as the infant at this stage cannot understand love beyond a barely burgeoning narcissism, and never lost, to the extent that his matrixial sustenance depends on a sense of their having been nothing to lose. I think here, of course, of the work of psychoanalyst and artist Bracha Ettinger (2006).

The mother's efforts are devoted to the infant's sense of omnipotence — that whatever he needs might be availed nearly before even the recognition of need (Winnicott 1971, 285). This maternal aesthetic, which is an environment the infant habits without perception of its difference from himself, seeks to nullify the boundary between the imagined and the actualized. The mother (more specifically, the mother's breast) arises as the infant's first encounter not with the female element (he already is this), but the male element (the mother's unceasing *doing* for the sake of doing's own evaporation in the field of what the infant rudimentarily *is*). Such a formulation suggests the residuum of this primal aesthetic implication which leads to weaning and autonomy but unsurprisingly remains as ghost-structure; that which was never there remains never there. Beneficently haunting and heuristically audible in least discernible of whispers, the aesthetic unconscious subtends any subsequent form of ontology, betrays the extent to which *being* and *doing* can't help but braid and unbraid subjectivity's nostalgia for and unawareness of its fundamentally aesthetic condition.

Winnicott's contribution to an ethics of psychoanalysis would therefore complicate Lacan's account of measurement of action, at very least because of action's insolubly confused relation with being, of the salutary and ingenious insistence on an ethics necessarily predicated on a psychoanalytic aesthetics in excess of the rhetoric of dreamwork, the artistic permutations of a repetition compulsion's serial structure, the inaccessible Platonic figura from which the empirical, in most contexts, depressively is withdrawn. If ethics, in our current political duress, conjures an agonistic relation to omnipotence, Winnicott clarifies an omnipotence beholden less to ideology or hegemony than to aesthetic fragility. Omnipotence, for Winnicott, quite literally (and figuratively) is *work in progress.*

Winnicott's insights illuminate the thinking of Eve Kosofsky Sedgwick (2008), whose most recent work gravitated to the idea, in both Marcel Proust and C.P. Cavafy (2006) of *queer little gods.* Conceived on some level as a form of Roman *penates,* Sedgwick's queer little gods, nominally and otherwise, speak to the condition of Winnicott's aesthetically enabled infant, whose queerness resides in both the factitiousness of its omnipotence, as well as in the veracity of that factitiousness: the queerness of being without capacity, of belief in capacity without conscious cognizance of omnipotence's own complicated repertoire. Conscious cognizance, even as an unconscious organized in aesthetic terms would both harrowingly and/or ebulliently remonstrate any form of autonomy unaware of its own contingency.

There is, alas, not enough of Sedgwick's work on queer little gods. After many years living with cancer, Eve died in the summer of 2009. *I wish there were more,* as a way of wishing Eve were still here. As a good-enough mother — father of queer theory, incessantly *doing* in such a manner that we might think we were doing; doing so much that we ourselves felt enabled by her own luminous industry — Eve has been teaching us her imminent withdrawal for several decades. What will we do without her, as succinct and inadequate formulation of theoretical weaning. *I shall not be here forever,* as perhaps the most awful and important of her points of departure. I both thought of and think of Eve as good-enough mother, allowing me in fleeting, miraculously irrational moments, to feel like a queer little god, the Winnicottian infant for whom aesthetic play arose as ethical lynch-pin. Eve's consideration of queer little gods is as non-ideological as Winnicott's sense of unduly (or, ethically, duly) empowered infants, for whom delusion is synonym for safety, for whom delusion never encounters the normative binary of the veritable. Non-ideological, to the extent that Eve's *doing* inspires her queer infants (myself included) to become queer little gods aspiring to become good-enough mothers. If there were a way to mourn Eve's awful extrication from the empirical world, it would be in the sense that her mode of imaginative capacity, in producing us, has become our world, such that an imagined Eve might approximate the Eve we have lost. Eve, nominally, of a sudden feeling as allegorical as Henry James's naming May Bartram, *May.* Eve on the brink, and in following her into a world of aesthetics and figuration, we realize that we were as much enabling as we were enabled.

That queer little gods might dream of becoming good-enough mothers describes a queer pedagogy for which Winnicott paves the way. Way and away, utility and distance, brought together by somatic exhaustions and sublimations recalled as axiomatically aesthetic. To mourn the loss of a good-enough mother (and here I defer to Freudian melancholy, or at least some less strictured version of it) is to find a good-enough mother inhabiting one's own egoic vantage. Weaning (of the Winnicottian mother, of Eve) would in the most sublimely ethically fashion guarantee one's own balletic instruction as element of one's own eventual doing, borne of one's own floundering but hopeful being. The incorporated object isn't chiding so much as inspiring. If weaning, following Winnicott, is a form of never loved/never lost, we have here, between Winnicott and Sedgwick, a form of melancholy so magnificently capacitating to deserve another word. The Roman *lares*, watching over the family. We are both the family and the watchful. We tend and are tended, touch and are touched. Taken-for-grantedness in the infantile regime is the precondition for allowing into one's psyche the cultivation and care that made this take-for-granted possible in the first place. Melancholy isn't the suspension of work, but the non-shattering inheritance of unfinishable labor. Unfinishable, partly because it is a fiction borne of fictive premises. And simultaneously, because the good-enough definitionally soars far beyond "enough's" own limited expectations.

Drawing Lines

Again, the implausible extricability of ontology and aesthetics describes the domain of both Winnicottian theory and ethics, writ large. Aesthetics recalibrates ethics as the hinterland between being and doing, subject and object. If to speak of an ethics of psychoanalysis compels reconsideration of an aesthetics of psychoanalysis, then it is necessary to consider further how aesthetics informs Winnicott's clinical practice, as metaphor and technique. Much has been made of Winnicott's maternal aesthetics (and this art's coextensive relation to the aesthetic desiderata of an analytic session[3]) even as this form of environmental holding has yet adequately to be imagined in the context of Winnicott's clinical predilection for what he called the squiggle game (Winnicott 1992[1964–68], 299–317). The squiggle game goes as follows: Either Winnicott or his patient makes a squiggle on a sheet of paper. Whoever makes the first squiggle passes the paper to the other person, and that person sees in the squiggle something — a woman wearing a rakish hat, a bird in a nest — which, through additional lines is realized. The person who has "realized" the first squiggle then is responsible for enacting the next doodle, which is passed for "realization" to the person who initiated the prior doodle. The rules of the game are succinct. Someone begins. Someone turns the squig-

---

3   See Mavor (2007).

gle into something more or less intelligible; in either an additive fashion, or (in the spirit of Michelangelo's sculptures) in having discovered in the squiggle something that already had resided within it. Winnicott distinguishes, throughout his papers, between games and play, the former as the inhabiting and negotiation of pre-conceived structure, versus the latter as fruitful, digressive loss in imagination freed from structure. The squiggle transaction is posited as a game whose implicit goal is to free its participants *from* the game, to free the two into play.

Squiggle, an excellent, childish word for a mode of communication Winnicott forged with his child patients. There is nonetheless more to the squiggle game than its childishness, or even its analytic utility. The squiggle game, as I shall argue, literalizes interpersonal necessity as aesthetics distilled to irrevocable contingency. And the multiple mobilities of this aesthetic humbly offers a model of aesthetic ethics from which both psychoanalysis and queer theory might learn. The squiggle literalizes what Sedgwick, in the context of Cavafy's queer little gods, imagines as ontological indeterminacy—the squiggle simultaneously is and is not. While the squiggle's completion may seem the more conventionally aesthetic gesture, the production of the squiggle itself is the more aesthetically demanding. Where is the pencil headed, and how to defer the pencil's vagrancy from prematurely understanding its possible pulsions toward intelligibility, when the latter, strictly (and non-strictly) speaking, is the responsibility and pleasure of the initiator's artistic participant? How to withstand the desire for completion, and how to leave open what might be foreclosed, for the sake of the other person's imagination. The squiggle game relies less on artistic prowess than on a particular form of self-withholding imagination predicated on the eventually generous gift of its own motivated or happily self-abandoned incompletion. The squiggle is aestheticized by its inscriber's collaborator. The relational energies, here, recall those of both the Winnicottian maternal aesthetic apparatus, as well as the more familiar affective particularities of analytic transference and counter-transference. What will one person give the other? How to share in the creative phenomenon of the squiggle-transformation having been offered as either incomplete or ineluctably implicit, or some unspeakable conjunction of the two?

The squiggle game replicates on a graphic level the transactions of infant and good-enough mother, transactions themselves replicated in the analyst's role as good-enough mother. Beyond this, the squiggle game allows the child analysand, graphically, to assume the role of mothering to Winnicott's own squiggles. The analysand, that is, realizes what Winnicott's squiggle already needed, or on only a slightly different register, already potentially was. The aesthetics of holding and being held are materialized in literal aesthetic venture, even as the squiggle itself suggests the mother herself, shared by two queer little gods. As Winnicott writes, "the mother (or part of the mother) is in a 'to and fro' between being that which the baby has a capacity to find and (alternately) being herself waiting to be found" (47). The squiggle, as correlative to both materfilial magic and to the mother without whom that magic is possible, always nearly exists on several personificatory registers, even as its avowed innocuousness (innocuousness in part dependent on the aesthetic production's contingency) relies on its sheer materiality, passed between persons. Nearly existing as personification coincides with the squiggle's nearly existing as art, as communication. The virtue of the squiggle in part lies in its nearliness, in which approximation brings persons and aesthetics closer together than definitiveness could. The squiggle in its metaphorical and literal traversals, offers the possibility of psychoanalytic subjectivity as the nearliness of being a person as that approximateness moves toward adjacent proximities of being art. We find ourselves in this juncture removed from Bersani's account of pastoral therapies attached to the corrective realization of clinical accounts of fictiveness. The squiggle, at its most certain, remains a squiggle, even as what it *might* be flourishes in multiple simultaneous directions. This approximateness importantly revises accounts of incoherence and ontological dubiousness espoused as queer theory's ethical aspirations. Incoherence can't help but lean on a fiction of coherence. This binary dissolves (what Bersani recently has called conversation's liquifying speech) in the field of approximateness, in which one cannot choose between fabrication and non-fabrication because each category is equally approximate to the other.

Winnicottian nearness (only nominally distinguishable from Winnicottian spaciousness) arises in a form of graphic collaboration that enriches our understanding of Lacan's account of the unconscious as being structured like a language. Language, syntactically, is governed by rules, capable of evasion as much as confession, of succinctness (the Freudian joke) as much as volubility (free-association). Language, likewise, minimally is shared between two people, and like a Freudian joke, achieves greatest intensity in the confluence of lucidity and surprise, or what Freud (1990), in the context of jokes, calls bewilderment and illumination (9). The squiggle, as a form of language, rewrites talk of the unconscious as predicated on memory inseparable from its immanent or futural materialization as something else. I think, here, of Bersani's account of subterfuge in the work of Henry James: the possibility of a lie living long enough in its particular environment to justify if not erase its own opening prevaricatory gambit. The squiggle's linguistic bravura — the following of non-syntactic rules for the sake of flirting with a syntax of association inseparable from the disarticulation from those original rules — resides in its humility, and in the strangeness of the squiggle only barely existing, communicatively speaking.

In this sense, the squiggle recalls the graphically, fastidiously dalliant works by Cy Twombly. Following Roland Barthes, Twombly's graphic executions — like Winnicott's squiggles — both precede and follow methodologies of intelligible writing: Twombly's graphemes anticipate writing in their stern incompleteness and solemnly mark what of writing remains, in the wake of its own foundering. An unconscious structured like a language, versus a squiggle, versus a Twombly. In the latter two examples, the unconscious — what can be imagined in ethical terms — withholds itself on the brink of volubility; is interested in the rhetorical plethora onto which it opens, without committing to it. We are approaching and even caring for something like an unconscious without presumption, *prima facie*, of its architecture or contents. We return, again, to Bersani's account of psychical virtuality, in which the strength and utility of an unconscious depends on its inability to see beyond its own immanent and futural opacities. A psychoanalysis wed to this literally sketchy psychical landscape would require an exegetical language as mutational as the unconscious' own fitfulness, a language or repertoire always on the verge, whose veracity falls *toward* the plausibility of veracity. The fictive is won from itself only in the offing, rather than being embedded in a psychical lexicon which it can only bolster or betray. In lieu of Hamlet's inability to read his own lines in advance of speaking them, we have fallen into the near-coterminous formation and deformation of lines being read across two persons.

Works Cited

Austin, John L. *How to Do Things with Words.* Oxford: Clarendon Press, 1962.

Barthes, Roland. *The Responsibility of Forms: Critical Essays on Music, Art, and Representation.* Berkeley: University of California Press, 1991.

Bersani, Leo. *The Freudian Body: Psychoanalysis and Art.* New York: Columbia University Press, 1986.

———— and Adam Phillips. *Intimacies.* Chicago: University of Chicago Press, 2008.

———— and Ulysse Dutoit. *Forms of Being: Cinema, Aesthetics, Subjectivity.* London: BFI, 2004.

Bollas, Christopher. *The Shadow of the Object: Psychoanalysis of the Unthought Known.* New York: Columbia University Press, 1987.

Butler, Judith. *Giving an Account of Oneself.* New York: Fordham University Press, 2005.

————. *Antigone's Claim.* New York: Columbia University Press, 2002.

———. *Gender Trouble: Feminism and the Subversion of Identity.* New York: Routledge, 1999.

———. *Excitable Speech: A Politics of the Performative.* New York: Routledge, 1997.

Cavafy, C.P. *The Collected Poems of C.P. Cavafy,* trans. Aliki Barnstone. New York: W.W. Norton & Company, 2006.

Dean, Tim. *Beyond Sexuality.* Chicago: University of Chicago Press, 2000.

Edelman, Lee. *No Future: Queer Theory and the Death Drive.* Durham: Duke University Press, 2004.

———. *Homographesis: Essays in Gay Literary and Cultural Theory.* New York: Routledge, 1994.

Emerson, Waldo Ralph. "Experience." In *Essays and Lectures,* ed. Joel Porte, 471–92. New York: Library of America, 1983.

Ettinger, Bracha L. *The Matrixial Borderspace,* ed. Brian Massumi. Minneapolis and London: University of Minnesota Press, 2006.

Foucault, Michel. *Ethics: Subjectivity and Truth,* ed. Paul Rabinow. New York: The New Press, 1997.

Freud, Sigmund. *Jokes and Their Relation to the Unconscious* (1905). New York: W.W. Norton & Company, 1990.

Jacobus, Mary. *The Poetics of Psychoanalysis: In the Wake of Klein.* Oxford: Oxford University Press, 2005.

James, Henry. "The Beast in the Jungle." In *The Complete Stories 1898–1910,* 496–541. New York: The Library of America, 1996.

Khan, R. Masud. M. "Introduction." In Donald W. Winnicott, *Holding and Interpretation: Fragment of an Analysis,* 1–18. 1986; rpt. New York: Grove Press, 1994.

Lacan, Jacques. *Book VII: The Ethics of Psychoanalysis* (1959–1960), trans. Dennis Porter. New York: W.W. Norton & Company, 1992.

Mavor, Carol. *Reading Boyishly: Roland Barthes, J.M. Barrie, Jacques Henri Lartigue, Marcel Proust, and D.W. Winnicott.* Durham: Duke University Press, 2007.

Mills, Catherine. "Normative Violence, Vulnerability, and Responsibility." *differences* 18, no. 2 (2007): 133–56.

Phillips, Adam. *Winnicott.* Cambridge: Harvard University Press, 1989.

Sedgwick, Kosofsky Eve. "Queer Little Gods, a Conversation." Interviewed by Michael D. Snediker, *The Massachusetts Review* 49, nos. 1–2 (2008): 209–18.

———. *Touching Feeling: Affect, Pedagogy, Performativity.* Durham: Duke University Press, 2003.

Winnicott, Donald W. *Holding and Interpretation: Fragment of an Analysis.* 1986; rpt. New York: Grove Press, 1994.

———. "The Use of an Object and Relating through Identification." In *Playing and Reality,* 115–27. New York: Basic Books, 1971.

———. "On the Split-Off Male and Female Elements." In *Psychoanalytic Explorations,* ed. Clare Winnicott, 1966; rpt. 168–92. Cambridge: Harvard University Press, 1992.

———. "The Squiggle Game." In *Psychoanalytic Explorations,* ed. Clare Winnicott, 299–317. 1964–68; rpt. Cambridge: Harvard University Press, 1992.

_____. "Deductions Drawn from a Psychotherapeutic Interview with an Adolescent." In *Psychoanalytic Explorations,* ed. Clare Winnicott, 325–40. 1964; rpt. Cambridge: Harvard University Press, 1992.

6 | DISCOURSE

Discourse and the History of Sexuality

Will Stockton[1]

Following the French historian and philosopher Michel Foucault, contemporary queer scholars frequently maintain that
sexuality is a product of discourse. At its most basic, *discourse*
means speech, but for Foucault (1972) discourse is "the general domain of all statements, sometimes as an individualisable
group of statements, and sometimes as a regulated practice that
accounts for a number of statements" (80). In the first volume of
The History of Sexuality, Foucault (1990a) frames the relationship
between sexuality and discourse in this way: sexuality is "the
correlative of that slowly developed discursive practice which
constitutes the *scientia sexualis*" (68) — the Western "regulated
practice" of classifying, monitoring, and disciplining individuals based on what Freud would call their choice of sexual objects
or the directions of their sexual aims. The *scientia sexualis* has
its roots in the Catholic practice of confession, which from the
Middle Ages enjoined people to speak about sex in extraordi-

---

1   I wrote this chapter in 2009, and since then have come to dislike it. This
chapter is dated, overly quotational, and altogether inadequate in its reading of Shakespeare's Sonnet 20. For many years, I believed *Clinical Encounters in Sexuality* to be defunct, and in truth, I would prefer this piece remain
stuck in a desk drawer. I agree to its publication now, in relatively unrevised
form, only because I realize that the volume as a whole depends on it, and
may indeed depend (although I am not sure, as I have not read the responses) on the way I originally expressed ideas.

nary detail, to seek out "all insinuations of the flesh: thoughts, desires, voluptuous imaginings, delectations, combined movements of the body and soul" (19). In the nineteenth and twentieth centuries, psychiatry and psychoanalysis contributed to the secular appropriation of the church's insistence that each person transform his or her sex into discourse. As Foucault wryly notes, "Ours is, after all, the only civilization in which individuals are paid to listen to all and sundry impart the secrets of their sex: as if the urge to talk about it, and the interest one hopes to arouse by doing so, have far surpassed the possibilities of being heard, so that some individuals have even offered their ears for hire" (7).

For many queer scholars, Foucault's location of psychiatry and psychoanalysis in the history of sexuality undermines the claims of both discourses (or regulated practices) to speak universal, often plainly heterosexist, "truths" about sex. From 1952 to 1973, for instance, the American Psychiatric Association's *Diagnostic and Statistical Manual* (DSM) classified homosexuality as a mental disorder, effectively exempting homosexuality from history by ignoring the different ways that other cultures have understood and evaluated same-sex desire. (The DSM still includes sexual sadism, sexual masochism, and transvestic fetishism among the sexual disorders or "paraphilias," and it pathologizes one's identification with the opposite sex as "gender identity disorder.") Psychoanalysis, especially in Anglo-American practice, has not necessarily been any more historically self-aware. The work of Sandor Rado (1940 and 1949), Edmund Bergler (1956), and Irving Bieber (1962), among many others, advanced sexual conversion therapy, predicated on the idea that homosexuality is an aberration, a curable mental condition, rather than something invented by the very disciplines that aimed to treat it. To be sure, many psychoanalysts have worked over recent decades to develop more queer-friendly practices (Dean and Lane 2001). Yet the conversation between queer historians and psychoanalysts remains underdeveloped, and the image many of the former have of the latter — an image perpetuated by figures such as the late, vocal advocate of conversion therapy Charles Socarides (2005) — remains one of homophobia and ahistoricism.

This chapter's effort to foster the conversation between queer historians and psychoanalysts begins with an invitation to consider the history of the term "sexuality." According to the *Oxford English Dictionary* (1989), the use of the term to mean "sexual identity in relation to the gender to which [one] is typically attracted" dates from late in the nineteenth century (specifically, from Havelock Ellis's 1897 *Studies in the Psychology of Sex*), while the use of the term to mean the possession or expression of "sexual nature, instinct, or feeling" is only fifty years older. As David Halperin (1998) writes, without the nineteenth-century:

[C]onception of the sexual instinct as an autonomous human function [...] our heavily psychologized model of sexual subjectivity — which knits up desires, its objects, sexual behavior, gender identity, reproductive function, mental heath, erotic sensibility, personal style, and degrees of normality or deviance into an individuating normativizing feature of the personality called "sexuality" or "sexual orientation" — is inconceivable. (96–97)

The fact that *sexuality* does not, as a term or a psychological model, exist in pre-nineteenth-century contexts is one reason Foucault (1990a) argues that the "history of sexuality [...] must first be written from the viewpoint of a history of discourses" (69). To historicize sexuality is to historicize the discourses — medical, theological, judicial, ethical, philosophical, pedagogical, popular, etc. — that underwrite a concept of relatively recent advent.

Foucauldian historicism thus opposes itself to the "essentialist" assumption that sexuality is a transhistorical feature of human beings, something that can be analyzed without attention to cultural, linguistic, and ideological differences. Indeed, from this Foucauldian perspective, the effort by some contemporary scientists to locate a "gay gene" is not unlike the effort of some psychoanalysts to locate the cause of homosexuality in a "perverse" deviation from a "normal" path of psychosocial development: neither the geneticist nor the psychoanalyst acknowledges or attempts to explain homosexuality's (and hetero-sexuality's) historical belatedness. Like *sexuality, homosexuality* first appears in sexological discourse in the late nineteenth cen-tury, and only enters into popular discourse in the twentieth. Furthermore, what most people now mean by *homosexuality* can often be quite different from what was earlier meant by *in-version* (a woman's soul in a man's body, or a man's soul in a woman's body) or *sodomy* (a broad category of deviant, usually non-reproductive sexual acts, not simply male–male anal sex). By focusing attention on such differences, Foucault's historicist calibration of sexuality as a product of discourse unsettles — or queers — essentialist discourses of sexuality, including the often essentialist discourses of psychoanalysis.

Rather than advocate historicism at the expense of psychoa-nalysis, however, I want in this chapter to distinguish a psycho-analytic approach to sex and discourse that could itself be useful in historicizing sexuality. This approach differs from Foucault's, but it is not simply ahistorical, nor should it be understood as entirely antithetical to the Foucauldian project. To accomplish this task, I need to define *sex* and sexuality, like *discourse,* in Fou-cauldian terms. Sex includes "anatomical elements, biological functions, conducts, sensations, and pleasures" (154) — a set of acts and experiences deemed relevant to sexuality: a "historical construct [...] in which the stimulation of bodies, the intensifi-cation of pleasures, the incitement to discourse, the formation of special knowledge, the strengthening of controls and resist-ances, are all linked to one another" (105–6). In the modern and perhaps only historically accurate sense of the term, sexuality is frequently synonymous with sexual orientation, understood as central to individual identity. When I speak anachronistically of sexuality, I am therefore referencing an organization of erot-ic meanings that are comparatively less identitarian. Foucault points out — and I will return to this point — that discourses of sexuality often determine what qualifies as sex in the first place (54–57). Yet as a queer literary critic and historian, I am particu-larly invested in a line of Lacanian criticism that maintains that discourses of sexuality are always failed discourses, or discourses that fail to secure sex's significance. I will illustrate this failure by way of short survey of the critical controversy surrounding Shakespeare's famously "perverse" Sonnet 20. In the chapter's final section, I outline a specifically Laplanchian approach to sexuality's discursivity that contributes to the current queer theoretical conversation about "temporality," or the demarcations of historical time that regulate the significance of sex (what can be said about it and how it can be understood). I premise this approach on Laplanche's concept of the enigmatic signifier, which I will also suggest is useful in theorizing the similar historical work of queer literary studies and psychoanalysis.

Ahistorical Psychoanalysis

By training, I am a scholar of English Renaissance literature. As an undergraduate student in the late 1990s, when queer theory was reshaping the study of sex in literature, I was drawn to this field in part by my desire to historicize my own subject position as a gay male. More specifically, I was drawn by my desire to historicize this subject position with reference to the emergence of "modernity" — "Renaissance" and "early modern" often being synonymous terms. From a reading of the first volume of *The History of Sexuality,* I understood that historicizing homosexuality meant tracing the relationship between the modern discourse of sexual identity and Renaissance discourses that governed the meaning of "sexual" acts. Especially pronounced among these Renaissance discourses was the Christian discourse of fallen humanity. This discourse made no distinction between the types of people who committed sexual sins, as it held that everyone was potentially vulnerable to the same temptations. As the historian Alan Bray (1995) writes, "To talk of an individual in this period [the Renaissance] as being or not being 'a homosexual' is an anachronism and ruinously misleading. The temptation to debauchery, from which homosexuality was not clearly distinguished, was accepted as part of the common lot, be it never so abhorred" (16–17).

As one of the most influential discourses in the modern "deployment" of sexuality, psychoanalysis represented for many scholars in the 1990s the discourse from which Renaissance discourses had to be distinguished. An extensive consideration of such critical attitudes towards psychoanalysis lies outside the scope of this chapter. Suffice it to say that many Renaissance scholars have dismissed psychoanalysis as a monolithic discourse historically suspect at its Freudian core. In *Homosexual Desire in Shakespeare's England* (1991), for instance, Bruce Smith writes, "In the standoff between essentialists and social constructionists Freud figures as the most important and influential essentialist of them all. He assumes that the human psyche has an existence outside history and that human sexual development follows the same pattern in all times and in all places" (25). From Smith's perspective, Freud's ahistorical approach to psychic and sexual development fundamentally undermines the interpretive portability of psychoanalytic concepts. As variably defined as the concepts may be among psychoanalysts themselves, and as applicable as they may be to modern, Western subjects (two concessions that Smith himself actually does not grant), psychoanalytic concepts are almost or entirely useless when it comes to the task of "analyzing" Renaissance subjects and their "sexualities." To psychoanalyze the pre-psychoanalytic subject is to distort that subject in its historical specificity, to obscure the historically available network of discourses that produce a historically specific form of subjectivity and sexuality.[2]

---

2   For an example of such distortion, one has only to think of Freud's (and Ernest Jones's 1910) interpretation of Shakespeare's *Hamlet*. In *The Interpretation of Dreams,* Freud (1900) asserts that the solution to the problem of Hamlet's delay lies in Hamlet's Oedipal jealousy of Claudius (265). For many Renaissance scholars, such a claim is hermeneutically simplistic and historically problematic. It relies on the anachronistic importation of interpersonal dynamics that Freud observed in late-Victorian bourgeois families. It overlooks, or reduces to the level of a symptom, Hamlet's concern that the ghost might be a demon. And it assumes that Hamlet's delay even is a problem — an assumption that Margreta de Grazia (2007) has shown originates only in the early eighteenth century.

Although most historians of sexuality continue to distance themselves from psychoanalysis, arguing that Renaissance discourses "speak sex" in ways that psychoanalysis silences, I was drawn towards the historiographic possibilities of psychoanalysis by a graduate school encounter with a 1977 conversation between Foucault and a group of analysts. In the middle of this conversation — or discourse — published in English as "The Confession of the Flesh," the Lacanian analyst Jacques-Alain Miller objects to Foucault's assertion that sexuality has a history. In Miller's words, "Sexuality isn't historical in the sense that everything else is, through and through from the start. There isn't a history of sexuality in the way there's a history of bread" (Foucault 1980, 213). Miller makes this claim by way of explaining the Lacanian axiom that "there is no sexual relation" — a claim of which Foucault claims to be unaware. Foucault then states that the history of sexuality is a history of discourses about sex as the "truth" of the subject (as the core of the self, the determinant of who one is), and the conversation moves on. Yet this instance of discursive collapse (as Miller fails to explain himself and Foucault fails to address the objection) flagged an alternative, Lacanian approach to sexuality's history.

In *Read My Desire: Lacan Against the Historicists* (1994), Joan Copjec elaborates on this alterative approach as follows:

> Sex is the stumbling block of sense. This is not to say that sex is prediscursive; we have no intention of denying that human sexuality is a product of signification, but we intend, rather, to redefine this position by arguing that sex is produced by the internal limit, the failure of signification. It is only there where discursive practices falter — and not at all where they succeed in producing meaning — that sex comes to be. (204)

In other words, the Lacanian axiom that "there is no sexual relation" speaks to "*the radical antagonism between sex and sense*," to the fact that "sex is never reducible to any discursive construction" (204; emphasis in original). This translation makes sense of the fact that Jacques-Alain Miller invokes the axiom as support for Foucault's (1980) claim that psychoanalysis transforms the study of sexuality by formulating "the logic of the unconscious" (213). In Miller's Lacanian terms, the sexual relation — not simply between man and woman, but also between sex and discourse — is purely symbolic, and its inevitable failure is properly attributed to the order of the real. At the same time, Miller also invokes the axiom to suggest that Foucault denies the "reality" of the unconscious by focusing only on sexuality's emergence as a discourse of human "truth." By historicizing sexuality as if there were nothing outside of discourse, Foucault misses the Lacanian point that sex itself is not simply discursive — that in its relation to the unconscious, sex rather confounds the discourses of sexuality that mark its presence and delimit its significance.

To be clear, I do not understand Miller to mean, baldly, that there simply is no history of sexuality. Overstatement is, after all, a key element in Lacanian rhetoric. Rather, I understand Miller to mean that sexuality is not simply historical. As Charles Shepherdson (2000) has argued, we need to "distinguish between the *particular historical forms* that a given culture may institute for sexuality (that is history), and that *inevitability* of symbolic inscription that is constitutive of the human animal" (34; emphasis in original). For Lacan, all human beings are subjects of sexuality, irrespective of their place in history or culture, for all human beings are subjects of language. As Foucault's work illustrates better than Freud's or Lacan's, however, symbolic inscription takes different forms, and the terms of each inscription do not necessarily translate into other discourses. These two approaches to sexuality and history need not be set in irreducible opposition. Indeed, the tendency of many literature scholars (like Smith) and psychoanalytic critics (like Copjec) to exacerbate the differences between psychoanalysis and "historicism" works against the formation of mutually informative analytical methods. I seek in the next two sections of this chapter to illustrate one such method with reference to Shakespeare's Sonnet 20. While contextualizing the sonnet within particular Renaissance discourses of sexuality, I will also use the sonnet to illustrate the Lacanian point that sex is always in part inimical to symbolic inscription.

The Indeterminacy of the Sexual

First published in 1609, Shakespeare's 154 sonnets have long been recognized as literary heirs to the medieval confessional practices that are so instrumental for Foucault in constructing and regulating sex as the truth of the self (Smith 1991, 232–3). In these highly introspective sonnets, the confessional becomes fourteen lines of verse, the theological imperative a literary one: "Not only will you confess to acts contravening the law, but you will seek to transform your desire, your every desire, into discourse" (Foucault 1990a, 21). Much of the critical conversation about these sonnets has focused on the type of relationship the speaker has with the young man who, in the first 126 poems, occupies the place generally reserved in sonnet sequences for the mistress.[3] Much of the critical conversation about Sonnet 20 in particular has focused on the extent to which it, more than any other sonnet, reveals a specifically sexual relationship. Here is the sonnet in its entirety:

> A woman's face with nature's own hand painted
> Hast thou, the master mistress of my passion;
> A woman's gentle heart, but not acquainted
> With shifting change as is false women's fashion;
> An eye more bright than theirs, less false in rolling,
> Gilding the object whereupon it gazeth;
> A man in hue, all hues in his controlling,
> Which steals men's eyes and women's souls amazeth.
> And for a woman wert thou first created,
> Till nature as she wrought thee fell a-doting,
> And by addition me of thee defeated
> By adding one thing to my purpose nothing.

---

3 The assumption that the young man is the addressee of all 126 sonnets has been challenged. See Dubrow 1996.

But since she pricked thee out for women's pleasure,
Mine be thy love and thy love's use their treasure.

The difficulty critics have making sense of this sonnet is a difficulty making sense of its puns, especially those in the third quatrain and couplet, beginning with "for" in line 9: the youth was created to be a woman's lover or (and?) as a woman. If one reads "for a woman" as "to be a woman's lover," the speaker seems to be saying that nature's "addition" of a penis (line 12's euphemistic "thing") ensured that the youth and the speaker could not be lovers. Yet the pun on "pricked" (line 13) complicates this gloss. On the one hand, the youth was given a prick to pleasure women, such that the final line's distinction between "love" and "love's use" is the distinction between same-sex friendship and opposite-sex love, the latter of which is associated with the genitals, reproduction, and, in the sequence's economic lexicon, "use"/usury and financial accrual. On the other hand, recalling the pun on "for" as "as" in line 9, the couplet also allows that the youth was "pricked [...] out"/indented so that he could be pleasured/penetrated like a woman. (The couplet's opening conjunction might thus be read as a negation of the admission of defeat. It is also tempting, though anachronistic, to hear "But" as an anatomical reference that follows on line twelve's "nothing," a euphemism for the vagina.) In a sequence that later explores "heterosexual" non-monogamy between the speaker and his female mistress, this sonnet may suggest that the speaker and the youth have (or at least the speaker wishes they had) a sexual relationship that does not conflict with women's "treasure" of the youth's "use" (his semen).

As cryptic as these lines are, they provide a particularly good example of Bruce Smith's (1991) claim that "sexual experience in the sonnets resides largely in puns" (252). To amend this claim somewhat, I would argue that these lines more pointedly exemplify the way the sonnets both attempt and fail to translate sex into discourse. Certainly, Sonnet 20 can illustrate Foucault's argument that sexuality is a product of discourse. Sexuality is an organization of erotic meanings, and notwithstanding the fact that such meanings here are multiple, any argument about sexuality in the sonnet must attempt to make the puns mean something. Yet the sonnet's refusal to specify who is having sex with whom (and how) also illustrates the Lacanian qualification of sexuality's discursive production. This qualification is two-fold. First, the sex in Sonnet 20 is not simply ambiguous. This ambiguity rather points to the difference between discourses of sexuality and what James Penney (2006) calls "'the real of sex' — actual sexual behaviors in concrete sociohistorical situations" (3–4). The real of sex is ultimately "unavailable to the epistemophilic sexological gaze" (4); it is, in short, the sex the sonnet does not reveal the speaker and the youth as having or not having, the sex the reader ultimately cannot "see." Apropos of Miller's objection to Foucault, the second qualification of sexuality's discursive production requires hearing "the real of sex" as a reference to the unconscious — to that opacity, that void of signification, around which the poem's proliferation of possible readings takes shape. Shakespeare's sonnets speak sex in a network of interconnected discourses (of economics, theology, friendship, etc.), as well as through puns and other rhetorical devices that "play off experience itself against the words that would inscribe it" (Smith 1991, 252). Confusing rather than clarifying the speaker's relationship to the young man, however, Sonnet 20 and its enigmatic ilk also gesture towards the gap between discourses of sexuality and the real of sex. In Copjec's terms, they gesture towards the fact that sex is or "comes to be" where discourse falters: in the disjunction between the symbolic and the real.

Shakespeareans usually approach the ambiguity of the sonnets by locating them within particular homoerotic discourses that allow for historically informed speculation about what the sonnets might "really" be saying, to whom, and how. Katherine Duncan-Jones (1997), the editor of the Arden edition of the sonnets that I use here, contextualizes their "compromising or 'disgraceful' elements" (xiii) within the political discourse of the court of King James I — a homoerotic discourse of male mentorship and patronage.[4] Gregory Bredbeck (1991) maintains that the final lines of Sonnet 20 "mean *too much*" (177; emphasis in original) to be reduced to a single interpretation, and he argues that their semantic profusion reflects Shakespeare's poetic relationship to what Foucault (1990a) called the "utterly confused category" (101) of sodomy: "For Shakespeare, the sodomite destroys or uses up language and thereby establishes a space different from language for the poet" (Bredback 1991, 180). For Bruce Smith (1991), these sonnets are somewhat ahead of their time. He argues that Sonnet 20 and the sequence itself exhaust period discourses for policing male bonds and distinguishing them from transgressive homoerotic affections. Folding sex back into discourse, however, he also argues that as "expressions of desire" that were "highly idiosyncratic to its author and its historical moment," these sonnets participate in the invention of "a new mode of discourse about sexual desire" (267) now recognizable as the discourse of modern homosexual subjectivity: a discourse of secret confession, of "the love that dares not speak its name."

I share such contextualizing aims, and I would argue that Bredbeck's and Duncan-Jones's readings are especially important correctives to the assumption that the sonnets speak sex in the contemporary discourse of homosexuality. Jones's reading additionally pressures the supposed perversity of the sonnets by locating them within a relatively normative political discourse. Yet I am arguing that the sonnets, and Sonnet 20 in particular, also redirect the critic's "sexological gaze" to something outside discourses entirely: the "real of sex" that no discourse can translate. Bredbeck suggests that the space outside discourse may itself be historically accessible through the discourse of sodomy, and I think he is correct. But that claim in itself does not answer the question I now want to pursue: the question of what qualifies as sex, and thus as sexual, in the first place. Is "master-mistress"

---

4   See also de Grazia (1994), who argues that the sonnets to the young man were not nearly as scandalous in the period as those addressed to the Dark Lady. In the Renaissance, interracial eroticism was much more controversial than homoeroticism.

simply an ironic, not a sexual, notation of the young man's status as the sonnet's addressee? Is there actually a pun on "pricked," or am I hearing something that is not there? These questions speak not only to Foucault's claim that the discourses of sexuality determine sex's definition and the conditions of its representation, but also to what the Renaissance scholar Mario DiGangi (1997) calls the "indeterminacy of the 'sexual'": "[W]e cannot always be entirely confident that we know which bodily acts count as 'sexual.' When is kissing an expression of sexual desire, of affection, or of a social bond? Under what circumstances might our ability even to distinguish these realms be frustrated? In a patriarchal culture, is intercourse always more 'sexual' than kissing? Is it more *erotic*? Might nonpenetrative eroticism, such as kissing between women or 'sport' between men, subvert patriarchal sexuality? These questions cannot be answered outside of particular contexts, and even then with reservations" (11; emphasis in original).

By scrupulously attending to "particular contexts" to answer such questions, DiGangi himself practices a kind of skeptical historicism. He foregrounds his reservations about his entire critical project (on the homoerotics of early modern drama), cognizant of his inability to definitively distinguish sexual desire from affection and social bonding, or to classify and render fully — discursively — significant acts such as kissing. Even as I therefore want to claim that in DiGangi's cautionary notion of the "indeterminacy of the 'sexual'" lies Joan Copjec's claim that "sex comes to be where discursive practices falter." DiGangi's questions also cast into relief the difference between his own and a Lacanian approach to sexuality. Whereas DiGangi offers reserved interpretations of signifiers within particular discursive contexts, Lacanian psychoanalysis posits that by definition sex and the sexual exceed these contexts. After all, any critical effort to actually determine the sexual status of friendly affection and social bonding, or the difference between sexuality and eroticism, in pre-nineteenth-century contexts cannot ultimately escape the anachronistic assumption a definition for the sexual — an assumption that relocates outside history the very thing it attempts to analyze.

Enigmatic Historicism

In *Sexuality and Form: Marlowe, Caravaggio, and Bacon* (2000), one of the first books in Renaissance Studies to challenge historicist efforts to analyze sex within singularly Renaissance discourses, Graham L. Hammill argues that "the reduction of sex to historical information does not constitute interpretation as such" (2). Instead, sex constitutes "a horizon of interpretation and a threshold of thinking" (1), and it "urges the problem of historiography" (2), calling "for modes of critical analysis that maintain external relations with the historical" (3). Hammill's own mode of analysis effects a careful rapprochement between Foucauldian historicism and Lacanian psychoanalysis. Both, Hammill demonstrates, avoid reducing sexuality to sexual identity, and the history of sexuality to the history of the homosexual's invention. Both also avoid reducing the history of sexuality to the history of what has previously been thought about sexuality: Foucault and Lacan evince "a passion for producing as such the unthought (or the unhistorical)" (19). (Foucault's [1990b] description of the goal of his history could apply equally well to Lacan's own efforts to cast the history of sexuality in terms of the impossibility of the sexual relation. Both histories aim "to learn to what extent the effort to think one's own history can free itself from what it silently thinks, and so enable it to think differently" [9].) In the spirit of finding similar common ground between psychoanalysis and Foucauldian historicism, I would like to demonstrate how Jean Laplanche's particular recovery of Freud's seduction theory also distinguishes sex from "historical information," affording analysts and literary scholars alike a series of conceptual tools for studying sex's queer temporality.

Over the last decade, an increasing number of queer literary scholars (Renaissance and otherwise) have begun to argue, like Hammill, that sex challenges "conventional" historiographic models. This argument emerges in part from historicist critiques of the "supersessionist" (and ostensibly Foucauldian) distinction between a pre- and early modern discourse of sexual acts and a modern discourse of sexual identity. Invariably, this distinction simplifies a much more complex and uneven historical shift (For a critique of supersessionist historicism, see Sedgwick 2008, 44–48). The argument that sex challenges conventional historiographic models also emerges from the critical sense that a dually temporal and discursive distinction between sexual acts and identities is thoroughly inadequate to containing the analytic of queerness, which Judith Butler (1993) defines as a "collective contestation, the point of departure for a set of historical reflections and futural imaginings" (228). Most recent works of queer historicism utilize queerness as a vehicle for contesting discourses of the normal and the natural rather than as a synonym for gay and lesbian identity. Similarly positioning queerness in opposition to "official" sexual and historiographic discourses, queer histories also now frequently contest the discourse of the modern divide so often coterminous with the division between acts and identities. The result has not only been a wider attention in queer studies generally to the conceptual work of terms like *modernity,* but an arguably belated recognition (relative to other sub-disciplines of critical theory and cultural studies) that time is always, as Shakespeare's Hamlet says, "out of joint" (2008, 1.5.189).

Introducing a 2007 special issue of GLQ: *A Journal of Lesbian and Gay Sudies* entitled "Queer Temporalities," Elizabeth Freeman takes Hamlet's expression of time's "heterogeneity" and "asynchrony" as her own point of departure in contemplating the future of queer studies:

If we reimagine "queer" as a set of possibilities produced out of temporal and historical difference, or see the manipulation of time as a way to produce both bodies and relationalities (or even nonrelationality), we encounter a more productively porous queer studies [...]. Indeed, this queer studies meets critical race theory and postcolonial studies in its understanding that what has not entered the historical records, and what is not yet culturally legible, is often encountered in embodied, nonrational forms: as ghosts, scars, gods. In this sense we are also (re)turned to a queer studies among whose definitional moves has been a turn to the "premodern," not only to moments in time before the consolidation of homosexual identity in the West but also to how the gaps and fissures in the "modern" get displaced backward into a hyper-sexualized or desexualized "premodern." (159–60)

This rich provocation potentially resonates with the psycho-analytic project in several significant ways. We can think, for instance, of the focus in queer studies on issues of (non)rela-tionality and the body, issues often framed in conversation with psychoanalysis, and which are discussed in other essays in this volume. My interest here lies in how Freeman's description of the turn of queer studies towards "what has not entered the historical records," towards what is "culturally illegible" but "en-countered in embodied, nonrational forms," resonates particu-larly with psychoanalytic historiography. For many queer crit-ics, this turn will seem distinctly Derridean — a turn towards the practice of "hauntology," which Derrida elaborates apropos of *Hamlet* in *Specters of Marx* (2006). Hauntology is the study of the way the past presents itself in the present, often in the form of a demand (as, in Shakespeare's play, the ghost of Hamlet's father demanding revenge). Carla Freccero (2006) has related this Derridean practice to queer historicism's "affective invest-ments of the present in the past," an investment that "harbors within itself not only pleasure but also pain, a traumatic pain whose ethical insistence is 'to live to tell' through complex and circuitous processes of working through" (79). I claim that pre-cisely because queer historicism is a "working through" of the relationship between past and present discourses of sexuality, the turn of queer studies towards what has not yet entered the historical records can likewise correlate with a turn towards the enigmatic signifiers with which the historical work of psychoa-nalysis begins.

In his essay "Time and the Other," Jean Laplanche (1999) writes that "thinking about time, whether philosophical or scientific, develops on four levels": (1) "cosmological time," or "the time of the world"; (2) "perceptual time," or the time "of immediate consciousness"; (3) "the time of memory and of the individual project, the temporalisation of the human being"; and (4) "the time of history," which entails not only "temporalisation [...] but recapitulation" (237–38). The Foucauldian work of historicizing sexuality generally operates at the fourth level, "recapitulating" a network of evolving and interrelating discourses, while psychoanalysis operates most immediately at the second and third levels, relating consciousness to memory and to the history of an individual's development. Psychoanalytic historicism is not limited to these levels, however, or to individuals. Psychoanalysis also operates at the fourth level by developing "case-histories" of individuals as social, collective beings — as subjects within a larger discursive milieu. Texts like Freud's *Totem and Taboo* laid the foundation for considerable psychoanalytic work at the fourth level as well: work with "nonrational" cultural phenomena like taboos set against the names of the dead. The continuing relevance of psychoanalysis to cultural studies suggests that despite its relatively recent arrival on the historical scene, psychoanalysis is uniquely situated to join the level-four history of sexuality with the history of an individual's sexuality, with his or her entry into the symbolic order of a given culture. Differences between symbolic orders should prompt consideration of the portability of particular psychoanalytic concepts, but the potential jointure I have in mind hinges precisely on the temporality of sex as such, on the level-three temporality of the enigmatic signifier.

Laplanche locates the origin of human sexuality at the moment of the enigmatic signifier's reception — a moment Freud frequently found impossible to fix in his recapitulation of a subject's history. As is well known, the enigmatic signifier is most immediately the "seductive" signifier: adult gestures, words, and looks not understood by the child (nor even by the adult), but later subject to a coming-into-sense as the child matures.

The persistent elusiveness of these originating moments, the way one recovered scene simply revealed itself through further analysis as the translation of another scene, was partly responsible for Freud abandoning seduction theory and replacing it with the more universal theory of human sexual development that he outlines in "Three Essays on the Theory of Sexuality" (1905). Yet besides demonstrating that traces of seduction theory nonetheless remain in Freud's case histories (and in the "Three Essays" themselves) Laplanche (1976) argues that in seduction theory resides Freud's original, most revolutionary idea: that the unconscious, as the repository of the enigmatic signifier, operates like an "alien internal entity" in the subject (48). The unconscious is fundamentally other, and human sexuality originates in the self's relationship to this other. As is perhaps equally well known, this recovery of Freud's most radical idea also leads Laplanche (1999) to translate Freud's *Nachträglichkeit* as "afterwardsness" rather than as James Strachey's "deferred action." In their relation to consciousness, enigmatic signifiers are subject to both deferred and retroactive understandings. They constitute both the "deposit of something which will only be reactivated later" and something "registered in the first time and then understood retroactively" (261). Akin to Butler's "queer," they are objects of both "historical reflections" and "futural imaginings."

Despite the practices of psychoanalysis that have reduced homosexuality to a curable or manageable perversion, Laplanche queerly recognizes that the meaning of sex is not straightforward (pun intended). Rather, the meaning of sex — which as a signifier is ciphered at its moment of origin — partially results from a preposterous reconstruction, the work of a certain type of analytical and historical *inversion*. For the historian whose task has long been understood as the repudiation of anachronism — the scrupulousness of one's repudiation being directly proportional to one's success in distinguishing the discourses through which different cultures speak sex — approaching sex as an enigmatic signifier reconfigures anachronism as a structural condition of historicism, subordinating the search for a given signifier's first or nascent discursive appearances to the recognition of the always enigmatic signifier's temporal movement from present to past *and* past to present. (As Valerie Rohy [2006] has argued, "[A]nachronism represents not a foreign threat or radical alternative to queer historicism, but an inherent aspect of it" [71]). Laplanche's account of the enigmatic signifier has also led me to argue, in my own work (2011), that queer historicism is less the work of interpretation than detranslation — the reiteration, for present but never complete clarification, of an enigmatic message in another discourse. This difference between interpretation and detranslation is central to Laplanche's (1996) understanding of the psychoanalytic method as one of tracing the transmission of messages, the other's message being the "object of the proto-comprehension or proto-translation" (11). As Laplanche states in an interview, "Interpretation may mean that you interpret some factual situation. Translation means that there is no factual situation that can be translated. If something's translated, it's already a message" (Caruth 2001).

Texts like Sonnet 20 bear these messages: hence the potential for a productive collaboration between what Laplanche (1996) calls "anti-hermeneutic" (or anti-interpretative) psychoanalysis" and queer literary-historical criticism. In the Lacanian and Laplanchian approaches that I have sketched here, the signifiers of sex are distinct from the real of sex, whereas Foucault's productive model of sexuality risks foreclosing this distinction. But recognizing the limits of Foucault's model does not prevent the practice of a mutually informative approach to the history of sexuality. Indeed, the value of Foucauldian historicism for psychoanalysts lies in the former's effort to historicize the procedures of the latter, beginning with its demand that analysands speak about sex. A history of psychoanalysis also has the potential of placing psychoanalytic approaches to homosexuality and perversion in the much broader context of power's production of sexuality as a mechanism of social control — a context in which psychoanalysis often appears complicit with the production of heterosexuality as a normal, natural, and thoroughly ahistorical form of sexuality. The value of psychoanalysis for

Foucauldian historicists lies in turn in the unique attention psychoanalysis gives to what lies outside discourse — an outside variously demarcated as the unconscious and the real. Whereas Foucault erects a theoretical apparatus for historicizing the injunction to transform sex into discourse, psychoanalysis argues that sex is not fully discursive, that sexuality is a network of enigmatic signifiers. As something subject to repeated translation, to continuous comings-into-sense, the enigmatic signifier is also always out of place, always throwing time out of joint.

Indicative of Freeman's observation about the sexually polarized construction of the pre-modern is the critical tradition of defending against the "hypersexual" detranslation of Sonnet 20. My students sometimes object that I am "reading the poem wrong," for the speaker's suggestion of having or wanting to have sex with his "friend" does not make sense within their own ostensibly asexual discourse of amity. In response, I usually point to hundreds of years of critical unease with these lines, citing in particular Edmund Malone's 1790 pronouncement, quoted in Smith (1991): "Such addresses to men, however indelicate, were customary in our author's time, and neither imported criminality nor were esteemed indecorous" (230). Malone would be right that *certain* expressions of affection were common between men, especially male friends, but one can hardly agree that addresses like the one in Sonnet 20 are "customary." At the same time, Malone's efforts to de-sexualize these lines admits that they have "crossed the line" — making nonsense of the distinction between "friendly" and "sexual" relations. Bruce Smith similarly observes that as the speaker attempts to describe his feelings for the young man throughout the sequence, he appropriates and exhausts three "heterosexual" discourses: Horation eroticism, courtly love, and Christian marriage. At the moments where these discourses falter, the sonnets call our attention to "the void between sexual experience and the metaphors we have to talk about it" (266) — a void in which Smith locates the emergent discourse of homosexual identity. My point here is that regardless as to whether one follows Smith in enlisting these sonnets in the invention of the homosexual, this new discourse, like the period discourse of friendship, cannot make complete sense of the enigmas they present. To whatever interpretation is offered, the psychoanalytic critic can only respond, "That is not *it*." No interpretation can itself resolve these enigmas to identify what the speaker is *really* saying, how he *really* conceives of his relationship with the young man, and what he is *really* experiencing. The poem's message, the sex it translates into discourse, remains irreducibly enigmatic.

If this anti-hermeneutic thesis sounds like the translation of a cautionary statement made by any responsible literary historian, then this essay has succeeded in one of its goals: demonstrating that psychoanalysis should not simply be juxtaposed to historicism in the analysis of sex, and that psychoanalysis can inform, rather than oppose, the study of sex's transformation into discourse. To translate Smith's historicist reading into Laplanchian terms, the meaning of Sonnet 20 is both deferred to a future discourse of homosexuality that develops to make sense of it, and is retroactively understood in light of this discourse. In light of more anti-identitarian discourses of queerness — for example, Lee Edelman's (2004) claim that "queerness can never define an identity; it can only ever disturb one" (17) — the poem might also be read for the ways it defers its opposition to, and in retrospect seems opposed to, clarification of "the sexual." Ideally, both readings recognize that they do not establish what the poem is definitively saying, though they are no less useful as readings (as detranslations) for that reason. What I call enigmatic historicism simply foregrounds Hammill's (2000) critical gesture of "fracturing relations between the phenomenon and the supposed nomenon" (19), between the discourses of sex and the real of sex, so as to sustain queer criticism's orientation towards producing the "unthought."

By way of again distinguishing the unique contribution psychoanalysis makes to historicizing sexuality, I will suggest in closing that the persistent resubmission of the sonnets to critical detranslation is itself sufficient grounds for thinking the history of sexuality as something that includes but exceeds the history of discourses. The history of sexuality is a history of discourses, and psychoanalysts need to be cognizant of this history as a check on their field's tendency towards essentialism. Yet into this conversation about sexuality's history psychoanalysts should interject an awareness of the way sex comes to mean in something other than straight(forward) time. With respect to Sonnet 20, one should not be required to deny the critical utility of the discourse of homosexuality. Nor should one deny the equally useful historical discourses of sodomy, political patronage, and friendship. When these contexts are provided, however, the truth of the sonnets is not simply "outed." The real of sex is always something different from the discourses of sex — something, the psychoanalytic historian can point out, that Sonnet 20, like any utterance, ultimately fails to speak.

Works Cited

Bergler, Edmund. *Homosexuality: Disease or Way of Life?* New York: Hill and Wang, 1956.

Bieber, Irving, et al. *Homosexuality: A Psychoanalytic Study.* New York: Basic Books, 1962.

Bray, Alan. *Homosexuality in Renaissance England.* 1982; rpt. New York: Columbia University Press, 1995.

Bredbeck, Gregory W. *Sodomy and Interpretation: Marlowe to Milton.* Ithaca: Cornell University Press, 1991.

Butler, Judith. *Bodies That Matter: On the Discursive Limits of "Sex."* New York: Routledge, 1993.

Caruth, Cathy. "An Interview with Jean Laplanche." *Postmodern Culture* 11, no. 2 (2001). https://muse.jhu.edu/article/27730.

Copjec, Joan. *Read My Desire: Lacan Against the Historicists.* Cambridge: MIT Press, 1994.

Dean, Tim, and Christopher Lane. "Introduction." In *Homosexuality and Psychoanalysis,* eds. Tim Dean and Christopher Lane, 1–42. Chicago: University of Chicago Press, 2001.

De Grazia, Margreta. *Hamlet without Hamlet.* Cambridge: Cambridge University Press, 2007.

———, "The Scandal of Shakespeare's Sonnets." *Shakespeare's Survey* 46 (1994): 35–49.

Derrida, Jacques. *Specters of Marx: The State of Debt, the Work of Mourning, and the New International,* trans. Peggy Kamuf. New York: Routledge, 2006.

DiGangi, Mario. *The Homoerotics of Early Modern Drama.* Cambridge: Cambridge University Press, 1997.

Dubrow, Heather. "'Incertainties now cron themselves assur'd': The Politics of Plotting Shakespeare's Sonnets." *Shakespeare Quarterly* 47, no. 3 (1996): 291–305.

Edelman, Lee. *Queer Theory and the Death Drive.* Durham: Duke University Press, 2004.

Foucault, Michel. *The History of Sexuality, vol. 1: An Introduction,* trans. Robert Hurley. New York: Vintage, 1990a (1976).

———. *The History of Sexuality, vol. 2: The Use of Pleasure,* trans. Robert Hurley. New York: Vintage, 1990b (1984).

———. "The Confession of the Flesh." In *Power/Knowledge: Selected Interviews and Other Writings, 1972–1977,* ed. Colin Gordon, 194–228. New York: Pantheon Books, 1980.

———. *The Archeology of Knowledge and the Discourse on Language,* trans. Alan Sheridan. New York: Pantheon, 1972.

Freemen, Elizabeth. "Introduction." GLQ: *A Journal of Lesbian and Gay Studies* 13, nos. 2–3 (2007): 159–76.

Freud, Sigmund. "The Interpretation of Dreams." In *The Standard Edition of the Complete Psychological Works of Sigmund Freud, vol. 4,* trans. James Strachey in collaboration with Anna Freud and assisted by Alix Strachey and Alan Tyson, 1953; rpt London: Vintage, 2001.

Halperin, David M. "Forgetting Foucault: Acts, Identities, and the History of Sexuality." *Representations* 63 (1998): 93–120.

Hammill, Graham L. *Sexuality and Form: Caravaggio, Marlowe, and Bacon.* Chicago: University of Chicago Press, 2000.

Jones, Ernest. "The Oedipus Complex as an Explanation of Hamlet's Mystery: A Study in Motive". *The American Journal of Psychology* 21, no. 1 (1910): 72–113.

Laplanche, Jean. *Essays on Otherness.* New York: Routledge, 1999.

———. *Life and Death in Psychoanalysis,* trans. Jeffrey Mehlman. Baltimore: Johns Hopkins University Press, 1976.

———. "Psychoanalysis as Anti-Hermeneutics," trans. Luke Thurston. *Radical Philosophy* 79 (1996): 7–12.

Oxford English Dictionary. 2nd ed., 1989.

Penney, James. *The World of Perversion: Psychoanalysis and the Impossible Absolute of Desire.* Albany: SUNY Press, 2006.

Rado, Sandor. "An Adoptional View of Sexual Behavior." In *Psychosexual Development in Health and Disease: The Proceedings of the Thirty-eights Annual Meeting of the American Psychopathological Association, held in New York City, June 1948,* eds. Paul H. Hoch and Joseph Zubin, 159–89. New York: Grune and Stratton, 1949.

———."A Critical Examination of the Concept of Bisexuality." *Psychosomatic Medicine* 2, no. 4 (1940): 459–67.

Rohy, Valerie. "Ahistorical." *GLQ: A Journal of Lesbian and Gay Studies* 12, no. 1 (2006): 61–83.

Sedgwick, Eve Kosofsky. *Epistemology of the Closet.* 1990; rpt. Berkeley: University of California Press, 2008.

Shakespeare, William. Hamlet. In *The Norton Shakespeare.* 2nd edition, eds. Stephen Greenblatt, Walter Cohen, Jean E. Howard, and Katharine Eisaman Maus. 1683–1784. New York: W.W. Norton & Company, 2008.

———. *Shakespeare's Sonnets,* ed. Katherine Duncan-Jones. London: Thomas Nelson and Sons, 1997.

Shepherdson, Charles. *Vital Signs: Nature, Culture, Psychoanalysis.* New York: Routledge, 2000.

Smith, Bruce R. *Homosexual Desire in Shakespeare's England: A Cultural Poetics.* Chicago: University of Chicago Press, 1991.

Socarides, Charles. *Homosexuality: A Freedom Too Far: A Psychoanalyst Answers 1000 Questions About Causes and Cures and the Impact of the Gay Rights Movement on American Society.* Phoenix: Adam Margave, 1995.

Stockton, Will. *Playing Dirty: Sexuality and Waste in Early Modern Comedy.* Minneapolis: University of Minnesota Press, 2011.

PSYCHOANALYTIC RESPONSES

7

On Not Thinking Straight:
Comments on a Conceptual Marriage

R.D. Hinshelwood[1]

[T]he engagement of queer theory with psychoanalysis [...] is pre-
dominantly critical, psychoanalysis being seen as a theory and set
of practices that rigidify rather than open up the sexual field.
— Frosh 2006, 248

It is ironic. Psychoanalysis was born in the context of sexual
transgression — the theory of seduction, and the Oedipal theory. The plethora of sexualities was suddenly open to be known,
and in principle to be known in all of us. But, for normative
reasons, powerful a hundred years ago, in no time at all, that
opening door spawned the "Three Essays on the Theory of
Sexuality" (Freud 1905); it became a classic that could easily be
read as experts in the clinic normalizing categories of sexuality, and defining the abnormal. No wonder queer theory has a
thoroughly mixed reaction — but to be fair, the selection in this
book is a respectful one. On being asked to add a comment on
the chapters in section one, I looked forward to the challenge.
They amass a "report" on the progress of the two innocent suit-

---

1   I need to acknowledge the help of Aaron Balick's comments on a previous
version of this chapter.

ors in finding a way forward together. What can one add to the promise of their new relationship?

Changing Tack

The emphasis on sexuality and libido was solidified in the dispute with Carl Jung and Alfred Adler, so that sexuality and the Oedipus complex were promoted as the exclusive foundation of the human personality, transcending culture and history. However from 1911, Freud's trajectory was already changing. His analysis of the Schreber "case" had led him to pursue an increasing interest in identity, the ego, and the reality-principle. More recently, with the demise of ego-psychology and drive theory, and with the increasing importance of Kleinian psychoanalysis, self-psychology and the relational turn in general, the psychoanalysis of sexuality has become secondary, or at least contingent on the analysis of narcissism, personal identity, and the relatedness to others. This does not mean that orgasmic and non-orgasmic sexualities lack attention, but that sexuality is an ingredient, rather than the whole cake-mix. What is foremost now in a psychoanalysis is to outline the shape of a human personality, its coherence and its inner core of identity.

In this book which questions the nature of desire, it might be worth considering a move towards an object-relations approach and relinquishing the territory occupied by desire theories. Sexuality is nothing if not desire and ecstasy, but that is not at issue. It is the paraphernalia of identity that goes with it, both personal identity and social identity. For these purposes it is necessary to be clear about the postulate on which object-relations theory is grounded — the libido is primarily object-relating, rather than drive satisfying (Fairbairn 1944).

As a Kleinian, the consistent resort to Lacanian psychoanalysis and some post-Lacanians (notably Jean Laplanche and Luce Irigaray) in these texts seems a little one-track, all the eggs in one basket — almost equivalent to a straight phallic identity! A degree of flexibility might be warranted. Jacques Lacan and his audiences were molded in the climate created by Michel Foucault and the post-war suspicion of social engineering in France. But across the Channel, welfarism in Britain implied a very different view of the individual within his society — perhaps a maternal view of a nurturing culture (Zaretsky 1999). A different psychoanalysis burgeoned.

Fluid identities

In the object-relations approach, identity is a matter of relations, and to a degree follows Freud's (1921) view that psychology is more or less always social psychology; i.e., it is always about relations with the family, first, and then expanded into social relations growing out of those early ones. Freud quoted Gustave LeBon (1895) to the effect that a person is not quite the same in a group as he is when alone. The fact that social relations affect personal identity therefore has a long history in classical psychoanalysis. Freud (1921) put a lot of effort into understanding how this happened. He used his notion of introjection, which at the time he called "identification" (Freud 1917). Something of society, in the form of the people to whom the subject relates, gets inside the person, and significantly affects the way that person feels, thinks, and behaves. Not only is personal identity influenced by a group, but it is influenced in different ways according to the group of which one is presently a member. Thus personal identity has a potential to reshape itself as one moves from group to group during one's day. I can say that when I write my academic papers sitting in my sun-lounge, I am reaching for a particular identification, and that is somewhat modified from the "me" that goes and feeds the horses in the stables, or the "me" that reads a bed-time story to one of my grand-children. These are performances; the fluid movement between each is absolutely in line with the queer theory proposition about the fluidity of human sexuality. Thus identifications may be chosen, and chosen from a social context. However, identity itself is a little different.

Identity and Identifications

The dominant notion of the individual is a discrete, stand-alone individual, with satisfactions to satisfy, and ambitions to achieve. No matter that the nature of this identity has varied from the rationalist "Cogito ergo sum" to the consumerist, " I am what I buy," the individual is expected to experience himself as a relatively inflexible monument of human nature. In contrast, since 1917, when Freud used the term "identification," a psychoanalytic version of a highly flexible inner world of identifications has become relatively commonplace. A kaleidoscopic representative world inside each person, suggests that psychoanalysis is counter-cultural, not positing a from-the-beginning unitary individual. Freud (1923) referred to the ego as "a precipitate of abandoned object-cathexes" (29), a kind of psychic wardrobe of potential identities. Through the day I am selecting from the "identity-wardrobe" of my unconscious, what I will "be" for the moment. There is a sense in which the individual is a truly disaggregated person.[2] Psychoanlysis never developed this into a proper theorization that could have helped queer theory.[3]

Within and amongst this whirlwind of possible identifications where is "identity" found? A sense of personal identity is socially prescribed out there; and at the same time, psychoanalytically-speaking, there is a churning mass of possibilities inside here. And yet, for most of us, some "thing" holds all the possibilities together, and for that we might continue to use the term "identity," as opposed to the separate potentialities of the identifications. Through all these variegated identifications, there is a thread which knows it is me all the time. There is a kind of "core" left, which keeps safe the knowledge of who it is that performs unconsciously in these identification roles (Hinshelwood 1989, 1997). One might think of Donald Winnicott's

---

2　The serial assumption of identifications might be better called multiple rather than fluid (Balick 2008)

3　Judith Butler (Salih 2002) has made significant headway in thinking through this notion of internalized identities.

(1960) phrase, a sense of "the continuity of being" (591), which if interrupted leads potentially towards psychosis. This is a very slimmed-down role for the notion of "identity," the stability of which is an existential necessity. In this sense identity is to be distinguished from "identification." Identity is thus a potentiality, a hitching post onto which different identifications may be hung, according to the unconscious influencing of social groups and relationships.

I offer this as a working model to render the war between essentialism and constructivism more manageable then it normal is between disciplines across the social/individual boundary. As Ian Craib (1995) remarked:

> My professional life is divided between sociology and psychoanalysis (as a group psychotherapist) and I have become used to the idea that these two worlds know nothing about each other and that when sociologists comment on emotion, they do so with the same sensitivity and understanding that psychoanalysts display when commenting on society — which is (to put not too fine a point on it) none at all. (151)

This book is dedicated to straddling the disciplines and therefore the antagonism of the essentialist/constructivist battleground. In the formulation in this section, there exists some sort of essential experience of identity — though at the outset it is empty; whilst there is no doubt that what fills in the empty category of identity is a set of multiple identifications, precipitates of relational experiences as they have been performed and experienced, and moreover as they have been implicitly required by the prevailing discourse. The value of such a distinction between identity and identifications has not, to my knowledge, been as productively explored in queer theory as it might.

Sexuality and Stability

However if the stability of personal identity is necessary to avoid consequences as bad as psychosis, then fluidity is likely to be personally threatening. The nature of the ego and other aspects of personal identity have become the focus of psychoanalytic examination since Freud's (1911, 1914) consideration of narcissism, and have over the years become a more dominant tradition. The stability of the ego has taken precedence in the treatment situation over the conflicts within it.

In some cases, sexuality may be a support to an identity where it is felt by the subject to be weak or inconstant or fragmented. Certainly, sexual identity is a common enough notion, and something which many people feel a need to be sure of in themselves and others (Balick 2010). It can bolster the sense of self, and the relatedness in one's environment. Perhaps the sexual revolution of the twentieth century, which psychoanalysis helped to promote, may have in fact enhanced the need in many quarters for a clear sexual identity. To adopt a strategy of fluid sexual identity may therefore be problematic by undermining some more foundational sense of stability and inner security. One major support to stable identity is the physical entity of the body. This might be less well expressed by, "who am I?" than if we changed it to, "where am I?" I am where this organic, lumpish body of mine is. My sense of being is indissolubly glued to this physical mass. So, one of the massive resources for bolstering a sense of identity is one's body, its felt existence, and most intensely, the sexual feelings which are as glued to the body as the sense of identity.

The view of identity as a core element of psychological stability is essentialist, and so works against the basically Foucauldian notion of the social construction of identity. One problem is that social constructionism equates identifications (performances) with identity. On that score, its undermining of enduring identifications with specific sexual performances makes sense as a campaign against sexual prejudices of various kinds. At the same time it threatens the sense of identity. But if we unhook identity from identification, then a campaign against a stable identification does not destabilize a core sense of identity.

I would claim in fact that I am following Freud by describing identifications as fluid, whilst identity is a stable fulcrum. It is important therefore in promoting a "fluidity of sexual identity," that it is sexual *identifications* — i.e., performances — that should be fluid. Such a conceptual strategy entails acknowledging an essentialist basis for identity; it is an innate potential, a given; but in the formulation I propose, identity is content free. That is, the ego may freely explore a wide variety of identifications (including sexual performances) without loss of its needed stability.

Freedom and Ethics

Identifications are mostly constituted by performance. And sexuality is a performance with another who is equally performing within an identification. So, sexual identifications are performative and relational. Because they are actions in the context of relationships with other sexual "actors," they therefore have an integral ethical aspect. Thus an identification sought by one person, implies a complementary identification accepted by their partner. As a result good/bad evaluations creep back into sexual preferences and performances. What does one partner press his other to perform? It is unrealistic to plead for a non-judgmental attitude to all sexual acts since, clearly, some sexual relations can be violating, either bodily, financially or psychologically.

And license for even straight sex can only be seriously allowed between consenting adults. In addition, some relations, even when sexual satisfactions are freely agreed, e.g., extra-marital affairs, have to be carefully negotiated with an eye to the benefits and deficits for all concerned. In short, the identifications taken up require the consenting agreement of partners to reciprocate. In many cases of course — no problem. Very many straight couples are happy enough to divide up the binaries: active-passive, thrusting-receptive, etc., etc., in a relatively long-standing arrangement — though some couples will alternate in various imaginative inventions. However such performative compliance could be forced on the partner — and sado-masochism is a case in point. In the extreme, a rapist will automatically require his "other" to suffer the identification of a rape victim. As is well known, the fantasy of being a rape victim is not uncommon at all, but the ethical situation makes the actual performance of such an identification very problematic.

So there are inevitably limiting conditions to performative identifications since they require compliance with a complementary identification. This ethical aspect to sexuality as relational may not sit well with the standard notion of self-actualization for everyone. But self-actualization carried to extremes can warrant exploitative violations of others.[4] Identifications which require the other's compliance with a complimentary identification should be limited by the usual informed consent. Finally, there is a question if sexual performers should be fluid, and whether that is already a directive on the way to a sort of rigid counter-prejudice. Such a requirement needs to be permissory, not obligatory — that is to say, society could permit fluid sexualities, rather than oblige people to be more fluid.

Inner Performance and Ethical Boundaries

Even with solitary masturbation, there is invariably an accompanying "masturbatory phantasy" about some sexual object however inanimate or fetishistic. The adoption of an identifica-

---

4   The severe restriction of identification, including sexual identifications, is a violation of the personality. Such constriction of others into performances could be the basis of a psychoanalytical formulation of unethical action at an unconscious level. That is a principle of personal integration, and can be a basis for professional and general ethics (Hinshelwood 1997), as well as being applicable to an ethics of sexual roles and performances. A Kleinian version of this principle would involve the notion of splitting; the complementary identifications are separated (split) apart. The phenomenology of unconscious splitting in a Kleinian mold would allow more subtle understanding of the adoption of one or other complementary identifications. A splitting that is permanent and unhealing, leaving the partners wedded to a particular identification, would probably be unethical, whereas a splitting in which the identifications are fluid would be ethical (perhaps even identification with non-compliance). Whether such a principle of unconscious splitting could ever be part of a formal ethics is debatable; as is the question whether (given the human unconscious) such an unconscious principle could even be completely excluded from a workable ethics.

tion implies at the outset an inner performance with an other (internal object). Inward performances are potentially as arousing and as satisfying as proximity with an actual other. In fact, no sexual action takes place without it being action with the "other in the mind." In the inner arena, the ethical constraints are relaxed. Murder in the mind is not murder. So too are exploitation and violation in the mind. Ethical issues arise when inner fantasy is transferred to an actual partner. Then freedom and ethics may clash.

However this "innocent" internal activity becomes an important consideration because some people may have a weak sense of that boundary between inner and actual. For them it is easy to overstep the mark. And it may be the case that for most of us, at high levels of intense arousal, the boundary is much more easily breached — people are tempted to "let go" if extremely excited. As a result, society has taken on itself a policing function as a means of protecting the vulnerable. And perhaps it should, but it seems to have stepped from policing a boundary to controlling the inner life of personal fantasy. Maybe that inward policing is exemplified in the actual policing of sexual material on the internet.

However the social policing job is strongly assisted by the subject himself. Even to imagine oneself a homosexual can become a self-loathing. This is understood by psychoanalysts as the function of the super-ego. However, on occasions — and non-straight sex is one of those occasions — the super-ego overfunctions through being socially supported. Both internal factors and external social forces aim at "civilizing" individuals. Excessive policing over and above the real requirement is not uncommon, and was termed "surplus repression" by Herbert Marcuse (1955). This civilizing principle seems to derive from the economic requirements of society — and repression of sexuality is sublimated in labor activity. The apparatus of the super-ego appears to be the point of access by which the social exerts its intrusive influence over the individual, whether economic or ethical. The essential plasticity and polymorphous nature of human sexuality is the site upon which social forces most easily and frequently play.

Queer theory engages with the judgmentalism about sexual performances, and it can deploy a counter-judgement, a prejudice against prejudice! It requires a stronger theory of prejudice. Invalid evaluations of conduct, normalizing and pathologizing need some reference to the psychoanalytic theory of the superego. That is to say we need to understand exactly how social norms get inside the individual. A straightforward appeal to the pressurizing effects of power may not be sufficient. It would seem at least necessary to consider that there are internal mechanisms for receiving and accepting such socializing pressures. It would seem at least necessary to consider that such a two-sided knife sustains the wounds of prejudice. Given the resistance that prejudice always displays towards dissolving away, it would seem a little lacking in flexibility not to consider all the possibilities.

Prescription versus Description

Restricted to a social power theory of personality construction, there are therefore equally restricted possibilities for action. Power theories are one of the reasons for the temptation to counter-judge others, and to attempt to create a "powerful" restatement of sexual norms and mores, in order to change the dominant class and the dominant language traditions. Such a prescriptive approach is understandably tempting. But queer theory itself is culture-bound and socially located. Are there alternatives to a confrontation of power — a frequently sterile confrontation between the traditional and the progressive?

A kind of praxis that is not prescriptive — for instance, descriptive — must be a possibility. At its best psychoanalysis itself is a descriptive "science," not a prescriptive brainwashing (though psychoanalysis can often seem so). In fact, what psychoanalysts do is to give a description as best they can of internal states, addressed to the very state of mind itself.[5] There is a power in simply revealing the state of affairs. To turn once again to the old-fashioned terminology of Western Marxism, pointing out the falseness of a false consciousness is empowering (Lukács 1920); and this prompted the development over the years of a strategy for "consciousness raising." Queer theory might adopt such a program of its own; that is to gain the conscious awareness of at least a Western population, of the polymorphous nature of human sexuality. This is the message of Freud's (1905) early ambiguous book, "Three Essays on the Theory of Sexuality." There is passivity buried in the most active of sexual actors, there is sado-masochism in all-loving encounters, there are aspects of homosexuality that are foundational in heterosexual relationships.

Conclusions

Queer theory applies where queer prejudice is. Psychoanalysis has not always been a solid ally. But there is a radical and critical leverage in the British object-relations tradition. It brings the pre-occupations with relationships into the inner reality of the individual, and at the same time, a much closer correspondence with the social relatedness of human beings to each other. The notion results in a picture of a changing, fluid world of unconscious connections to others, to groups. That this everyday journey around one's inner population is relatively freer as far as non-sexual living is concerned should promise the possibility of a continual loosening up of the sexual identifications. This implies a stabilized identity (without specific characteristics) within a world of identifications.

As Stephen Frosh (2006) concluded in his not-unsympathetic critique of psychoanalysis, "That psychoanalysis has a long

---

5 It is true that psychoanalysts do not address themselves to the social influences of power and privilege in the context in which their analysands live, but that is because psychoanalysis is not about that. It is about internal states. That is what psychoanalysis is good at, but analysts should not deny the impact of factors and forces outside their own ken.

road to travel before it comes to terms with homosexuality can hardly be in doubt, but perhaps the journey begins here" (250). He meant that sexuality should allow for differences and multiplicity. The fact that the broad potential for sexualities may be prematurely and unnecessarily cut off in many people, seems to be a matter of social prescription, and psychoanalytic description.

Though psychoanalysis has a reflective and descriptive intent, this has not prevented it being used in that normalizing way — given the powerful prejudicial tendencies in all members of (at least Western) society. Nor have psychoanalysts been particularly reticent about the use of psychoanalysis itself as gatekeeper to the profession and its Institutes. Instead of the knee-jerk reaction, homosexuality bad, heterosexuality good, it would be better to investigate if there are patterns of unhealth specific for homosexuality, and moreover the patterns of unhealth specific for heterosexuality, as well. Don't we need the courage to explore on either side?

Rightly queer theory has not always been respectful of psychoanalysis and it is laudable that a serious attempt to engage with psychoanalysis has been promoted. Psychoanalysis has become accustomed now, like queers, to the odium of being socially off-center. There appear to be grounds for an encounter between the two which might give both more substance, or will each continue to emphasize the other's oddity? Psychoanalysis when abroad from the treatment situation, needs the reminder that we are all social beings; whilst queer theory needs the help to understand the disavowed "essence" of people's identity. We can hope with the help of this book that the mutual sensitivity and understanding that Craib called for might be forthcoming.

Works Cited

Balick, Aaron. *The Multiplicity of Gender: An Integrative Psychoanalytic Approach to Theorising Gender and Sexual Identities.*Doctoral Dissertation. University of Essex, 2008.

———. "Speculating on Sexual Subjectivity: On the Application and Misapplication of Postmodern Discourse on the Psychology of Sexuality." *Psychology and Sexuality* 2, no. 1 (2011): 16–28.

Craib, Ian. "Some Comments on the Sociology of the Emotions." *Sociology* 29 (1995): 151–58.

Fairbairn, W.R.D. "Endopsychic Structure Considered in Terms of Object-Relationships." *International Journal of Psycho-Analysis* 25 (1944): 70–92. Republished in Fairbairn, W.R.D. *Psychoanalytic Studies of the Personality.* London: Routledge and Kegan Paul, 1952.

Freud, Sigmund. "The Ego and the Id" (1923). In *The Standard Edition of the Complete Psychological Works of Sigmund Freud,* vol. 19, trans. James Strachey in collaboration with Anna Freud and assisted by Alix Strachey and Alan Tyson, 3–66. 1953; rpt. London: Vintage 2001.

———. "Group Psychology and the Analysis of the Ego" (1921). In *The Standard Edition of the Complete Psychological Works of Sigmund Freud,* vol. 18, trans. James Strachey in collaboration with Anna Freud and assisted by Alix Strachey and Alan Tyson, 67–143. 1953; rpt. London: Vintage 2001.

———. "Mourning and Melancholia" (1917). In *The Standard Edition of the Complete Psychological Works of Sigmund Freud,* vol. 14, trans. James Strachey in collaboration with Anna Freud and assisted by Alix Strachey and Alan Tyson, 239–58. 1953; rpt. London: Vintage 2001.

———. "On Narcissism" (1914). In *The Standard Edition of the Complete Psychological Works of Sigmund Freud,* vol. 14, trans. James Strachey in collaboration with Anna Freud and assisted by Alix Strachey and Alan Tyson, 67–104. 1953; rpt. London: Vintage 2001.

———. "Psycho-Analytic Notes on an Autobiographical Account of a Case of Paranoia Dementia Paranoides" (1911). In *The Standard Edition of the Complete Psychological Works of Sigmund Freud,* vol. 12, trans. James Strachey in collaboration with Anna Freud and assisted by Alix Strachey and Alan Tyson, 3–82. 1953; rpt. London: Vintage 2001.

———. "Three Essays on the Theory of Sexuality" (1905). In *The Standard Edition of the Complete Psychological Works of Sigmund Freud,* vol. 7, trans. James Strachey in collaboration with Anna Freud and assisted by Alix Strachey and Alan Tyson, 123–245. 1953; rpt. London: Vintage 2001.

Frosh, Stephen. *For and Against Psychoanalysis.* London and New York: Routledge, 2006.

Hinshelwood, R.D. "Social possession of identity." In *Crises of the Self: Further Essays on Psychoanalysis and Politics,* ed. Barry Richards, 75–83. London: Free Association Books, 1989.

Hinshelwood, R.D. *Therapy or Coercion.* London: Karnac, 1997.

LeBon, Gustav. *Psychologie des foules/The Crowd.* Brunswick and London: Transaction Publishers, 1995.

Lukács, György. *History and Class Consciousness.* London: Merlin, 1967 (1920).

Marcuse, Herbert. *Eros and Civilisation.* Boston: Beacon Press, 1955.

Salih, Sara. *Judith Butler.* London and New York: Routledge, 2002.

Winnicott, D.W. "The Theory of the Parent-Infant Relationship." *International Journal of Psycho-Analysis* 41 (1960): 585–95. Republished in Winnicott, D.W. *The Maturational Processes and the Facilitating Environment.* London: Hogarth, 1965.

Zaretsky, Eli. "'One large secure, solid background': Melanie Klein and the Origins of the Welfare State." *Psychoanalysis and History* 1 (1999): 136–54.

8

Queer as a New Shelter from Castration

Abe Geldhof and Paul Verhaeghe[1]

Introduction

Somewhere in his diaries, Søren Kierkegaard (1998) wonders about how Jesus Christ would react when asked to prove that he is really the son of God. If he really is, Kierkegaard says, then he would *not* prove it, because his existence is the proof. If Jesus were to comply with the request to prove it, he would make himself appear not to be the son of God. Lacan (1986[1959–60]) says something similar about the perversion of Sade. In his seventh seminar on ethics he notes that the more Sade shouts not to be bound by any law, the more it becomes clear that the Law remains indestructible at its core (225–41).

Jesus Christ doesn't prove he is Jesus Christ because he is Jesus Christ: his existence is the proof. Sade, on the other hand, has to prove ceaselessly that he is not bound by any law, but in producing transgression after transgression, it becomes obvious that his pleasure is only possible because of the law. Without the law no transgression is possible. The silence of being contrasts sharply with the shrieking noise of discourse.

This train of thought is very instructive for queer theory and for psychoanalytical practice. If somebody were to *be* really queer, then he would have no reason to prove it. The fact that

1   We would like to thank Sue Feldman, who was our first reader.

some people try to prove to others they are queer, again and again, only reveals ever more sharply that they aren't. They only work their fingers to the bone for some obscure Other. They remain bound to some *queer* God.

To be or not to be, that's still the question. Different approaches are proposed through the different chapters in the first section of *Clinical Encounters*. Queer gives some people an identity. Queer is also a discourse that started as an underground movement, and that in the meantime has been recuperated by the university discourse. For others, queer is a name for their perversion. Other perspectives are possible. We put ours forward in a deliberately provocative way: queer is a new shelter from castration. Just as Lacan (1973[1964]) says on atheism in his eleventh seminar that the myth that *God is dead* is nothing but a shelter from castration (29; 45), queer also is a way to refuse castration, proving how speaking beings are bound to castration.

People who identify with the signifier queer can only love queer because it's a name for their *jouissance*. What else is queer, if it is not *jouissance*? It is the *jouissance* of the body that is considered to be queer. One can never fully identify with one's own body and can never totally control the *jouissance* that erupts from this body. One's body remains always to some extent strange to oneself, it remains *heteros*. Using the word queer for one's identity seems to be nothing more than a failing attempt to control one's *jouissance* (Lacan 1986[1959–60]; Declercq 2004; Verhaeghe 2001, 65–132).

Queer as One of the Names-of-the-Father

This is one of the most important aspects of queer: it's all about the act of naming. In this sense queer might be considered one of the Names-of-the-Father. It gives a name to one's *jouissance*. By saying this, we must realize that the act of naming in itself is not "good" or "bad." Sometimes it can have pernicious effects when naming pins one down to the signifier. Nevertheless, everybody (every body) needs to be named via the Other, or otherwise no subjectivity is possible. Still, the radical split between the Symbolic and the Real remains. The act of naming always fails at a certain point. In the case of the signifier queer we must ask where the act of naming fails. While the ordinary signifiers of homosexuality and heterosexuality refer to an object choice, queer is a signifier used for another kind of identity, one that tries to escape being defined by this object choice. The signifier queer refers to a choice for an enjoyment; implicitly, queer is opposed to "the straights" who are often seen as people who do not enjoy.

Queer theory therefore seems to have enlarged Immanuel Kant's three fundamental philosophical questions: What can I know? What do I have to do? What may I hope? Queer theory doesn't answer Kant's questions, but adds a fourth one: How can I enjoy? And more specifically: How can I reach *my* enjoyment?

The question is interesting, but by giving an answer to it we find ourselves immediately in a deadlock. There lies an important difference between queer theory and psychoanalytic practice. Queer theory tries to sell itself as a new answer to a question that is not explicit in Kant, although it is as old as humanity itself. Psychoanalysis for its part does not answer this question, but tries to make it conscious while accepting that absolute enjoyment is not attainable for any speaking being. Lacan (1966[1960]) insists a lot on this impossibility: "jouissance is forbidden for the one who speaks" (821).

Today, it becomes clear that people have abandoned the old ideals, seen as conservative. Ideals are normative, and thus they are bad. In the place of the ideal, the contemporary subject has the object *a* that steers his life, which is typical for a capitalistic era. This is a remark Lacan (2001[1970]) made in *Radiophonie*. He called this switch "the rise at the social zenith of the object called by me small *a*" (414). Jacques-Alain Miller (2002) formalized this as follows: I < *a*. With these remarks in mind, we can consider *Queer* as one of the Oedipal vicissitudes in an era during which the belief in the Other of the Other declines, and in which as a consequence the object *a* emerges.

Being born as a male or female is one of the most contingent factors in life, but no matter how obvious this contingency might be for some subjects, one still has to do something with it. Even more so: it is a necessity to do something with the contingencies of life. And one always clashes with the impossibility of a final answer. With this, we have introduced three terms Lacan (1975[1972–73]; 1991[1969–70]) places in mutual relation: contingency, necessity, and impossibility.

Necessity is, so to speak, the upper layer. Every speaking being is confronted with the Real of the drive and the question of how to handle the *jouissance* of the body. Gender is already an answer to this question, and thus a defense to the impossibility that lays beyond. Introducing gender as a solution is thus nothing but another formulation of the same problem (Verhaeghe 2004). Impossibility therefore can be considered as the lower layer and is much more difficult than necessity.

Some extreme representatives of the queer movement seem to refuse the classical distinction between man and woman. By doing this, they avoid not only the impossibility, but they also avoid the necessity to set about the task of doing something with the contingency of gender. Meanwhile they install, in their refusal of this classic dichotomy of man and woman, a new dichotomy, the one of straight and queer. In this way queer is nothing other than an illustration of its own failure. One difference between two categories is replaced by another difference between two categories. While in the first dichotomy the identification with one of the sexes is central, in the second dichotomy the identification with a way of enjoying is central. But both of them show the same deadlock of every binary dichotomy. To say it simply: the first element needs the second element to be placed in opposition to it.

Other binaries that have been made in psychoanalytical theory are the ones between passive and active, and between Eros and Thanatos. Both of these binaries introduce more problems than solutions. Lacan's critique of the active/passive opposition is that in identifying masculinity with activity and femininity with passivity, one tries to make man and woman a complementary couple. Implicitly this distinction hides a belief in such things as a sexual relationship between man and woman. For Lacan (1966[1958]) femininity must not be thought of as complimentary to masculinity, but as a supplement, what is also referred to as the not-all (*"le pas tout"* of Lacan). As for the distinction between a life drive and a death drive, Lacan says the opposition is true as long as it is considered two aspects of the same drive. For Lacan (1966[1960]) there is only one drive and this drive is virtually a death drive. When pushed through, every drive is a death drive.

As several authors in the book note, the attempts to define what queer means conflicts with what queer would like to be. The attempts to define something undefinable show us how radically we are cut off from it. Queer is an impossible position. We can redefine it with Lacan's terminology where he distinguishes subject and object. The subject is radically cut off from the object, i.e., from the *jouissance* of his body. Psychoanalysis now defines its position in the failure of the identification of the subject with his body, while queer theory attempts to identify the subject with his body, i.e., its *jouissance*.

Symbolic Castration and the Logic of the Not-All

By choosing *not* to identify with the symbolically determined difference between man and woman, one tries to hide from castration. Here one has to distinguish between real, imaginary and symbolic castration. Real castration is something Lacan focuses on in his tenth seminar. It points to the fact that the body has its limits, with the penis as paradigm, in which it's clear that men can't enjoy without limit because the orgasm is at the same time typically its limit. Imaginary castration is stressed by Lacan in his fourth seminar. It is the classic neurotic fantasy about the father frustrating the child by taking away his object of *jouissance*. This is a fantasy in which neurotics often believe in order to avoid a primordial symbolic castration. The latter is the effect of the Symbolic: the subject ex-sists outside the Real. As a result, every discourse is ultimately a semblance. To understand the discussion about queer we must remember that the Symbolic order with its castrating effect is already there, before the entrance of any subject. By refusing the phallic distinction between man and woman, it's this symbolic castration that is whisked away. "Not choosing is not losing," might be their hidden motto. Identifying with one signifier within a binary reasoning automatically means the impossibility of identifying with the opposite signifier. Identifying as a man means you're not a woman. This interpretation of queer now creates the illusion of mending the not-all. At least that is the hope. But for queer subjects, *jouissance* is just as unreachable as it is for others. The fact that they have to affirm over and over again that they are queer shows us that they are not that queer after all and that *jouissance* slips through their fingers as it does for everyone.

In this line of reasoning, queer does not indicate the presence of a perverse structure. Queer is just a signifier that can be used by every subject, whatever its structure: neurosis, psychosis or perversion. Identifying with the signifier queer doesn't say anything about the structure of the subject.

In a certain sense the discourse about queer is both the opposite of and the same as the scientific discourse. Whereas the scientific discourse believes fully in biological determinacy, the queer discourse stresses that everything is socially constructed. In both cases there is a tendency to a logic of the "all." The scientific discourse tends to put all belief in a biological cause, while the queer discourse tends to place their bet fully on cultural constructions. This leads queer theorists to invent concepts like "determined indeterminacy," to recover the deadlock in their theory. But just because everything is socially constructed doesn't mean that there are no real limits that the sexed subject must recognize. Both these discourses can't be maintained. Not all is biological, not all is socially constructed.

Clinical Illustration: The Case of Michel H.

To illustrate our line of reasoning and its implication for psychoanalytic practice, it is interesting to refer to one of Lacan's lesser known case studies, the case of Michel H., a psychotic transsexual man. Michel H. is presented in the same period as his seminar on the *sinthome,* in a clinical presentation at which Lacan (1996[1976]) assisted. Michel H. would not have called himself queer, nor would Lacan have done so, but we introduce this case study because it is clear that Michel H. is at odds with himself at the point of sexual identity and object choice, and because his solution is not a typical one.

Michel H. tells Lacan that from infancy he has been jealous of his sisters. He would have liked to have been in their shoes, or even more particularly, their clothes. Secretly he dressed up as a woman, and upon Lacan's questioning, he clarifies that the accent is on the underwear. "Having clothes on my body, gives me pleasure. Not a sexual pleasure, but a pleasure at the level of the heart, for my inner self" (313). He stresses that he has the character of a woman and enumerates some stereotypical characteristics, like "I am soft" and so on. According to his own account, he has botched up his school time, because he always had to think about "that problem there." Once he tried to castrate himself literally with a rusty knife, but he didn't dare to. "After all," he says, "I didn't have such a bad infancy because I could dress up secretly" (313).

On his sexual relations with men or women, he says he couldn't feel like a woman in the arms of a man, nor could he feel like a man in the arms of a woman. Finally he had to conclude that he didn't feel attracted to men or women. He describes sexual acts as pleasures he cannot refuse. Once he is driven into the arms of a woman, he gets in a spiral he can't get out of anymore and he must go on. It's a point of no return for him. "You don't get out of it anymore. I had to do it" (329). When asked by Lacan who primed this spiral, he answers: "both," but then he thinks for a moment and answers that she might be the one who started it. We can see illustrated here how in his sexual relations the initiative comes from the Other. It's the Other who starts an act that is experienced by the subject as pressing and difficult to stop. An intervention of the analyst could be at this point to say that he doesn't have to comply with the demand of the Other. At first sight one could see a similarity here between psychoanalysis and queer theory. Queer theory is saying that subjects do not need to organize their sexuality around the demand of a contingent, socio-historical construction of sexuality by foregrounding different ways sexuality has been or could be conceived. The point we must stress here is that this intervention doesn't aim arbitrarily at a social construction, but at the *jouissance* of the Other. For this psychotic subject the *jouissance* of the Other is traumatic, and the intervention aims at emptying out the *jouissance* of the Other.

Masturbating is something he doesn't do in a typical male manner, but rather in a female way. He can only come to a climax by keeping his hand between his thighs and pushing on his penis. Twice in his life he tried to masturbate in a male way, but this had hurt him too much. For the same reason he doesn't slide the prepuce backwards. In this phenomenon we can see that there is no libidinal investment in the organ, but rather there is a radical foreclosure of the phallic function. Hence, *jouissance* remains all around the body, and is not regulated by its openings.

"I never felt as a male [...] I only live to be able to be a woman, I'm not interested in anything else" (317, 331). To be able to feel more like a woman, he takes all kinds of drugs. Being slightly doped helps him to better feel his character. "I forgot everything, except that I was a woman" (325).

His attempts to create a sexual identity are very unstable. The only options that remain after many years are an operation or suicide. He is quite radical in this. If he cannot become a woman, he chooses to stop his life. Earlier he had actually tried to commit suicide, and at the time of his interview with Lacan, he had stopped almost all social interaction. Because people jeered at him too much, he didn't come out anymore. Once he stayed in his room for a week, and as a consequence he didn't eat, even though there was a store nearby. One day, dressed as woman, he smashed a mirror to pieces.

Lacan seems to be pessimistic about a psychoanalytic treatment for this man, but that doesn't mean one can't do anything.

The analyst might function as a guarantor for castration, as a guarantee for what Lacan calls the "*pas-tout,*" the "not-all." In this case, one can confirm that the body and gender identity is problematic for everyone, and that an operation will not solve everything, let alone provide a final solution. Other, less radical solutions might be invented, even though one doesn't think about them immediately. The expectation that a surgical treatment at the level of the real of the body can solve everything is very pernicious for the subject. If this expectation is not fulfilled after the operation, nothing remains. An analyst shall therefore never subscribe to this hope, but places himself at the side of the "*pas-tout*" to help the subject to find other solutions, without the certainty or the finality.

Conclusion

What is really queer, is *jouissance.* In the last resort the whole discussion about gender and queer is nothing but a defense against the queerness of *jouissance* and the contingencies of life. Beyond gender and queer, a much more difficult problem hides. Lacan's differentiation between the other *jouissance* and phallic *jouissance* permits us to rethink the classic mind/body deadlock in a larger topological structure. There is no binary opposition between body and soul, between being and Other, between man and woman, between phallic *jouissance* and the other *jouissance*. In each case there is a gap between the two that causes a further evolution to yet another binary, in which one of the terms tries to regain the other but never succeeds because of a structural incompatibility, thus forcing this attempt towards yet another level.

In this way, the gap between being and signifier is reproduced in the gap between woman and man. In our opinion, what we have here is the complete elaboration of the ontological structure announced by Lacan in 1949 in his paper on the mirror stage. Human beings are always divided between something that they are not or do not have, and something that they will never be or never have. The Lacanian subject lacks all substance and its supposedly underlying "being" is always lost at the very moment it is supposed to appear. That is why it is condemned to a structurally-determined form of never-being-there. Hence the paradoxical fact that the essence of the Lacanian subject comes down to its lacking any kind of essence whatever, and that the whole accent has to be put on its divided character.

Works Cited

Declercq, Frédéric. "Lacan's Concept of the Real of *Jouissance*: Clinical Illustrations and Implications." *Psychoanalysis, Culture & Society* 9 (2004): 237–251.

Kierkegaard, Søren. *The Diary,* ed. Peter Rohde. New York, Citadel, 1998.

Lacan, Jacques. "Radiophonie Autres" (1970). In *Écrits,* 403–47. Paris: Seuil, 2001.

———. "Entretien avec Michel H" (1976). In *Ouvrage Collectif. Sur l'identité sexuelle: à propos du transsexualisme,* 311–53. Paris: Association Freudienne International, 1996.

———. *Livre XVII: L'envers de la psychanalyse* (1969–70). Texte établi par Jacques-Alain Miller. Paris: Seuil, 1991.

———. *Livre VII, L'Éthique de la psychanalyse* (1959–60). Texte établi par Jacques-Alain Miller. Paris: Seuil, 1986.

———. *Livre XX, Encore* (1972–73). Texte établi par Jacques-Alain Miller. Paris: Seuil, 1975.

———. *Livre XI, Les quatre concepts fondamentaux de la psychanalyse* (1964). Texte établi par Jacques-Alain Miller. Paris: Seuil, 1973.

———. "Propos directifs pour un Congrès sur la sexualité feminine" (1958). In *Écrits,* 725–36. Paris: Seuil, 1966.

———. "Subversion du sujet et dialectique du désir dans l'inconscient freudien" (1960). In *Écrits,* 794–827. Paris: Seuil, 1966.

Miller, Jacques-Alain. "La théorie du partenaire." *Quarto 77* (2002): 6–33.

Verhaeghe, Paul. *Beyond Gender: From Subject to Drive.* New York: Other Press, 2001.

————. "Phallacies of Binary Reasoning: Drive beyond Gender." In *Dialogues on Sexuality, Gender and Psychoanalysis,* ed. Irene Matthis, 53–66. London: Karnac, 2004.

9

The Redress of Psychoanalysis

Ann Murphy

> Poetry does not intervene in the actual, but by offering conscious-
> ness a chance to recognise its predicaments, foreknow its capacity
> and rehearse its comeback in all kinds of venturesome ways, it of-
> fers a response […] which has a liberating and verifying effect upon
> the individual spirit.
> — Heaney 1995, 2.

Seamus Heaney's eloquent apologia on behalf of poetry captures more accurately than most psychoanalytic texts my own
way of thinking about the practice of psychoanalysis. Thinking
through poetry may be my antidote to some tendencies in psychoanalytic theory, language and practice towards institutionalized rigidity, with its focus on the adaptive and the normative, as
opposed to the radical sense of the singularity and uniqueness
of the individual, which is the gift of psychoanalysis at its best.

Postmodern, social constructionist critiques of gender, sexuality, and identity have challenged essentialist psychoanalytic
notions of psychosexual development, fixed gender identity,
and stable sexual orientation. Such critiques challenge psychoanalysts to recognize and interrogate assumptions that we hold
about sexuality, identity, gender, and subjectivity, and to address
the contradictions that have permeated psychoanalytic think-

ing on these questions, all the way back to Freud's radical, conflicted, disorderly, multiply revised, and exuberantly footnoted "Three Essays on the Theory of Sexuality" (1905).

The first part of this volume offers an exploration of queer theory ranging from considerations of identity, desire, and pleasure, through perversion, ethics, and discourse. These texts invite the practicing analyst to engage in a dialogue with queer thinking on gender, sexuality, and identity, to explore the potential insights offered by the undermining of simplistic binaries, and to question familiar narratives of psychosexual life. My initial encounter with the ideas that have informed queer theory was in *Gender Trouble* (1990). Judith Butler's text had usefully challenged the simple binaries of sexual and gender identity, and argued that, far from being natural or inevitable expressions of an essential femininity or masculinity, gender roles are performative, a series of citations that constitute us as gendered subjects — "gender is always a doing, but not a doing by a subject who might be said to pre-exist the deed" (33).

From the point of view of a clinician, while aptly critiquing the exclusionary impact of restrictive and oppressive gender normativity, the apparent political voluntarism of her position appeared to leave little space for a concept of the unconscious, and seemed to announce a utopian project for a new, gendered way of life promising freedom from constraint. It appeared to propose a menu of options to be consumed, gender as commodity, with the implicit specter of this newly gendered subject as commodity par excellence. While challenging simplistic dualities and binaries within psychoanalytic and cultural narratives of identity, she proposed the alternative norms and binaries of fluid versus fixed, incoherent versus coherent. In her preface to the 1999 edition of the text, she addresses some of these criticisms, stating that "the positive normative vision of this text [...] cannot take the form of a prescription: 'subvert gender in the way that I say and life will be good'" (xxi), and further that "subversive performances always run the risk of becoming deadening clichés through their repetition and, most importantly within commodity culture where 'subversion' carries market value" (xxi).

It was of great interest to me to have this opportunity to encounter a range of contemporary thinking on queer theory. Rather than attempting, in this brief response, to address the richness, diversity and complexity of the papers individually, I have opted to pick up certain of those strands I found most relevant to my thinking and practice, addressing from time to time some of the individual contributions.

Alice A. Kuzniar, in her chapter on identity, "Precarious Sexualities," maps the contested territory between classical psychoanalytic conceptions of sexuality as "stable, fixed and […] identifiable as an integral part of the self" and a definition of queer sexuality as "quintessentially defined by its inexplicability, incoherence, volatility, and contingency." There has been an uneasy oscillation and contestation between similar paradigms within psychoanalysis itself, dating back to Freud's "Three Essays" (1905). He states here that "what is known as normal sexual life" is a consequence of "effective restriction and other kinds of modification" (172), and that heterosexual object love is by no means a natural, inevitable development, but a learned, unstable process (223), and that "the exclusive sexual interest felt by men for women is also a problem that needs elucidating and is not a self evident fact" (145–46). He further challenges commonly-held notions of masculinity and femininity, claiming that it "is essential to understand that the concepts of 'masculine' and 'feminine' whose meaning seems so unambiguous to ordinary people, are among the most confused that occur in science" (219), that "pure masculinity or femininity is not to be found either in a psychological or biological sense," and that bisexuality is the decisive factor" (220) in understanding human sexuality. He startlingly backtracks from these radical insights, however, in proposing the desiring subject as exclusively masculine, and giving an account of female sexuality defined by a shift from active to passive, thus rendering the woman acceptable and desirable to men, who idealize "a woman who holds herself back and denies her sexuality" (221).[1]

Adam Phillips (1996) elaborates the disjunction between what he terms "the Enlightenment Freud," in search of a universal theory of human development and committed to the project of building a strong and undivided ego in his patients, and the "post-Freudian Freud," who "was questioning the very idea of the self as an object of knowledge" (7). The latter was the poet of the divided self, of the unconscious which perpetually destabilizes us and makes us strangers to ourselves. Many other writers have commented on the oscillation between the radical Freud and what we might think of as the panicked Freud, who did not have the courage of his most revolutionary ideas (Dimen 1999; Bersani 1986).

Kuzniar's juxtaposition of such binaries as stable versus mobile and fixed versus fluid, raises again the extraordinary difficulty of escaping the tyranny of binary thinking, and the sense in which queer theory is haunted by the very dualities it seeks to deconstruct. I wonder whether they are inescapable because they form the basis and bedrock of our early mental processes, and carry the traces of the development of our capacity for thinking and representation. Melanie Klein's (1946) concept of the paranoid-schizoid position, which posits a constellation of anxieties and defenses characteristic of early mental life, suggests that such binaries represent the most primitive attempts at differentiation and serve to locate us *vis-à-vis* the other and the environment. And while we may develop more subtle and complex ways of representing ourselves and our experience with what Klein (1935) describes as the depressive position, the capacity to appreciate the ambiguity of the twenty-first century novel co-exists with the enduring appeal in popular culture of

---

1   Many of these quotations appear as footnotes, added at various dates. There is something extraordinary about the abundance of footnotes in this text (88 in a work of 125 pages), perhaps revealing something of Freud's struggle in getting the full measure of desire, and in particular of female sexuality.

narratives of good and bad, heroes and villains. Adam Phillips (1997) links this dualistic logic with the fact that:

[I]n one way or another [...] there are only two sexes. [...] Starting with two sexes, as we must — described as opposites or alternatives or complements — locks us into a logic, a binary system that often seems remote from lived and spoken experience and is complicit with the other binary pairs — inside/outside, primary process/secondary process, sadism/masochism, and so on — that are such a misleading part of psychoanalytic language. We should be speaking of paradoxes and spectrums, not contradictions and mutual exclusions. (158)

Quoting David Halperin's (1995) definition of queer as "by definition whatever is at odds with the normal, the legitimate, the dominant" (62), Kuzniar introduces a difficulty inherent in all categories, suggesting the potential for queer to become another category of the kind it calls into question, and further that it depends on its relationship to a category of the normal and the legitimate for its existence, since outside that relationship there is "nothing in particular to which it refers. It is an identity without an essence" (62).

Lisa Downing, introducing her chapter on perversion, also contrasts queer with psychoanalytic thinking on sexuality: "for queer theorists, especially following Michel Foucault, sexuality is a constructed epistemological category that functions to normalize the behaviours and bodies of social subjects [...] it is a pervasive and power-laden lie to be exposed." For psychoanalysts, "it is a source of truth to be tapped," "Queer takes the theory of performativity as its explicatory model to account for the ways in which subjects learn to 'do' their genders and sexualities."

She highlights and critiques the paradoxical binary thinking I commented on above, focusing on a pair of concepts that are central to both psycho-analytic and queer thinking on sexuality and its perverse forms — namely *fixity* and *fluidity*. She sees the privileging of the idea of fluidity in queer theory as a deficiency, referencing Brad Epps who proposes that it is the *fetish* of queer thinking: "Privileging the concept of fluidity leads to a concomitant stigmatization of the idea of fixity, establishing an unhelpful binary in a body of thought that usually attempts to deconstruct such dualities." She argues convincingly that this imposes on queer thought a programmatic tyranny that runs counter to the epistemological and political aims of queer theory.

Downing's critique extends to the prescriptive tendencies within queer theory that I noted in *Gender Trouble,* remarking that:

> [I]t becomes a discourse in which the ghost of what it disavows — normalization — returns surreptitiously in the prescription to desire appropriately, plurally, fluidly and openly. The embalmed object of fixity haunts the queer position behind the shiny fetish of fluidity that it promotes.

The "exemplary plural subject" proposed in queer theory, appears "performing the right number of appropriately dissident and different sexual practices in the correctly plural and queer relationship configuration."

In his mostly appreciative commentary on "Melancholy Gender" in *The Psychic Life of Power* (Butler 1997), Adam Phillips makes a similar point:

> Butler [invites us] to multiply our versions of self as some kind of psychic necessity, as though we might not be able to bear the loss of not doing so. But how many lives can the analyst recognise in, or demand of, his patient, and what are the constraints on this recognition that so easily becomes a demand? (156)

Charles Levin (2004), in his paper "Sexuality as Masquerade," discusses David Cronenberg's *M. Butterfly,* a film adapted from a play by David Henry Hwang. It is loosely based on a spy scandal involving a French diplomat (M. Gallimard) who was stationed in mainland China in the 1950s, and who became sexually involved, and obsessed with a Chinese Communist spy (Song Liling), a singer with the Chinese Opera. The film and the play, with which I am more familiar, offer a powerful exploration of gender performativity and the enigma of desire.[2] Song was actually a man impersonating a woman, and apparently succeeded in concealing this fact from Gallimard throughout their intimate relationship. Levin comments on the difficulty of determining "the nature of the gender relationship in the actual sexual encounter:

[N]ot just referring to the fact that Song is masquerading as a woman, which is confusing enough, but also to the much more profound sense in which Gallimard may be impersonating a man. [...] Is this a man with a woman, or a man with a man, or a man pretending to be a man with a man pretending to be a woman. (121)

Levin refers to the impenetrability of the psyche and the hidden fantasies that render the actual anatomy no more revealing of the truth than the costumes. It is only many years later, at the espionage trial, that Gallimard is forced to confront what he had disavowed about the nature of their relationship. At the end of the play and film, imprisoned for revealing state secrets, Gallimard commits suicide while performing the role of Madame Butterfly for the other inmates. Levin comments:

Having given himself over entirely to the pursuit of Song, the impossible realization of his unconscious sexuality, he has no choice in the end but to turn himself into the object of that sexual desire, to actually become *my butterfly,* and to kill the elusive butterfly [...] himself.

---

2   The film *M. Butterfly* was directed by David Cronenberg and released in 1993; the play of the same name was by David Hwang, based on Puccini's opera.

> Our temptation to believe that the enigma inhabiting the soul [...] can be found and resolved in a figure of the real world [...] is very great. The logic of submitting to this sublime lure is to undertake, wittingly or unwittingly, the arrangements for the destruction and disposal of the self and its social representative, the ego. (125)

What, then, can the psychoanalyst bring back to the clinic from the encounter with queer theory? Most centrally, I think, a renewed recognition of the ethical imperative of acknowledging and confronting the fact that psychoanalysis, in common with all institutionalized bodies of knowledge and practice, is embedded in a web of cultural, social and political regimes of power. That we are always at risk of participating in regimes of discipline, regulation, and control, and, through enforcing or upholding corrective, conventional, prescriptive and normative approaches to human subjectivity, of becoming agents of oppression.

Butler's (1997) reminder "we are never one thing or another, but a miscellany" (84) recalls us to Freud's claim that the unconscious always speaks more than one dialect and restores our sense that we are not just one thing and that we have more than one thing to say. As Jack Halberstam (2005) observes, "The power of Butler's work [...] lies in her ability to show how much has been excluded, rejected, and abjected in the formation of human community, and what toll those exclusions take on particular subjects" (153).

However, while many individuals in the clinic present narratives of suffering from the oppression of sexist, homophobic, racist and restrictive regimes of control and authority, my view of what it means to be human does not permit me to hope that even the most benign social and political conditions will offer a cure for human misery. While oppressive regimes must and should be contested, the human subject remains fundamentally tragic, subject to loss, lack and contingency. In an effort to evade the psychic pain of facing loss, limitation and ultimately, mortality, many analysands have restricted their own possibilities through constriction and sterile repetition. To quote Adam Phillips (1996), "Psychoanalytic theory is a theory of the unbearable, of what one prefers not to know" (13).

Desire remains stubbornly elusive, anarchic, enigmatic and resistant to agendas of improvement. It in no way undermines the ethical imperative of social and political engagement to bear in mind the paradox that while social approval and permission may have a bearing on the possibilities of pleasure, desire refuses to be tamed or domesticated. It continues to be tantalized and thrilled by what is forbidden, dangerous and subversive. As Katherine Bond Stockton reminds us in her chapter on *jouissance,* "sex is queer — riddling, elusive, excessive, and estranging — for anyone, for everyone." In the words of that bard of melancholy, (Leonard Cohen) "there ain't no cure for love."

While some women and men who engage in a range of non-normative sexual behavior suffer primarily as a result of social oppression, exclusion, and often additionally from the punishment inflicted internally by a cruel and harsh superego, others enter analysis in the hope of finding relief from the torment of compulsive wishes, fantasies and behavior that they find morally repugnant, in conflict with their ethics, dangerous, or conflicting with and threatening other valued aspects of their lives. Others suffer because the restrictiveness and fragility of a particular sexual scenario makes it difficult for them to enjoy a desired — by them — mutuality and playfulness in their sexual encounters.

It can be even more difficult for a self-identified homosexual man or woman in a satisfactory relationship to face up to and acknowledge the emergence of heterosexual attraction, than for their heterosexual counterpart. This is understandable in terms of what has often been the cost of acknowledging and claiming their homosexual identity in the first place.

The challenge for contemporary psychoanalysis must be to remain committed to what is unique and particular in the individual subject, to the slow and careful work of allowing her to symbolize in language previously unrepresented, conflictual, forbidden or disavowed wishes, desires and thoughts, and to face and bear the previously evaded psychic pain of lack, loss and limitation. What is at stake is what Heaney (1995) also claims for poetry, the possibility that "consciousness can be alive to the different and contradictory dimensions of reality and still find a way of negotiating between them" (xv). Psychoanalysis is in a unique position to "provide the conditions where," to quote Heaney again, "*lacrimae rerum,* the tears of things, can be absorbed and re-experienced" (xv).

And the redress of which Heaney speaks is nothing less than "a glimpsed alternative, a revelation of potential that is denied or constantly threatened by circumstances" (4). Psychoanalysis, like poetry, speaks to "the continual need we experience to recover a past or prefigure a future .... [offering] a sensation of arrival and of prospect" (9). When the language of psychoanalysis fails me, or has becomes over-saturated, I turn to poetry to re-articulate where it is I want to situate myself in the uncertain but privileged encounter that is the analytic project — "a place where the co-ordinates of the imagined correspond to and allow us to contemplate the complex burden of our own experience" (10).

Wilfred Bion (1970) reminded us that certainty is the enemy of psychoanalysis, and quoting another poet (John Keats) recommended the cultivation of negative capability, the ability to bear "being in uncertainties, mysteries, doubts, without any irritable reaching after fact or reason" (125). Poetry, like psychoanalysis, may be subject to expectations or demands that operate in a different territory: "[the activist] will always want the redress of poetry to be an exercise of revenge on behalf of *their* point of view" (Heaney 1995, 5).

Relatively recently, the spread of new media and the internet was being hailed as the development that would loosen the hold of repressive regimes on their subjects — acts of oppression could no longer be kept secret, tyranny would be exposed, and people increasingly free to protest. That was a grave underestimation of the capacity of oppressive regimes to infiltrate and appropriate developments in technology and society. As it turns out, it is considerably more efficient and cost effective, to gather information via Facebook and other social media, than through traditional methods of surveillance.

Many colleagues have concurred with my own observation that, increasingly, the sexual difficulties one encounters in the clinic today relate not so much to forbidden or transgressive desires, but to the absence or lack of sexual desire and libido. Under the more subtle tyranny of global capitalism, faced with the increasing commodification of our most intimate wants, needs, desires, and preferences, it might not be surprising if, when we are invited to choose from the menu of possibilities and "choices" available to us, we should say, with Melville's Bartleby, "I would prefer not to" (1987, 22).

In *Bartleby, the Scrivener,* Melville renders the dilemma of a subject so radically trapped in the tyranny of regimes of circulation that from the beginning he is a spectral presence, until he takes his refusal to its ultimate conclusion, since there is no "outside" to the circuits of exchange he wishes to escape.

Since psychoanalysis concerns itself with individual subjectivity, we might hope that it can offer those with whom we have the privileged and unique conversation that defines the analytic relationship "a fleeting glimpse of a potential order of things *beyond confusion,* a glimpse that has to be its own reward" (Heaney 1995, xv).

Works Cited

Bersani, Leo. *The Freudian Body.* New York: Columbia University Press, 1986.

Butler, Judith. *Gender Trouble: Feminism and the Subversion of Identity.* 2nd ed. New York: Routledge, 1999.

———. *Gender Trouble: Feminism and the Subversion of Identity.* London and New York: Routledge, 1990.

Dimen, Muriel. "Between Lust and Libido: Sex, Psychoanalysis, and the Moment Before." *Psychoanalytic Dialogues* 9 (1999): 415–40.

Freud, Sigmund. "Three Essays on the Theory of Sexuality" (1905). In *The Standard Edition of the Complete Psychological*

Works of Sigmund Freud, vol. 7, trans. James Strachey in collaboration with Anna Freud and assisted by Alix Strachey and Alan Tyson, 123–245. 1953; rpt. London: Vintage, 2001.

Halberstam, Jack. *In a Queer Time and Place: Transgender Bodies, Subcultural Lives.* New York: New York University Press, 2005.

Halperin, David M. *Saint Foucault: Towards a Gay Hagiography.* New York: Oxford University Press, 1995.

Heaney, Seamus. *The Redress of Poetry.* London: Faber and Faber, 1995.

Klein, Melanie. "Notes on Some Schizoid Mechanisms." *International Journal of Psycho-Analysis* 27 (1946): 99–110.

———. "A Contribution to the Psychogenesis of Manic-Depressive States." *International Journal of Psycho-Analysis* 16 (1935): 145–74.

Levin, Charles. "Sexuality as Masquerade: Reflections on David Cronenberg's M. Butterfly." *Canadian Journal of Psychoanalysis* 12 (2004): 115–27.

Melville, Herman. "Bartleby the Scrivener: A Story of Wall Street." In *The Writings of Herman Melville,* vol. 9, eds. Harrison Hayford, Alma A. McDougall, and G. Thomas Tanselle, 13–45. Chicago: Northwestern University Press, 1987.

M. Butterfly, dir. David Cronenberg (1993).

Phillips, Adam. "Keeping It Moving." In *The Psychic Life of Power* by Judith Butler, 152–59. Stanford: Stanford University Press, 1997.

———. *Terrors and Experts.* Cambridge: Harvard University Press, 1996.

Rowe, John Carlos. *Through the Custom-House: Nineteenth-Century American Fiction and Modern Theory.* Baltimore: Johns Hopkins University Press, 1982.

10

Queer Directions from Lacan

Ian Parker

Queer functions at its most radical as an activity rather than as a noun, and, as many queer activists have noticed, the reduction to noun-form threatens to sediment what queer "is," especially to sediment it in the adaptable identities that neoliberal heteropatriarchal capitalism now works with so well. So, "to queer" as an intervention, as transformational process, already transcends the opposition between noun and verb while refusing to rest, refusing to accept a transcendent position that pretends to have escaped that opposition. Three moments in this transformational process, in a little history of queer, lead us directly to psychoanalysis, perhaps back to the psychoanalysis from which it first sprung, but with which, against which, queer has an uncannily-appropriate suspicious relationship.

The first moment rehearses the unravelling of binary oppositions that secure sexual identity in ostensibly biologically-wired distinctions between "males" and "females" and in gender categories that either replicate these distinctions or surreptitiously confirm their value. First wave queer, which was also a sublation of first and second wave feminism and pulsed through third wave feminism, took another binary opposition that underpins the relationship between man and woman — that between heterosexuals faithful to the coupling of one of each and homosexuals preferring one to the other — and emptied our attachment to our objects of at least that potent ideological content. Lesbian and gay activism underpinned much of what was queer in this first moment, and it also questioned what straights took to be "same-sex" and showed that every sexual relationship is structured and inhabited by what is "other" to it.

The second moment, already coterminous with the first for many authors and readers of the key queer texts, saw the implications of the critique of heteronormative sex, gender and sexual orientation realized in political action. It has been from the political dynamic of queer that signifiers such as "bisexual" and "transgender," to note but two, have enrolled many more curious allies, including from feminism and even the left, so binary oppositions that also underpin colonialism and racialization could be cracked open. This working through of queer, a comprehension of what had begun to be articulated which was grounded in practice, disturbed the opposition between "queer theory" and the movement which gave it body, gave it life. Proliferation of queer through the academic and sub-cultural political landscape now takes it to a third moment in which we might conclude what it means for us now as something rather singular, if not also at the same moment, perhaps, universal.

The question psychoanalysts face now, one that not everyone faces but which does have a bearing on what they might expect to find in analysis, is how to manage what is referred to in the Anglo-American tradition of psychoanalysis as the "boundary" between the inside and outside of the clinic. Are the rippling effects of queer as theory and practice to be channeled into first wave feminist demands for the rights of women, and now of those claiming rights as "queer" to be represented in the training of analysts and access to therapy? Are queer claims as to the nature of shifts in sexual orientation to be contained by second wave feminist arguments that what is personal is always-already a version of a political question? Or are the distinctions between clinical space and public space themselves to be queered, to be viewed as problematic distinctions that maintain the questionable integrity of the individual talking about itself to one other supposed to know?

One might imagine that Lacanian psychoanalysis would open its doors to a queering of the boundaries that define clinical space, keen to disrupt such boundaries between "inside" and "outside" the consulting room. A line runs through Lacan's own work, from the early engagement and then reformulation of "intersubjectivity" to the argument that the unconscious is the discourse of the Other, from the "extimate" status of the object *a* to the Moebius strip as image of the shifting status of inner and outer domains of the subject. This line redraws the boundaries of psychoanalysis so that the "subject" no longer corresponds to the individual, and this divided subject then becomes the site of an act that could be that of one or two or more bodies. On condition that this encounter is not reduced to two, any more than psychoanalysis reduces itself to the therapeutic adjustment of one, the analysand, to what they think they know about their sex.

However, the conditions of possibility that makes sex — heterosex, homosex, bisex, intersex — less personal are that the analyst is installed as subject "supposed to know" and that this figure is coated and then stripped of personal characteristics that enable the transference to work and be worked through. This means that the clinical "frame" is crucial to the work, and it is only against the frame that transgressions of it become disturbing, enervating, and fruitful. A variable length session, for example, provokes a degree of anxiety and urgency that has some calculated and some unpredictable effects by virtue of its organization around a nominal length of time for the session as such. This is a conceptual practical innovation that we learnt from Lacan, but it does not mean that we thereby simply repeat, even less imitate him when we "cut" a session and thereby mark an opposition between the inside and outside of the clinic. We do not as a rule, for example, follow Lacan's occasional practice of leaving the door of the consulting room open during a session, for while this would make what goes on between analyst and analysand public — at least to those in the waiting area — it would do so in a conventional rather than queer way.

Psychoanalytic space actually has to mark itself out against a public sphere in which psychoanalysis, for some, for many, forms a conventionalized grammar in which individual subjects speak about themselves and try to define who they are. For some subjects in some places, there is now more psychoanalytic discourse outside the clinic than inside it, a discourse that saturates the way we account for misdemeanors and reflect on what we want, that infiltrates a sense that what we do and feel are not what they seem and that there is something unconscious at play. The danger is that the success of psychoanalysis thereby becomes its undoing, for as a discourse it then turns from being a clinical practice into a worldview, which is something that Freud warned against but which many psychoanalysts have been keen to embrace. It is when psychoanalytic discourse sucks lesbian and gay activists into it as a worldview that it takes shape as something normative, which is then, of course, antithetical to queer. This is when it also sabotages ostensibly queer-friendly psychoanalysis, embedding interpretative activity in well-meaning therapeutic support for alternative life-styles which then reduce ethics to what the analyst believes to be right and wrong. A psychoanalytic worldview may not be a bad one, but it is then ideology not analysis, it maintains a frame instead of working inside a frame to shake things up. It repeats rather than questions psychoanalytic discourse as such.

This psychoanalytic discourse is fractured and politically ambiguous, at one moment reinforcing the taken-for-granted sexual division of labor and pathologizing sexual orientations that do not correspond to that sexual division, and at the next disconnecting sex from gender and sexuality from sex-role so as to pathologize those who shut out fantasy and reclaim the unconscious in different forms of counterdiscourse. This is one reason why the queering of sexuality as a historically-constituted epistemological category "becomes a discourse in which the ghost of what it disavows — normalization — returns surreptitiously in the prescription to desire appropriately plurally, fluidly and openly" (Downing, this volume). Queer theory repeats psychoanalytic rhetoric because it is embedded in that rhetoric as a pre-existing discursive frame; this is what will lead some writers to claim that "psychoanalysis is arguably already queer" (Stockton, this volume), or that "Lacanian theory lies at the heart of much queer thought" (Bond Stockton, this volume).

This much is evident in the oscillation between fixed point and free play, between "fixity and fluidity" (Downing) in queer discourse, a replication of conceptual anchor points in psycho-analytic theory — the Oedipus complex, the Name-of-the-Fa-ther — that were always in tension with the hope that the flow of discourse would itself provide some kind of freedom, as "talking cure" or "speaking well." The attempt to recruit Donald Winni-cott as "the father of queer theory" (Snediker, this volume), for example, requires that we resignify "Winnicott" after treating him as one of the "squiggles" for which he has become known, for it is only after this reconfiguration of him as a site of "onto-logical indeterminacy" (Snediker) that it is possible to pin him down again somewhere else. Another attempt has its sights on Jean Laplanche as an unwitting avatar of queer, but it seems that he will not himself provide the "inexplicability, incoherence, volatility, and contingency" (Kuzniar, this volume) that is asked of him; instead, for that, we are asked to turn to a creature more biddable, and look to "the unconditional nature of the dog's af-fection of its human companion" (Kuzniar). For some it could be love of a good dog, or, for others, it could be love of God which would, it is true, bring him closer to Lacan, with or with-out Luce Irigaray, as a "lacking that is a having," "the wound of our relations but also the only hope for the lack that, fracturing us, allows us to touch ourselves" (Bond Stockton). The queer turn could, some hope, entail a celebration of "intoxication," the hope that the analyst might be "drunk on love" (Farina, this vol-ume), which would at least be better than mainstream psychoa-nalysis in the English-speaking world which seems to be drunk on knowledge.

We must now, as we have for some time with respect to psy-choanalytic discourse, attend to queer discourse that circulates in the public sphere, circulates in some forms in opposition to psychoanalysis and in some forms intertwined with it. What was said of psychiatric categories of sexual disorder — perversion and suchlike — was always as important, if not more important than what psychiatrists actually believed, for what was said always entered into the clinic as an explanation and position for the subject. Now the psychoanalyst needs to know what is said of the different "affective communities" that are available as symbolic forms to which the analysand may attach themselves, this as much as they needed to know something about the nature of the family.

So, inside the clinic Lacanians refuse to feed psychoanalytic discourse with a series of well-rehearsed interpretations that whet the appetite of the analysand for more of the same, that merely serve to keep the unconscious busy with the rhetorical forms that it enjoys so much in the outside world. Psychoanalysis did, once upon a time, frustrate the demands of the analysand for advice, and the explanations elaborated along with interpretation were out of kilter with commonsense enough for them to queer as well as normalize the subject. Now psychoanalysis, paradoxically, needs to frustrate the demand of the analysand for more of what they already know of themselves from psychoanalytic discourse, to "cut" that discourse and so re-mark the frame of the clinic in order to make it function as a queer space.

Let us turn to a clinical case to illustrate how the psychoanalytic frame permits a number of different moves, and how the analyst holds the frame so that what happens is what the analysand makes of it. This case is one of the very few of his own that Lacan describes, which may in a curious way be a function of the complex boundaries he needed to draw between his "private" practice and "public" teaching. The case is itself framed by the paper in which it is contained, "The Direction of the Treatment and the Principles of Its Power," in which Lacan (2006[1958]) argues against directing the patient and so also against molding the patient to any particular predictable psychoanalytic discourse.

At first sight the scenario is really quite straight, and classically psychoanalytic. An obsessional neurotic who once suffered the conflicts between his parents is now impotent with his mistress, but a dream then becomes the scene for an image of a phallus which then reenergizes him, reawakens his desire. The inclusion of the case in a psychoanalytic paper by Lacan is also very conventional. Narrative as such is reassuring to a subject, suturing a place for the subject from which they spin a story about where they have come from and where they are going. In psychoanalytic case reports, narrative slots us into a linear track which takes us from a critique and a problem to an example and lessons for good theory and practice. And it works all the better if it is the type of case that psychoanalytic readers will recognize and feel comfortable with. They already know what an obsessional neurotic is — one of the least queer characters to appear in the clinic — and so the clinical account replicates, in a clear self-contained narrative, the nature of the analysand described there.

A little more detail will help us begin to unravel this account. Lacan tells us that this analysand had at least come to recognize "the part he had played in the destructive game foisted by one of his parents on the other parent's desire" (526), but he does not tell us which parent is responsible; the issue here is that the analysand is starting to see how his desire is enmeshed in the desire of the Other: "He surmised his powerlessness to desire without destroying the Other, thus destroying his own desire insofar as it was the Other's desire" (526). There has already, it seems, been a hystericization of the analysand, a shift from obsessional position in the treatment and then, beyond that, a questioning of a typical hysteric's attempt to put all the blame on others. Note that this shift of position from stereotypically-masculine position — as obsessional neurotic — to stereotypically-feminine position, particularly in relation to a man, is something quite queer that happens in every analysis.

The analysand appears to be well-enough versed in psychoanalytic discourse to believe that his impotence might have something to do with "repressed homosexuality" and that if he can persuade his mistress to sleep with another man this might reactivate his libido. Lacan comments that he refuses to play along with these ideas, with "the demand for fables ... sated with the truths spread by analysis itself" (527). He does not feed this psychoanalytic discourse with interpretations that will satisfy his analysand, and in fact Lacan does not report anything he says at all. Perhaps he merely shrugs and demurs to agree with his analysand. Instead, Lacan describes a dream that the mistress has the night after the analysand "suggested that she sleep with another man to see": "In the dream she had a phallus — she sensed its shape under her clothing — which did not prevent her from having a vagina as well, nor, especially, from wanting this phallus to enter it" (527). This does the trick, for on hearing the dream "my patient's powers were immediately restored and he demonstrated this brilliantly" (527). He performed "brilliantly," Lacan says, "to his shrewd paramour," which raises a question about who was performing what for whom in this little game.

It should be said that a male analysand successfully treated by a male psychoanalyst for impotence with a female partner can be rendered into something queer. It certainly is not queer if gender positions are mapped directly onto the sexed bodies of those involved, even less so if sexual orientation is viewed as corresponding to those positions and bodies and as requiring some kind of correspondence between them, what Lacan will later speak of and refuse as "sexual rapport." How might it be queer? The key lies in the subversion of the subject of these statements about sexuality that are relayed through the representation of the case. Not in the description or knowledge that we obtain from the case but in the position of the subject in relation to that knowledge. It is the mistress who has the dream, and so the phallic powers that were "immediately restored" to the analysand opens up yet more questions about the terms in which his performance of masculinity was successful.

The phallus here is not possessed outright by the analysand, but is the semblance of power dreamt into being by another, a woman. Lacan comments that the dream and "its effect on my patient" was "an opportunity to get the patient to grasp the function the phallus as a signifier serves in his desire" (528), and the man is confronted with his desire to "be" the phallus — a normatively feminine position — rather than to "have" it, as normatively masculine; the mistress's "desire yields to his desire here, by showing him what she does not have" (528). We are therefore faced here with the separation of sexed subject from that which they perform "as if" they were a sexed subject, with the performance and reiteration of sex as "drag," which, remember, for queer theorists also includes the drag performance of men and women playing at being the men and women of their conventionally-assigned sex.

The odds are that this obsessional character will himself stumble upon the rock of castration at some point in his analysis, and this will keep him locked on the side of the man keen to hold on to what he has of the phallus and reassuring himself that even if he does not have complete mastery there is some man somewhere who does have it and in whose image he can keep himself together. Or, as subject he might or might not conclude from this episode that he is not the "man" he thought himself to be, and the space is opened up for a different outcome in which there is a shift from one kind of gender identification to another or beyond to something altogether more queer. Among the lessons of "The Direction of the Treatment" is that the analyst does not pretend to know how things should end up. This is why Lacanians do not, as a rule, interpret the transference, and in this case Lacan speaks instead of "exhausting [...] all the artifices of verbalization that distinguished the other from the Other" (526), by which he seems to mean that the mother is distinguished from the father and the performance of a relation to one or the other is no longer for the analyst as Other in the "spectator's box" (526).

If queer operates as an ideal, whether as an identity or affective community, fixity or fluidity, it will start to function ideologically rather than as a critique of ideology outside of the clinic. It will also threaten the space of the clinic itself, and this through recruitment of psychoanalysts who may be tempted to inject their own ideological suppositions into the speech of their analysands. This is why we do not treat Lacan as an "example" of a queer intervention in psychoanalysis, but rather as a discourse through which we might trace our own queer line, or not. Lacan was no friend of feminism, but, by the same token, and partly as a function of the elision of feminism and femininity in most French psychoanalysis, no friend of normative femininity, still less of normative femininity inside the clinic. He is not "social" in his approach nor is he "anti-social," and so Lacanian psycho-analysis need not be mired in a peculiar binary opposition of those two signifiers that informs queer theory today. If Lacan-ian psychoanalysis is treated as a clinical strategy instead of a worldview, then it is possible to make something radical with that strategy, to make of it a place where we are freer in our tac-tics than other types of psychoanalysis, potentially a good deal queerer in our practice for that.

Work Cited

Lacan, Jacques. "The Direction of the Treatment and the Principles of its Power" (1958). In *Écrits: The First Complete Edition in English,* trans. Bruce Fink in collaboration with Héloïse Fink and Russell Grigg. New York: Norton, 2006.

11

Queer Theory Meets Jung

Claudette Kulkarni

Introduction

I will begin by disclosing my own prejudices since they surely have shaped my reactions to these chapters.

Psychological Prejudices. In spite of the sexism, heterosexism, and racism that invade Carl Jung's theorizing, I am a Jungian — or, more accurately, a post-Jungian[1] — and a feminist. The challenge for me as a lesbian Jungian has been *not* to defend, reinterpret, contort, or reformulate Jung and his theories — but, rather, to use Jung, often against himself, in ways that seem "truly Jungian" and thus, hopefully, to follow through on the "subversive possibility that Jung opens up" (Samuels 1989, tape) when we take him "beyond" himself.

Philosophical Horizons. My reading in queer theory has been motivated mainly by the work of Judith Butler and has focused on queer theory's usefulness in understanding LGBTQI experience in a heterosexist and genderized world. My philosophical prejudices derive from the work of Hans-Georg Gadamer, especially his approach to hermeneutics and the problem of understanding.

---

1 A term coined by Andrew Samuels (1985) "to indicate both connectedness to Jung and distance from him" (19).

Problems with Freudian Psychoanalysis. Reading Freudian psychoanalytic theory does not come easily to me, so the most challenging aspect of writing this response has been to negotiate the language of Freudian thought, especially as it gets morphed through French psychoanalysis. While I sincerely appreciate Freud, as most Jungians do, the language of Freudian discourse simply does not speak to me — as a person, as a lesbian, or as a Jungian. Its focus on sexuality seems too reductive and universalizing, and its male-centered explanatory principles not very explanatory. Undoubtedly, my resistances will show as I attempt to engage with the viewpoints expressed in the chapters in the first section of this book, as will my dependence on each writer's interpretation of their favored theorists. All of which leads me to this question: Is psychoanalysis always and only Freudian? That seems to be the consensus of these writers. While it *might* be true, as some claim, that Freudian psychoanalysis offers the only systematic theory of desire, I do not believe that Freudian thought equals psychoanalysis, nor that Freudian psychoanalysis is capable of theorizing sexualities other than heterosexuality — and I am not sure it does that very well.

My Dilemma as a Therapist. The concept of "perversion," as it is discussed in these chapters and in queer thought, often comes into conflict with my own current context, namely, my clinical work with convicted sex offenders. While the lesbian part of me is delighted with the idea of challenging sexual norms, the therapist side of me fears that this cannot be done adequately without addressing the issue of sexually-offending behaviors. While some of the writers in this volume hint at this problem, none address it.

Logistical Limits. With all of this as a backdrop and given space restrictions, I have opted to focus on the three chapters that deal with identity, desire, and perversion.

Identity: A Concept in Need of Expansion

I welcome the efforts of some queer theorists, like Alice Kuzniar, to incorporate the unconscious into theory making. However,

Kuzniar's suggested alternative to traditional Freudian theory, namely, the theory of Jean Laplanche, seems as problematic to me as the theory she wants to supplant, i.e., "the Oedipal narrative of identity formation" (Kuzniar, this volume). The problem from my perspective is that Laplanche continues the conflation of sexuality with identity. Limiting identity to sex/ual/ity is actually what makes the concept of identity so justifiably vulnerable to queer critique. Sex/ual/ity is one vital subset of identity, but it sits alongside many other aspects of human existence. So, while the concept of *das Andere* would pose no problem for many Jungians — since it seems to parallel Jung's idea of anima/animus (the "contrasexual" other in the unconscious) — Laplanche's continuation of a sexualized unconscious is as problematic as Jung's genderizing of it (Kulkarni 1997). While we cannot take the sex out of sex/ual/ity, it does not follow that sex/ual/ity is *only* about sex. If queer "is an identity without essence" (Kuzniar, quoting David Halperin), why would we restrict it to sex/ual/ity? Laplanche's de-genderizing of the Oedipal scene *might* be sufficient to allow "the child's imagination" to fantasize "gender variation" (Kuzniar), but it still does not relativize the role of sex in identity formation. In fact, Laplanche's theory seems centered on sex/ual/ity at the exclusion of all else. At one point, Kuzniar does mention the parent's "sexual unconscious," as if hinting that the unconscious might include other aspects, but she never makes this explicit. And is sex really so enigmatic — or do we make it so by our theorizing? Is homosexuality *really* so different from heterosexuality (other than in defying societal norms)? Are all sexualities *really* so problematic that we need elaborate theories to justify *every* manifestation of human diversity?

When Kuzniar argues that "all identity, seen as an attempt at self-centering, will necessarily be destabilized by the unconscious," she is acknowledging, perhaps inadvertently, that there is *something there to be destabilized*. She implies, however, that because identity is always being destabilized, attempts at identity formation are somehow fruitless. From a Jungian perspective, however, it is precisely these efforts at identity formation (i.e., at integrating split-off aspects of oneself) that make decentering possible. This never-ending process is, by its very "nature," fluid. It becomes rigid only if one refuses to individuate, that is, when "the impervious ego [...] clings to" old identity labels (Kuzniar). But the ego is not always impervious. However we conceptualize it, the function we call "the ego" plays a vital role in terms of consciousness and reflects the individual's capacity to differentiate her/himself from the collective (something essential to feeling queer). But perhaps this is a difference between the Jungian ego and the Freudian ego.

In any case, Kuzniar seems to settle for declaring this entire process a failure and turns to Jacqueline Rose for support:

> The unconscious constantly reveals the "failure" of identity. Because there is no continuity of psychic life, so there is no stability of sexual identity, no position [...] which is ever simply achieved. [...] "Failure" is not a moment to be regretted in identity: [...] "failure" is something endlessly repeated and relived [...] [T]here is a resistance to identity at the very heart of psychic life. (Kuzniar, quoting Rose)

Significantly, Rose puts "failure" in quotes, signaling recognition of the importance of *attempting* to build an identity, even if it is an endless process. However, where Rose claims that "there is no continuity of psychic life," I contend that the endless process she describes *is* the evidence of continuity; and where she imagines this process as "a resistance to identity," I envision it as a resistance to a *fixed* identity, so that this resistance, paradoxically, embodies the very "essence" of identity.

While Jung did not expound a formal theory of identity formation, he did posit that we come into the world with the seed of a personality/identity that develops/individuates over the individual's entire lifetime in a never-ending movement toward an ever-expanding and always "becoming" sense of self. This process, undergone in response to an "inner necessity" (Jung CW7[1970], para. 369), is fueled by the continual tension between the ego (the center of consciousness) and the unconscious (particularly the archetypal Self — the Jungian equivalent of "the Other who 'wants' something of me" (Kuzniar, quoting Laplanche) — which presses the ego into its service). For Jung, the unconscious is "creative in character" (CW11[1969], para. 875), a kind of fountainhead of possibilities that are *both* productive *and* destructive. So, while the unconscious is "other" in one sense — it includes unintegrated qualities that one must integrate in order to individuate — in another way, the unconscious also *is* me and, so, is not so "other" at all.

My post-Jungian understanding of identity is like Butler's idea of "queer": "never fully owned, but always and only redeployed, twisted, queered" (Kuzniar, quoting Butler) or Eve Kosofsky Sedgwick's: "continuing moment, movement, motive — recurrent, eddying, troublant" (Kuzniar, quoting Sedgwick). However, to assert that identity must be only fluid is problematic. As a therapist, I have seen what happens when a person is not grounded in a sense of ego/self/identity that is fixed/stable enough to tolerate fluidity. To deconstruct identity, one must first have one. To take that possibility away from others seems to me both elitist and disingenuous. Individuation proceeds when one holds the tension between what Jung calls "the opposites" (a concept I do not take literally but understand as a tug-of-war between divergent forces). According to Jung, "there is no energy" without this tension (CW7[1970], para. 78) and holding it is what allows something else to emerge. So, to deconstruct one's identity, one needs to hold the tension between fixity and fluidity. And because any identity which emerges from this is always already immersed in a never-ending process of adjustment, change, and integration (i.e., individuation), it is full of possibilities. That's the paradox. *Fluidity and fixity need each other.* The tendency of many queer theorists to resist anything "stable," or "fixed" results too often in their taking positions that are just as normalizing, rigid, and absolute — if not quite so stable — as some of the oppressive theories they are attempting to deconstruct.

Kuzniar seems intent on salvaging a place for psychoanalysis in queer theory, asserting that psychoanalysis "adopt or develop hypotheses such as Laplanche's that would help articulate why one feels queer" and asking: "What new vocabulary does psy-choanalysis need to adopt to adequately help women organize their fluid sexual desires?" It seems to me, however, that until someone explains "why" some people "choose" to be heterosex-ual, there is no need to explain "why one feels queer." And while psychoanalysis might do well to adopt a new vocabulary, I do not know why women need to "organize" their desires — much less, why they would need the help of psychoanalysis to do this.

Finally, a comment about Kuzniar's attempt "to draw out the queer implications" of queer theories via a discussion of pet love. In spite of my being an animal lover myself, I did not find this section very convincing. Love of animals certainly can be deeply meaningful and does not fit into any binaries that I know of, sexual or otherwise — but is it "queer" just because it chal-lenges "self-definitions based primarily on sexual preference"? Well, that's my point. Identity comprises more than sex/ual/ity.

Desire: Our Engagement with the World

Lara Farina seems intent on finding a theory of desire that can adequately encompass same-sex desire. She reasons convincing-ly that theories of desire founded on lack are problematic. How-ever, I think she is mistaken in dismissing efforts by some queer theorists to rehabilitate narcissism. She claims that any theory based on a "longing for sameness" (Farina, quoting Leo Bersani) is ethically disconcerting. But why does she equate a desire for sameness with narcissism? There are other ways of theorizing sameness. Two examples: Christine Downing's (1989) idea that same-sex desire be theorized on the basis of "analogy rather than contrast, on mirroring rather than the complementation of opposites" (xvii); and Jungian analyst Lyn Cowan's (2013) re-minder that in alchemy (a major source of inspiration for Jung and Jungian thought) "alchemical conjunctions may happen be-tween 'sames' as well as between 'opposites'" (2).

In any case, Farina finds the work of Elizabeth Grosz to be the most useful in theorizing desire. I was taken by Farina's not-ing that Grosz has provided "a way of thinking about desire in which the body [...] comes first, leading the 'self' along with it as a current of 'continuous excitation' constantly remakes it." This excited my post-Jungian sensibilities because it challenges the traditional psychoanalytic tendency to ignore the lived body and because it hints at an unconscious that functions dialectically, not just from the inside out. In spite of this, however, I am reluctant to privilege any one factor in desire, even the body. I want to propose instead that desire be imagined as a spectrum of factors and modes, *including* lack, and I want to cite Judith Butler as my authority: "I think that crafting a sexual position [...] always involves becoming haunted by what's excluded. And the more rigid the position, the greater the ghost, and the more threatening in some way" (Downing, this volume, quoting Butler).

Like Grosz, I do not see why queer theorists would want to devise a unified theory of desire. If the task of queer theory is "the queering *of desire*" by "the dismantling of sexual norms" (Farina), that cannot be done by establishing a norm that excludes lack just because we do not like it or because it has been used against us. Also, to imply that desire ought to be *only* "productive, rather than the result of negation" (Farina) privileges one side of the opposition and thus misses the possibilities that might be "produced" through holding the tension between them.

Which brings me to the problem that any theory of desire faces: How to understand those forms of desire that go awry and take the path of sexual violence. There *are* "*so-called* sexual perversions," (Farina) but there are also *perverted* desires, sexual or otherwise, what Jung calls "blind instinctuality" (CW8[1969], para. 108). Farina refers to this: "Of course, perverts (homosexuals, fetishists, pedophiles, and others) and women of all kinds don't fit neatly into the most simple formulation of Oedipus." But, while she comments on how psychoanalytic theory has had to contort itself to make room for women, male homosexuals, and fetishists, any similar consideration of pedophiles is noticeably lacking. *This is a major omission.* How can we discuss desire and reclaim certain categories of "perverts" without addressing those whom we, presumably, do not take along with us, and without acknowledging that, at times, desire is expressed in *truly* twisted ways? — that is, without exploring the shadow side of desire?

In comparing desire with intoxication, Farina gives us an enticing image of desire in its ego-dissolving mode — romantic, exciting, passionate — but again fails to explore the shadow side of this image. Instead, she conflates sobriety with pessimism and intoxication with Utopianism. This may be poetic, but it is untenable. Sobriety is not pessimistic or gloomy; it is thoughtful and grounded. Intoxication is not poetic or optimistic; it is dissociated and self-centered. Of course, I am literalizing these states of mind whereas Farina is employing a seemingly playful metaphor, intending, I presume, to evoke a mood of exhilaration. Like any good Jungian, I love metaphors, but this one seems precarious. For example, Farina critiques sobriety because it "wants fixity [...] boundaries" — but doesn't desire *need* boundaries at times? Isn't that a problem of desire gone awry? She also seems to confuse intoxication with inspiration when she implies that intoxication somehow "make[s] room for [the] reader's experience of affect." In reality, intoxication runs roughshod over others, affect and all. And while I can't speak about "the pessimism of Freudian/Lacanian psychoanalysis," Farina's suggestion that we "allow for ways in which the analyst, too, can be drunk on love rather than remain at a remove from the erotic object of analysis" seems to me to mistake drunkenness *for* affect. As a Jungian therapist, I am not "at a remove" from my clients, nor do I see them as "the erotic object of analysis." That, it seems to me, would be just another example of desire gone awry.

Perversion: Is There No Such Thing?

I rather like the idea of redeeming the word "queer." I do not mind twisting it for political purposes (as Butler suggests in 1993, 19). I do not even mind conceiving of it as "perverse," that is, as "a defiant performance of excess that shows up the constructedness and arbitrariness of the category of the 'normal'"

(Downing, this volume). What I do find troubling, however, is the lack of questioning related to how this subversive use of "perverse" can be distinguished from other uses. As someone who has worked clinically and fairly extensively with both the victims and perpetrators of sexual offenses, I would like to know: if everybody is queer and "desire is always perverse," (attributed by Downing to Jacques Lacan/Tim Dean), how do we differentiate the perversions that create victims? While I could argue that such behaviors are not *really*, theoretically, a perversion of *sexual* desire, I could also argue that they are. And although, like Jung, I resist the concept of "normal," I do not think that it is sufficient simply to reclaim, resignify, and celebrate the term "perversion" and re-label certain behaviors as "paraphilias" without somehow addressing that other term: "normal." Maybe there is no such a thing as "normal," but there certainly is something "abnormal" about sexual offending! We need to find some way of differentiating queerly "perverse" behaviors from *really* "deviant" and "abnormal" behaviors. How else can we, ethically, "embrace the energies of the 'perverse'?" In 1914, Jung declared that "We are not yet far enough advanced to distinguish between moral and immoral behaviour in the realm of free sexual activity [...]. All the repulsive hypocrisy [...] we owe to the barbarous, wholesale legal condemnation of certain kinds of sexual behaviour, and to our inability to develop a finer moral sense for the enormous psychological differences that exist in the domain of free sexual activity" (CW4[1970], para. 666). I believe Elizabeth Grosz is challenging us to develop that "finer moral sense" when she suggests that the term "queer" not be used to subsume all "perversions." Sadly, Downing characterizes Grosz's position as "binaristic — and covertly identitarian" and critiques it as "a rather un-queer gesture of hierarchy-of-oppression-building." I think that this is an unfair rendering of Grosz's position and that maligning her thinking simply evades her point: that the universalizing use of "perverse" lumps many people together who ought not be lumped together. For example, it could be argued — perhaps misappropriating Lacan's idea that because there is no gender in the unconscious, there is "no 'proper' object of desire" (Downing) — that pedophiles are simply expressing a unique form of "perverse" desire. I am not claiming that Lacan or any queer theorists believe this. I am only highlighting a problem that Downing gets close to, but does not address: "Queer theory has always had an ambivalent relationship with what — in a different discourse — would be called the perversions or paraphilias [...]. In some ways, non-normative bodily practices (what I do) [...] are the very stuff of queer [...]." I only wish she had examined this "ambivalent relationship" between *problematic* "non-normative bodily practices" and "the very stuff of queer."

On the other hand, I very much admire how Downing challenges the tendency of queer theorists to privilege fluidity and stigmatize fixity, thereby propagating "a strikingly normative directive." She quotes Butler to make her case against this kind of absolutism: "This is not to say that I will not appear at political occasions under the sign of lesbian, but that I would like to have it permanently unclear what precisely that sign signifies" (Downing, quoting Butler). In Jungian terms, Butler is arguing to keep the sign (in this case, *literally* a sign) a symbol:

> A symbol [...] [points] to something not easily defined and therefore not fully known. But the sign always has a fixed meaning, because it is a conventional abbreviation for [...] something known. (CW5[1976], para. 180)

> So long as a symbol is a living thing, it is an expression for something that cannot be characterized in any other or better way. The symbol is alive only so long as it is pregnant with meaning. But once its meaning has been born out of it [...] then the symbol is dead [...]. (CW6[1971], para. 816)

> [It has become] "a mere sign." (CW6[1971], para. 817)

I think this speaks also to the concern expressed by queer theorists, that "as soon as an identification is taken up, that identification stagnates into recognizable meaning" (Downing).

Alluding to Butler's cautionary statement (quoted above) about the ghost of what is excluded, Downing issues a stern warning: as long as queer theory excludes fixity, it "becomes a discourse in which the ghost of what it disavows — normalization — returns surreptitiously in the prescription to desire appropriately plurally, fluidly and openly." She argues against the pathologizing of fixity and in favor of legitimizing "both plurality and singularity, not in a dialectical configuration, but as infinitely equal and different." While I am totally sympathetic to the thrust of this argument, I would point out that legitimizing these opposites is not the same as holding the tension between them because it accepts the underlying binary and thus creates another shadow in which ghosts can lurk.

Downing laments that the stigmatization of fixity "persists in the psychiatric model" and that "[g]eneralizations about personality are adduced from facts [fixations] of sexual behavior." I have no wish to defend psychiatry — and I do not know the source of Downing's opinions about clinical practice — but, as a therapist, I can say that behaviors do indicate something about people and, as a therapist in a forensic unit, I can say that in that context and in real life "perversion" is not defined simply by fixity, but on the basis of criminal behaviors. Nor, in my experience, is it "variety" that has made "sexual behavior and identity acceptable [...] in mental health discourse from the turn of the twentieth- to the turn of the twenty-first centuries" — though perhaps that is true of traditional psychoanalysis? Fixity can be a factor in assessing problem behaviors, e.g., it *can* indicate how difficult it will be for a person to change certain behaviors. On the other hand, to my knowledge, no sex offender has ever used "variety" as a defense.

Downing is right to critique queer theorists, including Butler, for demonizing fixity and idealizing fluidity, but that is not the only problem. Would Butler take the standpoint that "all sexual norms" are doubtful, and suggest that one counter them by "occupying a position that you have just announced to be unthinkable" (Downing, quoting Butler), if we were discussing things like sexual violence and pedophilia?

Downing is persuasive when she argues that fixity be restored to its rightful place as a valid psychological principle. She challenges psychoanalysis to question its prejudice against fixity and to ask itself "what investments are really at stake in making a symptom out of a pleasure." That is a good question — at least as long as the pleasure under consideration *really* is not a symptom. But how do we determine that? How do we know when a pleasure *is* a perversion? What is at stake, at those times, if we do not recognize *that* pleasure as a symptom?

Clinical Application and Conclusions

Although I gratefully acknowledge an intellectual debt to queer theory, and appreciate its power as a form of cultural critique and a tool for self-examination, I must admit that I remain doubtful of its usefulness to clinical practice — *except* in terms of shaping the attitude and thinking of the therapist. The insights of queer theory can inspire the therapist to resist cultural imperatives and to keep an open and questioning mind. That, in turn, can inform how a therapist conceptualizes both the client and the work to be done. In that sense, queer theory has a lot to offer to psychoanalysis and psychotherapy. In other ways, however, queer theory frustrates me — much like it frustrates a good friend of mine, also a therapist, who wrote me that what bothers him is "the mental spinning that seems dislocated from the world that people live in."[2] I guess what I really yearn for are theories and intellectual challenges that hold the tension among all the various factors and concepts while staying grounded in the real world of people's everyday suffering.

So, does psychoanalytic theory have anything to offer queer theorists? I am not sure. Admittedly, I came to this project with some deep reservations about Freudian psychoanalysis and, while I have tried to overcome these, I find myself thinking like Grosz (1995), that "too heavy a reliance on psychoanalytic theory" (167) is problematic:

---

2   Mickey Landaiche, private communication.

While an immense amount of […] feminist thought, ingenuity, and labor has gone into this project of stretching or extending the tolerable boundaries of male discourses so they may be useful for or amenable to feminist projects, the long-term benefits of continuing to prop up or support a discourse which has well-recognized problems are not clear. (167)

Certainly, the writers in the first section of this book have tried to "both face and expose what is problematic about psychoanalytic discourses, and then show that these problems are not so overwhelming that they entail the abandonment of its frame" (167). But, like Grosz, I have concerns about efforts to preserve psychoanalytic theory and continue to grapple with this myself in relation to Jung:

One cannot simply buy into a theoretical system (especially one as complex and as systematically conceived, in spite of its inconsistencies, as psychoanalysis) without at the same time accepting its basic implications and founding assumptions. […] Problematic implications cannot be contained and prevented from infiltrating those considered unproblematic. (168)

I especially share Grosz's concerns "about the capacity of the framework of psychoanalysis to explain precisely that which it must exclude in order to constitute itself as a system or a discourse" (167). I am not arguing that anyone abandon Freud or his theories. I certainly have no intention of discarding Jung. Rather, my hope would be that queer thinkers (with or without the insights of any version of psychoanalysis) focus less on theorizing sex/ual/ity and more on exploring meaning(s), contesting normative assumptions, asking provocative questions, challenging the institutions of compulsory heterosexuality, and wrestling with the problem of perversion.

Works Cited

Butler, Judith. *Bodies that Matter: On the Discursive Limits of "Sex."* London and New York: Routledge, 1993.

Cowan, Lyn. "Dismantling the Animus." On *The Jung Page: Reflections on Psychology, Culture and Life* (2000). http://cgjungpage.org/learn/articles/analytical-psychology/105-dismantling-the-animus?showall=1&limitstart=.

Downing, Christine. *Myths and Mysteries of Same-Sex Love.* New York: Continuum, 1989.

Grosz, Elizabeth. *Space, Time and Perversion: Essays on the Politics of Bodies.* London and New York: Routledge, 1995.

Jung, Carl. *Symbols of Transformation. The Collected Works of C.G. Jung,* vol. 5, eds. Sir Herbert Read, Michael Fordham, and Gerhard Adler, and William McGuire; trans. R.F.C. Hull. Princeton: Princeton University Press, 1976 (1956).

———. *Psychological Types. The Collected Works of C.G. Jung,* vol. 6, eds. Sir Herbert Read, Michael Fordham, and Gerhard Adler, and William McGuire; trans. R.F.C. Hull. Princeton: Princeton University Press, 1971.

———. *Two Essays on Analytical Psychology. The Collected Works of C.G. Jung,* vol. 7, eds. Sir Herbert Read, Michael Fordham, and Gerhard Adler, and William McGuire; trans. R.F.C. Hull. Princeton: Princeton University Press, 1970.

———. *Freud and Psychoanalysis. The Collected Works of C.G. Jung,* vol. 4, eds. Sir Herbert Read, Michael Fordham, and Gerhard Adler, and William McGuire; trans. R.F.C. Hull. Princeton: Princeton University Press, 1970.

———. *The Structure and Dynamics of the Psyche. The Collected Works of C.G. Jung,* vol. 8, eds. Sir Herbert Read, Michael Fordham, and Gerhard Adler, and William McGuire; trans. R.F.C. Hull. Princeton: Princeton University Press, 1969.

———. *Psychology and Religion: West and East. The Collected Works of C.G. Jung,* vol. 11, eds. Sir Herbert Read, Michael Fordham, and Gerhard Adler, and William McGuire; trans. R.F.C. Hull. Princeton: Princeton University Press, 1969.

Kulkarni, Claudette. *Lesbians and Lesbianisms: A Post-Jungian Perspective.* London and New York: Routledge, 1997.

Samuels, Andrew. *Jung and the Post-Jungians.* London: Routledge & Kegan Paul, 1985.

———. "Jung, Anti-Semitism, and the Fuehrerprinzip" (Cassette Recording 4.2.89), Pittsburgh: Pittsburgh Jung Society.

12

Queer Troubles for Psychoanalysis

Carol Owens

As a critical psychologist in Britain in the mid-1990s, I experienced many of the effects that queer theory, critical feminism and post-structuralism had upon social science research and discourse theory at this time. Wide-ranging debates about materialism, essentialism, and biological reductionism revolved around the purloining of the human subject by mainstream social, psychological and biomedical science. The critical project's devotion to decentering the same subject, destabilizing the taken-for-granted, and deconstructing the practices warranted by the mainstream contributed to the writing of thousands of research articles and conference presentations, not to mention hundreds of books and as many careers launched in the mobilization of the critical agenda. My own doctoral work on the examination of "compulsory heterosexuality" at the site of the "couple" as constituted by and within the psy-discourses was typical for the time. People like me were usually referred to disparagingly within the mainstream as "social constructionists" or worse "constructivists." We moved through our doctoral years occasionally caught up with dilemmas over relativism which would spur a whole other rake of research articles and papers dedicated to the declaring of the reality of death, the holocaust, and furniture. Some of us were labelled "critical realists" when we got too concerned about the political, "unreconstructed feminists" when we worried overly about "woman," and unreflexive allegiance to any of the great "isms" (Marx, Freud, "Femin") necessitated some serious time spent in the careful study and contemplation of Donna Haraway's (2013) groundbreaking work *Simians, Cyborgs, and Women* where we would be firmly reminded that all knowledge is situated, all identities fractured, and that the "local" tops the "global" every time when it comes to theorizing. *In general,* at this time, "psychoanalysis" was at best a foolish word, at worst, a bad word.

However, over time, and ironically in some ways (of course), the ultimate modality for me of working with local, situated knowledge *par excellence* was to be the psychoanalytic clinic. In my reading of the six queer chapters in this book I inevitably "read" from that peculiar historically and subjectively fractured location as a former critical psychologist, critical polytextualist, post-structuralist, and, psychoanalyst trained in the Lacanian school. I won't pretend now that formulating a response out of my reading of these essays is either straightforward (*sic*) or unproblematic. Indeed, in working on this piece I have felt provoked at times into mobilizing a grand-scale defense of Lacanian psychoanalysis (where I think that the Lacanian baby is being thrown out with the bathwater of "classical [*sic*] psychoanalysis"); occasionally wanting to address what I consider to be misused or misunderstood fragments of Lacanian theory (where I have detected a singular, decontextualized, and/or unreflexive usage of concepts such as "lack" and "*jouissance*" for instance) and even moved into a position where I want to demonstrate precisely just how queer Lacanian psychoanalysis is (especially when Lacan's theories are reduced to an improbably monolithic rendering, taking no account whatsoever of the reception of his work from the late 1960s as having consequences at theoretical, clinical, practical, and political levels [see, e.g., Soler 2014; Tomšič 2015]). These are the dilemmas of my "response" and of course even as I recognize my own desire in each of these dilemmas I need really to consider the elements in these essays that engage me in this dilemmatic trajectory.

First Thing: (The Game Is Rigged)

This entire project is staged: it seeks to bring together essays by "specialists in queer theory," responses to these essays by psychoanalytic "clinicians," and responses to those responses by "theorists" on a "stage" which is described as a "clinical encounter" between psychoanalytic practice and queer theory. I realize that some of my difficulty here consists in my being located singularly and most unqueerly as a "clinician." From that particular location I am invited to "reflect on my engagement with the six queer chapters and to include a clinical input if possible." It occurs to me that there are inevitable tensions in play here and indeed that they come into being precisely because of the structuring of the "encounter." What after all is being staged? An encounter between two sets of theories? No, since the encounter is between queer *theory* and psychoanalytic *practice*. An encounter between two sets of practices? No, since not all queer theorists are queer "practitioners," not all queer theorists are homosexual or lesbian even, and not all psychoanalytic theorists are psychoanalytic practitioners, obviously. So there are — at least — some fundamental problems here of combination and incommensurability. And this is something which I would say arises out of the actual structuring of the project but then (re-) emerges in the six queer chapters in so far as authors variously conflate "queer" with "homosexual" identity, psychoanalytic theory with psychoanalytic practice, and in their critique of psychoanalysis — undifferentiated here as to theory/practice - demand of some homogeneous big Other of psychoanalysis that it come up with something that heretofore is missing.

Kuzniar, for example, in the chapter on identity emphasizes that the task of current psychoanalysis is *not simply* to acknowledge the failure of previous conceptual psychic models but to adopt or develop hypotheses (such as Laplanche's, for this author) that would help articulate "*why one feels queer*" (Kuzniar). At the same time though, the author remarks that it is crucial to keep in mind "the uniqueness of every individual's circuitous path which resists generalization into a theorem." Here is the crux of the matter then: on the one hand, psychoanalysis must explain why one feels queer but on the other hand, the emphasis must be precisely on the singular queer subject, it must not attempt to re-foundationalize what queer theory has de-foundationalized in its critique of psychoanalytic psycho-social-developmental theories and grand narratives of sexualized identity. But is it a question of a reformulation on a grand-scale that is necessary for "psychoanalysis" in order to address this demand or is it rather, as Kuzniar seems to suggest later in the chapter that a "new vocabulary" needs to be adopted? This demand amounts to something like an ontological impasse: on the one hand psychoanalysis must explain why some people feel queer and on the other hand it must not come up with any kind of universalist statement. Many psychoanalytic practitioners — and especially those that teach on various training courses — know very well the difficulties and tensions of working case by case, with the absolute singularity of subjectivity and resisting public domain demands to discourse some kind of psychoanalytic universal.

In what form then, can a specifically psychoanalytic discourse prove palatable to queer theory given this too little/too much motif? In this vein, I was wondering to myself why Laplanche has proved so appealing to many queer theorists and to Kuzniar and Will Stockton in this collection. It occurred to me that Laplanche himself was someone who was keen to establish a new "vocabulary" of psychoanalysis, one which significantly re-words Freudian and Lacanian concepts in order to produce his own set of theories. This is perhaps also part of Donald Winnicott's charm for Michael Snediker in this collection. Neither Laplanche nor Winnicott pushed themselves into establishing what we might think of as "doctrines," however each analyst has become well known in terms of segments of their theories — for Laplanche it is often his "enigmatic signifier" that represents him, and for Winnicott the "good enough mother," for instance. Ultimately, do we not see in this collection that parts of Lacan, parts of Laplanche and parts of Winnicott are press-ganged into service, in other words, that strictly speaking, when it comes to queer theory, psychoanalysis can only ever be palatable *à la carte*?

Second Thing: (The Ethics of Transformation)

While it is true that queer theory and psychoanalysis (theory and practice) share an interest in subjectivity, desire, identity, relationality, ethics, power, discourse and norms, it is not true that their interest is dedicated in the same direction, with let's say, a common objective, or common interpretations. Indeed this isn't even true for psychoanalysts of different traditions! Queer theory is a specific set of analytics put to the service of deconstructing the constitutiveness of identities insofar as those identities become fixed and hardened entities with very real consequences for living. As such, it is overtly political, concerned with the destabilizing of warranted practices and ideological discourses. It is concerned with the disturbing of monolithic treatments of identity, the troubling of the taken-for-granted *vis-à-vis* "identity" and causal links to behavior,· and the demobilizing of the so-called signs of identity in order to open up rather than foreclose the possibility of future significations (Butler 1991, 19). This account of queer theory suggests an ideology (of course, it is *anti-ideologically* ideological). Ideologically speaking, psychoanalysis *should absolutely not* be invested in subjectivity and desire and identity and so forth with the same stakes as queer theory. Queerly speaking, the consequences for identity of "deconstruction," "destabilizing," and "demobilizing" are at the very least transformative, both at the level of subjectivity and (ideally) at the level of practice and discourse (e.g., Watson 2009). Whilst the whole question (oft debated and mostly controversial) within psychoanalysis (and within and between different "schools") of the extent to which (if any) psychoanalysis may be transformative is variously contested; Lacanians take the rather more suspicious view that as far as psychoanalytic treatment is concerned, "transformations" normatized into a set of therapeutic objectives are always an index of a "desire to do good" and/or a "desire to cure." And for those queer theorists so fond of Laplanche it is worth pointing out here that he too was vehemently anti-programmatic declaring that psychoanalytic practice cannot propose an aim of practice, no matter what, otherwise it risks becoming marshalled into a form of social adaptation. Lacanian psychoanalytic ethics insists that those analysts who would go about normatizing or normalizing (that is, wishing to transform their patients into "happier," "better-adjusted," "more secure in their identity" patients, etc.) believe themselves to be working for a sovereign good — that is to say — the good of the patient. Indeed, as an index of our direction of the treatment, whenever we find ourselves desiring to do good (according to some transformative trajectory), it is at that moment that we are likely to be led astray (Lacan 1986[1959–60], 218–19).

It is but a short and terrifyingly direct move from the desire to transform a patient's life according to what a well-adjusted (*sic*) analyst would seek to achieve while working for the "good" of his/her patient, to a kind of "thinking straight" which would iron out any quirks in the patient's thinking altogether. Not even Freud (1951) condescended to straighten out (*sic*) the son of one mother concerned about his homosexuality. And in fact Freud spoke out most vehemently against those who would seek to transform others into "better" versions of themselves. In his 1919 paper, "Lines of Advance in Psycho-Analytic Therapy," Freud defines the ethical dimension of the analyst as a renunciation of the directing of the patient's conscience. He writes: "We refused most emphatically to turn a patient who puts himself into our hands in search of help into our private property, to decide his fate for him, to force our own ideals upon him, and with the pride of a Creator to form him in our own image and see that it is good" (164–65). He goes on to reject the notion that psychoanalysis "should place itself in the service of a particular philosophical outlook on the world" and force this view upon the patient with the intention of improving him/her. Freud insisted that this would be a violence, notwithstanding the idea that it would be carried out with the most "honourable of motives."

Ethically speaking, Lacanian practice is basically at odds with the idea of the psychoanalytic clinic as a site of re-insertion, reduplication, re-production or re-presentation of any norm, including heteronormativity. A specifically Lacanian ethics not only shies away from a transformational ideology, it radically contests the grounds that give rise to transformative politics as always involving at least some degree of patronage which assumes for itself the (identitarian) knowledge of what is best for the one it seeks to transform.

Butler has remarked that understanding gender as a matter of *doing* rather than *being* allows for the transformation of its very meaning, that performing gender "self-consciously" rather than unconsciously has transformative effects on "gender" and therefore on gendered subjectivity. I am reminded of a patient who told me that regarding sex she has certain difficulties. Sex is a performance where she attempts to *indicate something* to her sexual partner. What was it she was attempting to indicate? That she is a woman. I asked her if she felt she gave a convincing performance. To the partner she thought she sometimes did, to herself she never did. Where do you learn to perform "woman" I asked her. She told me: from other people, from TV: what sounds to make, what moves to make. "Doing" gender for this person hardly seems to have the transformative effects that Butler imagines, even for all that it is "self-conscious." What this woman suffers from is not the idea that she comes up short as a woman, that — in the words of the song — she isn't made to feel like a "natural" woman, but, rather that there is no such thing as natural when it comes to gender/identity, that in fact it is all performance, all doing. There is no playfulness here, this is a serious kind of business after all. This kind of destitution of identity is increasingly seen in the contemporary psychoanalytic clinic (Owens 2010). A question that Lacan (1976–77) poses in his *Seminar XXIV* might thus paraphrase a contemporary predicament: "How is a subject, with all his weakness, his infirmity, able to hold the place of truth?" (39). Besides he notes later on in the same seminar, we are forever wandering about in the dimension of the love of truth and that is why, he wryly remarks, the real continues to slip through our fingers. There isn't in fact any truth about the real, since the real excludes meaning (44).

Here, we can begin perhaps to see one of the sharp differences in "interpretation" between queer theory and (Lacanian) psychoanalysis: for my patient it is that "essence" itself has to be performed and is what fails for her. Far from sustaining any notion of "woman" as emanating from her female sexed body it is rather that being a woman in the sexual act allows her to feel real […] full stop! In the movie — *The Truman Show* (1988) — *being* (a) tru(e)man is obtained by doing all the things that "true" men do unconsciously. When Truman finally discovers the staged fakery of his existence and chooses to exit the stage, it is at that moment that we can say that he is truly a fake along with all the other fakes in the real world — performing self-consciously that is — rather than the falsely true-man he had been up until then in his fake world. If this is a moment that we might celebrate as the moment of his discovery of his authenticity, then we would be misguided, since his very "authenticity" resides in his knowing that as he leaves one show it is to enter, indeed, another.

Third Thing: (The Trouble with Jouissance, Lack and Desire)

In the chapter on *jouissance*, Kathryn Bond Stockton remarks that psychoanalysis benefits from the conceptual engagement of "bliss" with queer theory and contemplation, themselves "shot through with psychoanalytical suggestions and perspective." Yes indeed. Of course! Any self-respecting psychoanalyst should be reading any/all of the works Bond Stockton mentions in her chapter. Roland Barthes, Georges Bataille, Leo Bersani and so on. It is really impossible to read Bersani's "Is the Rectum a Grave" (2010) without cause to *really really* try to think through and about the *jouissance* at stake in what he (2008) has elsewhere described as "apparently suicidal and murderous behavior." And precisely, in his chapter in the book co-written with Adam Phillips (2008), he attempts to think it and moreover to come up with some kind of conceptual key which would allow him to reflect on the effects of a barebacking "self-divestiture" not merely as ego-annihilation but also as ego-dissemination (56). But then what I find largely un-thought in the chapter on *jouissance* in this collection is precisely this other side of *jouissance* — suicidal/murderous, dangerous/fatal. Instead, *jouissance* is largely reframed via Barthes's translator as bliss and it is bliss we are stuck with then until the end — notwithstanding the rehearsing of Bataille's visions of excess. We are told that if it didn't exist, queers would invent it. Please! Liberated of its more painful connotations and as such from any sense of Lacan's multiply nuanced glosses — it is simply wrong to present Lacan's account of *jouissance* as only and ever "bound to mysticism" (Bond Stockton). *Jouissance* in Lacan's hands here is sketched as the tragically elusive (or excessive) in the case of feminine *jouissance* or as the tragically fantasmatic (or disingenuous) in the case of phallic *jouissance*. Stockton invites the "analytic scene" to venture the question of whether certain desires are more desirable than other more staid versions of pleasure. I would say, that regarding *jouissance* we don't get much of a choice! Clinically, psychoanalysts tend to hear more about the ravages of *jouissance* than it's "glistening," "dark glamour of rapture" etc., and even that can cause a *jouis*-sens that itself further ravages the subject. We are probably mostly familiar with descriptions of *jouissance* which invariably make it a sexy topic and then it is so difficult for us to bear in mind all of the other practices which guarantee *jouissance* for the subject even as they herald her/his destruction (Owens 2015; 2016). Myself, I like Lacan's (2007[1969–70]) definition of *jouissance* that he suggests in his *Seminar XVII*: "It begins with a tickle and ends in a blaze of petrol. That's always what a *jouissance* is" (72). After all, tickling is fun up to a point, but nobody really wants to be tickled (burnt?) to death.

In accusing Bond Stockton above of being too blissed-out in her working of *jouissance*, I surely help to add weight to Lara Farina's accusation that Freudian and Lacanian psychoanalysts remain too sober in their theorization of desire. Like Socrates — she says — they remain "at a remove from the erotic object." The analyst rather, should be or could be "drunk on love." Instead however, the analyst is sketched as a party pooper and a boring teetotaller. But what is this sober business about?

First take: "Lacanian psychoanalysis preserves and even magnifies the role of lack in desire." By and large, "lack" is simplistically synonymous with "loss" for many critics of Lacanian theory. Lack — become loss, is then mobilized and marshalled into discourse as "tragic," "sober," and so on. This kind of pathetic state of affairs for the human subject — who "strives (unsuccessfully) to fill the void with an endless series of objects" is itself endless as the satisfaction of lack — were it ever possible — would cause desire to cease and with it, symbolic existence. As such we need to keep desiring desire as a way to stay inscribed within the symbolic. Here we can't say that if lack didn't exist, Lacan would have invented it! Let's think about lack a little bit differently but where its role in desire is still preserved. Let's take the "fifteen puzzle" as an example of contingency: specifically whereby it is lack itself that guarantees any form of desire, movement, enjoyment. The fifteen puzzle is a sliding puzzle that consists of a frame of numbered square tiles in random order with one tile missing. The object of the puzzle is to place the tiles in order by making sliding moves that use the empty space.[1] Quite simply, if there is no lack, there is no question of solving the puzzle (satisfaction), if there is no lack, there is no question of desire, it just doesn't arise. Those of us who witness the satisfaction of children at play with quest/puzzle type games can observe too that once the game/puzzle has become solved, there is a nostalgic twist: a wishing to be back at the start again. Desire for desire needn't be pathologically tragic, rather, it is when there is the fantasy that satisfaction (with an object, with a theory perhaps?) could be obtained if only the right [...] object/ theory could be found, that it seems to me (non-clinically and clinically) there is a tragic dimension.

Second take: "Psychoanalysis itself is often given the role of policing giddiness in queer theory" (Farina). Farina claims that even in Bersani and Grosz's accounts, Freudian and/or Lacanian analysis is hailed as a "necessary agent of sobriety." Why is it

---

1   I am grateful to Carlos Gomez for sharing this great demonstration of desire with me in Copenhagen in 2008.

necessary, she asks, to be sober and/or pessimistic when think-ing about queer desire? Why is it so great (paraphrasing Ber-sani) that aggression is theorized as inevitable for *jouissance*? In fact this is a somewhat misleading representation of Grosz's comment (cited in Farina as Grosz, 1995, 242, n. 1). She doesn't "hail" Lacanian analysis as a "necessary agent of sobriety": what Grosz actually says is that Lacan "provides a *necessarily sobering* counterbalance" to a retrospective idealization of mother/child relations (my emphasis).

It is interesting to note then what Grosz (1994) says else-where regarding the inevitable ambivalence in one's relationship to one's body, i.e., precisely what emerges as a consequence of the imaginary as the site of rivalrous as well as of narcissistic identifications. She argues, following Lacan, that the subject al-ways maintains a relationship of love/hate towards the subject's own body precisely because every body is invested with libidinal value. *No* body is ever simply or solely functional but rather, psychically and libidinally invested (32). The frustration and ag-gression attendant at the "mirror phase" in Lacan are the in-evitable experiences of firstly, the infant's biologically premature helplessness when comparing itself with the gestalt image in the mirror, and secondly, as Lacan puts it — more or less — when compared with this excellent little version of the self (this little other/counterpart), it's either me or her... one of us is fucked. We do very well indeed to heed the aggression inherent in a *jouissance* that has as its center a focus upon the body, however variously that body is theorized.

Last Thing:

In my response here I wanted to articulate something of the di-lemmas of my responding in a series of interwoven moves:

By reflecting on what seems to trouble queer about psycho-analysis in the collection and,
finding some surprising recuperations but,
not throwing out Lacan with lack and,

finding that *jouissance* is not(-all) nice and,
challenging a queer = cool/psychoanalysis = fool motif as well as,
noticing what queer demands of psychoanalysis.

Works Cited

Bersani, Leo. "Shame on You." In Leo Bersani and Adam Phillips, *Intimacies,* 31–56. Chicago and London: University of Chicago Press, 2008.

Bersani, Leo. "Is the Rectum a Grave?" In *Is the Rectum a Grave and Other Essays,* 3–30. Chicago and London: University of Chicago Press, 2010.

Butler, Judith. "Imitation and Gender Insubordination." In *Inside/out: Lesbian Theories, Gay Theories,* ed. Diana Fuss, 13–31. New York: Routledge, 1991.

Freud, Sigmund. "Historical Notes: A Letter from Freud." *The American Journal of Psychiatry* 107, no. 10 (1951): 786–87.

———. "Lines of Advance in Psycho-Analytic Therapy" (1919[1918]). In *The Standard Edition of the Complete Psychological Works of Sigmund Freud,* vol. 17, trans. James Strachey in collaboration with Anna Freud and assisted by Alix Strachey and Alan Tyson, 257–68. London: Vintage, 2001.

Grosz, Elizabeth. *Volatile Bodies: Towards a Corporeal Feminism: Theories of Representation and Difference.* Indiana: Indiana University Press, 1994.

———. *Space, Time, and Perversion: Essays on the Politics of Bodies.* New York and London: Routledge, 1995.

Haraway, Donna. *Simians, Cyborgs, and Women: The Reinvention of Nature.* 1991; rpt. Routledge: London and New York, 2013.

Lacan, Jacques. *Book XVII: The Other Side of Psychoanalysis* (1969–70), trans. Russell Grigg. 1991; rpt. New York: W.W. Norton and Company, 2007.

———. *Book VII: The Ethics of Psychoanalysis* (1959–60), ed. Jacques-Alain Miller, trans. Dennis Porter. 1986; New York and London: Routledge, 1992.

———. *Book XXIV: L'insu qui sait de l'une bévue, s'aile à mourre,* [Love is the Failure of the Unconscious] (1976–77), ed. Jacques-Alain Miller, trans. Dan Collins, unpublished.

Owens, Carol. "Danger! Neurotics at Work." In *Lacan and Organization,* eds. Carl Cederstrom and Casper Hoedemaekers, 187–210. London: Mayfly, 2012.

———. "'Sex-folly-ation': Don Juan's Desire and the *Jouissance* of the Nymphomaniac." *Lacunae* 10 (2015): 139–50.

———. "Not-in-the-Humor: Bulimic Dreams." In *Lacan, Psychoanalysis and Comedy,* eds. Patricia Gherovici and Manya Steinkoler, 113–29. Cambridge: Cambridge University Press, 2016.

Soler, Colette. *Lacan: The Unconscious Reinvented.* London: Karnac, 2014.

Tomšič, Samo. *The Capitalist Unconscious.* London: Verso, 2015.

The Truman Show, dir. Peter Weir. Scott Rudin Productions, 1988.

Watson, Eve. "Queering Psychoanalysis/Psychoanalysing Queer." *Annual Review of Critical Psychology* 7 (2009): 114–39. http://www.discourseunit.com/arcp/7.htm.

13

Clinique

Aranye Fradenburg

Academic writing about psychoanalysis does not often engage the practice of psychoanalysis in today's USA, or vice versa. There are many reasons for this, and one is always wishing there were more mutual interest. The canons differ; academics still read a lot of Freud and later continental theory, less often Anglo-American object relations theory, and much less often, Thomas Ogden, Robert Stoller, Muriel Dimen, Joe Natterson, or Mark Leffert. In my experience, American psychoanalysts too often abdicate their intellectual responsibilities and the social implications thereof; too few of us regard ourselves as minds shaping and being shaped by the urgent questions of our time. In turn, academic psychoanalytic work does not, in my view, grapple closely enough with the reasons why particular people seek treatment, and with the ethics of responding or not responding to misery experienced as "personal," that is, felt to be "inside." Queer theory has, remarkably, been to-and-fro-ing all over this ground, in its *agōn* with psychoanalysis, powerfully critiquing it, and equally powerfully re-thinking it, finally changing policy and helping to usher in "an exciting [era] of discovery" of sexuality's range and resourcefulness (Roughton 2002, 757, referring to the first decade of the twenty-first century). The chapters to which I'm responding here show that the ground shared by queer theory and psychoanalysis is still something of a battleground, but they also show that the debate is a highly creative one, born of a provocatively uneasy intimacy.

The stakes of knowledge for "the institute" or "the clinic" are, in truth, not identical to those that motivate the academy. The academy's interest in psychoanalysis stems chiefly from the latter's vast cultural influence. We want to know what its history means, why it was so influential, what were its main ideas about the mind, how it has changed thinking about the arts, about social behavior and indeed all human endeavors, for good and for ill. We see its power. We employ its insights as well as elements of its technique in interpreting dreams and films and literary texts, historical catastrophes, social movements, and funeral rituals in distant lands. We remain, for the most part, committed to making knowledge, in as unconstrained a fashion as possible. The clinic, on the other hand, wants knowledge that changes us. It wants to know which ideas, techniques and medication will save lives, relieve suffering, enrich our capacity for introspection, and deepen our understanding of our real circumstances: we're mortal, we need other people, and yet we are only intermittently capable of togetherness. Moreover, "each" of us is in reality just a highly impressionable and constantly changing procession of affective, cognitive and somatic events, experienced as "self-states." The clinic wants to know how these "truths" *transform* us (Snediker).

I taught psychoanalytic theory for more than twenty years before I decided to train as a psychoanalyst. I went into training partly because I couldn't answer my students' questions about medication, substance-abuse, sexual abuse, ADHD, cutting, and eating disorders. I could imagine what Lacan might say about them—note that Lacanian or neo-Lacanian psychoanalysis is practiced vigorously in many parts of the world, if not so much in the USA — but I knew little about the vast overlapping networks of pharmacology, social work, inpatient and outpatient treatment, or the twelve-step and life-skills programs which currently address our addictions. However, I did know some things about my students' lives. My students, straight or gay or transsexual, live in, or at minimum must cope with, a very hard-drinking, substance-abusing, status-sensitive world of date-rape, overdose, suicidality, STDs, depression, anxiety, binging, and purging. Many grew up with parents who smoked pot or drank or fought or divorced or had to work double shifts. Others grew up with parents who abused prescription drugs (Oxycontin, Xanax) and relied on antidepressants, not psychotherapy, to make their feelings bearable. These students tend to see psychotherapy as the solution rather than the problem. Many were themselves (over-)medicated as children for "hyperactivity." They are familiar with self-destruction — as *jouissance,* as tragedy.

And of course it gets worse: parents who abuse their children in every way possible; children who respond by mutilating or starving themselves and scratching themselves raw, or abusing or even killing their parents in later life, should they survive the latter's post-partum depression, explosivity, drunkenness and cultism. These lives are not "the norm"; but they are widespread for all that. So there are those who suffer, from unbearable and yet unavoidable thoughts and affects, from uncontrollable impulses. How should we (when not ourselves overbusy with suffering) care (for them)?

One of my first patients, "Jerry," was a sex offender, schizophrenic, alcoholic (in recovery), raped at the age of sixteen, whose father, a lifelong alcoholic, had sexually abused his sister, who in turn developed multiple personality disorder and was taken from the home, along with the rest of the children. Jerry spent most of his teen years in group homes. After his father's death, his mother married a man now in prison for child molestation. Jerry once invited a fourteen-year-old boy to come over to his apartment and watch porn, and when he was subsequently convicted of sexual assault against a disabled eighteen-year-old girl, he was sent to a "treatment facility" for sex offenders. Once-a-week psychotherapy could not do much to help him reduce the intensity of his sexual "urges." What psychotherapy could do was to help him bear his chaos, by learning to consider alternatives — ways of mattering, ways others might matter — so that his struggles with his *jouissance* might be experienced differently. "What investments are really at stake in making a symptom out of a pleasure?" (Downing). Good question. But what is a pleasure? Do pleasures not also involve "investments" (perhaps "cathexes")? Can it be a pleasure to make symptoms out of pleasure? Could doing so be a certain registration of the reality principle, or of the superego gone mad? The question of who is doing the making is also relevant to what is at stake in making symptoms. *Pace* Foucauldian leveling, does it make a difference if the symptom-maker is the sufferer, the intake specialist, the teen group? Foucault turned to a genealogy of "self-care" in volumes two (1992) and three (1990) of *The History of Sexuality* for good reason. Care is a resonant and disturbing word. If one is a clinician, one is committed to caring for persons deeply hurt by the people who are supposed to care most about relieving their cares but don't (their family, their country). The clinic is one of many interlinked versions (daycare centers, hospices, peer counseling) of the affective and somatic caring humans render as so many arts, rights, and responsibilities. Families retain importance here, as highly overdetermined points of intersection and transmission in vast networks of "caring." Care also has a long political history, e.g., as premodern *cura,* the love sovereigns are supposed to show their "*belovit*" subjects. So does carelessness: Oedipus's belief that he had solved his problems by leaving home brings plague to Thebes; George W. Bush's dislike of having to do chores blew up as Katrina. We also hate and fear care. We distrust its motives; it threatens impingement.

A number of the chapters in this collection investigate the caring practices that join and separate us. For Kuzniar, pets are "non-human object choices," which diminish "the power of sexual identity categories that socially regulate the individual." "Caring" assembles practices we use to do up and undo our shifty affiliations; it gives standing to the creature being cared for, and thus changes affective/political maps. (This is of course the import of Ronald Reagan's well-known reluctance to fund AIDS research — well-known, at least, to all but Hillary Clinton, who, at Nancy Reagan's funeral, forgot about the 1980s.) Perhaps because of its longstanding commitment to "the talking cure," psychoanalysis has been slow to extend its understanding of attachment to nonhumans. There is the famous example of Lacan's valorization of human language, but the story is really longer and more mystifying than that: As Bennett Roth (2005) points out, despite the great love Freud and other analysts have felt for their pets, in the analytic literature, there is a subtle tendency to diminish the importance of human-pet relationships and accent the pathology of pet attachment. In fact, psychoanalytic writing leaves unexplained the quality of shared psychic environment between animals and humans.

When psychoanalysis does attend to animals, all too frequently it forgets the implications of "shared psychic environment"; intersubjectivity is thrown out the window and replaced by older intrapsychic and transference approaches, such that the contribution of the animal to shared experience is largely ignored. Increasingly, however, attempts to communicate have intensified; whisperers speak to horses and dogs; pugs and pussycats help the elderly cope with anxiety. Lab researchers tickle their rats and discover rat laughter. The "animal turn" and the ecological sensitivity that often accompanies it have begun to make inroads in psychoanalytic theory too, under the influence of Gilles Deleuze and Félix Guattari, and enactivist psychology. The work of Deleuze and Guattari (2002) on "Becoming Animal" (232–309) is in the nature of a response to the notion of identification as well as to the narrowness of Freudian understandings of subjectivity. If we can *become* human, we can also become animal. There is no important role for a house-pet in the Oedipus legend, though the Sphinx's questioning of "man" would seem be relevant here.

Freud's theory of the Oedipus complex is widely regarded in queer theory as an attempt to shore up (and therefore re-produce) gender distinctions and distinctions between normative and heteronormative sex practices. If Freud gave us infantile sexuality and polymorphous perversity, if he pointed out the queer elements in all sexualities, if he proclaimed the bisexuality of all humanity, acknowledged the homoeroticism of his friendships with men, and refused to try to turn homosexuals into heterosexuals (a practice he regarded as "cruel"), nonetheless Oedipal teleology consigned all sucking, sniffing, tickling, looking, and listening to vestigial status (regression, foreplay, perversion), instead of regarding genital sexuality as simply one of many potential erotic constructs and construals — including fixations (Downing).

A number of these essays criticize psychoanalysis for deploying "pathologizing identity label[s]"; the "gendered Oedipal scenario" still dominates psychoanalytic discourse (Kuzniar). If thinking about Oedipus is just part rather than the main event of thinking about sexuality and identity, however, I think it remains thought-provoking. From the standpoint of the clinic — and this holds true regardless of our role in eliciting the phenomena — incest and transgenerational sexuality are forms of queerness that disgust many queers and challenge the boundaries of queer ethics. A surprising number of people do *not* think it's okay for a brother and sister to sleep together, even consensually and using protection. Defenses of pedophilia are rare in academic circles. The family remains a powerful delivery system for caring and not-caring, partly because it makes use of age (hence time, mortality) as well as kinship in the ways it tries to wrap itself around *jouissance*. One thing Oedipus means now: If we eroticize care, that is because enjoyment is designed by our attachments to lifesaving superpowers we can't do without.

Moreover, it's arguable as to how long the sway of Oedipus really lasted in psychoanalysis; in fact the notion of the Oedipus complex is scorned by many us psychoanalytic practitioners today. Its interest has been eclipsed by many new developments, including the challenge posed to drive theory by "deficit" models in self-psychology ("deficits" in self-structure replace the "conflicts" of drive theory and ego-psychology), and by trauma and attachment theory. "Intrapsychic" experience, which reached a certain zenith in Kleinian theory, still has many adherents, but relational and intersubjective models of psychical process have gained enormous ground over the last few decades (Snediker). Many of us now do our thinking with the notion of "neuroplasticity," and think of plasticity and entrenchment as inevitable concomitants of each other. As Catherine Malabou (2008) notes, once poured into its mold, plastic does, or is, this or that, largely undisturbed. But it can be re-molded, with effort. Perhaps it is because sexuality must be neuroplastically designed that it is *both* (as Freud understood) mobile and capable of fixation. Perhaps sexuality is *pliable,* like all the other neuronal patterns in the brain that derive from experience.

The critique of ontology should not be abandoned, however. It keeps us from settling into complacency about our mobility. It remains a highly generative form of interplay between queer theory and psychoanalysis, as these chapters exemplify. Their fresh de-sequestrations of "ontology and action" open up new pathways of thought — from Snediker's elegant discussion of "the vicissitudes of personate veracity" and the virtues of approximation, to Farina's reflections on the erotic cast Georges Bataille gives to "ego-dissolving practices," to Frommer's (2000) essay on the (intersubjective) eroticizing of domination, to Bond Stockton's exploration of Jean Laplanche's "enigmatic signifier" — "in relation to the unconscious, sex [...] confounds the discourses of sexuality that mark its presence and delimit its significance" — and Luce Irigaray's "failure" to fuse that enjoys possibility: "Sex, then, is fracture." Downing rings a further change in her analysis of the idealization of fluidity in both queer theory and the Freudian discourse on perversion (God forbid that we should get so stuck on any one erotic prop or activity that we couldn't get off without it). But can signifiers ever be pinned down? It has been fourteen years since Roughton (2002) looked forward to the renewal of "the intellectual struggle to redefine what we [psychoanalysts] mean by sexuality" (757). Do we keep on trying to define, as opposed to seeking the mastery of definition?

In the case of perversion, we certainly need to continue redefining. Some quality of obsession or ossification is still linked to perversion by many clinicians today: perversion is pathological when the need to satisfy perverse wishes overtakes all other life goals. Extremely risky behavior likewise indicates that Thanatos has come out to play. Or the pervert cannot or will not give up his or her part-objects in order to reconstitute them as a loving and loveable "whole person." Arguably, however, what gives these activities their life-consuming aspect is not the erotic dimension but the death drive, in its driven reconstructions of the borderline between caring and hurting: *The Night Porter* (1974), *Misery* (1989), *One Flew Over the Cuckoo's Nest* (2012).

The death drive likes to entwine itself with highly intimate practices like care and sex. Is this the "fault" of care or sex? I think not. But is it so bad to do perverted things that we have to blame them on the death drive to make us feel better about getting off on handcuffing someone to the radiator? Surely we don't want to take all the naughtiness out of queerness. Queer theory struggles regularly with two wishes that are often at cross-purposes: the one to undo demonization, the other to speak for *jouissance*. Sex is, or can be, fantasy-laden, furtive, slimy, painful, unflattering, exploitative. We want to restore dignity, or at least value, to a wide variety of erotic experiences, but another goal, not always comfortably co-aligned, is to question the very value of dignity. I think psychoanalysis can help with both. Bergmann (1974) avers, following Freud, that (re)finding and being found are part of every relationship (or relational style) (2). This is a moving and important way to think about partying in general and in specific the importance to many queer lives of clubs and cruising (which we now feel all the more keenly post-Orlando). But are we trying to sanitize, to tender-ize, sex clubs because we find in their unfamiliar familiarity the trace of a wish to be found? But then, orgiastic behavior really should not frighten psychoanalysts as often as it seems to do. As Alain Cohen once remarked, in a meeting of the University of California's Psychoanalytic Consortium years ago, "we are not the Red Cross." Lacan may be credited for noticing that Freud meant to clarify the always non-"pastoral" nature of our modes of enjoyment (or *jouissance*), including probity. The prominence of caring means now that not-caring, especially not-self-caring, behavior, is peculiarly, multiply, affectively invested. As Farina puts it, in slightly more inspiring terms than I can muster myself,

Perhaps what "queer" theorization of desire needs is not to remain sober […] but to allow for ways in which the analyst, too, can be drunk on love […]. How splendid it would be to rejoin the party, sitting at the side of beauty, among all the others.

(I am tempted to say, with Dorothy Parker, "and I am Marie of Romania" — but I so approve of banqueting).[1] Even the ecstatic can be understood in terms of disassociation. Sometimes we want to scatter or hurt our "selves." We can't even say the words "hurt our 'selves'" without evoking pathos or pathology. But *jouissance* lies far beyond the Good or the goods, says Lacan (and I agree). It may be neighborly, but that's why we think we need good fences, mace, and bars on the window. Or, it's all in the family, but the family is always-already abject, owing to the dimension thereof that does *not* honor particular subjectivities, as well as the factor of entrenchment that makes its repetitions so compulsive. Today's clinic must appreciate the power of attachment — hence of caring and not caring — to design desires of widely varying consequences for the well-being of others as well as oneself.

Works Cited

Bergmann, Martin S. "On Love and Its Enemies." The *Psychoanalytic Review* 82 (1995): 1–19.

Deleuze, Gilles and Félix Guattari. *A Thousand Plateaus: Capitalism and Schizophrenia.* 1987; rpt. New York: Continuum, 2002.

Foucault, Michel. *The History of Sexuality, Vol. 2: The Use of Pleasure,* trans. Robert Hurley. 1984; rpt. London: Penguin, 1992.

———. *The History of Sexuality, Vol. 3: The Care of the Self,* trans. Robert Hurley. 1984; rpt. London: Penguin, 1990.

---

1   "Oh, life is a glorious cycle of song,/ A medley of extemporanea;/ And love is a thing that can never go wrong,/ And I am Marie of Romania."

Frommer, Martin S. "Offending Gender: Being and Wanting in Male Same-Sex Desire." *Studies in Gender and Sexuality* 1 (2000): 191–206.

Kesey, Ken. *One Flew Over the Cuckoo's Nest.* London and New York: Penguin, 2012 (1962).

King, Stephen. *Misery.* London and New York: Penguin, 1989.

Malabou, Catherine and Sebastian Rand, *What Should We Do with Our Brain?* New York: Fordham University Press, 2008.

The Night Porter. Dir. Liliana Cavani. 1974.

Parker, Dorothy. "Comment." In *Enough Rope.* New York: Boni and Liveright, 1926.

Roth, Bennett. "Pets and Psychoanalysis." *The Psychoanalytic Review* 92, no. 3 (2005): 453–68.

Roughton, Ralph E. "Rethinking Homosexuality: What it Teaches us about Psychoanalysis." *Journal of the American Psychoanalytic Association* 50 (2002): 733–63.

14

From Tragic Fall to Programmatic Blueprint: "Behold this is Oedipus…"

Olga Cox Cameron

In the first flush of his discoveries Freud (1900) was much given to inventing mottoes for himself and for this new praxis which both excited and disturbed him. "*Flectere si nequeo superos, Acheronta movebo,*" he inscribes as epigraph to *The Interpretation of Dreams*: "What have they done to you poor child?" he suggests to Fliess as he attends to stories of shocking childhood abuse (Masson 1985, 289). Reading this collection of queer responses to psychoanalytic theory I am tempted to affix Barthes's (1975) statement, "we are scientific because we lack subtlety" (61), less as a motto than as a caveat to the large swathes of psychoanalytic theory which Alice Kuzniar challenges in her opening chapter "Precarious Sexualities."

It is as astonishing to psychoanalysts as to non-analysts that a theory predicated on the existence of the unconscious and therefore committed to the radical undercutting of an abiding undisturbed notion of the self should have lent itself with such stalwartness and consistency to a version of the Oedipus complex which in Kuzniar's words presumes as its telos "a stable fixed identity of personhood that rests solidly within a unitary gender role and unwavering sexual object choice directed to the opposite of one's own gender."

How has this come about and why? I would like to approach these two questions from a number of angles, historical, aesthetic and psychoanalytic, perhaps condemning myself to a degree of superficiality and overview. To do so, I will look briefly at this tendency firstly in Freud's own thinking and at the later Lacan's attempts to formulate a beyond of the Oedipus complex; secondly, in a dominant current in literary history at the time of Freud's writing; then crucially at the need for psychoanalysis to remain alert to its own susceptibility to slippage here.

If, passing the wine at a dinner party, one were to mention Oedipus, where would the conversation go? Towards Sophocles or towards Freud? The stark intractability of *Oedipus Rex* and *Oedipus at Colonus* would be an unlikely reference in the jokes, anecdotes and discussion which might ensue. This in itself should give us pause. What had to happen for one of the greatest tragedies of Western literature to become traduced and banalized into a checklisted blueprint for heteronormative identity formation?

Far from being a narrative of identity formation Sophocles's great play carves through accumulating layers of foreboding to etch a trajectory in an exactly contrary direction. Re-reading it now in the twenty-first century it is impossible not to be struck by the thought that it is not so much a "queer" tragedy as a tragedy of "queering" in the sense indicated by Kuzniar (quoting David Halperin): "Queer is by definition whatever is at odds with the normal, the legitimate, the dominant." One of the most relentless narrative currents in the play is the ousting of Oedipus from a position of normalcy, legitimacy and dominance to that of arch outsider, reviled, ejected and unsupported in the pitiless glare of universal abhorrence. The opening description of himself: "I Oedipus, renowned of all" (Sophocles 1938, 369), endorsed by the Chorus who name him 'first of men, king glorious in all ages" (370) is slowly leached of its lustre, darkened by gathering horror until the point where everything that was world is stripped from him, and he is found to be "a pollution which neither earth can welcome nor the holy rain nor light" (413).

Is the theoretical tamping of tragic import in the so-called Oedipus complex an almost perfect example of what psychoanalysis calls repression? In one of his later seminars Lacan refers to the Oedipus complex as Freud's dream, with its "classic" version functioning as manifest content. To juxtapose the starkness of Sophocles' text, the throat-constricting ferocity of its performative power with the steady forward march from oral to anal to genital heteronormativity outlined by Freud and stolidly installed by classical post-Freudian psychoanalysis is indeed to evoke this duality, but here we should attend to Freud's caveat and look for the unconscious not as lodged in either manifest or latent content, but in the turbulent energy of the relation between them.

What attracted Freud's attention was indeed the power and subjective resonance of *Oedipus Rex.* "There must be something which makes a voice within us ready to recognize the compelling force of destiny in the Oedipus," he writes in *The Interpretation of Dreams* (1900, 262). Musing on this will very quickly lead him onto the terrain of unconscious desire, but as many careful readers of Freud, including Derrida, Bersani, and Lacan have noted, Freud was both an extraordinarily innovative thinker *and* a nineteenth-century man, deeply immersed in the intellectual trends of his day and limited by the difficulty of accommodating twentieth- and even twenty-first-century insights within the inadequate conceptual apparatus of nineteenth-century thought. This is very visible along the axis of one of his favourite metaphors for designating unconscious activity, the fragment and the fragmentary. In *The Interpretation of Dreams* the narrative fragment is quintessential to the non-sense of unconscious desire, and in recent years has been brilliantly theorized by Guy le Gaufey (1995) as part object which is not part of any object (1). But it is impossible for Freud (1896) not to oscillate between the implications of this ground-breaking discovery and the nineteenth-century archeological excitement of seeing in this fragment the necessary clue to a recoverable and coherent completeness (193). In the "Three Essays" (1905) one can see how the seduction of this summative gesture comes into play in his account of sexuality. Anarchic, polymorphous, perverse; pleasure-seeking rather than object oriented, all this wild enjoyment cannot be left to its own devices, but must somehow be "organised," retrospectively labelled as the "components" of a larger whole and its energies channelled into a universally acceptable solution. Post-Freudian psychoanalysis has privileged this summative gesture. Lacan (1992[1959–60]) puts it well in his seminar on ethics: "It seems that from the moment of those first soundings, from the sudden flash of light that the Freudian experience cast on the paradoxical origins of desire, on the polymorphously perverse character of its infantile forms, a general tendency has led psychoanalysis to reduce the paradoxical origins in order to show their convergence in a harmonious conclusion" (4). This harmonious conclusion will not be queer. As Eve Watson (2011) convincingly demonstrated in her doctoral thesis, despite very impressive insights and the fact that his theorization of sexuality and oedipal formation changed considerably over the years, Freud's ultimate bias was towards heteronormativity. So the assertion in the "Three Essays" (1905) that "the exclusive sexual attraction felt by men for women" is as much a problem as homosexual attraction (57) will disappear disappointingly a hundred pages later in the postulation that "one of the tasks implicit in object choice is that it should find its way to the opposite sex" (229).

It is however extremely difficult to do justice to the breadth of Freud's often contradictory thinking about sexuality and sexual identity. The totalizing tendency, the channelling of sexuality into the safe harbor of heterosexual fulfilment, though dominant, is also seriously shafted by his view that there is no safe harbor for this anarchic force: "It is my belief that, however strange it may sound, we must reckon with the possibility that something in the nature of the sexual instinct itself is unfavorable to the realization of complete satisfaction" (258), while his heterosexual bias, also dominant, is pushed somewhat off course by blurring its terms of reference; "pure masculinity and femininity remain theoretical constructs of uncertain content" (1925, 258).

Lacan (1992[1959–60]), speaking about the Oedipus complex in the late 1950s as part of his seminar *The Formations of the Unconscious* emphasized its normativing and normalizing role, but even in those early years of his teaching, he was scathing about a proposed route to fulfilment via the channelling of desire which he refers to as "the ideal of genital love — a love that is supposed to be itself alone the model of a satisfying object relation: doctor love I would say if I wanted to emphasize in a comical way the tone of this ideology; love as hygiene" (8). Not only is this project tainted with an optimistic moralism, but it is in fact ludicrous: "To say that the problems of moral experience are entirely resolved as far as monogamous union is concerned would be a formulation that is imprudent, excessive and inadequate"(8).

By the 1970s, possibly influenced by feminist analysands such as Antoinette Fouque (founder of the publishing house *Les Femmes*). Lacan (2007[1969–70]) was-somewhat(!) re-thinking masculinism and was writing the word "normal" as "nor-male." He had also begun to question Freud's appropriation of Sophocles's *Oedipus Rex*: "The Oedipus complex as it is recounted by Freud when he refers to Sophocles is […] Sophocles' story minus its tragic component" (113). Like many interrogations of canonical "truth" the remarks Lacan goes on to make in this seminar are both startling and (once made) obvious. He draws a clear distinction between Freud's theorization of the Oedipus complex (alongside his other mythologies of the powerful murdered father such as "Totem and Taboo") and what he was actually, simultaneously, hearing from his hysterical women patients. These were all stories of powerless impotent "degraded" fathers. Instead of attending to this and its possible implications, Freud seems to have been tempted by a masculinist fantasy of unlimited potency which he purveyed as fact. Lacan scoffs at this: "Above all he clings strongly to what actually happened, this blessed story of the murder of the father of the horde, this Darwinian buffoonery. The father of the horde — as if there has ever been the slightest trace of this father of the horde" (112–13). Lacan asks how this masculinist myth has been so persuasive:

Isn't it an odd thing when one knows how it actually is with the father's function? To be sure this is not the only point at which Freud presents us with a paradox, namely the idea of referring this function to some kind of *jouissance* of all the women, when it is a well known fact that a father barely suffices for one of them, and even then- he musn't boast about it. A father has with the master — I speak of the master as we know him, as he functions — only the most distant of relationships since in short, at least in the society Freud was familiar with, it is he who works for everybody. (100)

Lacan seems to be suggesting here that the oedipal myth as purveyed by Freud is a mask, a "master-ized" discourse (acting the master is to think of oneself as univocal (103) eliding the truth of the hysteric's discourse which is divided into "on the one hand, the castration of the idealized father, who yields the master's secret, and on the other hand, privation, the assumption by the subject, whether feminine or not, of the *jouissance* of being deprived" (99). This double-hinged truth might have led him very far, but Freud, Lacan says, diminishes these truths by opting for what has become the Oedipus complex. Furthermore in the psychoanalytic theory which this diminishing has fostered, the elision of the tragic mainspring of Sophocles' play has facilitated the bizarre troping of castration itself as the necessary and educative curtailment of desire preparatory to its channelling into normativing channels. Lacan returns us to the horror of the Sophoclean denouement:

[W]hat happens to him is not that the scales fall from his eyes, but that his eyes fall from him like scales. Don't we see Oedipus being reduced to this very object, not by being subject to castration but as I would prefer to say, by being castration itself? — namely being what remains when one of the privileged supports in the form of his eyes, disappears from him. (121)

The history of psychoanalysis provides one instance of this repressive gesture. It is worth pointing out however that this gesture is equally visible in the history of literature, and may arguably have functioned as an influential backdrop to Freud's thought. The eighteenth- and nineteenth-century metamorphosis of tragic vision into *Bildungsroman* has been extensively charted. From the point of view of psychoanalysis and queer theory (if they can be said to share a point of view) two aspects of this metamorphosis may usefully be highlighted, in the first instance what appears to be its structural necessity, and in the second, its propensity to lend itself to coercive ideologies, such as precisely the classic heteronormative version of the Oedipus complex.

It is tempting to begin with the second point first (who can resist a rant?). Historically tragedy has been the art form which has most uncompromisingly engaged with the anarchic forces, among them sexuality, which disrupt human destiny. Shakespearian tragedy like the great Greek plays, bears witness to the radical impossibility of a sustained and benign ordering of desire, to the irruptive and destructive otherness which severs the continuities installed by social institutions. This starkness is profoundly anti-Enlightenment, and it is interesting to note that it is at the juncture which Lacan designates as that of the birth of modern science and of the subject of psychoanalysis, in other words, the seventeenth and early eighteenth century that literary history locates the decline of tragedy and the rise of the novel. Terry Eagleton (2003) rather caustically describes this moment as a shift from the martial to the marital, from destiny to domesticity (178). There are several ways of theorizing its impetus, among them an analysis of the rise of a pragmatic progressive middle class. Since Lacan so emphatically links the appearance of the subject of psychoanalysis to the birth of modern science, one might also consider the refusal of the new scientific spirit to entertain the concept of impossibility. It is said of Galileo that he urged his contemporaries to measure everything that could be measured and to render measurable that which could not. Tragedy is of course the domain of the impossible, and impossibility is at the heart of queer theory's non-definitions and athwart positionings with respect to sexuality.

A certain type of novel on the contrary, in particular the *Bildungsroman,* highly popular in Freud's lifetime, thematically embraces possibility, progress, and self-determination, alongside the harmonious integration of individual desire and the social good. As Franco Moretti (1997) puts it, this is an art form which tends "to make normality interesting *as* normality" (55). The *Bildungsroman* is classically a narrative of education whose teleological impetus is underpinned by some kind of reconciliatory or recuperative myth permitting suffering pain or evil to be instrumentalized in the service of a wider social good. This very ancient teleological curve (Aristotle's *anagnorisis*) was put to work in quite specific ways in the eighteenth and nineteenth centuries. *Bildungsroman,* which focused to great effect on the complexity and individuality of its hero/heroine, tracing out very varied and intricate narrative paths, all of which, tended to fetch up on the same marital shores. As both Sigi Jottkandt (2005) and Martin Swales show in their masterly discussions of the novels of Henry James, all the singular potential of the protagonist's desiring quest had somehow to recognize as its destination, the socialized outcomes of marriage, family and (if male) career. In Jottkandt's words,

> the ultimate telos of the *Bildungsroman* […] lies in the way it promises to realize the ideal synthesis of freedom and necessity, uniting under one term both individual desire (sensuous impulses) and the larger social Good (an ethical or moral community). In marriage, the individual's desire coincides with society's law, transforming what is essentially […] an economic transaction into an expression of personal freedom. (20)

The important thing here is that this trajectory is in no way imposed, but freely chosen: "the marriage contract elicits *voluntary* consent to society's limitations on the individual's erotic freedom by revealing how, what appeared initially to be opposed (individual desire and duty) are really one and the same thing" (20). How have the ideological underpinnings of this myth remained so invisible for so long? Jottkandt is trenchant:

> When the protagonist leaves home and embarks on a series of painful adventures, only to emerge from these experiences with a greater sense of self and ethical destiny — when that is, the teleology of the Bildungsroman teaches the individual to sacrifice her presumptuous individuality and voluntarily submit to the greater Good of an ethical destiny within the larger social group by troping it as the realization and expression of her singular desire — the very same aesthetic ideology is at work which makes us blind to the potentially very real violence that may be inflicted in the name of that social Good. (21)

Indeed it is on this violence that all such idealizing tropes such as narratives of sacrifice and recuperation depend, as she goes on to say. The runaway success of this ideological torsion which funnels anarchic perverse polymorphous sexuality into the safe channels of the marriage contract is extravagantly evident in the millions of women who batten hungrily onto the romantic fiction of Mills and Boon as the truest, most subjective expression of their deep desire.

The forces which create this torsion are not then to be lightly dismissed. The history of tragedy as an art form would suggest that the scandal of human desire is almost invariably tamped and blurred into recuperative and normalizing narrative variants. In *The Birth of Tragedy* (2008), Nietzsche blames Socrates for sanctioning these attempts to impose intelligibility and a kind of anodyne moral didacticism on the unruly turbulence of tragic form (64). In a recent discussion of the long history of this theory-driven dilution, Terry Eagleton (2003) rather witheringly suggests that "knowledge in the long aftermath of tragic theatre is no longer mythical or mystical but coupled to the groveling English values of virtue and morality, happiness and self-transparency" (18). The discrepancy between tragedy and theories of tragedy is largely due to a jagged refusal of amenability on the part of tragic truth. As another commentator observes; "Tragic plays, rather than bearing out the salient principles of traditional dramatic theory resist them and withstand the modes of understanding they make possible" (Gellrich 1988, 7). Eagleton, like Jottkandt, is not unaware of the ideological underlay of this tendency to dilution, and is suspicious of attempts to press gang the disruptive destabilizing energy of tragedy into the muted contours of the cautionary tale.

From tragedy to *Bildungsroman,* from performative intransigence to moralizing theories, the analogy with what has happened in psychoanalytic theory is easily sketched. And rightly evokes queer protest. The challenge here as Kuzniar points out is to psychoanalysis. It seems to me that psychoanalytic theory actually goes some way towards explaining its own narrative slippage, via its pinpointing of repression, which sometimes works in the direction of a kind of sedative reductionism. Part of this project consists in an attempt to erase or at least to offer illusory solutions to the troubling enigma of sexuality. There are formidable, probably insuperable obstacles to reversing the normativing slippage from Sophocles to Freud, from Oedipus Rex to the Oedipus complex, since this slippage is structural and not simply historical. Indeed it is not even necessary to invoke psychoanalytic theory here since in both Greek and Shakespearian tragedy, this normativing gesture frequently appears in the play itself as an attempt at closure. In the final moments of the great tragedies, the hero no longer speaks but is spoken about. He or she has become the object of a commentary which passes between chorus and audience. But it is worth pausing over the status of this commentary. If one looks at some of the instances in both ancient Greek and Shakespearean tragedy where commentary is passed to the other it is a striking fact that the commentary of this other is at an altogether different and radically inferior level to what has occurred on stage. At the moment of ultimate stasis, there where the audience is confronted with the image of Lear as he falls dead with the dead Cordelia in his arms, it would appear that some semblance of continuity must be assured, even if this semblance is itself rendered derisory by the contrast between the stark grandeur of the final image and the plodding rhythms of the words with which Edgar closes the play:

> The weight of this sad time we must obey;
> Speak what we feel, not what we ought to say.
> The oldest hath borne most: we that are young
> Shall never see so much nor live so long.
>
> (Shakespeare 1979, 1113)

As Franco Moretti (1983) points out the extraordinary dramatic efficacy of these lines consists precisely in "their chilling stupidity, in the drastic banalization they impose on the play" (52). At the point of ultimate non-sense, "in the very work that has unhinged our trust in the meaning of words, there reappears the obtuse assurance of sing-song proverb and of dead metaphor" (52). The notion that a kind of universalizing summary could possibly be adequate to the catastrophic happenings we have just witnessed is savagely undercut by these sing-song rhythms, these rhyming saws, whose blind mediocrity can only indicate, as Moretti points out "the chasm that has opened between facts and words, or more properly between referents and signifieds" (53). While Moretti rightly sees this commentary as plodding, sing-song and inadequate, it is nonetheless almost always there, marking the need for continuity, an attempt at re-installing the status quo by compressing what is completely untellable: "a tale/ Told by an idiot, full of sound and fury/ Signifying nothing" (Shakespeare 1979, 1025) into a banalizing narrative of universal moral import.

The drive to restore the status quo, to cover over the lack in being laid bare by tragedy is, I would suggest, ultimately anxiety driven, which accounts for its extraordinary tenacity and its capacity to reassert itself almost, one might say, regardless of the severity of the challenges encountered. Fiercer than the will to power which in fact derives from it, this flight from the non-being which underpins our existence insists on the coherence of ordered identities and the safety of a corralled and defined *modus vivendi*. This is as clearly visible in the great catastrophes of history as it is in the tragic form just discussed. As Žižek (2000) says of this tenacity which he calls "the Oedipal order": "it is a gargantuan symbolic matrix embodied in a vast set of ideological institutions, rituals and practices" in which all possible dissensions and transgressions are already taken into account, since it is composed both of "symbolic forms *and* their codified transgressions" (314).

Psychoanalysis exists to examine the anxiety-laden roots of this hegemonic will and not to let itself be co-opted and enrolled in its service. The facility with which this anxiety translates into the will to power and the brutal suppression of otherness is a way marker testifying to the ever-present fragility of the narcissistic identifications underpinned by this violent tenacity. What Samuel Beckett (1987) has wonderfully called "that most necessary and most monotonous of plagiarisms, the plagiarism of the self" (33) should of course be put in question by psychoanalysis, but this plagiarism is persistent, and identity markers are never more categorical than when unexamined. (While writing this paper I heard a jubilant farmer on the radio announcing that his cow's "alluring femininity" had won her first prize at the Tullamore Agricultural Show!)

Lacan (1958–59) defines the unconscious in *Desire and Its Interpretation* as "this something which always puts the subject at a certain distance from his being, and which means precisely that this being never rejoins him" (Session 12/11/58, 15). How then can psychoanalysis position itself otherwise than athwart? Its history however shows it to be dangerously susceptible to subsumption by conformist ideologies. In his incisive and insightful critique *For and Against Psychoanalysis* (2006), Stephen Frosh points to two ways in which psychoanalysis can function in society. One, the "positive" one focusing on what psychoanalysis can offer to social values — "prescribing particular ways of organizing society that will produce social and individual health (a position that can certainly lead to progressive policies but can also be sucked into normative prescriptiveness of the right way to be)"; the other "negative," which refers to "its capacity to sustain a critical attitude constantly exploring the underpinnings of the individual and the workings of the social order" (175). The work of Lacan has gone some distance along this negative axis. As one commentator has put it: "what has been especially influential in Lacan's writings is the point that the imaginary and symbolic dimensions of psychical life are themselves the ideological carriers of culture and history" (Elliott 2005, 35).

In the most groundbreaking of all his books, *The Interpretation of Dreams* (1900), Freud reversed the totalizing gesture by privileging the dream fragment and de-throning narrative coherence. Laplanche goes further seeing in these attempts at completeness and closure a defensive process, and "the guarantee and seal of repression" (Frosh 2006, 176). As Kuzniar has pointed out the so-called narrative of psychogenesis is seriously suspect in this regard. One of the tasks of contemporary psychoanalysis is to disrupt its coherence, and queer theory is perhaps our most important ally in this venture.

Works Cited

Barthes, Roland. *The Pleasure of the Text,* trans. Richard Miller. New York: Hill and Wang, 1975.

Beckett, Samuel. *Proust and Three Dialogues.* London: Faber and Faber 1987 (1931).

Eagleton, Terry. *Sweet Violence: The Idea of the Tragic.* Oxford: Blackwell, 2003.

Elliott, Anthony. *Psychoanalytic Theory: An Introduction.* London: Palgrave, 2002.

Freud, Sigmund. "Some Psychical Consequences of the Anatomical Distinction between the Sexes" (1925). In *Standard Edition of the Complete Psychological Works of Sigmund Freud,* vol. 19, ed. and trans. James Strachey in collaboration with Anna Freud and assisted by Alix Strachey and Alan Tyson, 248–58. 1961; rpt. London: Vintage, 2001.

———. "On the Universal Tendency to Debasement in the Sphere of Love" (1912). In *Standard Edition of the Complete*

Psychological Works of Sigmund Freud, Vol. 11, ed. and trans. James Strachey in collaboration with Anna Freud and assisted by Alix Strachey and Alan Tyson, 179–90. 1957; rpt. London: Vintage, 2001.

———. "Three Essays on the Theory of Sexuality" (1905). In *Standard Edition of the Complete Psychological Works of Sigmund Freud,* Vol. 7, ed. and trans. James Strachey in collaboration with Anna Freud and assisted by Alix Strachey and Alan Tyson, 135–245. 1953; rpt. London: Vintage, 2001.

———. *The Interpretation of Dreams* (1900). *The Standard Edition of the Complete Psychological Worksof Sigmund Freud,* Vols. 4 and 5, ed. and trans. James Strachey in collaboration with Anna Freud and assisted by Alix Strachey and Alan Tyson. 1953; rpt. London: Vintage, 2001.

———. "The Aetiology of Hysteria" (1896). In *Standard Edition of the Complete Psychological Works of Sigmund Freud,* Vol. 3, ed. and trans. James Strachey in collaboration with Anna Freud and assisted by Alix Strachey and Alan Tyson, 191–221. 1962; rpt. London: Vintage, 2001.

Frosh, Stephen. *For and Against Psychoanalysis.* London and New York: Routledge, 2006.

Gellrich, Michelle. *Tragedy and Theory.* Princeton, New Jersey: Princeton University Press, 1988.

Jottkandt, Sigi. *Acting Beautifully.* New York: State University of New York Press, 2005.

Lacan, Jacques. *Book XVII: The Other Side of Psychoanalysis* (1969–70), trans. Russell Grigg, London and New York: W.W. Norton and Co., 2007.

———. *Book VII: The Ethics of Psychoanalysis* (1959–60), ed. Jacques-Alain Miller, trans. Dennis Porter, London: Routledge, 1992.

———. *Book VI: Desire and Its Interpretation.* Private trans. Cormac Gallagher (1958–59). http://www.lacaninireland.com/web/wp-content/uploads/2010/06/Book-06-Desire-and-its-interpretation.pdf.

Laplanche, Jean. "Narrativity and Hermeneutics, Some Propositions." *New Formations* 48 (2003): 26–29.

Le Gaufey, Guy. "The Object *a.*" *The Letter: Lacanian Perspectives on Psychoanalysis* 4 (1995): 1–12.

Masson, Jeffrey Moussaieff. *The Complete Letters of Sigmund Freud to Wilhelm Fliess,* 1887–1904. Cambridge and London: Harvard University Press, 1985.

Moretti, Franco. *Signs Taken for Wonders.* London: Verso, 1997.

———. *The Way of the World.* London: Verso, 1992.

Nietzsche, Friedrich. *The Birth of Tragedy,* trans. Ian Johnston. 1872; rpt. Nanaimo: Vancouver Island University, 2008.

Shakespeare, William. *Complete Works.* London and Glasgow: Collins, 1979.

Sophocles. "Oedipus Rex." In *The Complete Greek Drama,* eds. Whitney J. Oates and Eugene O'Neill, Jr. New York: Random House, 1938.

Žižek, Slavoj. *The Ticklish Subject.* London: Verso, 2000.

15

Enigmatic Sexuality

Katrine Zeuthen and Judy Gammelgaard

Introduction

It was not without hesitation that we agreed to take part in the discussion initiated by the editors of this book. We are only very superficially acquainted with queer theory, and as clinical practitioners we are not quite at ease with postmodern and post-structuralist thinking, and thus we felt ourselves to be unfamiliar with the perspectives presented by those who are more well versed in this field.

In some ways our apprehension was confirmed when we read the texts, but at the same time our curiosity was piqued when we realized that psychoanalysis was being both used and challenged by deconstructive readings of the Freudian theory of sexuality. As we gradually familiarized ourselves with this line of thinking, we found several perspectives we wanted to address. Because of the limited space, our answers to the many interesting and provocative ideas are of course only preliminary. To this we want to add that we have confined ourselves to commenting on the ideas presented in this book and only occasionally on the ideas quoted in the book, many of which we are not familiar with.

The authors of this book take a postmodern, deconstructive approach, reading classical Freudian psychoanalysis from a certain critical perspective. Most of the authors follow the Lacanian and post-Lacanian return to Freud in an attempt to promote a subversive and queer theory of sexuality. Lisa Downing makes this very explicit in her chapter, when she states that sexuality is the common theme of interest in psychoanalysis and queer theory. "In the former," however, "it is a source of truth to be tapped; in the latter it is a perversion and power-laden lie to be exposed."

This lie to be exposed — according to Lara Farina — is Freud's concept of the Oedipus complex, the focal point of his theory of infantile polymorphous sexual development. Freud saw this concept, so the argument goes, as a "foundational structure of modern Western society (which) produces the opposition of gender and the experience of desire as lack."

Later when we discuss Laplanche's concept of "the sexual" we shall comment on the distinction between gender and sex which does not have the same bearing in most European languages where the two concepts tend to be typically expressed with the same word.

Furthermore, queer theorists challenge Freud's developmental model of sexuality and not least his theory of perversion "as sexuality gone awry" (Downing). A prominent spokeswoman for this approach is Judith Butler, who combines feminist and queer theory to give substantial political and ideological weight to the concept of gender as performance rather than essential. Defined as performance, gender and sexuality "are a series of performances that habitually *do us* (implying that) we can turn around and do them back" (Downing). We can in other words "*transform* the meaning of gender by performing it self-consciously, playfully and with self-awareness rather than unconsciously and in ways that shore up the idea that gender emanates naturally from an essentially sexed subject" (Downing). We wholeheartedly support Butler and others in their political opposition to oppressive and ideological crusades against sexual minorities and find the deconstruction of what is often taken for granted enriching. However, we also see the shortcoming of this strategy when working with patients, whether homosexual or sexually perverted.

While we greatly appreciate a theory of sexuality and desire which escapes the binary concepts of male and female that haunt Western conceptualizations of gender, we want to underline that Freudian theory only concerns itself in a very limited way with gender, focusing rather on repressed, infantile sexuality. We shall return to this.

While reading through the chapters of different queer theoretical accounts of sexuality we found ourselves caught in a dilemma. On the one hand, we were genuinely attracted to the many poetic notions of a sexuality pointing to a desire, as Kathryn Bond Stockton puts it, "over the staid nature of pleasure." Introducing the term "bliss" as one of the meanings of the Lacanian term *jouissance,* gives desire the touch of queering, which according to Farina endows it with the critical potential for "the dismantling of sexual norms." More importantly it makes sexuality what Bond Stockton captures poetically as "sexy, intimate, scandalous, and bodily, while it's evasive of capture and speech." We would also willingly take part in the imagined party inspired by Plato's *Symposium* where love, philosophy and intoxication are gathered in the picture of Socrates drunk in love. Farina hopefully transfers this picture to the analytical situation, wanting the analyst to be drunk in love, "rather than remain at a remove from the erotic object of analysis." Analytic work could hardly take place if we weren't intoxicated by love and philosophy.

However, we must respond to what Farina describes as the pessimism of psychoanalysis, when we are confronted with descriptions of what queer means for our understanding of sexuality. Queer is supposedly "wonderfully suggestive of a whole range of sexual possibilities" (Kuzniar, quoting Ellis Hanson) or according to Alexander Doty "a flexible space for expression of all aspects of non (anti, contra-) straight production and reception" (Kuzniar, quoting Doty). Maybe we are too serious or literal, but we sense in these and other attempts to delimit the essence of sexual queerness an idealization which contradicts our experiences of the pain and suffering which many patients — homosexual as well as heterosexual — associate with coming to grips with the unconscious part of sexuality. Alice Kuzniar proposes that instead of understanding the homosexual, psychoanalytically speaking, as someone who has failed to adopt a heterosexual identity, we should instead see him or her as "dis-identif[ying with heterosexuality and the coerciveness and predictability of the oedipal ego formation all while acknowledging the pains it produces." From a clinical point of view, this sounds like a political and ideological aim that is not in accordance with psychoanalysis, which abstains from defining the aims of the cure except of course for the goal of relieving the patient's pain.

We find ourselves on familiar ground with the suggestions of Lisa Downing, Will Stockton and Kathryn Bond Stockton. To overcome the false dichotomy between, for instance, "fluidity" and "fixation" as signifying the vicissitudes of drive, we need a theory, as Downing argues, that dissolves both and comes up with a more nuanced way of thinking about the concrete ways people find towards pleasure. When fluidity is used as an uncritical weapon against the psychoanalytical idea of fixation it may turn out to be just the other side of the coin rather than giving way for a dissolving of limiting boundaries.

We also need the kind of discussion we see in Will Stockton's chapter of the book which critiques psychoanalysis for its a-historical conceptualization of sexuality. Using Lacan and Laplanche to critique Foucault, Stockton shows that "Foucault denies the 'reality' of the unconscious by focusing only on sexuality's emergence as a discourse of human 'truth.'" Thereby, he argues, we ignore that "sex [...] is not simply discourse [...], sex rather confounds the discourses of sexuality."

Following Stockton we will focus the rest of our discussion on unconscious sexuality as the object of clinical and theoretical psychoanalytical investigation. After a brief clinical vignette we go on to discuss Laplanche's reading of Freud's concept of sexuality, supplementing it with a discussion of what Ruth Stein (1998, 2008) refers to as the excess, the poignant and the enigma of sexuality, taking a different perspective on Laplanche.

Unconscious Sexuality

Anna sought analysis not because of her homosexuality but due to the difficulties she experienced in ordinary interpersonal relationships, including the give and take in her love life. The way to her sexual life had been very long and troublesome, from the moment she dimly realised that she was different from her girl-friends in that she could not take part in their budding interest in and orientation towards the opposite sex. Now, while Anna probably did not differ from others who had to fight their way through the constraints of normative gender roles and was pain-fully aware of the comprehensive constraints these norms and conventions imposed on her search for her own sexuality, this was not the main issue in the analytical situation where another aspect of her sexuality came up in the transference. Anna started analysis with what at first appeared as a strong erotic transfer-ence. The remarkable thing about these eroticized transference fantasies was how stubbornly she insisted on addressing them to the analyst, giving reasons for the analyst's countertransfer-ence questions like: "what is it, she wants from the analyst?" In sharp contrast to Anna's inhibitions against communicating about herself and sharing her thoughts and feelings with others including her analyst, she was remarkably open about her erotic fantasies, seemingly due to the pressure and vital importance of their meaning, which however, was not available to conscious-ness.

Anna grew up in a family where sexuality was non-existent in meaning, i.e., neither visible nor mentioned. Even though her mother cared for the physical needs of her small daughter, there was an absence of libidinal investment, corresponding to the image of the mother of the hysterical patient described so incisively by Christopher Bollas (2000). A distinct modesty and insecurity relating to her own sexuality prevented the mother from normal seduction and made it difficult for her daughter to find her way to the erotic playfulness of the body. Finding no answers to her infantile curiosity about the parental couple, Anna turned her investigation of sexuality inwards in an attempt to find the object and aim of desire in fantasy. The result was a kind of overheating in the inside world that complicated genuine reciprocity and blocked her ability to communicate in words. Experiencing her desire as "too much" for the other to meet and feeling awkward when trying to decipher the other's desire, Anna was and is often desperately unhappy when her attempts at seduction fail. Allowing herself to address the question of the other's desire in a concrete way in analysis, Anna encountered the legitimacy of this kind of question for the first time.

Space does not allow us to go into greater detail about Anna. We want to illustrate that sexuality in the Freudian meaning of the term is deeply woven into the texture of mutuality; unlike gender, however, it is not assigned to the child in his or her up-bringing but produced as a residue of what remains non-understood in the erotic communication. This leads us to Laplanche and to Stein's concepts of the excess, the poignant and the enigma of sexuality.

Otherness

In their attempts to explain how our sexual identity affects who we are, queer theorists tend to focus on society and its oppressive dualistic norms of sexuality that equate sexuality with gender. In our opinion the deconstructive strategy of queer theory focuses too one-sidedly on society when searching for answers to questions such as "who am I if I do not fit into these categories?" or "why do I feel queer?" In her essay, Kuzniar suggests the theory of Laplanche as a possible frame for finding "a language to reflect feelings of disjointedness." We think that if the above-mentioned questions are to be addressed in a Laplanchean framework we must turn to the small child and its early relations with important caregivers. It seems that the queer focus has lost sight of the fact that society *is* these primary relations, which are cultural expansions of the biological womb. This focus is expressed most uncompromisingly by Leo Bersani whose work is cited by most of the contributors to this book.

Thus Bond Stockton refers to Bersani stating "that sex keeps one free from the 'violence of relationships.'" In visualising sex as beyond object-choice and even personhood altogether, Tim Dean — quoted by Farina — follows the same line of thought with the aim of liberating the sexual from any kind of relationship. Laplanche begs to differ.

Laplanche's theory (1989, 1997, 1999, 2002) expands and enriches the focus of queer theory by turning our attention to the early relation between child and adult and the development of meaning that takes place here. He does so without losing the deconstructive focus characteristic of queer theory, but also without dissolving the creation of meaning into powerful yet arbitrary constructions. When the adult gratifies the child's needs, the child is confronted with the adult's desire. The child is seduced by the adult other through its attempt to understand the desire when the adult addresses the child; an address full of meanings that are inaccessible and thus enigmatic to the child.

What Kuzniar calls "lack of intelligibility," Laplanche refers to as an enigmatic message or signifier. There is a difference, we want to emphasize, between that which lacks intelligibility and that which presents itself as an enigma to be solved. Laplanche's focus is thus the hidden and enigmatic signifier of the adult's care-giving; a focus that embeds infantile sexuality in a real lived relation rather than surrounding it with "an aura of sexual mystery," a signification that too easily leads to other and similar vague descriptions of sexuality as "being mystifying and unexplainable" (Kuzniar). Desire is directed towards what we lack, Farina asserts. We agree, but at the same time we want to point out that the specific experience of lack is always embedded in what we have experienced in our real and lived mother-child relation. The construction or translation of meaning is not arbitrary but has as its starting point the adult's enigmatic signifier and thus the adult's *otherness,* rather than sheer lack of intelligibility.

In her work on the poignant, the enigmatic, and the excessive, Ruth Stein (1998) emphasizes the child's fundamental need for bodily care, thus making explicit that sexuality comes into existence and develops in real and lived relations. First of all there is a body and with it bodily excitations and sensations that are overwhelming or *poignant* (263). Secondly there is the enigmatic object, the caretaker "whose otherness, transmitted via enigmatic, unconscious, seductive messages helps the infant's psyche build itself through the infant's efforts to 'translate' and fantasize about these messages" (2008, 47). And finally, that which cannot be given meaning is by Stein defined as excessive, in so far that "the mother's enigmatic message vaguely attracts and excites the child, but it can only belatedly become symbolised" (1998, 263). Often this symbolization takes place not only very late but is also very painful, as Anna's story reflects.

Anna's relations to others and the meaning or lack of meaning she experiences in these relations are marked by the enigmatic address of the adult other as well as the adult other's failure to answer Anna's question: "what do you want from me and who am I in relation to your enigmatic address?" Stein's concept of sexualization — i.e., the ability of the infant to deal with the painful gap between herself and the excessive adult — has been very useful in working with Anna, since it gives meaning to the powerful libidinal excitement which found a kind of solution in her sexual fantasies. Sexualization, thus understood, is a capacity, a positive achievement and not only a defensive manoeuvre. Admitting that we need to add to the concept of sexuality, inherited from Freud, some other dimensions to take into account the extraordinary impact of sexuality, Stein turns to queer theory and the work of Georges Bataille and, as she puts it, his idea that eroticism by "undoing us [...] is a device for carrying us beyond the toll of our separate individuality" (255). In Stein's renewal of psychoanalytic writings on sexuality we find similarities between her approach and the many fresh perspectives expressed by the authors of this book. Thus we see a similarity between her concept of excess (2008) and the concept of bliss introduced by Bond Stockton. Stein, however, like Laplanche cannot envisage sexuality outside the relation between the subject and the other, even though it is both enigmatic and excessive.

We shall give a clinical account of how a child's unconscious sexuality can be seen as a result of the communication between mother and child, leaving the child with an excessive sexuality as a consequence of his attempt to respond to his mother's enigmatic messages.

Tom, Sexuality and Gender

In the analytic work with the eight-year-old Tom it became evident that what at first appears to be a story of a boy whose sexual identity *as* a boy was prevented from developing by sexual abuse and by his mother's attempt to protect him, turns out instead to be about a child whose mother did not let him find his way to his own infantile sexual fantasies of what it means to be Tom in relation to his mother.

A male pre-school teacher that Tom had been very attached to had abused Tom anally, when Tom was six years old. His condition was worrisome as he suffered from chronic constipation, withdrew from his classmates, and stayed in his room when he was at home. His parents had been divorced since Tom was two and his relation to his mother was very close; their symbiosis had been reinforced by the abuse and his bad health. At the same time the mother was disgusted by the close relationship her son had had to the pre-school teacher as well as by the sexual abuse.

The mother protected her son by shutting out the outside world, thus preventing him from being in the world independently, but the world that obtained between mother and son was potentially threatening. To Tom, faeces were dangerous, symbolizing the inverted penis and penetrating him when he held it back. If he let it go, he feared it would penetrate his mother, yet holding it back kept him at a pre-genital stage. Thus faeces became identical with the penis, which mother and son conspired to ban from their relationship. Thus the mother was able to maintain a relation to her son that was without sexuality. Holding back the faeces and thus his development, however, prevented Tom from creating social relationships with children of his age.

First of all Tom's case is a nasty example of perverse seduction, which inflicts on the child a brutal reality that takes the place of the child's infantile fantasies. These infantile fantasies should have carried out the work of interpreting the enigmas given to the child through maternal seduction. Tom was forced to cling to his mother who seemed simultaneously both available in reality and inaccessible. The mother repeated the trauma he had suffered by binding him to their relation and denying him the right to give their relation meaning in fantasy. Tom missed the moment where he should have developed his infantile sexual fantasies as interplay between fantasy and reality, an interplay that should have separated him from the relation to his mother. Instead, he met his mother's enigmatic address, an approach that was already filled with significance, but a significance that was totally beyond the reach of Tom's translations. Thus, Tom could neither answer his mother nor give their relation a meaning of his own. Fantasy was not put to work but rather was locked by the mother's gaze. Tom's holding back of faeces as an inverted penis is not to be interpreted as a holding back of gender, but as a holding back of the mother's enigmatic address and her refusal to let him give their relation a meaning of his own. The faeces prevented Tom's creation of infantile sexual fantasies.

Continuing the Copernican Revolution

While we were reading the attempts of the authors of this book to seek out the queerness of psychoanalysis through the work of Lacanian and post-Lacanian analysts, we found an interesting article, written by Laplanche (2007), which takes us directly to the subject under consideration.

In this article, Laplanche presents an outline of how the triad of gender, sex and the sexual functions in the early history of the human being, suggesting that "the sexual" as such "is the unconscious residue of the repression/symbolization of gender by sex" (202). In other words, the sexual becomes the repressed through the societal or parental need to define gender as twofold by letting biology and genital difference assign gender a duality. With his interest in and talent for dissolving givens in our understanding of what it means to be human, Laplanche argues that "conceptual distinctions are valid not in themselves but for the conflictual potentialities they conceal" (202). Binary distinctions often hide a forbidden middle that does not automatically fit into the categories which we use and allow to define the world and its possible identities. Laplanche states that: "the question of sexual identity" is displaced "onto the question of gender identity" (202).

In a society with a "forbidden middle" or a lack of room for that which falls between false dichotomies we should focus on the relation between subject and object, and the difficulties and pain that the otherness of relating holds. How can we keep expanding the Copernican revolution, its unfinishedness, its openness? If Laplanche gives queer theory a hand we can keep our focus decentralized, that is to say that we can shift between the intersubjectivity of the child and the adult other, as well as between the intersubjectivity of subject and society. The Ptolemaism or self-centeredness of the human psyche is a conviction acquired by the psyche itself — as is that of society.

Queer theory opposes duality; first and foremost that which is founded on the argument that biology determines sexual identity. It argues that society leaves out categories that are queer — that is, not dualistic or defined by having or not having a penis, being or not being male — and tries to capture a world of identities not categorized in stigmatizing dualities and categories.

Such identities do not maintain dualities by falling inbetween them, but dissolve duality by pointing at the many ways of being that cannot be understood within the dualistic categories supposedly determined by biology. Queer theory points to the excess of sexuality by reminding us how very difficult it is to categorize sexuality in acceptably delineated dualistic definitions.

While queer theory helps us question the categories of sexual identity by turning to society, psychoanalytic theory and its clinical practice can help us understand how identity is embedded in the relation between the child and the adult and how this decentralized subjectivity is a driving force of development that is facilitated in the relation; that is, the relation between child and adult as well as the relation between analyst and analysand. Psychoanalysis lets us focus on the enigmatic character of sexuality and helps us maintain that enigma as defined by that which cannot be categorized. Psychoanalysis can explain to us why sexuality or the sexual is not twofold or dualistic but rather plural or polymorph.

Works Cited

Bollas, Christopher. *Hysteria.* London and New York: Routledge, 2000.

Laplanche, Jean. *New Foundations for Psychoanalysis,* trans. David Macey. Oxford: Basil Blackwell, 1989.

———. "The Theory of Seduction and the Problem of the Other." *International Journal of Psychoanalysis* 78 (1997): 653–66.

———. *Essays on Otherness.* London and New York: Routledge, 1999.

———. "Sexuality and Attachment in Metapsychology." In *Infantile Sexuality and Attachment,* ed. Daniel Widlöcher, 37–45. New York: Other Press, 2002.

———. "Gender, Sex, and the Sexual." *Studies in Gender and Sexuality* 8, no. 2 (2007): 201–19.

Stein, Ruth. "The Poignant, The Excessive and The Enigmatic in Sexuality." *International Journal of Psychoanalysis* 79 (1998): 253–68.

———. "The Otherness of Sexuality: Excess." *Journal of the American Psychoanalytic Association* 56, no. 1 (2008): 43–71.

16

The Transforming Nexus:
Psychoanalysis, Social Theory, and Queer Childhood

Ken Corbett

Twenty-first-century clinical psychoanalysis surely has as much
to do with feminism, queer theory, and social philosophy as
it does with Freudian tenets, postwar British object-relations
theory, American ego psychology, or even modern attachment
models. The social critique of the normal is now developing developmental theories. Questioning the rigid necessity of a normative symbolic order has led not only to rethinking human
development, but also to the re-conception of psychotherapeutic care.

This modern frame of mind has only been articulated in a
relatively small quarter of psychoanalysis[1] (a guild of small sec-
tors), yet it reaches into virtually every mode of psychoanalytic
practice.[2] Psychoanalysts have begun to rethink life as a complex

---

1   See for example, Aron and Starr (2011); Corbett (2009, 2010); Dimen (2003,
    2011); Dimen and Goldner (2005), Fairfield (2002); Goldner (2010); Harris
    (2005), Layton (2004); Rozmarin, (2010); Saketopoulo (2010); Stein (2010);
    Suchet (2010).

2   See, for example, how Françoise Davoine and Jean-Max Gaudilliere (2004)
    incorporate social theory into their largely Lacanian inflected considera-
    tions of trauma and history, and in so doing argue for modes of psycho-
    therapeutic care that are outside the dictates of classical technique. Or con-
    sider how Fonagy (2001) approaches the press of a social world in his most
    recent theorizing about attachment and sexuality—albeit troubled by his

psyche-socio-soma field, open to multiple points of reference, normative expectation, and inimitable relational bonds.

Theorists now place the evolving human in an evolving relational world. They do so by leaning into bedrock psychoanalytic presuppositions as to the ways in which fantasy is inter-implicated with embodiment and mind. Bodies and minds are seen as open to a range of fantastic expressions and relational dynamics, including traumatic intromissions, as well as, non-normative openings. If one accepts that relational dynamics create varying inter-subjective spaces, spaces from and through which humans emerge, spaces that are more or less coherent and more or less organizing and loving, spaces that inflect the manner of the enigmatic transfer of fantasies and attributes, then one also has to be open to considering the ways in which the evolution of the human is open to a range of relational organizations and coherence.

Further, if one also accepts that the human is never outside social regulation (even before birth, even in resistance), and if it is additionally accepted that humans are formed and constituted by cultural norms, then one is left to question the attribution of that which is called "originary." There is no pure psychology of the protagonists (mother and child). There is no pure authority of the past. Intromissions, both traumatic and nurturing, are always and already socially and historically constituted, and thereby open to a variety of nuance and complication (even contradiction).

---

failure to problematize the imagination through the social. Or look at Kulish's (2010) effort to integrate social and relational concepts into the frame of modern ego psychology, as she reviews modern theories of gender. Or consider how Straker (2006) integrates social theory into her contemplation of race and hatred, specifically hate within the transference and countertransference — theorizing that rests mainly on Freudian propositions. Or bear in mind Tronick's (2007) efforts to reflect on parent-child attachments as they are interimplicated with cultural orders. Or how Widlocher (2001), in conversation with Jean Laplanche, contemplates the world beyond the parent and infant, and how that world and the history it carries infects every parent, and is, in turn, enigmatically transferred between every parent and child.

We look now toward a wider arc of livable lives; ideality is not reserved for the more normative among us. And in so doing, we have begun to theorize lives built in-and-through social praxis and regulatory forces. We reflect on the anxious press of normative regulation. We consider how social orders and symbolic registers are enigmatically transferred in idiomatic parent-child relations.

Without a theory that locates such perception and assessment within the constituting frame of the social, we are left with no social demarcation for the clinical scene of address. We are left with a "neutral" analyst, who appears as if he magically lives outside the inside, as if he is not regulated by cultural orders and twisted by the drill of the normative. The ethical insufficiency that issues from this lack is that it leaves the therapist inadequately prepared to address counter-transference, and to recognize if counter-resistance or counter-anxiety is being repeated through normative presumption, and reactive pathologizing.

At stake here is nothing less than how we measure the well-being of our fellow citizens. And, in turn, how we are rethinking the sphere of the psychological, including the ethics and the modes of care that constitute the therapeutic scene of address.

Rethinking the psychological sphere has been intertwined with a reconsideration of psychotherapeutic action. Focusing on the work of reverie and potential space has been central to these considerations. A premium is placed on discerning the role of fantasy as it builds potential space between analyst and patient. This technique is not distinguished from the longstanding classical mode of suspension that grounds (or more precisely ungrounds) psychoanalytic listening. We listen with free-floating ears; we suspend and hover; we look toward manifest expressions of the re-cathecting unconscious.

Modern technique, however, is distinguished from classical modes of apprehending the patient in that the *free* in free floating is problematized even as it is sought. It is understood that no one lives outside the inside, and that fantasy, interiority, and relationality are always-and-already constituted by cultural norms — for both patient and analyst alike. The work of normative regulation, as it regulates affective and ethical dispositions, is held in view — held as regulatory force comes to bear (via anxiety and aggression; via attachment and security; via love and hate) on any narrative. The frame of psychotherapeutic action has also been rethought as a potential field open to both the patient and analyst, one that necessitates a broader based analysis, one that includes the relational exchange between patient and analyst, not just what has come to be called the "one person" psychology of the patient.[3]

Transforming Nexus

I have come to think of one technical feature of this practice as seeking what I refer to as a transforming nexus. I move forward here to illustrate this process. I do so because I could not think about this process outside of my doubled education in psychoanalysis and queer theory. The congress and accomplishment of this union, this potential space, if you will, seems important to catalogue and consider. What is more, it is suspension, the knitting nexus, and the transfers that unfurl to shape this space that clinical psychoanalysis has to offer, as it may be similar to and/ or distinguished from queer literary, theoretical or textual analytic instruments, aims and spaces. In speaking of distinction I do not aim toward the differences between a text and a patient.

Frankly, I don't find the blunt distinction between a patient and a text to be productive. Yes, in the consulting room analysts are posed with the pressing reality of the other. But are we not also pressed by the immanence of Anna Karenina as she makes her way to the train station? How different is our affective range, reach, and even consequence with a patient or with a fictive character? Indeed, a patient may demand something immediate, a response that hinges on our immediate affective

---

3 This technique, broadly referred to as "relational," is open to a variety of technical expressions and variations. For good overviews of this tradition, see Mitchell and Aron (1999); Aron and Harris (2005); Suchet, Harris and Aron (2007); Mitchell (2003); Aron (2001); Benjamin (1997); Bromberg (2001); Cooper (2010).

resonance employed in the service of reciprocal action/speech/ interpretation. But might a fictive character also press for immediacy? Fictive creations demand, pull at us, and are not so easily pushed aside. Our responses may be impotent (as is true with patients as well). We can warn Anna (I would go so far as to argue that we are warning her in the act of reading), but it will do no good. Still and all, might it be the case that our affective resonance and reciprocal experience found in a textual realm operates on a different temporal register? Does Anna come back to us, unknowing, unbid, as we struggle to meet the pressing reality of the other in the consulting room? I not only think she does. I am glad she does.

I take the time to make these points about texts and patients, because in my view there are differing and yet overlapping modes of reality and reciprocity: theory can be built in the relational rush of reading; theory can be built through relational bid(s) with a patient. I do not think we can so easily cleave the theoretical promise and intervention of clinical psychoanalysis from what is gleaned through the practices of textual analyses. The distinction that interests me is not the patient or text, but the quality of the analysis brought to bear.

The clinical/textual project of theory making is more productively approached as we consider how the modern shift in analytic instrument and aim open onto considerations of interpretation: modes of interpretation, interpretive technique, how interpretations are offered, and to what end. Are interpretations offered as a way to name a gap (a discursive lack)? Or are they offered within a field? Might they do both? Are they offered in accord with well-known signposts of depth, modes of understanding that may dutifully repeat classical psychoanalytic presuppositions with too little regard for the vicissitudes of the human and the evolving social order? Or is the interpretive arc paced in an idiomatic/speculative manner (offered, not declared)? Is room left for the rebounding transference? Is room made to play between psychic and material realities? Is depth found and re-found and re-found through the affect of what is said, and the charge of the relational bid that is made?

I ask these questions not because I think they distinguish queer theoretical textual analyses from clinical analyses. I don't. I ask these questions because clinical psychoanalysis does not only bring a mode of knowing — a set of propositions through which theorists can glean philosophical positions or tenets. Clinical psychoanalysis also brings a mode of practice that rests on the action of interpretation, and modes of interpretation that are different from modes of knowledge. I am reluctant to know the other. I prefer to keep company, to *play in reality* — keeping present, where keeping present has an unexpected relationship to the limits of knowing.

How one works with the limits of knowing and the action of play are, in my view, part of any good-enough psychoanalytic practice; an unknowing that affords the exploration of the relational possibilities to be discovered in the transference and counter-transference; play that opens into a mode of suspension and holding, a complex potential space that allows for and depends on reverie.

An intriguing example of the tensions between knowing and unknowing can be found in a founding queer theory text, Michael Moon's (1998) *A Small Boy and Others,* where he offers readings of both Henry James and Andy Warhol's boyhoods. In approaching James, Moon zeroes in on repetitive themes, fantasies, and scenes of repressed and enacted desires, as well as offering a keen reading of the social order in which James found himself as a boy. Through a cautiously constructed interpretative arc, Moon articulates a set of processes he holds to have been formative of James's queer childhood: daring, dramatic uncanniness, risky weirdness, erotic offcenteredness, uniquely tuned perception and imitation (hypermimesis), unapologetic perversity, and a precocious acquaintance with grief.

The pace of the interpretations rendered by Moon could be called Winnicottian. Moon takes care to stay one step behind James, not ahead of James. Speculation is offered not declared. Room is left for the rebounding transference. Suspension (playing between psychic and material reality) is key here as one seeks to live in the complex matrix of relational potentialities.

In the same text, Moon moves on to contemplate Andy Warhol's childhood. This analysis follows not on the basis of a book
length autobiography, but on one paragraph of one of Warhol's
autobiographies, a paragraph Moon reads as a screen memory,
a condensed scene that draws on actual events but is also composed of imaginary elements.

At odds with the Winnicottian pacing of his analysis of
James, Moon approaches Warhol in a manner more in keeping
with Melanie Klein's determination to interpret unconscious
processes quickly and with authority. Klein held that human life
followed and faltered on an endogenous sadistic instinct and aggressive responses to frustration. Good and bad are set up in the
psyche and undergo a complex play of projections. The authority offered here is declarative not speculative. Warhol's memory
is quickly named as indicative of sexually symbolic conflicts:
castration, phallic narcissism, anality, and the primal scene.
These interpretations may indeed be precise and direct. They
strike me, however, as interpretive moves that leap too far, are
hasty, and determined by the necessity of presumed sign-posts
of depth as opposed to depth that emerges through the affect of
what is said, and the charge of the relational bid that is made.

Symbolic interpretations that are offered without equal attention to the ways in which symbols emerge and merge with
affect and relational exchange do not afford a more subtle and
contingent symbolic reading. They also risk the foreclosure of
play, reverie, and the suspended mental-freedom found therein.
Consider here the unique and original names (the life!) Moon
offers as he catalogues the processes that underscore James's
boyhood, as opposed to the stations-of-the-cross classical psychoanalytic vocabulary he employs in describing Warhol.

I voice this critique with regret, because I believe these ideas
should be a point of debate. Mrs. Klein, as she was known, would
I am sure take issue with my position. And perhaps Moon too
would have good grounds to challenge my assessment of his
differing interpretive strategies. After all, Warhol was famously inarticulate, and virtually mute. Warhol could have left one
with little interpretive room beyond the declarative. Still, there

is cause for debate, and in relation to a project as complex as theorizing queer childhoods progress can only come from this confrontation of opinion, and the theoretical work it compels us to do.

Lincoln

I often find myself suspended. My mind rearranged through the reverberations of reverie. I find myself in this state with both adult and child patients. But at times it is made especially clear with child patients, as I am caught in the vista of a child's vision and led toward a *life suspended playing in reality,* moving as children are wont to move between material reality and psychic reality, moving as transference and counter-transference move in accord with varying relational potentialities. Moving as my mind circles around what they may be trying to tell me about their experience of being socially ordered.

The construction of this transforming nexus seems especially important in work with queer children. Outside a protected potential space within which a queer child may become, he is left to construct an anxious narcissistic approximation. He is left in the poignant pain of foreclosed space; he is left to beckon the mirror. While he may be able to turn toward a shadowed melancholic retreat, he is given little in the way of a progressive push, or the license of a queer imagination, through which he might hope for and work toward securing more productive attachments.

I have learned, along with a number of queer children, the importance of establishing a reliable potential space — one that opens unto practice — as well as the kind of reflection necessary to work through troubling states of anxiety and the shadow of shame. I sometimes wonder if this nexus, this place of practice — this safe return — may be the most important thing I have to offer the children I see.

My clinical experience with gender queer children and their families has afforded me the opportunity to consider how these children and their parents create moments within which the social order of gender is challenged. Within such moments a transforming nexus of gender transfer and malleability is created. Gender is resignified through collective intersubjective fantasies and terms; bonds are forged. These bonds, this challenge to the prevailing order, can be created through a wide range of relational dynamics, fantasies, material conditions, and beliefs (as is true for any parent–child bond). Slipping the symbolic can occur through freedom as well as through alienation. Moments of malleability open through loving protection, just as they open through malignant seduction. Speaking to power may follow mental freedom or mental anguish. How, and whether, a transforming nexus is fashioned is as individual as any parent–child pair.

It has been my overwhelming clinical experience that those children who can, along with their parents, create a holding environment fare much better as they move into the outside world. Across time, this parent-child dialogic is internalized and comes to serve as a voice that privileges the child's peculiar ideality, offers solace in the face of normative cruelty, and holds out the hope these children need to imagine themselves otherwise. I have consistently found it to be the case that those children who cannot establish this holding transforming nexus do not fare nearly as well as they move forward into the world of school and others outside their family. Many permutations of this parent-child breakdown can occur, and many psyches follow. But one pattern that I have had frequent opportunity to analyze is of an abject young person caught in a web of loss. This melancholic condition is usually accompanied by self-reproach and self-torment.[4]

In my second consultation with a boy I will call Lincoln, he discovered that I could draw, and asked me to draw some mice, which I did. He colored them (six pink, one green) and cut them

---

4   My capacity to think through this melancholic condition is indelibly informed by Judith Butler's (1990, 2002, 2004) work on melancholic gender. See also Sedgwick's (1994) theorization of queer childhood, and Salamon (2010).

out. He seemed less pleased with the green mouse, which he crumpled but then attempted to uncrumple. He did not animate them, give them voice, or "play" with them *per se*. He held them, shuffled them, and admired them. At the end of the hour he put them under my radiator, where, as it turned out, they lived for the next three years. During his visits to see me over those years, he would immediately go to the radiator, check on the mice, but never move them. He always seemed pleased to find them, though he did not say much about them.

I pondered the mice in many ways. Were they an illustration of majority rule — one odd man out? The majority in this case, though, was pink. Was that Lincoln's way of pushing back? Were the mice closeted? Was the green mouse the shunned character that would later appear in his games? Or was the green mouse the melancholic one — the aggrieved, the diminished, the shamed, the mouse crumpled by self-reproach; the one who could not speak his identity — the one who may paradoxically take refuge in suffering and, through a kind of circular insanity, ward off his suffering through the manic display of his difference. See me, I am green. Look away, I am crumpled.

In the end, I found that I said little about the mice. It was their security that appeared to matter most, and once they were secured and sustained, it seemed enough. It appeared in some sense to be a pledge. In retrospect, it seems that sheltering the mice served as an opening gambit, a marker of the task at hand — the task of creating a secure space, one that holds but does not immediately or perhaps ever fully articulate a complex set of affects, serving instead to open unto the practice to come.

I speak of practice to denote the practice of psychotherapy, but also, in this case, the practice of gender. Probably the most salient theme that developed across Lincoln's treatment was what I came to think of as "scenes of practice." Lincoln spent much of his first year in treatment dressing and undressing Barbie dolls, commenting on the success of Barbie's various outfits, making alterations to her hair, and eventually to her clothes. Initially, these scenes inevitably came to chaotic and aggressive conclusions. Lincoln would undress the dolls hurriedly, casting the clothes aside; the contents of the scene would be scattered and rendered "a mess." I began to think of these scenes as the "mess" of shame and the curtailing wreck of practice. I also pondered the ways in which these scenes could enact melancholic despair, remorse, and self-torment. Barbie was debased, made to suffer. Sadistic satisfaction was derived therein.

The dynamics of crossing and the constituting practice of gender are not addressed in the traditional discourse on gender queer children. The variety of affects and dilemmas that arise for the gender queer boy in his quest for social recognition are not examined as socially constructed or located. Rather, they are seen as the manifestation of a specific psychic pathology. They are not seen as honorable social, relational bids; they are seen as troubled psychic enactments. The boys are depicted as locked in persecutory compulsive imitations of their mothers, and interpretations are aimed at these enactments, and named as the boys' efforts to simultaneously express and disown their desperate attachment to their mothers.

I noted with Lincoln, as I have with other genderqueer boys, that the anger that emerged in the treatment was not directed at a traumatized and unavailable mother. The anger that emerged in the transference and in various play themes was anger at a mother (at an other) who could not consistently help him metabolize his variant subjectivity.

Lincoln's anger almost always voiced the plaint of grievance, what one might call the dialect of the melancholic. Complaints ("She's messed up." "Her hair is nasty." "Her shoes are ugly.") inevitably imploded, and sad rejection/withdrawal emerged (Barbie was undressed and dejectedly cast aside). It was important to follow this character who met such rough justice and was left with no ally, no voice. At one juncture Lincoln spoke of the unclothed "messy" Barbie as a "girl who wanted too many things," adding, "She deserves to be punished," revealing yet another feature of the melancholic's tendency toward self-reproach and self-hatred.

Initial efforts to compare this character to Lincoln, and to wonder whether he too might feel the same, were met by adamant refusal. Several weeks later, though, Lincoln returned to a similar scene, and this time, unprompted, began to describe the shunned character as "tired" ("That's why she is lying down") and "mad" ("That's why she is naked"). When asked whether she might not be "lonely." Lincoln said, "She was too mad."

I was struck by this response, and by the ways in which it might capture the abjection of melancholy: "Don't disturb my angry withdrawal." "Don't disturb my self-reproach and shame." Through these emotional states the melancholic guards his lost love/identity. But, slowly, Lincoln approached his melancholy. We began to give voice to the shunned character's sense of loneliness and abjection. Eventually, we could approach the shunned girl, and were able to redress her, comb her hair, feed her, and let her rest.

In my final consultation with Lincoln I had the enlightening opportunity to question him about the "harsh things" (his phrase) in his mind. We were drawing together, and he was using colored pencils to draw an underwater scene, one that I recognized as mimicking the world of the "Little Mermaid," a character who intrigued Lincoln, as she has many of the gender queer boys with whom I have worked. I said that I wondered whether he liked Ariel only because she was pretty and had long hair, as he had previously indicated, or whether it might also be the case that he felt like her, "caught between two worlds." Ariel is caught between the world of the sea and her desire to join the earthly world of humans. I wondered whether Lincoln might not feel caught between the world of boys and the world of girls.

He sat silent for a while looking at his drawing, and then handed it to me. He said it was "a present." I thanked him. I then suggested that sometimes presents cover pain, "kind of like a trick." I went on to say that Ariel feels a lot of pain and sorrow. My mind was moving in at least two directions at this juncture. I was thinking of the gravity of the original Hans Christian Andersen story, of the weight of fateful decisions and how the pain of transformation is revealed. In order to gain her legs, the little mermaid agrees to endure great pain. Might this be a way, I was thinking, for Lincoln to express the pain of normative regulation — the price he was paying? I wondered further whether sometimes his "bright girl play" was not only fun, and, well, bright, but also a trick to disguise the anger, sadness, and pain that he felt. He was quick to remind me that "Ariel is happy in the end" — fortified as he was by the Disney camp romance that colors the studio's *Little Mermaid*. I acknowledged that that was in fact true, but added that day-to-day life does not always work out as well as does cartoon life. He gave me one of those looks children often do, as if to say, "Yes, yes, you adults and your reality." He did allow, though, that sometimes he felt "sad" and "mad" — states that he had been so very reluctant to recognize earlier in his treatment, offering, in turn, some recognition that had the potential to move toward the accomplishment of grief and out of the deadlock of melancholia.

I venture, though, that Lincoln was also pointing out that accommodation does not stop with a one-way adjustment. Reality bends. Many genderqueer boys seek to preserve their feminine identifications, to seize moments of mobility, to join forces within minority communities, and to imagine their ways into a world where the social life of gender is more malleable.

In that spirit, we did not move within this treatment toward a summarizing originary explanation. The treatment moved, if anywhere, toward less fixity, and toward the construction of reflective spaces and a social comity that can hold the probity of many origins. The narratives we pursued in the course of our work were in the service of Lincoln's need to establish better reflective resonance, less self-reproach, and greater mental-freedom. Surely, there were other narratives. Surely, there will be other narratives. And just as surely there will be future recontextualizations, relations, and fantasmatic spaces through which Lincoln will reweave.

Works Cited

Aron, Lewis. *A Meeting of Minds: Mutuality in Psychoanalysis.* Hillsdale: The Analytic Press, 2001.

———— and Adrienne Harris. *Relational Psychoanalysis: Innovation and Expansion 2*. Hillsdale: The Analytic Press, 2005.

———— and Karen Starr. *Defining Psychoanalysis: The Surprising Relevance of Racism, Anti-Semitism, Misogyny, and Homophobia*. London: Routledge, 2011.

Benjamin, Jessica. *The Shadow of the Other: Intersubjectivity and Gender in Psychoanalysis*. New York: Routledge, 1997.

Butler, Judith. *Gender Trouble: Feminism and the Subversion of Identity*. New York: Routledge, 1990.

————. *Antigone's Claim*. New York: Columbia University Press, 2002.

————. *Undoing Gender*. New York: Routledge, 2004.

Bromberg, Phillip. *Standing in the Spaces: Essays on Clinical Process, Trauma, and Dissociation*. Hillsdale: The Analytic Press, 2001.

Cooper, Steven. *A Disturbance in the Field: Essays on Transference and Counter Transference Engagement*. London: Routledge, 2010.

Corbett, Ken. "Gender Now." *Psychoanalytic Dialogues* 18 (2009): 838–56.

————. *Boyhoods: Rethinking Masculinities*. New Haven: Yale University Press, 2010.

Davoine, Françoise, and Jean-Max Gaudilliere. *History Beyond Trauma*. New York: Other Press, 2004.

Dimen, Muriel. *Sexuality, Intimacy, Power*. Hillsdale: The Analytic Press, 2003.

————, ed. *With Culture in Mind: Psychoanalytic Stories*. London: Routledge, 2011.

———— and Virginia Goldner. "Gender and Sexuality." In *Textbook of Psychoanalysis*, eds. Arnold Cooper, Glen Gabbard and Ethel Person, 93–116. Arlington: APPI Press, 2005.

Fairfield, Susan, ed. *Bringing the Plague*. New York: Other Press, 2002.

Fonagy, Peter. *Attachment Theory and Psychoanalysis*. New York: Other Press, 2001.

Goldner, Virginia. "Ironic Gender/Authentic Sex." *Studies in Gender and Sexuality* 4 (2001): 113–39.

———. "Trans: Gender in Free Fall." *Psychoanalytic Dialogues* 21, no. 2 (2011): 159–71.

Harris, Adrienne. *Gender as Soft Assembly.* Hillsdale: The Analytic Press, 2005.

Kulish, Nancy. "Clinical Implications of Contemporary Gender Theory." *The Journal of the American Psychoanalytic Association* 58 (2010): 231–59.

Layton, Lynne. *Who's That Girl: Who's That Boy?* Hillsdale: The Analytic Press, 2004 (1998).

Mitchell, Stephen. *Relationality: From Attachment to Intersubjectivity.* Hillsdale: The Analytic Press, 2003.

——— and Lewis Aron. *Relational Psychoanalysis: The Emergence of a Tradition,* vol. 1. Hillsdale: The Analytic Press, 1999.

Moon, Michael. *A Small Boy and Others: Imitation and Initiation in American Culture from Henry James to Andy Warhol.* Durham: Duke University Press, 1998.

Rozmarin, Eyal. "To Be Is To Betray: On the Place of Collective History and Freedom in Psychoanalysis." *Psychoanalytic Dialogues* 21, no. 3 (2011): 320–45.

Saketopoulo, Avgi. "Minding the Gap: Intersections in Gender, Race, and Class in Work with Gender Variant Children." *Psychoanalytic Dialogues* 21, no. 2 (2011): 192–209.

Salamon, Gayle. "Humiliation and Transgender Regulation: A Response to Ken Corbett's 'Boyhood Femininity, Gender Identity Disorder, Masculine Presuppositions, and the Anxiety of Regulation.'" *Psychoanalytic Dialogues* 19, no. 4 (2009): 376–84.

Sedgwick, Eve. *Tendencies.* New York: Routledge, 1994.

Stein, Ruth. *For the Love of the Father: A Psychoanalytic Study of Religious Terrorism.* Palo Alto: Stanford University Press, 2010.

Straker, Gillian. "The Anti-Analytic Third." *Psychoanalytic Review* 93, no. 5 (2006): 729–53.

Suchet, Melanie. "Crossing Over." *Psychoanalytic Dialogues* 21, no. 2 (2011): 172–91.

————, Adrienne Harris, and Lewis Aron. *Relational Psychoanalysis: New Voices,* vol 3. Hillsdale: The Analytic Press, 2007.

Tronick, Edward. *The Neurobehavioral and Social-Emotional Development of Infants and Children.* New York: Norton, 2007.

Widlocher, Daniel, ed. *Infantile Sexuality and Attachment.* New York: Other, 2001.

17

Clinical Encounters:
The Queer New Times

Rob Weatherill

"Let's get a few things straight," says a middle-aged man at the beginning of yet another fraught session, "I want you to accept that I am a married man; I am heterosexual and happy to be so; I love my wife and my children; I am good at my work. So can we return to what I sought these sessions for in the first place, namely my chronic anxiety? This is what I need to put right and I need your help." Of course, this demand for the analyst to get a few things clear — "straight" — is precisely the issue: the analyst simply repeats the guiding principle about free association.

Psychoanalysis, Freud makes clear, takes the middle way. It simply loosens the tangled (un-straight) threads (Gr: *analusis* — from *analuein*, to unloose, *ana*, up). It says to the analysand, "we are where we are — speak!" It does not proselytize. And where we are is in the post-modern, a metanarrative that spells the end of metanarratives (Lyotard 1979); referred to as "Integral Reality" (Baudrillard 2005). As Chris Turner points out in the introduction to this work, "a reality is being produced that is extreme in itself, extreme in the absence of critical distance it grants us, in the all enveloping nature of its short-circuited, real-time, asphyxiating immediacy" (Turner in Baudrillard, 8). This virtual reality absorbs every negation without judgment. This creates a fundamental problem for all former modernist critical movements because in the post-modern their critical insurgency is always being absorbed and reconciled as soon as it is produced. If modernity equates to loss, even tragic loss, post-modernity represents what Terry Eagleton has referred to as the "loss of loss." The post-modern subject is not even aware of loss. It may be no longer possible to fathom, to critique, the post-modern because of the continuous and rapid short-circuiting, updating that is inherent in and essential to late capitalism. It is always already too asphyxiatingly close.

Consequently, Gay Rights, for instance, is a done deal in many Western countries. What was significant about the Liberal-Democrat Minister David Laws's resignation in May, 2010 was not that his landlord was his male partner, but only that he had fiddled his expenses. His homosexuality was not an issue. On the contrary, in our times that combine a pan-spirituality with hedonism, queer theories and strategies have moved from the margin to the centre. Even Catholic clergy are onboard. There is a flourishing gay scene within the Holy See in Rome. According to an undercover reporter for *Panorama* (monthly news magazine in Rome) and report by Paddy Agnew in an *Irish Times* article also dating to 2010, there have been gay parties and brief encounters featuring openly gay priests.

Therefore, returning to our analysand, the analyst does not challenge his hidden hostility to homosexuality; nor does he try to get things straight; nor does he endorse his allegedly heterosexual position. He will encourage continued free association which will always tend to shadow this loss of loss. Precisely because gay rights is officially a done deal, queer theorists feel the need to pit a gay-queer insurgency on the straight world. So much so that actor Simon Callow quipped that, "the love that dare not speak its name has become the love that dare not shut up." The chapters in this book reflect this sometimes bitter ideological struggle. Officially, the struggle is for the human rights of an oppressed minority; entirely reasonable in a secular society and this is where the argument ends for the vast majority. However, this enervates queer academics to intensify the virtual struggle in order to re-establish a critical distance which is being continuously *absorbed* by Integral Reality.

My contention here is that this ideological attack on the so-called straight world can be profoundly anti-psychoanalytic. At worst, instead of a tentative freedom, polarities are generated and defences mobilized on every side. To blow apart "identity" and replace it with "fluidity," destroys what even Žižek (2009) refers to as "the ultimate difference, the 'transcendental' difference that grounds human identity itself" (8). Levinas (1987) suggests that this difference defines difference as such. He refers to, "an insurmountable duality," and the "absolutely contrary contrary [*le contraire absolutement contraire*]" (85–86). Again, psychoanalysis takes a middle position. As Elizabeth Wright (2000) puts it, "in the Freudian universe of discourse, sexual difference can neither be reduced to a biological given nor be *wholly* constituted by social practices" (17; my emphasis). Properly speaking, analysis emphasizes division, rupture and alterity. Psychoanalysis is a conflict psychology — *antagonism without resolution.*

However, if queer sexuality is defined by its inexplicability, incoherence, volatility and contingency, this is the sexuality best suited to urban, highly mobile subjects adjusted to living in late capitalism in the twenty-first century. Each identity is precarious and must be so. However, to co-opt Laplanche in support of queer theory, as Alice Kuzniar does in this volume, may be problematic. Kuzniar goes on to refute common psychoanalytic clichés. The assumption that gay desire is a desire for likeness or sameness and therefore narcissistic, is an assumption that ignores, she claims, the *actual* differences of lived life. And anyway, she points out, difference itself can be used defensively and narcissistically, like the heterosexual man who has sex with a woman *proving* that he is different to a woman. She further refutes the common assumption that female homosexuality arises regressively as a result of the father's rejection of the daughter who returns to her first love, her mother. She insists instead upon the possibility of the "discovery of a variety and coexistence of positive identifications that would explore shifting erotic desires and fantasies." She cites Jacqueline Rose's articulation of the constant "failure" of identity at the heart of psychic life. And this seemingly impossible and felt "disjointedness" makes the term "queer" helpful for those trying to find a language to reflect on this "failure."

Tim Dean (2000), in *Beyond Sexuality*, wants to "thoroughly deheterosexualise desire," and Lisa Diamond (2008) found that the women she interviewed, who belonged to a sexual minority, spoke of the radical contingency of their attractions to others, indicating that sexual fluidity was not just a male phenomenon. Likewise, Lara Farina sees Plato's *Symposium* as being co-opted, via the universal trope of "lack" into a normative gender binary system of complimentarity. Even homosexuals "rather than wanting a person like themselves, are represented as wanting a missing piece [...] their desire is structured no differently than heterosexual desire." Ultimately, she notes, the Socrates/Diotima formula is: we love our opposite, the perfect, eternal form of beauty. Even male homosexuality, the subject of the Symposium, is the love of an older man (active/male) for the beautiful youth (passive/female). Farina concludes that feminists and queer theorists have found in psychoanalysis "an unpalatable reliance" on the opposition masculine/feminine, with the feminine as the negation of the privileged masculine, at worst a death dealing absence (as in courtly love).

The attack being mounted on all fronts is aimed at the usual psychoanalytic tropes: the Oedipus complex, genital supremacy, castration, lack, narcissism and phallocentrism. Against "lack" and desire based on lack, Bersani and others want to take up Foucault's challenge to theorize "new ways of being together." Bersani and Phillips (2008) eschew the alleged negativity of lack in favor of the positive correspondences of being. Rather than find (self-serving and therefore ultimately violent) satisfaction in pleasure, participants seek self-shattering intensity — new intimacies that embrace shock and fragmentation, rather than repair and redemption. They allege that tuning into another person's "potential self" avoids the ego-driven "violent games of selfhood" (122). They specify "virtual being" beyond the ego which can reach out in love to other virtual beings, beyond gender and beyond the appropriation of the other's desire. Bersani is interested in how the pursuit of unprotected anal sex in highly ritualized situations can be understood as a critique of fixed gender-based hierarchical relationality. At sex parties, a man, called the King of Loads because he has received the ejaculations of dozens of men in one night is called a bug chaser in his apparent quest for AIDS, and his inseminators are known as gift givers (Dean 2009). Dean and Bersani see this as unlimited intimacy. Phillips is open to these new forms of intimacy that undermine mainstream norms (Bersani and Phillips 2008, 32ff).

Paradoxical concepts like "impersonal narcissism" (97) precisely anticipate and prepare for the post-human world in all its drug-fuelled techno-frenzy. Phillips, however, is careful to warn that no one should in any way promote non-consensual barebacking! He has to suddenly assert the old liberal notion of consent as a politically-correct gesture to cover the dissolute violence he has just been enthusiastically advocating. This is rather like the suicidal patient whose total indifference to her own death is chilling, yet when the same patient cuts her finger, she rushes to the doctor in panic. Psychoanalysis as such should be relatively unmoved by such fashionable virtual radicalism. Instead, these ideological demands should be met with critical resistance, not least because of radicalism's absolutely cool congruence with the contemporary atonal capitalist world and its loss of loss. Queer theory is all of a piece with what Virilio (2007) has characterised as the Dromosphere, the sphere of acceleration around the earth, with its cry of *everything right now,* "where everything crashes together, telescoping endlessly […] into this proximity that has nothing concrete about it except its infectious hysteria" (100).

However, there are theorists whose contributions are closer to a necessary clinical openness. Michael Snediker in his chapter, for instance, co-opts Winnicott to the cause. In Winnicott, "doing and being differently solicit queer theoretical attention, since the distinction between the two is a gendered one." Referring to Hamlet, as well as persons in clinical practice unable to feel real, Snediker says, "The sense of one's inauthenticity or self-depletion signals a psyche's queer stumbling." And to Sedgwick's queer little gods, Snediker links Winnicott's omnipotent infant, "beholden less to ideology or hegemony than to aesthetic fragility"; the infant god, fused with the mother, whose needs are met before he knows it. And where even the lack implied in "good enough," "definitionally soars far beyond enough's own limited expectations." Psychoanalysis and queer theory might learn from Winnicott's squiggle game in terms of ontological indeterminacy. "How to withstand the desire for completion... [and] the eventually generous gift of its own motivated or happily self-abandoned incompletion." What will one give to the other in the squiggle game? The play of what Snediker calls the "nearliness" of being a person, an incoherence which cannot help but lean on a fiction of coherence. This nearness is inseparable from "Winnicottian spaciousness," the transition space, the necessary space to be approximate. Even language (and Lacan's unconscious structured like a language) becomes playful with the joke with humor, with its "confluence of lucidity and surprise." What characterises the squiggle game is its humility and its barely existing.

We could learn much from François Roustang (2000), who also privileges being and becoming over doing and knowing. The symptom, he suggests, is a "narrow cyst," a blockage, a partial lifeless residue and "the key is to learn the tricks and detours that allow the symptom to return to the totality of the psyche — this is to restore the symptom to the general circulation of psychic life, by drawing it out of its narrow cyst in which it had become trapped" (99). By speaking in the analytic setting, the symptom is brought back from isolation, signalled by anxiety, and enabled to rejoin the circulation, the "fluidity" of life. Where queer theorists place stumbling, dislocation, queerness and so on, Roustang following Kierkegaard, places anxiety. "Anxiety is always present," wrote Kierkegaard, "as the possibility of a new state" (cited in Roustang, 99). "What psychoanalysis produces, and what makes it invaluable, is the return of the psyche to the dream state […] the coming into being of the individual totality of the soul" (100).

Roustang takes his cue from Freud, understanding Freud's style to exists in three registers, the analytical, rhetorical and poetic. He must be analytic so as not to exclude himself from the burgeoning scientific community, to develop coherent theories about the unconscious and so on as well as the need to constantly critique his developing work; rhetorical to persuade his readers and win them over to his cause; finally, poetic because he realized that the poets had said everything before him. Beyond the analytic, while including it, Roustang celebrates the mythological Freud. Psychoanalysis, according to Roustang, attempts "to uncover what Freud called the other scene […]. This is [ultimately] the scene of *unalienated* subjectivity, the one where life appears as suffering — a suffering that defines singularity because the manner in which we suffer is incommunicable, the thing to which we hold most dearly because it is the very essence of ourselves" (69). Queer theorists, on the other hand, tend to reject suffering or lack by trivializing and stigmatizing it as part of some heterosexist plot rather than understanding it as intrinsic to Being.

Michel Henry (1993), who quipped *contra* Lacan, "The unconscious is destructured like an affect," emphasized that, "Life never actualizes itself, never enters the finite locus of light. It stays entirely out of it, in the immediation of its self-omnipresence" (63). Life overflows any representation in its autoaffection. Henry makes a radical distinction between representation and life. Life cannot represent itself. Therefore, in our terms here: *life is queer; representation is straight.* Henry is thus set against structuralism and post-structuralism as the basis for psychoanalysis. Psychoanalysis fails to make the crucial distinction between representation and its radical Other, namely, *affectivity.* The Freudian concept of the unconscious has two fundamentally different meanings: the first pertaining to representations (present to consciousness or not); the second, to affects and affectivity or drive derivatives — more generally, part of the continuous upwelling of life itself and its inevitably *hidden* movement towards force and action in the world.

Life is disturbance, disequilibrium, proximity, suffering — more than the fluidity that queer theorists celebrate. The *power* that produces the dream, the joke, the slip, the commercial product, etc., is not the power of representational consciousness or of the universal code, but pure excess. This power opens onto representation's wholly Other. The Freudian unconscious, ceasing to be merely the formal negation of the quality "consciousness," takes on a life of its own, aiming at the very possibility of action — force, energy, power, madness, ultimately the death drive and what Baudrillard calls "Symbolic Exchange." Psychoanalysis, with its current focus on language, shows all the signs of being afraid of life. As Henry says: "Freudianism accounts for life only to liquidate it" (313), and "Psychoanalysis is the soul of a world without soul, the spirit of a world without spirit"(7).

What Henry is (re)claiming for psychoanalysis is the immediacy of the Real as irrecuperably closer to us than the equivocations of language, ideology or the repressive distractions and displacements of the code. Language cannot contain the anarchic plot, which is elicited by silence, by the disorganising effects of free association, by "unspeaking" (*deparole*), by the evolving ambivalent passions of transference and countertransference. A balance of forces emerges, a *hidden* order of ruse, challenge, game, suggestion, seduction, simulation, where each is hostage to the other: over-exposed, out of phase, out of sync, at risk — *sub-jectum*. "To catch the secret of our being," Henry asserts, "[w]e must hack back through a forest of symbols to find the great paths along which drives have tried to discharge themselves and by which life has tried to be rid of itself [...] exploded and dispersed across the ek-stasis of time" (325–26). Against the notion of a system, or, any kind of Idealism, Henry pits *auto*-affirmation, hyperpower, silence, immanance, presence, and suffering. Each subject is an ungraspable singularity, refusing registration and exposition while appearing to acquiesce (Winnicott's false self), playing the speech games and the castration games of loss and the "depressive position," all these apologies for living, while *being disturbance* (the imprisonment of which is neurosis), while being obsessed, being moved, to the point of outpouring.

With Henry and Roustang, as well as Winnicott, we have the other non-structuralist version of psychoanalysis that comes nearest to queer theory in its attempts to burst through difference and erase lack. However, as Freud (1933[1932]) very reluctantly makes clear again and again, civilization itself depends on some renunciation (180). Attempting to escape this leads to the *in*-civility of the contemporary life. Without difference, we are at the degree zero of sex. The brief history of sexuality is thus at an end.

However, Kathryn Bond Stockton reminds us, via Foucault's *History of Sexuality,* that sex did not even exist (as a discourse) prior to the nineteenth century. Ours is the only civilization to have discussed sex in intimate detail and even made therapies out of it! Foucault thus queers any essentialist or trans-historical reading of sexuality *per se.* However, Stockton acknowledges that beyond any psychoanalytically essentialist reading of sexuality, Lacan *still* regarded sexuality at a limit point beyond sense, meaning and discourse. In other words, as Stockton says, "by historicizing sexuality as if there were *nothing* outside of discourse, Foucault misses the Lacanian point that sex itself is not simply and solely discursive" (emphasis added). Stockton takes Shakespeare's Sonnet 20 to illustrate this limit point, or gap between the symbolic and the real, between discourse and its remainder, an opacity that is hard to translate and that remains an enigma. This where we should locate Germain Greer's forthright comments about transgender women: "Just because you lop off your d**k doesn't make you a ******* woman" (Saul 2015).

Philip Larkin said that sexual intercourse began between the lifting of the Chatterley ban and the Beatles' first LP. The conservative Irish Catholic politician, Oliver Flanagan, asserted, there was no sex in Ireland before television. Thus, for civilizations and individuals, what we call sexuality (what Henry calls life) ceases to be opaque at a certain key moment and thus becomes transparent and therefore potentially controllable. But as a statement of professed not-knowing, President Mahmoud Ahmadinejad asserted in 2007 in Columbia University, "In Iran we don't have homosexuals like in your country," he said, to laughter and boos from the audience. "In Iran we do not have this phenomenon. I don't know who's told you that we have this."

Finally, applying Baudrilliard's (and Noailles 2005) well known triptych, Illusion/Real/Simulation, might serve as a necessary situating of queer theory in the history of sexuality. Illusion is the domain of appearances, prior to meaning and thought. Here, what we later term sexuality is opaque and enigmatic, without truth or reality. It does not exist. At once threatening and primal, life (Henry), this enigma is at the same time enchanting and playful (*il-ludere*), prior, that is, to its growing *real*-isation and disenchantment. The Real of sexuality (not to be confused with the Lacanian Real), is the heyday of sexuality proper, maybe the golden age of sexuality, but also the beginning of the end of sex. Sex becomes thoughtful, meaningful and truthful, registered, classified, normalized, managed and scientifically controlled à la Foucault. Psychoanalysis has been central in this development. As Baudrillard (1990) says, "Freud abolished seduction in order to put in place a machinery of interpretation and sexual repression" (57). Sex is objectified, subjectified, repressed, and sublimated, broken down into its elements, all to reduce its seductive power of illusion, sin and superstition and bring it into the domain of health and safe functioning. Baudrillard (2007) speaks of "the incredible racism of truth" (42). Finally, at the most advanced stage, via Simulation, sex is perfected by becoming hyper-real. It surpasses itself hastening towards its end, by dissolving binaries, referents, essences, and becoming contingent, random, and recreational in a veritable explosion of hyperactivity. Sex like everything else goes 24/7. Baudrillard sees this as a partial return to Illusion and meaninglessness, by way of Illusion's revenge on it realisation. But it is not a return, but rather a hyper-realization, an excess of knowing, meaning, and interpretation. Here are all the ideological tropes of queer theory. Sex is neutralized via diffusion and diffraction within Integral reality thus turning a-sexual, virtual, and clithonic. This is the era of "total self-seduction," the era of "a digital Narcissus instead of a triangular Oedipus" (Baudrillard 1990, 175). Thus, we might usefully heed Lacan's (2005[1969–70]) warning in his seventeenth seminar: "A long time ago I observed that for the sentence of old father Karamazov, 'If God is dead, then everything is permitted', the conclusion that forces itself upon us in that the response to 'God is dead' is '*Nothing is permitted anymore*'" (120; my emphasis).

The Freudian clinic invites a loosening, *not* unbinding (*Unbindung*); fluidity but not superconductivity; remembering, repeating and working through, not consolation. Any agenda per se, gay or straight, radical or conservative, will be used by the analysand's resistance to end the work of analysis. And insofar as we are always already allegedly *within* a "scared straight" culture, that also needs loosening. The middle-aged man should connect his severe anxiety with his rigidity and loosen both.

Works Cited

Agnew, Paddy. "Magazine Exposes 'Double Life' of Vatican's Gay Priests." *Irish Times,* July 24, 2010. http://www.irishtimes.com/news/magazine-exposes-double-life-of-vaticans-gay-priests-1.626461.

Ahmadinejad, Mahmoud, "In Iran, We Don't Have Homosexuals," MSNBC. YouTube, September 24, 2007. http://www.youtube.com/watch?v=U-sC26wpUGQ.

Baudrillard, Jean. *Forget Foucault,* trans. Nicole Dufresne. Los Angeles: Semiotext(e) 2007 (1977).

———. *The Intelligence of Evil or The Lucidity of the Pact,* trans. Chris Turner. Oxford and New York: Berg, 2005 (2004).

———. *Symbolic Exchange and Death,* trans. Iain Hamilton Grant. London: Sage, 1993 (1976).

———. *Seduction,* trans. B. Singer. 1979; rpt. Montreal: New World Perspectives, CultureText Series, 1990.

Baudrillard, Jean, and Enrique Noailles. *Exiles from Dialogue,* trans. Chris Turner. London: Polity Press, 2007 (2005).

Bersani, Leo and Adam Phillips. *Intimacies.* Chicago: University of Chicago Press, 2008.

Dean, Tim. *Beyond Sexuality.* Chicago: Chicago University Press, 2000.

———. *Unlimited Intimacy: Reflections on the Subculture of Barebacking.* Chicago: University of Chicago Press, 2009.

Diamond, Lisa M. *Sexual Fluidity: Understanding Women's Love and Desire.* Cambridge: Harvard University Press, 2008.

Freud, Sigmund. "Lecture XXXV: The Question of a Weltanschauung" (1933[1932]). *New Introductory Lectures on Psycho-Analysis.* In the *Standard Edition of the Complete Psychological Works of Sigmund Freud,* vol. 22, ed. and trans. James Strachey in collaboration with Anna Freud and assisted by Alix Strachey and Alan Tyson, 158–82. 1960; rpt. London: Vintage, 2001.

Henry, Michel. *The Genealogy of Psychoanalysis,* trans. Douglas Brick. California: Stanford University Press, 1993.

Lacan, Jacques. *Book XVII: The Other Side of Psychoanalysis* (1969–70), trans. Russell Grigg. New York: W.W. Norton, 2005.

Levinas, Emanuel. *Time and the Other,* trans. R. Cohen. Pittsburgh: Duquesne University Press. 1987.

Lyotard, Jean-François. *The Post-Modern Condition.* Manchester: Manchester University Press, 1987 (1979).

Roustang, François. *How to Make a Paranoid Laugh,* trans. Anne Vila. 1996; rpt. Philadelphia: University of Pennsylvania Press, 2000.

Saul, Heather. "Germaine Greer Defends 'Grossly Offensive' Comments about Transgender Women: 'Just Because You Lop Off Your D**k Doesn't Make You A ******* Woman.'" *The Independent.* http://www.independent.co.uk/news/people/germaine-greer-defends-grossly-offensive-comments-about-transgender-women-just-because-you-lop-off-a6709061.html.

Virilio, Paul. *The Original Accident,* trans. Julie Rose. London: Polity Press, 2007 (2005).

Wright, Elizabeth. *Lacan and Postfeminism.* Cambridge: Icon Books, 2000.

Žižek, Slavoj. *Violence.* London: Profile, 2009.

18

Undoing Psychoanalysis:
Towards a Clinical and Conceptual Metistopia

Dany Nobus

It was not exactly Freud's birthday, but on April 27, 1995, the eminent French psychoanalyst André Green (1995) delivered the "Sigmund Freud Birthday Lecture" at the Anna Freud Centre in London under the title "Has Sexuality Anything To Do With Psychoanalysis?" In the opening sections of his paper, Green explained that his provocative question had been prompted by a twofold observation. On the one hand, he had noticed how since the mid-1980s sexuality had all but disappeared as a "major concept" and a "theoretical function of heuristic value" from the psychoanalytic literature, with the exception of "the ever problematic topic of feminine sexuality." On the other hand, he had ascertained how practicing psychoanalysts, when presenting case material, were more inclined to focus on the ego, inter-subjectivity and destructiveness, for example, rather than the role played by sexuality in the mental economy of their patients. In light of these considerations, and wishing the founder of psychoanalysis well for his birthday, Green went on to emphasize the value and significance of a thorough re-appraisal of Freud's key contributions to the psychoanalytic study of sexuality — libido, the Oedipus complex, genitality, the vicissitudes of the drives (Eros and Thanatos), narcissism — subsequently responding to his own call in the 1997 monograph *The Chains of*

Eros (2000) by newly integrating these and other notions into a hierarchical "erotic chain," starting from the drive and ending in language and sublimation.

Over the past seventeen years, quite a few psychoanalytic scholars and practitioners have echoed and amplified Green's words, and quite a few others have taken them sufficiently seriously to formulate various responses, and re-inject some sexuality into the allegedly de-sexualized body of psychoanalysis, as exemplified especially within the object-relations tradition (Budd 2001; Litowitz 2002; Dimen 2003; Lubbe 2008). Much could be said about the validity of Green's aforementioned observations, yet what concerns me, here, is rather the relevance of the response, which entails nothing less than a re-appreciation of Freud's original contributions, nothing more than what Lacan (2006[1955]) would have described during the 1950s as a mandatory "return to Freud." If, as Green (1995) contended, "today's sexuality is not Freud's sexuality" (880), what is the point of rekindling Freud? If psychoanalysis is to be rescued from extinction, on the assumption that it still has something to offer to contemporary debates on sexuality, why not start with its contemporary incarnations, despite their alleged de-sexualization of the mental sphere, because they may deservedly be regarded as constituting a better starting point than Freud's "outdated" conceptual paradigm? By way of "day dream," Green wondered whether Freud would have come up with the same theory had he been born in 1956, inventing psychoanalysis around the age of forty, immediately stating that the "answer would probably be no" (871). So how are we to accept, then, the reinvention of a theory and an associated clinical practice that even its inventor would not deem acceptable anymore? Today's sexuality is not Freud's sexuality. It is not Klein's, Lacan's or even Green's. And if the problem regarding the observed absence of sexuality in psychoanalysis is addressed by re-inserting the classic Freudian terminology (libido, drive, fantasy, sublimation, etc.) into its ailing corpus, the resulting picture is likely to appear as distinctively bland compared to the richness and complexity of the experiences, possibilities, performances, technologies and terminologies with which the still relatively young twenty-first century is equipping the human sexual condition. Sexuality may have little to do with psychoanalysis anymore, but a simple "return to Freud" may very well result in psychoanalysis having little to do with sexuality anymore, that is to say it may very well lead to psychoanalysis becoming sexually illiterate (Herdt 2007).

Discussions concerning the cultural relativity of psychoanalysis aside, shouldn't we at least expect, then, that it takes account of the changing face(book) of sexuality? Isn't a certain sexual *aggiornamento* of psychoanalysis required in order to prevent the theory (and its practitioners) from losing track of the Zeitgeist? It is worth pointing out, here, that some queer theorists have had no qualms drawing on (Lacanian) psychoanalysis in order to enrich and advance their own vocabulary. For example, in his polemical book *No Future,* Lee Edelman (2004; 2011) launched a searing diatribe against the ideological investment of the child as the guardian of human futurity, from the perspective of the deathbound, anti-futuristic image of the so-called "sinthomosexual," a self-identified gay man (homosexual) who identifies with and is bound by a point of lethal *jouissance* (the Lacanian *sinthome*) (Lacan 2005[1975–76]). Psychoanalysis itself, however, has been remarkably impermeable to the ever-changing and expanding, twenty-first century sexual lexicon. If psychoanalysis still wants to have anything to do with sexuality, shouldn't it start upgrading its conceptual software package, if not its entire operating system? The reader is no doubt expecting the answer to be a resounding "yes." And so it will seem rather odd if I suggest otherwise.

It goes without saying that psychoanalysis (as a theory, practice and method of inquiry) should engage with and reflect upon our new sexual realities, yet this does not mean that it should adopt all the associated terminologies and ideological principles. Psychoanalysis does not have to become queer theory or enter deep into the dungeons of our contemporary sexual subcultures in order to survive or maintain its respectability. As Javier Sáez (2005) has argued in an astute assessment of the strained relationship between psychoanalysis and queer theory, were psychoanalysis to regularly update its sexual vocabulary in keeping with changing social realities, or ideologically align itself with socio-cultural trends, values and institutions, this would drive the theory and practice (at best) into passive responsive mode and (at worst) towards a new form of intellectual propaganda. Psychoanalysis should not just be the recipient of newly established sexual wisdom, let alone align itself uncritically with either mainstream (normative) or critical (non-normative) discourses on sexuality. Instead, it should continue to play an active part in the critical elaboration of this very wisdom, its normative as well as its non-normative aspects, through the advancement of its own formulae and ideas. In a sense, this is what Lacan (1998[1972–73]) managed to do during the late 1960s and '70s, when he defined the logical operations of sexuation, proclaiming that "there is no such thing as a sexual relationship," that "woman does not exist," that "heterosexual, by definition, is the one who loves women, regardless of sex" (Lacan 2001[1972], 467) and, even, that psychoanalysts themselves are a *sinthome* (Lacan 2005[1975–76], 135). In addition, were psychoanalysis to improve its sexual literacy by assimilating and integrating the new lexicon, this in itself would not preclude these terms, and their associated practices, being re-excluded by way of pathologization.

In order to appreciate, then, the critical contribution that psychoanalysis may still make to the study of human sexuality, given the current state of affairs in the realm of sex research, gender studies and queer theory, it is imperative to start from a delineation of the various constitutive components that have been identified and discussed under this heading. Sexuality must include the anatomo-physiology of the sexed body. These biological areas of "sex," comprising the internal and external structures of the so-called reproductive system and the associated categories of "male" and "female" have always constituted a privileged hunting ground for male medical doctors, which no doubt explains why for centuries the female sexed body was described as isomorphic to the male, the clitoris was not "discovered" until the mid-sixteenth century (Laqueur 1990, 64–65;

Andahazi 1999) and the possibility of female ejaculation continues to divide the scientific community (Blackledge 2003, 198–
210). With the ascendancy of sexology in Germany and France
at the end of the nineteenth century, the medical study of the
sexed body was supplemented with the social, anthropological
and clinical investigation of human sexual behavior, with an
emphasis on the forensic-psychiatric significance of its "aberrant" forms. To this dual picture of the sexed body and its sexual
behavior (erotic practices), a new component was added during
the late 1950s and '60s, when John Money (1955) and Robert J.
Stoller (1968) coined the notion of (core) gender(-identity/role),
in order to account for a human being's intimate awareness of
being masculine or feminine, and the way in which this conscious realization affects the individual's performance of a particular social role. With this introduction of "gender," another
new element was added to the *tableau vivant* of human sexuality, seemingly emphasizing the hitherto underrated importance
of subjective experience. However, few debates within the newly
created "gender studies" have been more virulent than that concerning the exact status and precise origin of gender. Paraphrasing Judith Butler (1990), one feels inclined to say that gender
equals trouble, certainly for the individual who has to live with
it, but perhaps even more for the poor scholar who wants to examine it. Yet gender does not complete the picture. Since Freud,
and perhaps even to a large extent owing to Freud, our vision
of human sexuality has further expanded with the inclusion of
two additional factors: object-choice and fantasy. Of these two
components, object-choice has no doubt attracted most interest,
both within and outside the psychoanalytic movement, because
it concerns the vexed issue of sexual orientation, i.e., a human
being's positioning on the axis of homosexuality versus heterosexuality. The role of fantasy, on the other hand, has rarely been
debated outside psychoanalytic circles, perhaps because psychoanalysis is one of the few practices providing access to the
study of sexual fantasies, and even then discussions tend to be
descriptive, explanatory and categorizing rather than attuned to

the functionality and "logic" of fantasizing within the human sexual experience.

Human sexuality is thus made up of at least five different components: the sexed body, sexual behavior (erotic practices), sexual identity (gender), object-choice (sexual orientation), and fantasy-life. Each of these components stands in a meaningful relation to each of the other components, without any pre-determined unilateral causal connections. Whatever essentialist researchers may have tried to prove over the past hundred years or so, the sexed body does not determine sexual identity. Biological maleness or femaleness do not automatically trigger a sense of masculinity or femininity respectively, as is proven by the numerous accounts of people feeling that they were born with the "wrong body" and therefore opting to "transition" to a sexed body that is congruent with their gender. Likewise, the sexed body and sexual identity (even when they are "congruent") do not condition sexual orientation: a biological female with a strong sense of femininity does not by definition become heterosexual, and a biological female with a strong sense of masculinity does not by definition become a lesbian. Also, sexual orientation does not dictate sexual behavior: a self-identified homosexual man is not by definition more interested in pedophilia or sado-masochism. And sexual fantasy depends neither on sexual identity nor on sexual orientation: a homosexual man with a strong sense of femininity may very well entertain heterosexual fantasies in which he occupies the role of a male chauvinist macho character. Moreover, existing configurations may change over time, and depending on the sexual context and relational setting: a woman's seemingly established heterosexuality may be challenged quite unexpectedly and dramatically in response to her sudden falling in love with another woman (Diamond 2008). And with the emergence and proliferation of what I like to call "E-sexuality," existing sexual constellations in the real social space have become balanced against new, alternative sexual arrangements in cyberspace: someone's sexual identity may differ depending on where the social network in which he is moving is actually situated; off-line sexual identity does not necessarily translate into an identical on-line sexual identity.

Hence, what we are dealing with, here, is a set of components that does not represent a unified whole, for which there is no "normal" distribution, neither in the medical nor in the statistical sense, whose interrelations do not follow any preconceived paths, and which seems to be developing all the time. Instead of reducing the interactions between the various components of human sexuality to a series of predictable, mechanical, normal (average, ordinary) and pathological (eccentric, extraordinary) relationships, which is what many psychoanalysts have tended to do over the past century, it befalls upon psychoanalytic practitioners, theorists and scholars to appreciate these interactions in their irreducible unpredictability. At various points in his career, Freud referred to the vexed issue of the "choice of neurosis" (*Neurosenwahl*), that is to say the problem as to why an existing psychic economy develops into one particular direction rather than the other (1909, 240; 1911, 224; 1925, 36). Why, Freud wondered, does a particular male child whose Oedipal drama encompasses all the necessary pre-conditions for the emergence of a fetishistic sexual practice become homosexual instead, and most boys simply surmount castration anxiety (1927, 154)? Why does one girl's penis envy trigger a masculinity complex, whereas in another girl it elicits mature femininity (equaling motherhood, in Freud's book), and sexual inhibition in yet another (1933[1932], 129–30)? Sometimes Freud conceded that his explanatory powers were failing him in order to elucidate these issues, at other times he conjured up the *deus ex machina* of the constitutional predisposition, which evidently begged the question.

Rather than employing this apparent failure of Freud's intellect as an argument for discrediting its foundations, I believe it is much more appropriate to designate it as a cardinal psychoanalytic discovery. Freud was confronted, here, with the unpredictability of human development and this, more than anything else, is what the notion of "choice" intends to convey: not so much the formative power of conscious agency as the transformative ability of the unconscious to steer a given potential through a multitude of different options. In this context, "choice" does not reflect psychological "freedom of choice," but a logical selection amongst the plethora of available elements and the pleiad of possible relations between these elements. In attributing this logical process to the workings of the unconscious, one might still entertain the idea that it is determined, constructed, controlled by the socio-symbolic system to which the subject is alienated, and which Lacan (1988[1954–55] dubbed the Other (235–47). Yet one should not forget, here, that the unconscious itself cannot be determined, so that any suggestion of a determination by the unconscious inevitably entails the indeterminacy of this very unconscious and its formations. If psychoanalytic interpretation is capable of demonstrating, in retrospect, the unconscious determination of the manifest dream content, it is not able to determine the subsequent twists and turns of this determining unconscious. Psychoanalysis may explain why a particular dream has occurred, but it cannot predict whether this dream will re-occur, even less what the manifest content of future dreams will be made of.

In its recognition of "choice" as a synonym for the irreducible unpredictability of human development, including the way in which the various components of sexuality connect and reconnect over time, a psychoanalytically informed theory and practice of human sexuality may constitute a true "queer" alternative to each and every, ideologically dubious effort at rigid categorization, but it may simultaneously also enrich more complex approaches such as Anne Fausto-Sterling's (2000) developmental systems model, through its central emphasis on the determining yet indeterminable quality of the dynamic unconscious. The problem, of course, is that psychoanalysis itself has often been reluctant to accept the variations, diversity and unpredictability of human sexuality as what constitutes its actual norm. More often than not, psychoanalysis has endeavored to prescribe as "normal" a certain symbolic law of castration and an associated sexual order upon our subjective experience of sexuality, all the while pathologizing and marginalizing certain identities, orientations, fantasies and behaviors. In essence, this symbolic law (and the associated sexual order) is that of the Oedipus complex, which regards the recognition of sexual difference between man and woman as the necessary precondition for the normal (healthy) development of sexuality. In refusing to renege on the importance of sexual difference, psychoanalysts have regularly pathologized whole swathes of human sexuality, from homosexuality to fetishism, from anal intercourse to sadomasochistic relationships. Ironically, in unreservedly promoting sexual difference as the source and origin of normal sexuality, psychoanalysts themselves have done nothing more than reiterating (and imposing) a sexual principle of sameness, gathering and unifying human beings under the "same difference," which allows them to be classified, unified and homogenized.

This is what I would call the "homotopia" of psychoanalysis, which represents its body of knowledge as a locus of sameness and its own "sexual identity" as a phallic, normative and often normalizing doctrine whose epistemology leads to homo- and other phobias. Against this "homotopia," which could also be understood with reference to Lacan's logic of "male sexuation" in *Seminar xx,* it would be tempting to reclaim psychoanalysis as a Foucaultian "heterotopia," according to Lacan's (1998[1972–73]) formulae for "female sexuation" (78–89). In a "heterotopia," there is no such thing as identification, neither on the side of the doctrinal body of knowledge, nor on the side of those who fall under its spell. Much like "women" and the "Other *jouissance*" in Lacan's formulae, the "heterotopia" is characterized by flux, fluidity, flexibility, liquidity — precisely those characteristics which contemporary queer theorists hold dear as non-normative, emancipatory principles of human sexuality. A "heterotopic" psychoanalysis would no doubt be in the best position, then, to join hands with queer theory, in its conceptual framework as well as its clinical practice, attuned as it would be to the de-stabilization of sexual difference and any other hegemonic oppositional binary. If we take Lacan's formulae of sexuation seriously, the "heterotopic" strategy would also entail a de-masculinization and de-phallicization of psychoanalysis, in favor of its "feminization" and possibly its critical defamation. "She is called woman (*on la dit-femme*)," Lacan proclaimed "and defamed (*diffâme*)" (85).

The problem with this outlook, and in a sense also with queer theory — as Lisa Downing has argued so persuasively in this volume — is that its celebration of fluidity may very well lead to the re-pathologization of fixity, that is to say to the marginalization of those identities, orientations, fantasies and behaviors that appear as subjectively immutable, either within or outside a (hetero)normative paradigm. Put differently, a "heterotopia" does not exclude the pathologization of non-fluidity, of repetition, of sameness, identity, which are as much part of the potentialities and indeterminacies of human sexuality as fluidity. To argue that psychoanalysis should and can only ever be "heterotopic," and is therefore somehow by definition queer if it is to be truthful to the premises that have supported its clinical and theoretical edifice, thus misses the very point that I have been trying to make, insofar as it fails to acknowledge, as a fundamental and therefore "normal" principle, the irreducible unpredictability of the human sexual experience — its apparent fixities as well as its ostensible flexibilities.

What I propose, then, in order to ensure that psychoanalysis still has something to do with sexuality, and without compromising on Green's original call for a return to Freud, is neither a psychoanalytic "homotopia" nor a psychoanalytic "heterotopia," but a clinical and conceptual "metistopia" — a proteiform "postqueer" place whose epistemic parameters and body of knowledge are eternally shifting and changing, and which accommodates fluidity as much as fixity.[1] In its "metistopic" surroundings, psychoanalysis would not operate from any established source of wisdom, whether conservative or liberal, gay-negative or gay-positive, but act upon what Lacan (2013[1971]) called a "knowledge in failure" (*savoir en échec*) (329), which implies that it

---

1   "Metis" is Homer's most common epithet for Odysseus in the *Odyssey*. It is generally translated as "scheme," yet has connotations of an endless capacity for metamorphosis.

would approach each and every event in the sexual realm without prejudice and preconception, but with a spirit of discovery, a sense of wonder, and possibly a touch of irony. It would also imply that every attempt at situating psychoanalysis, clinically as well as theoretically, at the highest level of intellectual profundity would by definition be doomed to fail — not in the actual attempt as such, but in the objective to keep psychoanalysis within the boundaries of its own discourse. There is no guarantee that a "metistopic" psychoanalysis would make the discipline more respectable, yet historically some of the most significant psychoanalytic contributions were precisely those that did not command social or scientific respect.

Works Cited

Andahazi, Federico. *The Anatomist.* New York: Anchor, 1999.

Blackledge, Catherine. *The Story of V: Opening Pandora's Box.* London: Weidenfeld & Nicolson, 2003.

Budd, Susan. "No Sex Please — We're British: Sexuality in English and French Psychoanalysis." In *Sexuality: Psychoanalytic Perspectives,* ed. Celia Harding, 52–68. London: Brunner-Routledge, 2001.

Butler, Judith. *Gender Trouble: Feminism and the Subversion of Identity.* London and New York: Routledge, 1990.

Diamond, Lisa M. *Sexual Fluidity: Understanding Women's Love and Desire.* Cambridge and London: Harvard University Press, 2008.

Dimen, Muriel. *Sexuality, Intimacy, Power.* London and Hillsdale: The Analytic Press, 2003.

Edelman, Lee. *No Future: Queer Theory and the Death Drive.* Durham and London: Duke University Press, 2004.

———"Ever After: History, Negativity, and the Social." In *After Sex?* In *On Writing Since Queer Theory,* eds. Janet Halley and Andrew Parker, 110–18. Durham and London: Duke University Press, 2011.

Fausto-Sterling, Anne. *Sexing the Body: Gender Politics and the Construction of Sexuality.* New York: Basic Books, 2000.

Freud, Sigmund. "Notes Upon a Case of Obsessional Neurosis" (1909). In *The Standard Edition of the Complete Psychological Works of Sigmund Freud,* vol. 10, ed. and trans. James Strachey in collaboration with Anna Freud and assisted by Alix Strachey and Alan Tyson, 151–249. 1955; rpt. London: The Hogarth Press and the Institute of Psycho-Analysis, 2001.

———. "Formulations on the Two Principles of Mental Functioning" (1911). In *The Standard Edition of the Complete Psychological Works of Sigmund Freud,* vol. 12, ed. and trans. James Strachey in collaboration with Anna Freud and assisted by Alix Strachey and Alan Tyson, 213–26. 1958; rpt. London: The Hogarth Press and the Institute of Psycho-Analysis, 2001.

———. "An Autobiographical Study" (1925). In *The Standard Edition of the Complete Psychological Works of Sigmund Freud,* vol. 20, ed. and trans. James Strachey in collaboration with Anna Freud and assisted by Alix Strachey and Alan Tyson, 1–74. 1959; rpt. London: The Hogarth Press and the Institute of Psycho-Analysis, 2001.

———."Fetishism" (1927). In *The Standard Edition of the Complete Psychological Works of Sigmund Freud,* vol. 21, ed. and trans. James Strachey in collaboration with Anna Freud and assisted by Alix Strachey and Alan Tyson, 147–57. 1961; rpt. London: The Hogarth Press and the Institute of Psycho-Analysis, 2001.

———. "Lecture 33: Femininity, New Introductory Lectures on Psycho-Analysis" (1933[1932]). In *The Standard Edition of the Complete Psychological Works of Sigmund Freud,* vol. 22, ed. and trans. James Strachey in collaboration with Anna Freud and assisted by Alix Strachey and Alan Tyson, 112–35. 1964; rpt. London: The Hogarth Press and the Institute of Psycho-Analysis, 2001.

Green, André. "Has Sexuality Anything To Do With Psychoanalysis?" *The International Journal of Psycho-Analysis* 76, no. 5 (1995): 871–83.

———. *The Chains of Eros: The Actuality of the Sexual in Psychoanalysis,* trans. Luke Thurston. London: Karnac Books, 2000.

Herdt, Gilbert. "What is Sexual Literacy, and Why is it Needed Now?" In *21st Century Sexualities: Contemporary Issues in Health, Education and Rights,* eds. Gilbert Herdt and Cymene Howe, 17–19. London and New York: Routledge, 2007.

Lacan, Jacques. *Book II: The Ego in Freud's Theory and in the Technique of Psychoanalysis* (1954–55), ed. Jacques-Alain Miller, trans. Sylvana Tomaselli. Cambridge: Cambridge University Press, 1988.

———. *Book XX: On Feminine Sexuality, the Limits of Love and Knowledge, Encore* (1972–73), ed. Jacques-Alain Miller, trans. Bruce Fink. New York: W.W. Norton & Company, 1998.

———. "L'étourdit" (1972). *Autres Écrits,* 449–95. Paris: Éditions du Seuil, 2001.

———. *Livre XXIII: Le sinthome* (1975–76), ed. Jacques-Alain Miller. Paris: Éditions du Seuil, 2005.

———. "The Freudian Thing, or the Meaning of the Return to Freud in Psychoanalysis" (1955). *Écrits,* trans. Bruce Fink, 334–63. New York and London: W.W. Norton & Company, 2006.

———. "Lituraterre" (1971), trans. Dany Nobus. *Continental Philosophy Review* 46, no. 1 (2013): 327–34.

Laqueur, Thomas. *Making Sex: Body and Gender from the Greeks to Freud.* Cambridge and London: Harvard University Press, 1990.

Litowitz, Bonnie E. "Sexuality and Textuality." *Journal of the American Psychoanalytic Association* 50, no. 1 (2002): 171–98.

Lubbe, Trevor. "A Kleinian Theory of Sexuality." *British Journal of Psychotherapy* 24, no. 3 (2008): 299–316.

Money, John. "Linguistic Resources and Psychodynamic Theory." *British Journal of Medical Psychology* 20 (1955): 264–66.

Sáez, Javier. *Théorie Queer et Psychanalyse,* trans. Françoise Ben Kemoun. Paris: EPEL, 2004.

Stoller, Robert J. *Sex and Gender: The Development of Masculinity and Femininity.* London: The Hogarth Press and the Institute of Psycho-Analysis, 1968.

19

"You Make Me Feel Like a Natural Woman": Thoughts on a Case of Transsexual Identity Formation and Queer Theory

Ami Kaplan

This chapter is about a male to female transsexual[1] individual and some contemplation about her life through the lens of queer theory. I will introduce her shortly, but first I will outline my psychoanalytic orientation and clinical stance in regard to transgender clients. My psychoanalytic theoretical position is both Freudian (from an Ego Psychology perspective) and based in Object Relations. Within Object Relations, I am most informed by Winnicott and Fairbairn. I don't subscribe to any psychoanalytic or environmentally-based etiology theories that include such explanations of transsexualism as a defense against homosexuality; based on the mother's emotional state; stemming from insecure attachment to the mother or other problems in the family dynamic (Greenson 1966; Bak 1968; Greenacre 1969; Stoller 1970; Ovesey and Person 1973; 1976; Coates 1990). The type of work I do with these individuals takes a non-pathologizing stance and does not try to figure out how they

---

1 I use the term "transsexual" to denote individuals who feel their gender to be that of the non-natal sex and who desire to some degree to have the bodies of their non-natal or opposite sex. I use the term "transgender" to denote a larger group of gender variant individuals including cross-dressers and the intersexed.

became transgender. Rather it centers on helping gender variant individuals be who they authentically feel themselves to be.

As a lesbian analyst with a more androgynous gender identity, I might be more sensitive to queer issues and less likely to pathologize non-mainstream identities and behaviors. My approach is not necessarily at odds with mainstream Ego Psychology with its interest in ego functioning, strengths and weaknesses. In addition, Ego Psychology's emphasis on the ego function of synthesis does lend itself to thinking about the transgender experience, where often body dysphoria and anomalous social experiences must be tolerated for long periods of time. One might assume a case with transgender issues could be easily embraced by queer theory; however, I chose this case because it highlights areas where queer theory is both in sync with and problematic for this particular patient. It should be noted that I am not formulating a theory of transsexualism, rather I am describing work and offering ideas about a particular patient. The title suggests an intersubjective construction to a transsexual's gender identity. This refers to "mirroring" provided by the therapist and others who interact with Jenny as a woman and to the development of interpersonal skills developed in a social context. Work with this patient involved dealing with bias and stigma and negotiating shifts in relationships with family and partners. Therapy involved support for Jenny as she negotiated these tasks, as well as dealing with her feelings of having grown up with gender variance. Much of the therapy involved helping the patient construct and solidify a new gender identity to herself and the outside world.

James/Jenny[2]: History and Presenting Problems

I refer to James as both male and female in this chapter depending on how he or she was presenting at the time being discussed. James presented as a fifty-six-year-old genetic Caucasian man

2 Names and some identifying data have been changed to protect James's identity.

who contacted me as a therapist known to work with gender issues in order to explore his wish to be and live as a woman. He presented as a tall thin man dressed in business casual, with graying hair. He seemed somewhat awkward and self-effacing, smiling frequently and laughing in a sort of way that seemed to say, "don't take anything I say too seriously." I later understood his manner as a defense against shame of his gender variance. He struck me as educated, "old-fashioned," and shy. It became apparent early on that he avoided conflict and preferred not to draw attention to himself. He worked at middle-management level in a large New York firm. He is in a long-term relationship with a woman, who until recently did not know about his gender variance. He has children from a previous marriage and currently lives with a girlfriend.

Initial topics of concern to James included whether or not to go "full time" (transition to living as a women full time), his partner's ambivalence about his transition, coming out to family, shame about being transgender, and finding times and places to dress and be Jenny. James frequently voiced a (quite unrealistic) wish to be able to transition without anybody noticing: "well, if I just do it gradually enough maybe people wouldn't really notice," she would say with a little laugh, but it was clear to me that this was a real wish. I could feel Jenny's sadness, bewilderment and anxiety at being such a private person and having to face being an object of interest.

As a child, James's own understanding and consciousness of his gender variance was limited. He was mostly alone, shy and timid. He felt himself to be different from other boys with some awareness that he had certain feminine attributes which he understood as problematic as they drew attention to his being different. He alternated between being overweight and underweight as a teenager in an attempt to correct what he thought of as a feminine body.

Much of James's unconscious material had to do with shame. It could be seen outwardly in his extreme shyness and social awkwardness. Goldberg (1991) describes characteristics of shame as "a shrinking away from one's full presence in the world" and a "depleted sense of personal identity" (4). Jenny's wish to be "public" hasn't kept pace with lessening feelings of shame around her gender variance contributing to feelings of awkwardness and insecurity.

As a young adult James remembers being semi-conscious of his gender variance but he did not let himself dwell on it. He had no words for what he was experiencing. As a teenager and adult, James would cross-dress at times when he could, telling himself that "this was just something I like to do now and then." His wife "caught" him cross-dressing once and said she would divorce him if he continued with it. He hid it from her and his children. He describes having achieved satisfaction in the role of a nurturing father. He understood this as having been enough to sustain him during those years and the urge to cross-dress was lessened, although he still did it when he could, at times only putting on lipstick while alone in his car.

When James did decide to transition part-time he did it without first discussing it with his current partner "Kelly" in any depth. He simply began to take hormones he bought over the Internet and to accumulate and wear more women's clothing. This and other behaviors alerted me to what I believe is a significant problem — the state of James's object relations; specifically the lack of emotional intimacy, avoidance of conflict and the lack of depth in general in his communications with his partner and others. In fact, James has no close personal friends or colleagues outside of Kelly. It's possible that he didn't have the mental space to develop better object relations due to his having had to struggle with gender dysphoria alone throughout most of his life. For many transgender people (and for this person in particular) a good deal of psychic space is used up in dealing with the internal struggle of having an ego-dystonic gender assignment and body. The individual is both consciously and unconsciously preoccupied with the struggle, leaving fewer psychic resources available for such things as developing interpersonal skills, noticing and reacting to the feelings of others and a myriad of other maturational functions. Kelly had ambivalence over the transition. She was no longer attracted to James, and missed his masculine attributes such as body hair and more angular body. James was also upset at having lost Kelly as a lover, but didn't see any way to repair the situation.

The Concreteness of Identity as Necessary

Jenny embraces a traditional female identity that is almost stereotypical. When it is possible for her to do so she likes to wear skirts, sandals, earrings, French tip nails, makeup and jewelry. Jenny has constructed and wishes to embrace her vision of the female identity to its fullest. Certainly gender expression may fluctuate and often does after a period of transition; however, the identity of the *moment* must be taken with all due seriousness and respect, even if it does not end up as the ultimate or last gender identity. As with many trans people who are first transitioning, the gender expression can have a stressed and exaggerated feel to it. Raine Dozier (2005), a sociologist from Seattle Washington, comments on this phenomenon from his interviews with eighteen FTM (female-to-male) transgender people: "when sex characteristics do not align with gender, behavior becomes more important to gender expression and interpretation. When sex characteristics become more congruent with gender, behavior becomes more fluid and less important in asserting gender" (297).

The first issue grappled with in therapy was James' struggle to know to what extent he wished to transition. In the beginning of therapy, James reported "dressing" at least once a weekend and going out in public. These outings were very important to him and James often focused on relating them in detail. She often described what she wore, where she went, whether she was "read" or not (seen as a transsexual), her comfort level, etc. Jenny was engaging in "exploration" as described by Bockting and Coleman (2007, 185–208). In their "Developmental Stages of the Transgender Coming Out Process,"[3] they note that "exploration

---

3   The five stages are: 1. pre-coming out: crossdressing and "transgender feelings" but not the naming of the feelings; 2. coming out and acknowledging

is the stage of learning as much as possible about expressing one's transgender identity now that the secret has been revealed [...] ending social isolation [...] developing interpersonal skills through the newly adopted identity with peers, friends and family" (193). In addition, "exploration includes explicit experimentation with gender roles and expressions. This allows the transgender individual to find his or her identity (who am I?), and the most comfortable way to express it (how can I best actualize or express my gender identity?), often through trial and error" (193).

At the point in time I am writing about, Jenny was at the beginning of her transition and embraced a gender identity that was decidedly at one end of a gender continuum. Being at the extreme end can be seen to be somewhat problematic with some of the tenets of queer theory. Erin Calhoun Davis (2009), a sociologist from Cornell College in Iowa writing on transgender people and queer theory notes that, "identity has also been posited as something oppressive that individuals need to 'move beyond'" (101). A recurring theme in queer theory is the problem with gender binary and the associated labels of "man" and "woman." Bornstein (1994) notes that identifying as "male" or "female" perpetuates "the violence of male privilege" (74). Iain Morland (2009), in a piece on intersexed individuals, states that, "the identity claims 'male' and 'female', when made by people with non-intersexed anatomies, are morally indefensible because they constitute a commitment to the descriptivism that disenfranchises intersexed individuals" (45). Kathryn Bond Stockton, in her chapter, notes "two terms, 'man' and 'woman', that many queers would now regard as absurdly blocky, even totalizing, in their absence of further and finer specifications." The list of examples could go on and on.

How then do we understand this patient who wishes to embrace the label of "woman" given queer theory's privileging of gender fluidity and problems with the gender binary? I would suggest that despite queer theory's problems with labeling and

---

to self; 3. exploration; 4. intimacy; 5. identity integration.

binary gender labels, a stage of presenting with a non-fluid gender expression plays an important role in solidifying identity for this transitioning woman. Concepts such as gender queer, gender fluid, a-gender, etc., only came into public consciousness in the 1990s and as such, transsexualism was previously thought of in terms of the gender binary, that is, of women transitioning to be men or men transitioning to be women. The developmental objective in queer theory of *moving beyond* the gender binary has had the unfortunate side effect of tainting "binarism" as somehow unacceptable, even though it has important meaning and use for some people.

Mirroring of the Emerging Self

James has a history of being attracted to women. He had a few sexual encounters with men during college. In describing them, James's comment was a lackluster "it was OK," "it was really not that satisfying… I'm more into women." However, James added that he is "open to both sexes."

In transitioning James (Jenny) started seeking out men "you know, *admirers*," she would call them — these are men who are attracted to and seek out trans women, or male to female transsexuals. I wanted to understand the meaning of Jenny's going out on "dates" while still in a relationship. Did she want to leave Kelly? Did she wish to have a male partner? I think Jenny herself did not know the reasons other than having a strong desire to experience the world as a woman and have that mirrored or reflected back. Jenny discusses the dates with men as follows:

I like how they make me feel. They pursue me, they give me attention as a woman, and that feels good, they take the lead, after a first date I was going to just shake hands and maybe kiss the guy on the cheek, but he grabbed me and gave me a "full-on" kiss on the mouth. It was OK, I didn't find him attractive, but I liked his taking the lead.

In musing on a future date Jenny said: "I'm going to get dressed up for him, I like that, and they appreciate it, and if it leads to sex, that's OK, I'll go along with it, but its not really what I'm looking for, its more just for the experience of being out and dressed."

In short, Jenny's object choice at this point is not so much about whom she is attracted to but rather who treats her and thereby helps her to feel the most like a woman. The experiences help her to "construct" the female identity of Jenny. Dozier (2005) comments on object choice in interviews with eighteen FTM (female to male) trans people:

Respondents also challenge traditional notions of sexual orientation by focusing less on the sex of the partner and more on the gender organization of the relationship. The relationship's ability to validate the interviewee's masculinity or maleness often takes precedence over the sex of the partner, helping to explain changing sexual orientation as female-to-male transsexual and transgendered people transition into men. (297)

Others have written about similar phenomena. Diamond (2008) suggests the person rather than the gender of the person is the most important factor in desire for sexual minority women. Gagne and Tewksbury (1998, 92) note that the personal gendered state of mind during sex was of greater significance to male-to-female (MTF) transgender individuals than the actual sex of the partner. For some transgender individuals, the events of transitioning and changing so many things about oneself may, by association, act to give personal license to explore change in areas previously repressed or denied such as in sexual object choice.

Jenny's felt gender identity and the outward performance of the female gender helps her to construct and stabilize her identity as a woman while at the same time its exaggerated nature is an indicator of her current insecurity about it. The repetition of these "dates" allows her to practice and to be "mirrored" (in the

Winnicottian sense) in her new role. At first the inner state and later the outward performance were tenuous and their emergence has had to be nurtured, mirrored, and confirmed. In addition, positive mirroring by the analyst was extremely important due to the negative mirroring Jenny presumably experienced by her parents. Working backwards from the level of shame Jenny has about being transsexual; it can be assumed that her parents reflected back to the young child negative judgments and appraisals of James's gender expression. The disapproval helped to form the basis of a part of the self that was disassociated or repressed, namely her female self. When the female self was finally granted permission to emerge, one can reasonably expect there to be great ambivalence about it. The therapist's positive mirroring of the emerging female self is both healing and necessary for ameliorating what could be understood as Jenny's "internalized trans-phobia." Jenny's new identity is in part constructed with the help of others, i.e., intersubjectively. This can be seen in her need for the positive feedback and interplay of the other, be it companion or analyst.

I have mentioned shame several times in this account and made some suggestions as to its origin. The analysis and working through of shame for this patient was vitally important because of its debilitating effect on good object relations and on self-esteem. By "good" object relations, I am referring to the ability to have mutually satisfying relationships and to be wholly present or oneself in a relationship. This of course is very difficult to do when one is in hiding (and ashamed of) such a large part of oneself as one's gender. Shame results in alienation, feeling oneself to be unlovable, unwanted, embarrassed and inferior. The most typical reaction is withdrawal from interaction or the development of a "false self." Certainly any transgender individual who has kept their gender variance hidden has some experience of the "false self." In addition, because of the withdrawal or presentation of false self, the gender variant person has less time practicing good interactions with others when presenting the authentic self.

Queer theory is helpful in pointing out the awkwardness and imprecision of signifiers such as "straight," "gay," and "bisexual," which do not begin to address the complexity and subtleness of each individual situation. Queer theory benefits Jenny, transgender individuals and psychoanalysts in one obvious and significant way in that it advances society's awareness and acceptance of gender identities, expressions and sexualities outside of the hetero-normative. It has an important part to play in informing psychoanalytic practice by continuing to point out areas where we are making unhelpful assumptions about what is "normal" or desired for our patients.

Jenny, and other transsexual individuals in the process of transitioning may have a strong need to claim the *label* of "man" or "woman" which can be counter to queer theory's anti-identitarian politics. Queer theory's "nonnormalizing energetic trajectories" (Downing) are contrary to Jenny's wanting to appear normal. Lee Edelman (2004) states that "queerness can never define an identity; it can only ever disturb one" (17). That works well if one is perfectly secure and comfortable with an identity, but not so well when one is desperately trying to consolidate a gender identity, as with this particular individual.

Works Cited

Bak, R.C. "The Phallic Woman: The Ubiquitous Fantasy in Perversions." *The Psychoanalytic Study of the Child* 23 (1968): 15–36.

Bockting, Walter, and Eli Coleman. "Developmental Stages of the Transgender Coming Out Process: Toward an Integrated Identity." In *Principles of Transgender Medicine and Surgery,* eds. Randi Ettner, Stan Monstrey and A. Evan Eyler, 185–208. New York: The Haworth Press, 2007.

Bornstein, Kate. *Gender Outlaw.* New York: Vintage Books, 1994.

Coates, Susan. "Ontogenesis of Boyhood Gender Identity Disorder." *The Journal of the American Academy of Psychoanalysis* 18, no. 3 (1990): 414–38.

Davis, E.C. "Situating 'Fluidity': (Trans) Gender Identification and the Regulation of Gender Diversity." *GLQ: A Journal of Lesbian and Gay Studies* 15, no. 1 (2009): 97–130.

Diamond, Lisa. *Sexual Fluidity: Understanding Women's Love and Desire.* Cambridge: Harvard University Press, 2008.

Dozier, Raine. "Beards, Breasts, and Bodies: Doing Sex in a Gendered World." *Gender and Society* 19, no. 3 (2005): 297–316.

Edelman, Lee. *No Future: Queer Theory and the Death Drive.* Durham: Duke University Press, 2004.

Gagne, Patricia, and Richard Tewksbury. "Rethinking Binary Conceptions and Social Constructions: Transgender Experiences of Gender and Sexuality." In *Advancing Gender Research Across, Beyond, and Through Disciplines and Paradigms,* vol. 3, eds. M. T. Segal and D. Vasilikie, 73–102. Greenwich: JAI Press, 1998.

Goldberg, Carl. *Understanding Shame.* 1977; rpt. New Jersey: Jason Aronson Inc., 1991.

Greenacre, Phyllis. "The Fetish and the Transitional Object." *The Psychoanalytic Study of the Child* 24 (1969): 144–64.

Greenson, Ralph. "A Transvestite Boy and a Hypothesis." *International Journal of Psychoanalysis* 47, no. 2 (1966): 396–403.

Haldeman, Douglas. "The Practice and Ethics of Sexual Orientation Conversion Therapy." *Journal of Consulting and Clinical Psychology* 62, no. 2 (1994): 221–27.

Ovesey, Lionel, and Person, Ethel. "Gender Identity and Sexual Psychopathology in Men: A Psychodynamic Analysis of Homosexuality, Transsexualism and Transvestism." *Journal of American Academy of Psychoanalysis* 1, no. 1 (1973): 53–72.

Ovesey, Lionel and Person, Ethel. "Transvestism: A Disorder of the Sense of Self." *International Journal of Psychoanalytic Psychotherapy* 5 (1976): 219–36.

Stoller, Robert. "The Transsexual Boy: Mother's Feminized Phallus." *British Journal of Medical Psychology* 43, no. 2 (1970): 117–28.

Winnicott, Donald W. *Collected Papers.* New York: Basic Books, 1958.

20

Sexual Difference: From Symptom to Sinthome

Patricia Gherovici

"We speak therein of fucking, and we say that it's not working out" (Lacan 1998[1972–73], 32). Without splitting hairs, Lacan bluntly summed up what people talk about when they are on the analytic couch. If all what we talk about on the couch is sex, nothing much has been discovered in psychoanalysis since Freud and Lacan. Freud's major revelation that the unconscious is at root sexual is confirmed in our current practice. It is not just that, as Lacan has noted, one hears that something is wrong with sex. Consider the case of one of my analysands, Melissa, a twenty-four-year-old female, who felt that her analysis was progressing because she was "feeling pretty stable and calmer." She added however that "at the end of the day" she always felt anxious. "Perhaps it's this recurrent thinking, this unrelenting questioning," she added. Her problems, she knew, were about relationships. The trouble was not just her mother, looming large and overwhelming, or her father, weak and slightly perverse, but her current boyfriend, who overwhelmed her with his affection. "I want to figure out what Mike means to me. Sometimes I experience a sense of happiness because I love him; it can be really wonderful. Sex can be good but as soon as he expresses how much he loves me, I have only regret." Fundamentally, his love and support did not bring her satisfaction but rather a sense of loss and emptiness. "His intense admiration for me is overwhelming. As if I were cut off from him or myself. Something keeps me from connecting with him." Melissa had a suspicion about what the problem was: "It is the issue of seeing other people, but it does not seem worthwhile."

She had a confession to make: "I have had a couple of dreams in which I had wild sex with this guy. I felt as if I had betrayed Mike. His feelings for me are so monogamous; he has not been interested in anyone else. There again one can see in which ways we are so different. I have to accept the fact that I have desires; I may have dreamt about sex with a man, but in fact I have been wanting to be with a woman." That she had not acted upon those wishes nevertheless made her feel guilty for a transgression that had only taken place on her dreams. "What's wrong with me? I do love Mike. I do value our relationship. I wish I didn't fantasize about other people. […] I will have to make a choice about the relationship." Was her guilt justifiable? "Mike talked in such an emotional tone. When I heard him talk like that I cried, and almost immediately I felt distant. […] I fear it will become the devouring love I have for my mother." Separation from her first love had a cost: "I forged my own way outside my relationship with my mother by acquitting my own sexuality." Melissa was operating in the shadow of fear. "It is scary for me to have sexual desire for Mike. He is the main focus of my sexual attention. What feels really scary for me is that I haven't had any real relationship with a woman but this is part of my sexuality. It is really confusing. I would not identify as lesbian but I do not really know if I am really myself with Mike." Identity does not resolve the issue of desire for Melissa. Eventually, the logic of the unconscious takes hold and makes itself explicit in questions of sexual difference:

What's the difference between men and women? My mother would say that gender is societal. How much do I disagree? Men and women are different. Yes, there are women who are masculine and men who have feminine sides. But still this is very confusing for me […]. I feel attraction to both men and women. It is physical […]. I think that's how I know; this physical attraction to women is not going to go away. I also have emotional and intellectual attractions to women. Being around women feels right. What is the source of the attraction? It has to do with issues of gender and sexuality […].

As a variation on this universal theme, what follows is something quite familiar to psychoanalysts, an old question about sexual identity with a new twist: "How can I accept Mike's love? I feel dirty being sexualized by him. Actually, being with him is strange for me. I did feel comfortable with my sexuality before him. My sexuality was not a source of shame or anxiety. Maybe the issue is: am I straight or bisexual?" Are Melissa's statements motivated by a desire to understand an issue about gender and sex, or does she simply confuse object choice with identity politics? Is she bisexual because she fantasizes about having an affair with a woman? When she asks: "Am I straight or bisexual?" is she asking in fact: "Am I a man or a woman?" If that is the case, then the traditional question of sexual identity that we find at the core of hysteria is shifting from a question of gender identity ("Am I a man or a woman?") to one of sexual orientation ("Am I straight or bisexual?"). Melisa's comments seem to remap the whole terrain of sexual politics (compulsory heterosexuality, sexual choices, monogamy, love, reciprocity in relationships, attachment, sexual prejudice). She becomes aware of her boyfriend's love and while she admits that she is happy with him, this realization makes her experience regret and it is then that she questions her sexuality. Melissa become distant, or, as she puts it, "cut off from him or myself." Does her reference to being "cut off" echo old Freudian ideas about castration anxiety and penis envy? Can her account replay the classic Oedipal familial scenario of identifications and rivalries? Does she question her sexual identity as a phobic reaction to intimacy? Is her sexual ambiguity a strategy that defends her from desire while cancelling out the mother? If, as she stated, she forged a way out of a "devouring" relationship with her mother, "acquitting my own sexuality," can we say that her uncertainty about her sexuality is a sort of father substitute (a stand in for a name or *no!* which separates mother and child)? Are contested notions like phallic attribution and castration still valid tools in clinical practice?

Melissa's predicament, which is not uncommon, can be understood within the parameters of what Lacan (1966–67) called "the big secret of psychoanalysis" (Session 12/4/67). The secret is that "there is not such a thing as a sexual act," a dictum which tries to delineate the impossibility of a perfect sexual union between two people. Far from being harmonious, the sexual act is always a blunder, a mangled action, a failure, reminding one of the inconsistency of one's relation to sex. Lacan's later variation of the formula as "there is not such a thing as a sexual relationship" (1991[1969–70], 134; 1998[1972–73], 9) provides a condensed formulation of the sexual illness of humankind. Something about sex is intractable; it resists assimilation, it disrupts meaning.

Melissa is not the only case I have met of someone who seemingly breaks away from the paradigm of social conformity to so-called gender. An analysand came to see me with countless questions, since despite being a happily married woman, she had become restless, then had had sex with a woman — just once. This was just because, as she said, she wanted to find out how a woman's skin felt like, and also how it smelled. Was this an issue of identification since she admired and wanted to resemble the seductive, aggressive woman whom she had had sex with? Was she fascinated with an idealized femininity that would help her define her sexual identity on the basis of sexual practice? Or was she "done with men," as she once blurted out exasperatedly and had she, at last, followed her true desire?

I could also mention here the analysand who ran away from a marriage proposal from a man she thought she was in love with to rush into the arms of a lesbian friend, whom she claimed she was not even erotically attracted to. There was another declared feminist analysand who defined herself as bisexual but never had a sexual encounter with a woman. She detested makeup and "girly" things and insisted that she wanted to be loved for who she really was, without being "objectified by a male," but then she appeared smitten by a boyfriend who told her almost offensively that she should wear sexy clothes. Moreover, he was constantly comparing her to other women he was ogling. All these cases seem to be variations on a universal theme: the inconsistency of the relation of the subject to sex. Their agents seem to position themselves in a zone of sexual ambiguity, which forces us to rethink how we define sex and sexuality. We can contrast them with other cases that hinge more explicitly around issues of sexual attributes and seem to operate according to a binary of complementary opposites. Thus I treated a trans man who was deeply unhappy in his sexual life because in not having a penis, he believed he lacked a body part that was universally desired by all women and that would warrant their sexual enjoyment. There was also a new patient who explained that in the past someone like her would be thought of "as a man with a mental problem but that it's just the opposite, I am a woman with a physical problem." I have dealt elsewhere (2010) with the case of an analysand who said she had "the worst birth defect a woman can have, I was born with a penis and testicles" (190–93).

Psychoanalysis, with Freud, reveals the challenge of assuming a sexual positioning. As noted by Lacan (1981[1964]), Freud "posit[s] sexuality as essentially polymorphous, aberrant" (176). Freud "perverted" sexuality when he separated the drive from any instinctual function and described its object as "indifferent," that is, not determined by gender. Here, in my view, Laplanche's faithfulness to Freud is crucial. The normative slant in psychoanalysis, which has led to troubling standards of normalcy like elevating the genitals to the status of fetish organs of a mature heterosexual genitality or the pathologization of homosexuality, are post-Freudian deviations based on what Lacan (2006[1958]) aptly qualified as "delusional" notions of normalcy, an "absurd hymn to the harmony of genital relations" that have nothing to do with the reality of sex (507).

Any Sexual Identity Is Failed

To further contextualize our discussion, let's say that the subject's assumption of a sexual identity is always symptomatic because it is related to what psychoanalysts call the phallus — a defective tool to negotiate the Real that eludes us. Perhaps those analysands who confuse object choice with identity are searching for a totalizing answer that introduces a paradox: they ask whether they are straight or bisexual as if the simple fact of posing the question would mean that they are neither; but if they are neither, they feel obligated to choose what they are.

From a psychoanalytic perspective, as the mirror stage illustrates, identity is an artificial construct that results from imaginary identifications with an "other" who grants a "sense of self." As Tim Dean (2000) notes, "Human sexuality cannot be construed as in any way as the result of the mirror stage" (191). Identity relies on the assumption of an image and is something that eventually may come to an end during psychoanalysis because the subject emerges exactly where identity fails. In a well-known passage, Rose (1986) writes:

> The unconscious constantly reveals the "failure" of identity. Because there is no continuity of psychic life, so there is not stability of sexual identity, no position for women (or for men) which is ever simply achieved. Nor does psychoanalysis see such "failure" as a special-case inability or an individual deviancy from the norm. [...] [T]here is a resistance to identity at the very heart of psychic life. (90–91)

Rose's emphasis on the "failure" of identity is central because it contradicts the usual reading of "lack" as a loss or as an injury that women would have suffered and that men would fear. Lack is neither a negative "wound" due to the loss of an object, nor a deficiency, but rather a productive force. All subjects must confront and assume their lack; furthermore, the Lacanian subject is subjectivized lack. Such a lack carries several effects on the subject — it divides the subject; desire is born through lack and can never be finally fulfilled. I reiterate the importance of desire over identity because the desiring subject is produced by the impact of language on the materiality of the body — the subject of desire does not emerge from identifications with the mother, the father, or a signifier, but precisely when identifications stop working. In fact, identity is far from being stable because the foundational identification of the subject is with a signifier, which means, identification with difference (a signifier designates one thing in opposition to others). Due to the equivocal nature of language, identification is not unifying but rather it creates a split that eclipses the subject. As a result, I will depart from Farina's contention that theories of desire rooted in lack would understand "non-normative" forms of sexuality as excluded from sexual norms — assuming that they are "missing something" that supposedly a "normate sexual subjectivity" would posses. "Normality" is a questionable construct, a compensatory symptom, a norm of *mal* (evil) or the norm-of-the-male (*norme mâle*) as Lacan (2007[1972]) would say, playing with the fact that in French male norm and normal are identically pronounced, thus radically rejecting the notion of a normal sexuality.[1] How subjects relate to their sexual bodies is determined by the way they relate to lack: this is what psychoanalysis calls castration (another name for the "norm-male"). For psychoanalysis, a relation to lack will provide the foundation for diverse structures of desire, whether neurotic, perverse, fetishistic, or homosexual. We note here that perversion is taken as a structure and not as sexual practice. Downing's discussion of perversion in this collection makes evident that even though queer discourse and psychoanalytic discourse may enrich each other there may be unsurpassable chasms. Maybe the "The Woman does not exist" (Lacan 1998[1972–73], 7) of Lacan cannot compare with the "the category woman does not exist" of Monique Wittig (1992, 15). Dean (2000) argues well that Lacan "meets" queer theory but this meeting is not an overlap. Psychoanalysis may be queer but it is not queer theory.

---

1   Interview with Françoise Wolff at the Belgian television on "The great questions of psychoanalysis." MK2 video cassette under the title: *Jacques Lacan,* conference at Leuven followed by an interview with Françoise Wolff also known as "Jacques Lacan Speaks" (Lacan 2007).

Sexual Difference and the Paradoxes of the Formulas of Sexuation

For psychoanalysis, sexual difference is not a norm but a real impossibility, which is to say, it is a limit to what is sayable and thinkable; it is a failure of meaning. Our relationship to the body is structured by the symbolic system of language, yet language lacks a signifier to signify sexual difference. To complicate things further, sexual difference is neither just the body (as biological substrata) nor the psychic introjections of the social performance of gender (as a socially constructed role). Neither the perspective of biological essentialism nor that of social constructivism have been able to solve the problem of unconscious sexual difference. Since sexual difference is neither sex nor gender, sex needs to be symbolized, and gender needs to be embodied. This unconscious sexual reality about which the subject has no knowledge, i.e., does not know what is to be a man or a woman; it is a reality that psychoanalysis presupposes. Femininity or masculinity are both failed positions from which we inhabit our sexual bodies.

Lacan maps the implications of this in his formulas of sexuation. The formulas reiterate the dictum "there is no such a thing as a sexual relation" (1966–67, Session 12/4/67; 1998[1972–73], 9) which means that there can be sexual encounters between people, not between complementary beings, if any encounter takes place it is between partial places of the body, thresholds of localized *jouissance*. We are speaking bodies, that is, beings inhabited and exceeded by language. Language makes *jouissance* (a shattering mix of pain and pleasure) forbidden, setting limits and obstacles in the trajectory towards the full realization of desire. To answer Farina's question: "Why is it 'great' that we theorize aggression as inevitable for *jouissance*?" Because *jouissance* is experienced in the body in ways that cannot be signified, the body is transformed — the organism becomes a body of *jouissance*, a body of excesses resonating in the organic body.

With the sexuation formulas, Lacan is challenging a model of gender as a binary relation between two positive, representable and complementary terms. In fact he was grasping the impossible relation between sexuated beings of any gender. This is another way of saying that for the unconscious there is no representation of the female sex, that the unconscious is monosexual or homosexual; there is only one signifier for both sexes, the phallus. Tim Dean (2000) observes that, "it is not so important that the phallus may be a penis, or in Judith Butler's reading, a dildo, as it is a giant red herring" (14). As such, the phallus is clearly a misleading clue comparable to the use of smoked herrings to mislead hounds following a trail. To pun somewhat on the phrase, I would like to suggest that the phallus is less a red herring than a "read" herring — in fact, like gender, it is subject to interpretation, and it will always be read like a text. As Bond Stockton remarks, following Copjec, the Lacanian axiom "there is no sexual relation" speaks to a radical antagonism between sex and sense. We should keep in mind that sexual difference is intractable, and castration appears as a partial answer to this deadlock. For psychoanalysis, castration, lack, woman, phallus are ways of representing something that cannot be represented because they belong to the Real.

Can psychoanalysis talk about sexual difference without a direct reference to the notion of "phallus"? It would be just as impossible, Morel (2006) notes, to talk about Freudian sexuality without referring to sexual difference. However, to avoid the trappings of phallocentrism, we can make use of several psychoanalytic concepts that are not sexed and help define sexuality, such the unconscious, repetition, transference, object *a* (cause of desire and surplus *jouissance*) and symptom. Lacan returns to many of Freud's concepts and reformulates them, first in his elaboration of the dominance of the Name-of-the-Father in the Oedipus complex, and later, going beyond the Oedipus complex and proposing a new form of the symptom, which he called *sinthome* (2005[1975–76]). The *sinthome* is a way of reknotting in the psychic structure what has been left unknotted because of the father's failure. This applied to the case of James Joyce but can be generalized somewhat.

Beyond the Phallus

In order to think about sexual difference without a direct reference to the phallus, I propose to follow Lacan's later theory of the *sinthome*. As Bracha Lichtenberg Ettinger (2002) argues, it allows us to grasp the impossible relation between the sexes (91). Since the *sinthome* is not a complement but a supplement, it is a vehicle for creative unbalance, capable of disrupting the symmetry. The *sinthome* is what helps one tolerate the absence of the sexual relation/proportion (Lacan 2005[1975–76], 101). In contrast, the phallus is an obstacle. It is nothing other than a failed answer to the conundrum of sexual difference. This difference cannot be fully grasped (it is just speculation constructed on the real of the impossibility of a sexual rapport).

In this context, the clinical example of one analysand, whom I will call Ari, is helpful. Ari is a biological female who has had "top" surgery (breasts removed), prefers the pronoun "they" and takes testosterone. Ari is manipulating their body to transform it into a surface with an undecided readability: What they want is to pass as neither male nor female, thus rejecting altogether the phallus as a signifier of difference. If, according to phallic signification, we write two sexes with one signifier, Ari denounces the aporia of sex by refusing to be seen as either. The phallus is exposed as just a parasite, the conjunction of an organ and the function of language (speech). Ari elevates "the limp little piece of prick" (15) to the status of art and supplements it, transforming physical appearance into the art of divination. It is true that the phallus, often confused with the limp little prick, is not much more than a signified of *jouissance* that sexual discourse transforms into a signifier.

Certainly in some cases, sexual identity is of the order of the *sinthome*; it is acquired as achieving a reknotting of the three registers of the real, symbolic, and imaginary. Then, the *sinthome* shapes the singularity of an "art," a *technē* that reknots a workable consistency for the subject; this movement can best be evoked by saying that it moves the subject from a certain contingency to absolute necessity. Taking into account the complex relationship that transsexuals have to their body — they often say that their souls are trapped in a body of the wrong (opposite) sex — I claim that an art similar to that of actual artists, if not necessarily with the genius of Joyce, can be found in transsexual artificiality. In some cases, it gives birth to an art that, I argue, is tantamount to a creative *sinthome.* This can be clearly observed in Jan Morris's (1986) sex-change memoir *Conundrum* where Morris describes her trajectory as an inevitable, predestined act, as if the sex change had always been bound to happen (168–69).

One can see why her *sinthome* was necessary: it was necessity itself. A *sinthome* is what does not cease to be written. Thus Morris writes: "I see myself not as man or woman, self or other, fragment or whole" (191). Her continuing ambiguity is not a "solution" but a tolerable, permanent questioning, she can make do with: "What if I remain an equivocal figure?" (191); "I have lived the life of man, I live now the life of woman, and I shall transcend both — if not in person, then perhaps in art…" (190). In Morris's case, the *sinthome* has produced less a "woman" than a "woman of letters." Since sexual difference is real and resists symbolization, it creates a symptom, but this symptom is something that cannot be rectified or cured; it is nevertheless something with which every subject must come to terms. In Lacan's formulation of the *sinthome*, the idea of the symptom acquired a new meaning. The *sinthome* is a purified symptom; it remains beyond symbolic representation and exists outside the unconscious structured as language. In this sense, the *sinthome* is closer to the real. Lacan reached the final conclusion that there is no subject without a *sinthome*. Lacan's contention that there is no sexual relation entails that there is no normal relation, and therefore that the relationship between partners is a "sinthomatic" one.

I argue that in, what I provisionally call a push-towards-writing, a movement or passion that is often observed in transsexuals, the body finds its anchor in the sea of language. Many people who feel trapped in the wrong gender do experience the drive to write, to produce a text that narrates their experience, offering a testimony to their stories of transformation. It is in the writing of the sex change memoir that a final bodily transformation takes place, when the body is written.

The *sinthome* is a form of writing that offers a new relation to the body based on the possibility of assuming a sexual positioning without the phallus as absolute norm. The *sinthome* is a creation *ex nihilo*: "It is by this [the lack] that I try to meet the function of art, what is implied by what is left blank as fourth term, when I say that art can even reach the symptom" (Lacan 2005[1975–76], 18). The *sinthome* engages the lack but castration is vanquished; the constant weaving and unweaving of creation has nothing to do with the Oedipus complex or the phallus; it is even free from the Other (the Other may be just a semblance, someone's own personal myth). The *sinthome* creatively makes up for deficiencies linking body, ego, flesh, gender, *jouissance*, and subjectivity.

As we hear everyday in our clinical practice, the relation between the sexes is a screw-up (*ratage*) (Lacan 1998[1972–73], 121), and there is only a relation to the extent that it is symptomatic. This contention entails that there is no normal relation, and therefore that the relationship between partners can only be a "sinthomatic" one. This is because, in sexuality, the subject appears as a *sinthome* for another subject. It is at this anti-normative juncture that Queer Studies finally meets psychoanalysts.

Works Cited

Dean, Tim. *Beyond Sexuality*. Chicago: University of Chicago Press, 2000.

——— and Christopher Lane, eds. *Homosexuality and Psychoanalysis*. Chicago: University of Chicago Press, 2001.

Fausto-Sterling, Anne. *Sexing the Body: Gender Politics and the Construction of Sexuality*. New York: Basic Books, 1999.

Freud, Sigmund. "Three Essays on the Theory of Sexuality" (1905). In *The Standard of the Complete Psychological Works of Sigmund Freud*, Vol. 7, trans. James Strachey in collaboration with Anna Freud and assisted by Alix Strachey and Alan Tyson, 123–245. 1953; rpt. London: Vintage, 2001.

Frosh, Stephen. *For and Against Psychoanalysis.* London and New York: Routledge, 2006 (1997).

Gherovici, Patricia. *Please Select Your Gender: From the Invention of Hysteria to the Democratizing of Transgenderism.* New York and London: Routledge, 2010.

Lacan, Jacques. "The Direction of the Treatment and the Principles of Its Power" (1958). In *Écrits,* trans. Bruce Fink, 489–542. New York: W.W. Norton and Co., 2006.

———. *Livre XXIII: Le Sinthome* (1975–76), ed. Jacques-Alain Miller, Paris: Seuil, 2005.

———. *Book XX: Encore: On Feminine Sexuality. The Limits of Love and Knowledge* (1972–73), ed. Jacques-Alain Miller, trans. Bruce Fink. New York and London: Norton, 1998.

———. *Livre XVII: L'Envers de la Psychanalyse* (1969–70), ed. Jacques-Alain Miller. Paris: Seuil, 1991.

———. *Book XI: The Four Fundamental Concepts of Psychoanalysis* (1964), ed. Jacques-Alain Miller, trans. Alan Sheridan. New York: W.W. Norton and Co., 1981.

———. *Jacques Lacan Parle, Extraits d'une conférence donnée par Jacques Lacan à l'Université catholique de Louvain le 13 octobre 1972, suivis d'un entretien avec la réalisatrice Françoise Wolff.* DVD Video, 2007.

———. *Livre XIV: La logique du fantasme* [Book XIV: The Logic of Fantasy] (1966–67), unpublished.

Lichtenberg Ettinger, Bracha. "Weaving a Trans-Subjective Tress of the Matrixial *Sinthome.*" In *Reinventing the Symptom: Essays on the Final Lacan,* ed. Luke Thurston, 83–109. New York: Other Press, 2002.

Morel, Genevieve. "The Sexual Sinthome." *Umbr(a): Incurable,* no. 1 (2006): 65-83.

Morris, Jan. *Conundrum.* New York: Henry Holt and Company, 1986 (1974).

Rose, Jacqueline. *Sexuality in the Field of Vision.* London: Verso, 1986.

Soler, Colette. *La maldición sobre el sexo.* Buenos Aires: Editorial Manantial, 2000.

Wittig, Monique, *The Straight Mind and Other Essays.* Boston: Beacon Press, 1992.

RESPONSES TO PSYCHOANALYTIC PRACTICES ENCOUNTERING QUEER THEORIES

21

A Plague on Both Your Houses

Stephen Frosh

It is tempting to suggest that the staging of an encounter in this book has served mainly to dramatize the incommensurability of psychoanalysis and queer theory. Perhaps there are really two separate theaters, one in which queer celebrations of disruptiveness goes on, and one in which psychoanalysts and psychotherapists try to bring order to confusions of desire, identity and identification. Lisa Downing articulates one of the key oppositions in focusing on perversion:

> For clinical psychoanalysts, perversion is sexuality gone awry; the failure of the subject to attain adult genitality. For queer theorists, on the other hand, perversion may be construed as a defiant performance of excess that shows up the constructedness and arbitrariness of the category of the "normal," and it is centrally implicated in queer's rejection of the meaning of identity in favor of the politics of practice.

She is careful here, despite her affiliation to the queer theater, but the clinicians have their own worries. "Queer theory engages with the judgmentalism about sexual performances, and it can deploy a counter-judgement, a prejudice against prejudice!" exclaims Bob Hinshelwood, who is also troubled by the obsessive Lacanianism of much queer psychoanalytic thought. Where are relationships, where identity built out of identifications?

Carol Owens identifies a misrepresentation of the apparent parallels between queer and psychoanalysis which leads readers to believe they have much in common. Not so, she thinks:

> While it is true that queer theory and psychoanalysis (theory and practice) share an interest in subjectivity, desire, identity, relationality, ethics, power, discourse and norms, it is not true that their interest is dedicated in the same direction, with let's say, a common objective, or common interpretations.

Aligning themselves with each other results, she thinks, in radical misreadings, particularly over *jouissance* (blissful misreadings, we might say): "We are told that if it didn't exist, queers would invent it. Please!" And for some on the psychoanalytic stage, queer simply misses the point about what caring for patients means; that is to say, it fails to recognize reality. Katrine Zeuthen and Judy Gammelgaard, anxious enough about the encounter ("In some ways our apprehension was confirmed when we read the texts"), take the "maybe I'm old-fashioned" route:

> Maybe we are too serious or literal, but we sense in these and other attempts to delimit the essence of sexual queerness an idealization which contradicts our experiences of the pain and suffering which many patients — homosexual as well as heterosexual — associate with coming to grips with the unconscious part of sexuality.

Queer theory opposes the normativeness of psychoanalytic concepts. Psychoanalysis accuses queer of throwing the baby out with the bathwater — or at least, in Owens's words, there are places where "the Lacanian baby is being thrown out with the bathwater of 'classical (*sic*) psychoanalysis.'" For the "classical" group, whoever they may be, one problem is queer theory's tendency to reiterate binaries it appears to be opposed to: masculine–feminine transmigrates into heterosexual–homosexual; fluidity–fixity becomes another paean to the superiority of one side (fluidity) over the other. The consequence of this last point is particularly interesting and is well analyzed by Lisa Downing in her critique of how "Privileging the ideal of fluidity leads to a concomitant stigmatization of the idea of fixity, establishing an unhelpful binary (fluidity or fixity) in a body of thought that usually attempts to deconstruct such dualities." Promoting sexual fluidity — which as she knows is a truism in mental health work — leads to disparagement of those who enjoy fixity, repetition and sameness, the limited practice of sex time after time; yet why should this be excluded from the queer celebration of multifariousness and sexual variation? A nice paradox, indeed, here recognized by one of the players on the queer stage, apparently throwing a line across to the other theater.

Perhaps we are back in the terrain of a debate about continuous revolution. From the perspective of psychoanalysis, let us assume for a moment that the Freudian revolution was a real one and that everything changes as a consequence, leading not only to the saturation of culture by psychoanalytic discourse (as Ian Parker has repeatedly shown to have occurred, and does so again here) but also to a change in the extra-discursive domain, maybe even in the "real world" (it is too scary not to use these quotation marks). Freud turned things upside down and inside out; sexuality became "mal-normed" as Lacan once put it; discourses of and on the unconscious proliferated and the boundary between rationality and irrationality became blurred. Previous accounts of human subjecthood, and perhaps the experience of it too, were disrupted and queered. However, like most things, having made its revolution, psychoanalysis solidified, stagnated, found pragmatic solutions to bureaucratic necessities, created formal institutions, fought for its survival, made compromises to sustain a presence in the world of psychotherapy. It even seems that there is a strong inverse relationship between the radical subversiveness of psychoanalytic theory and the freedom of its institutional practices. That is, the more threatening is their theory of sexuality, the more focused psychoanalysts themselves have been on creating organizational cultures that are mired in conservatism and conformism, as if they had to protect themselves against the fall-out from their own daily encounters with unconscious life. Analytic abstinence was not enough; dress codes straightened out, ideologies hardened; bourgeoisification intensified. The resistance of many psychoanalysts to the depathologizing of homosexuality is famous, and relevant; along with a strong tendency, born of the individualism of much psychoanalysis, to back away from progressive political concerns.

On the other hand, when pushed to extremes we might also have to bear in mind that resistance to outrageous irrationality is not necessarily a sign of psychic rigidity. For instance, even the much-criticized ego psychologists of post-Second World War America may have had more integrity than Lacanian and leftist critiques have often allowed. Whilst ego psychology concentrated on that side of psychoanalysis that stresses the necessity for control of unconscious impulses and adaptation to society and hence seems clearly at odds with radical social critiques (e.g., Marcuse 1955; Frosh 1999), it can also be understood as an honest response to the destructive explosion of irrationality embodied in fascism and Nazism. That is, despite its many and obvious limitations, we should not be too single-minded about pillorying ego psychology's attempt to reinstate rationality as a moral force, given the historical context out of which it emerged. However, something more general is at stake here: not just ego psychology as a mode of conformist psychoanalysis, but the tendency for the most demanding, most difficult ideas of psychoanalysis to give way to a kind of conformist moralism, a common sense which one might argue it is precisely the task of psychoanalysis to disrupt.

At this point, queer theory can enter the fray as a new(ish) set of discourses "from the margins" that unsettles the psychoanalytic scheme. Ian Parker tries to maintain the value of such an unsettled psychoanalysis by refusing the tendency of Lacanianism to become too much of a system. Instead, he wants to hold onto its status as practice, as a way of doing things — or preferably, *un*doing them:

If Lacanian psychoanalysis is treated as a clinical strategy instead of a worldview, then it is possible to make something radical with that strategy, to make of it a place where we are freer in our tactics than other types of psychoanalysis, potentially a good deal queerer in our practice for that.

Abe Geldhof and Paul Verhaeghe, also Lacanians, are on the same lines when they claim, "What is really queer, is *jouissance*. In the last resort the whole discussion about gender and queer is nothing but a defense against the queerness of *jouissance* and the contingencies of life." Contingencies, unsettling practices: these are refusals to be brought into line with any pre-existing orthodoxy, whether that of psychoanalysis or queer theory itself. In this regard, it is noteworthy that what endears Jean Laplanche to some of the queer theorists is the enigmatic signifier and the disruptive presence of otherness that goes along with it. This is an important acknowledgement of the relevance of the theory of otherness to the construction of the subject, but as Carol Owens comments it might also miss the point that Laplanche "was vehemently anti-programmatic declaring that psychoanalytic practice cannot propose an aim of practice, no matter what, otherwise it risks becoming marshalled into a form of social adaptation." This aspect of Laplanche is perhaps central and is an aspect of his critique of the narrativism of much psychotherapy — by which he seemed to mean the attempt to create a meaningful story that would integrate the various strands of a person's suffering and consequently make that suffering more comprehensible and survivable. Of course this is a worthwhile "caring" aim; as a clinical practitioner, Laplanche (2003) knew that. But, he wrote:

The fact that we are confronted with a possibly "normal" and in any case inevitable defence, that the narration must be correlated with the therapeutic aspect of the treatment, in no way changes the metapsychological understanding that sees in it the guarantee and seal of repression. (29)

In opposition to this "reconstructive, synthesising narrative vector" he identified the truly "analytic vector, that of de-translation and the questioning of narrative structures and the ideas connected to them" (29).

Perhaps maintaining a broad idea of a "de-translating" analytic vector might be a way of thinking about these necessarily failed encounters. We would like the bringing together of psychoanalytic practice and queer theory to produce something new, an enlivened psychoanalysis, a deeper and less simplistically celebratory queer theory. But it cannot happen: they are in radically different places. The limit of what can be achieved has to be that of a bumping up against each other that pushes each one off course; more generally, we might wish a kind of "plague on both your houses" in the positive sense, resonant of the "bringing the plague" that Freud apocryphally promised America. That is to say, despite the danger that each approach will defensively close itself off in the face of the other's critique, psychoanalysis and queer theory need to actively needle each other and be destabilized from some other marginal place, or else they will each solidify still more into the kinds of orthodoxy that their own theoretical tenets would decry.

Works Cited

Frosh, Stephen. *The Politics of Psychoanalysis*. Basingstoke and New York: Palgrave, 1999.

Laplanche, Jean. "Narrativity and Hermeneutics: Some Propositions." *New Formations* 48 (2003): 26–29.

Marcuse, Herbert. *Eros and Civilization*. Boston: Beacon Press, 1966 (1955).

22

Something Amiss

Jacqueline Rose

There is something amiss. On that much queer theory and psychoanalysis agree. For both of these ways of engaging with the world, the dominant, normative, regulations of sexual life are a lie. Freud (1908) spoke of the "injustice" of expecting one form of sexual behavior from us all. "It is one of the obvious social injustices [*eine der offenkundigen sozialen Ungerechtigkeiten*]," he wrote in his essay "'Civilised' Sexual Morality and Modern Nervous Illness," "that the standard of civilisation should demand from everyone the same conduct of sexual life" (192). Except, he added, the injustice is normally wiped out by disobedience — *Nichtbefolgen* — or non-observance of the norm. The psychoanalytic subject is restless. She puts up a fight in her dreams. Nor is her rebellion restricted to the night time alone. She has thoughts she does not share. Sometimes she herself does not know what these are. Even in the putative calm of the day, when everything is meant to be safe, she can be surprised by herself. Such moments may allow a moment of escape from the norms that bind her — the norms of civilization which, as we see from his essay's title, Freud was careful to put in scare quotes. But these moments, inklings of another unconscious life, might also trail behind them ways of being which she would prefer not to know or to forget. Whatever her sexual orientation, this is likely to be the case. There is no clear or easy resting place in the mind. Fluidity, plasticity — the catch-words of recent theory — do not halt on request. The way-stations may be enticing or bleak. You cannot turn the unconscious into a manifesto (which is why Freud disagreed with the surrealists). For psychoanalysis, it is axiomatic that we never fully know who we are.

For a long time now I have been interested in what theory can "do." I am part of a generation who believed that mining the radical potential of psychoanalysis would have the power to shift the terrain of what was thinkable in social and sexual life. I still hold that belief. On this there is always more work to be done, especially in a climate increasingly hostile to psychoanalysis, where drugs and cognitive-based therapy are the officially sanctioned — dangerous and/or vacuous — approaches to mental life. But, for me, the belief in the transformative power of psychoanalysis was always accompanied by the recognition that there was something in its way of thinking which is recalcitrant to the world of knowledge. Psychoanalysis offers its own diagnosis of why, in the field of sexuality, there will always be something which refuses to submit to our political demands — why sexuality will never do or be what we want. In the early days of "psychoanalysis and feminism" — the title of Juliet Mitchell's path-breaking book of 1974 (2000) — some feminists felt that the force of sexuality had the power to disrupt the order of things, that in the confrontation between a scandalous unconscious and an ego deluded by its own seeming coherence, it was the ego — along with the heterosexual imperative — that would break (for psychoanalysis the ego is of course already broken, "split" to use Freud's own term). Juliet Mitchell was not one of them. She was far more interested in how patriarchy traced its lines indelibly across a woman's sexual life (an emphasis which if anything increased in her preface to the 1990 edition of her book).

But something of that early energy seems to have made its way into queer theory — Freud's polymorphous perverse infant now reappearing as queer (although only one essay in this collection actually talks of a "queer child"). As if the aberration of sexuality was isomorphic with the work of theory, or *theory at work,* as if the two — equally insistent, troublesome — were

somehow the same thing. The conceptual boldness, the eupho-
ria, then becomes its own testament to what the theory is trying to describe, to legitimate or release (the gash of bliss would
be the best example here). This is theory roused by itself, as a
path — if not *the* path — to freedom. And yet it often seems to
me that something has gone missing. Half the psychoanalytic
story is being left behind. Most simply, the ugliest part. In this
struggle of unconscious against ego — or in one formulation
here, "queer" versus "ego" — the agency of the mind that polic-
es our identities, the superego, has disappeared. The battle has
been won before it has truly begun. There is no hint of the sadistic force of social identifications — the cruel inner watchman
of the soul. There are few references to psychic pain. Queer performativity is mostly stripped of the melancholia and abjection
in which Judith Butler became so careful to embed it. Splitting,
denegation, foreclosure, denial, or even repression, one after the
other the insignia of how we struggle with our inner world appear to have been dropped. What is left of the whole repertoire
used by psychoanalysis to describe the shifting forms of identity
and loss of identity whereby we try, and fail, to exert psychic and
sexual mastery over ourselves?

Failure is, I realize, key. "Failure," I wrote in 1983 in lines
quoted several times here, "is something endlessly repeated and
relived moment by moment throughout our individual histories," there is a "resistance to identity at the very heart of psychic life" (2005, 91). I could not have anticipated then how this
moment would be taken up at a cost, allowed of course by my
own words, that failure would come to be aligned with resistance as if there were no gap between them. Failure thus becomes
a form of protest, before the discomfort, the anguish of failure,
has barely had a chance to be heard (to put it another way, in
the very moment it surfaces, failure re-represses itself). Reading
the essays in this collection, I repeatedly get the impression that,
for a politics of psychoanalysis, this was, and is, the deal — the
more unsettling concept of failure has to be absorbed, allayed
somehow, by its more political blood sister, resistance ("a more
productive resistance" in Alice Kuzniar's words). But resistance

is not only political, as I have had occasion more recently to explore — perhaps as a way of returning to, taking issue with, my own earlier formulation, although, till writing this, I had not made the link. For resistance too is freighted with ambiguity: a fight-back against oppression; but also, as Freud increasingly recognized, obduracy (another form of militancy), the mind's best defense against any demand that it might transform itself (Rose 2007). Which is the more powerful? Our revolt against the world's inhumanity, or our tenacity in holding onto the identities — even if we hate them — which we believe we have constructed for ourselves? Is the psychoanalytic unconscious on the side of freedom? If we look around the world, for example, at the more enduring and violent fantasies of national identification — which has been the increasing focus of my own work — it seems not. This must surely be the question of any psychoanalytically informed politics, the question around which the encounter between queer theory and psychoanalysis must be staged. But only, I believe, if we do not purport to answer the question too fast.

There are of course essays here in which this issue is central. The account of the post-surgery trans-gendered subject haunted by a body no medical intervention can sublate; or the story of another transgender patient who is not queer enough — his/her desire being not to escape "the drill of the normative" (to cite Ken Corbett's suggestive phrase in another essay) but to give it a more acceptable shape; or the stories of the patient whose suffering exceeds her social oppression, even if bound to that same oppression, as the flood of conflicting impulses overflow the heart. Think of Anna O, the first psychoanalytic patient, trapped at home with her dying father by a world that knows no other destiny for women, body steeled and frozen in protest, but who cannot reconcile her rage with her grief. I see all these moments as cautions — hence the value of this volume — against a psychic idealization of queer. What does it mean, for example, to describe the unconscious as a "psychic wardrobe of potential identities" from which, at any moment throughout the day, I select who I will "be"; or to suggest, via what is for me a misreading of Jean Laplanche, that the child's fantasy of seduction — seed-bed of potential violence, of the fraught bonds of love, in Jessica Benjamin's expression — is in itself queer? If queer is a form of relation to otherness, why would it be immune from the agonies of recognition — of embrace and revulsion — through which our reckoning with the other takes place?

These points are made by several of the clinical essays but I do not think it helpful to see this as a clash between theory and the consulting room. The more regulatory forms of psychoanalysis — on which many of these essays are rightly angry — forms which have not, to my mind, been attentive enough to the often conflicting nuances in Freud, still need to listen to queer theory. While for me, queer theory — once it enters the domain of psychoanalysis — can only be strengthened by engaging with the darker places of the psyche, where our capacity for transformation thwarts itself. Perhaps the relationship between queer theory and psychoanalysis — vital, uncomfortable, testy — has still not gone far enough.

Works Cited

Freud, Sigmund. "'Civilised' Sexual Morality and Modern Nervous Illness" (1908). In *The Standard Edition of the Complete Psychological Works of Sigmund Freud,* vol. 9, trans. James Strachey in collaboration with Anna Freud and assisted by Alix Strachey and Alan Tyson, 181–204. 1959; rpt. London: Vintage, 2001.

Mitchell, Juliet. *Psychoanalysis and Feminism: A Radical Reassessment of Freudian Psychoanalysis.* London: Penguin, 2000 (1974).

Rose, Jacqueline. *The Last Resistance.* London: Verso, 2007.

———. "Femininity and its Discontents." In *Sexuality in the Field of Vision,* 83–103. 1983; rpt. London: Verso, 2005 (1986).

23

Taking Shelter from Queer

Tim Dean

"Psychoanalysis may be queer but it is not queer theory," observes Patricia Gherovici, in a sentence that encapsulates the central tension structuring *Clinical Encounters in Sexuality*. As the chapters in this volume demonstrate, psychoanalysis looks different from a queer perspective, often disorientingly so. Yet even as the potential queerness of psychoanalysis is teased out and highlighted, some minimal difference between the two remains. What to make of that difference — indeed, what to make of various small differences — exercises all of the contributors in one way or another, eliciting a range of responses, from the intrigued and engaged to the disturbingly phobic.

Occasionally the narcissism of minor differences threatens to derail these encounters by turning difference into opposition — as, for example, when Rob Weatherill claims that queer theory's "ideological attack on the so-called straight world can be profoundly anti-psychoanalytic." Feeling attacked, perhaps outnumbered, the analyst perceives difference through an imaginary schema that frames the queer and the psychoanalytic as enemies. Never mind that queer functions as a critique of normalization (not as an "attack" on the "straight world"), Weatherill's paranoid response ignores all subtleties of distinction in the face of an overwhelming onslaught: "It is always already too asphyxiatingly close. Consequently, Gay Rights […] is a done deal in many western countries. […] [Q]ueer theories and strategies have moved from the margin to the centre," he claims. To give any space, any rights whatsoever, to the queers risks being completely overrun by them; loosening repression even slightly will open the floodgates to sexual chaos.

Given the perception of threat, it is important not — I repeat, *not* — to listen to what the "other side" is saying. Above all, one must stop his ears, lest any unwonted seduction occur inadvertently. Some of the analysts, especially the men, are astonishingly good at not listening. Lacanians Abe Geldhof and Paul Verhaeghe, along with the Kleinian R.D. Hinshelwood and the relational analyst Ken Corbett, all manage to avoid referring to, much less engaging, *any* of the contributors to whom they're ostensibly responding. With the exception of Corbett, these guys even succeed in keeping all queer theoretical works out of their bibliographies, thereby maintaining a strict univocal purity. It is so much easier to be certain about where one stands on messy issues, such as those involving sexuality, when he does not have to acknowledge the voices or the claims of others.

"Certainty is the enemy of psychoanalysis," writes Ann Murphy (quoting Wilfred Bion), in her thoughtful response. As I've suggested, framing any issue in terms of "the enemy" tends to imaginarize difference, polarizing matters within a binary framework that constrains thinking and meaningful exchange. One nevertheless appreciates the point that Murphy is making here. It is not queer theory that is "the enemy" of psychoanalysis but precisely the kind of certitude that would position the former as such. The trouble with certainty, from a psychoanalytic perspective, is that it too readily functions as a defense against the alterity of the unconscious; certainty represents both a practical and an ethical problem. When it comes to sexuality, certitude may be understood as a predictably symptomatic response to what several contributors eloquently describe as the irreducibly enigmatic dimension of sex. This is often, though not always, the case with Lacanian accounts of sexuality, which tend to couple their unwavering pronouncements about sex with projections concerning "the psychotic's certitude" or that of "the pervert" (it is the pervert's alleged certainty about how to enjoy that is a problem, never the analyst's) (Dean 2008).

The trouble with certitude as a defense against otherness needs be differentiated from the problematic of fixity that Lisa Downing tackles in her chapter on perversion. Justifiably skeptical about how queer theory's anti-essentialist commitment to sexual fluidity risks re-pathologizing erotic fixity, Downing wants to clarify from a different angle the crucial distinction between sexual identities and sexual acts. It is the fixity of identity, not that of any consensual pleasure-giving practice, that creates problems. Queer theory's critique of identity derives primarily from Michel Foucault's (1978) analysis of how, during the nineteenth century, erotic acts became construed as so many indices of discrete sexual identities. Reading an identity — or a definitional "structure of desire" — from any erotic act is an intrinsically normalizing gesture. As I've argued elsewhere, the queer critique of identity shares something fundamental in common with psychoanalytic critiques of the ego as a defensive structure.

This is all well and good, until our acknowledgement of the mobility of unconscious desire gets twisted into a normative prescription about sexual fluidity that re-pathologizes fixed erotic investments. What I find especially compelling about Downing's intervention is her directing our attention away from the obsession with sexual identities to a renewed focus on erotic acts and their attendant pleasures. To the volume's various discussions of pleasure, I would add the caveat that translating pleasure too quickly into *jouissance* risks relegating erotic pleasure to the domain of potential pathology. How do we adjudicate when sexual practice has gone beyond the pleasure principle and is tarrying with the death drive? How much pleasure is too much and who decides? The readiness with which certain of the contributors misrecognize sexual pleasure as a form of harm — as if non-normative pleasures were almost invariably at someone else's expense — might prompt reconsideration of how such misrecognitions themselves enact harm through the violence of stigmatization. When, for example, Claudette Kulkarni writes that, "maybe there is no such thing as 'normal,' but there certainly is something 'abnormal' about sexual offending!" we need to think about how psychoanalysis is being conscripted to the project of policing sexuality by segregating its manifestations into normal and abnormal. The concept of the abnormal cannot exist without that of the normal; indeed, the burden of queer theory is to demonstrate, in order to challenge, the pervasiveness of social normalization. Kulkarni's specious claim that "there is no such thing as 'normal'" may represent little more than a contemporary meta-ruse of normalization.

This problematic is framed especially cogently by Dany Nobus when he registers how "psychoanalysis itself has often been reluctant to accept the variations, diversity, and unpredictability of human sexuality as what constitutes its actual norm." To accept that variation is the norm requires, in tandem with a psychoanalytic perspective, some consideration of how social normalization actually works. Queer theory draws on the work of French medical historian Georges Canguilhem (1991) to distinguish statistical norms from evaluative norms and to show the troubling effects of conflating one with the other. A statistical norm describes mathematical averages in a population — for example, most men are heterosexual, or most North Americans are overweight — without commenting on the norm's desirability. Rather than descriptive, however, an evaluative norm is prescriptive; it articulates a normative ideal. We need not consider how evaluative norms feed into the superego to see how conflating them with statistical averages already creates problems. Nobus reminds us that even if, statistically speaking, most men identify as heterosexual, this tells us nothing about the ethical desirability of heterosexuality, the range of forms these men's sexual practice and relations may take, or their unconscious fantasies. Beneath the façade of normality lie fantasies whose eccentricity make a mockery of the very notion of sexual identity. Together psychoanalysis and queer theory permit us to grasp how oxymoronic the idea of sexual orientation actually is. No small measure of its pleasure comes from the capacity of sex to *dis*orient.

But what happens when sex disorients the paradigms through which we aspire to comprehend it? Psychoanalysis risks "becoming sexually illiterate," Nobus warns, when it declines to pay attention to "each and every event in the sexual realm without prejudice and preconception." It may be easier to suspend one's lingering prejudices than to approach sex without preconceptions. The danger is that psychoanalysts and psychoanalytically-oriented critics will interpret unfamiliar manifestations of *eros* either as unequivocally pathological, on one hand, or as totally intelligible according to established hermeneutic frameworks, on the other. In both cases, what we witness is psychoanalysis stopping its ears against — and hence refusing to encounter — the sexually alien. It is because so much pertaining to sex remains unconscious that sexuality persistently appears as opaque, enigmatic, alien, and queer. Every interpretive framework that makes sense of sex — whether through Oedipus, Antigone, or some other paradigm — risks annihilating the alien quality of sexuality by way of hermeneutic normalization.

Much of my own work has been devoted to exploring how its alien aspect renders human sexuality fundamentally impersonal, insofar as unconscious mental life exceeds individual personhood. Once the unconscious is taken into account, we can no longer really justify thinking about sex as interpersonal. Each person in a sexual encounter relates to an unconscious fantasy, to an imaginary image, or to an enigmatic signifier before he or she relates to the other person(s) present. Psychoanalysts know that their patients' relations to them are heavily mediated (there is always a "third" accompanying the analytic couple), and this is even more the case at moments of physical intimacy, when what may appear as unmediated bodily contact remains mediated by invisible formations that are at once unconscious and historical.

Enigmas from the sexual past haunt the gay bar's darkroom as much as they permeate the marital bedroom, and only the willfully ignorant persist in believing that sex takes place between couples. To take the unconscious into account enables one to appreciate how the group, not the couple, represents the sexual paradigm of psychoanalysis. It is like those moments in pornography when the camera pulls back to reveal that around two naked bodies stands a room full of people. Everyone is trying to ignore the extra bodies in the room but, like the unconscious, they continue to function irrespective of our awareness or belief in their existence. When it comes to sex, the unconscious is less like Baltimore in the early morning (as Jacques Lacan once said) than it is like a San Fernando Valley porn set. The limitation of the analogy is that, by appealing to an image of whole bodies rather than partial figures, it risks re-personalizing the eminently impersonal qualities of the unconscious. And it is because no image can capture the unconscious that sexuality and identity remain perpetually at odds. This does not mean, however, that psychoanalysts and queer theorists have to be at odds. *Clinical Encounters in Sexuality* initiates so many conversations that it offers a rich repertoire of possibilities for getting creative with the differences that divide and connect us.

Works Cited

Canguilhem, Georges. *The Normal and the Pathological,* trans. Carolyn R. Fawcett. New York: Zone Books, 1991.

Dean, Tim. "The Frozen Countenance of the Perversions." *Parallax* 14, no. 2 (2008): 93–114.

Foucault, Michel. *The History of Sexuality,* vol. 1, trans. Robert Hurley. New York: Random House, 1978 (1976).

24

Courageous Drawings of Vigilant Ambiguities

Noreen O'Connor

My aim is to elucidate ways in which analysts have responded to the challenges of queer theorists. Working with the operative distinction of analyst and queer theorist I draw out their shared vigilance of reductive classifications of foundational aesthetic, epistemic, ontological, ethico-political specifications of subjective/intersubjective relationships.

Corbett succinctly expresses the clinical ambiance of contemporary psychoanalysis in his first sentence describing the pivotal relationships between different models of analytic praxis and social critiques of normality. By "leaning" toward the generative grounding soil of psychoanalytic originality practitioners explore ways in which fantasy inter-implicates the body-subject and thereby challenge dualisms of mind/body, language/thinking. Psychoanalytic space is delineated as a place in which the enigmatic dynamism of transferences of fantasies and attributes highlight the courageous listening/speaking ethos present in the rigorous work of contributors to this book, namely, *encounters*. Analysis opens horizons of varying inter-subjective spaces and times for the emergence of individual speaking of a body-subject in their relational complexity (Ellis 2008, 187; 2010, 65–66).

This relational throwness into the implicit and explicit, conscious-unconscious resourcefulness of our common language(s) draws us out of the obsessionality of our egocentricity and moves us towards openness to the unexpected. Theories of human psychic lived experiences and their vicissitudes are formulated in socio-cultural contexts with their inevitable aesthetic, ethical, ontological, epistemological, which influence specifically methodological presuppositions (O'Connor 2010, 2).

Cultural Differences: Psychoanalyses?

Hinshelwood maintains that the history of welfarism in Britain implicitly influences perceptions of the individual as part of a maternal nurturing culture. This has facilitated the development of object-relations psychoanalysis which, he argues, is always a matter of relations, furthermore, psychology is inevitably social psychology. Are relationships constituted by interactive psychologies or by different ways in which we speak, listen, hear one another?

Abe Geldhof and Paul Verhaeghe argue that all of gender/queer theorizing is a defense against the queerness of Lacan's conceptualization of *jouissance* — "queer is a new shelter for castration." Beyond gender/queer specifications there are the contingencies of life irreducible to any Hegelian legacies of binary oppositions whether of body/soul or man/woman. Human subjectivity is not specified by any psychology, rather "selfhood" occurs through a series of linguistic shifts from imaginary identifications through fissures which insert us into the symbolic order of culture. As for example in recurrent recourse to myths: "Antigone can be productively analysed as symptomatic of hegemonic regimes of race and gender in which the nexus of sovereignty, state, law, and biopolitics [...] [operate together]" (Chanter 2011, 130).

Ian Parker's encounters with queer theorists conclude with his reflections on the operatively constraining binarisms of queer theory. He argues in favor of Lacan's directive against moulding the patient to any predictable psychoanalytic discourse. He refers to a clinical case in which Lacan holds the psychoanalytic frame enabling the male analysand to shift "from stereotypically-masculine position — as obsessional neurotic — to stereotypically-feminine position [...] [hysterical attempt to put all the blame on others] […] is something queer that happens in every analysis."

Lacanian Phenomenology?

Dany Nobus argues that ongoing critical contributions of psychoanalysis to the study of human sexuality "must include the phenomenology of the sexed body." He distinguishes different components: "the sexed body, sexual behavior (erotic practices), sexual identity (gender), object-choice (sexual orientation), and fantasy-life. Each of these components stands in a meaningful relation to each of the other components, without any pre-determined unilateral causal connections." Crucially Nobus holds that configurations can change over time. He concludes with a call to a "post-queer" place, not derivative of foundational truth claims, but opening shifting epistemic parameters which "act upon what Lacan called a 'knowledge in failure.'" For him this implies approaching every sexual event with a spirit of wonder and discovery.

How can we hear the implicit as well as the explicit questioning in the nuanced speaking of our patients if we stop wondering about the limits of our own convictions? To wonder about our relationships with our clients/analysands for example, not just in terms of countertransference, developmental assumptions, or the matheme(atic) elusiveness of *petit objet a*? Our investment in the play of archetypes?

The relationship between the theory, the story, and the narrator is commonly conflated in a univocal voice, that is, the analyst's presentation of "the case study." Different narrative strategies work with different assumptions. For every compelling interpretation of material, there are others which are equally valid. In recounting the relationship the storyteller analyst testifies to the triumph of psychoanalytic method in its clarification of the analysand's hitherto defeats in the face of woeful life. In the finitude of mortality can we speak of any "identity" of our fleeting selves? Psychoanalysis powerfully challenges the notion that we can fully control our desires, despairs, feelings, images, fantasies, loves, hatreds. With its emphasis on the interplay of psychic conscious/unconscious, psychoanalysis charts the limits of freedom and choice in our process of individuation.

For psychoanalysis the play of motivations are constellated by identifications which are described in the play of Sophoclean metaphors. They are explained by the variability of conscious/unconscious conflictual dynamisms of causes and reasons. Ann Murphy focuses on the centrality of repetition in our attempts to evade the psychic pain of "facing" loss, limitation, the contingency of mortality. What about the individuation, for example, of a person who is addicted and driven to distraction to find solace in that which is destroying them? This is the kind of question that guided Freud's thinking on neurosis in terms of his elaboration of the relationship between two principles governing mental functioning — the pleasure principle and the reality principle. Freud interprets subjective identity in terms of explanations of motivations that aim for identifications sought during the Oedipal stage of development and are reverberatively present/absent throughout one's life (O'Connor and Ryan 2003, 240–41). Murphy's encounter with queer theory alerts her to the clinical risks of participating in prescriptive normative regimes that are oppressive and betray a psychoanalytic practice which focuses on the unique *poēsis* of the individual.

Clinical/Textual Reverie

For Ken Corbett, clinical analyses evince different modes of knowing, interpretative actions which generate the unconscious transferential space of play between him and his patients, in this case queer children. His drawing of a number of mice for Lincoln which was left under the radiator, deeply shared and without discussion or reference, evokes the complexity of his different ways of speaking, including gesturally, his own patient presence to the melancholic abjection of his patient whose angry withdrawal was protecting his "lost love/identity." Corbett argues that the conflicts, dilemmas, of a queer gender boy desperate for social recognition are not explained by a specific psychic pathology in which "They are not seen as honorable social, relational bids; they are seen as troubled psychic enactments." His clinical aim is to "keep company," keeping present in play with its unexpected relationships to the limits of knowing.

In her readings of queer theorists, Ami Kaplan questions critiques of man-woman binarisms. James grew up with the confusion and secrecy of gender variance deeply ashamed of his wish "to be and live as a woman." In their therapeutic work together Kaplan focused on the unconscious shame, the alienation which had isolated him. His transition to stereotypical female identification involved negotiating different relationships with family, partners, who had thought they knew who "he" was. Jenny grappled with social/personal stigma. Kaplan acknowledges the crucial importance of queer theory for its critique of heteronormative renderings of gender, sexuality while also questioning its anti-identitarian politics. Jenny needed to have relationships with others as the female she felt herself to be: a woman. This emphasis on respect for an individual's struggle to speak is echoed in Kulkarni's "Queer Theory Meets Jung." Reflecting on responsiveness to the speaking of Others, she yearns for "theories and intellectual challenges that hold the tension among all the various [...] concepts while staying grounded in the real world of people's everyday suffering."

Focusing on recurrent neurotic questioning of one's desire, Patricia Gherovici wonders whether her patient Melissa is confused about object choice or identity politics. She reflects that, "the subject's assumption of a sexual identity is always symptomatic because it is related to what psychoanalysts call the phallus — a defective tool to negotiate the Real that eludes us." Following Lacan, she argues that identification eclipses subjectivity in the sense that rather than being somebody for someone we "represent a signifier for another signifier." Using the metaphor of "reknotting" of the registers of the Real, Imaginary, and Symbolic, Gherovici places the notion of sexual identity with that of *sinthome*, that is, a "purified symptom," and claims that its ontological existence is beyond the unconscious structured as a language. It creatively "makes up for deficiencies linking body, ego, flesh, gender, *jouissance*, and subjectivity" in the sense that it exists outside the unconscious structured as a language. She concludes that relations between sexes is constituted as symptomatic. This anti-normativity is the meeting place of queer studies and psychoanalysis.

Does Psychoanalysis Ever Let Go?

The haunting melody playing through Rob Weatherhill's "Queer New Times" is not evocative of consolation but of remembering, repeating, and working-through. Weatherhill challenges queer theories which trivialize suffering as part of a heterosexist plot rather than intrinsically vital in its variable instantiation, aiming beyond limits of rational transparency, logic, hermeneutics, rhetoric, structuralism. Along with both queer theorists and analysts, Weatherill points to the limits of language either as an excess of knowing or as the anarchic cut of free associations. Roustang (2003) argues that the speaking of the symptom in the analytic session expresses an isolation, anxiety which can existentially move someone from the prison of a repetitive present towards a future of new possibilities. I refer to the originality emergent in analytic speaking/responding as the an-archic dynamism of psychoanalysis: "The face-to-face is a saying that in being said at each moment breaks the definition of that which it says, and breaks through the totality that it embraces" (O'Connor 2010, 55).

Works Cited

Chanter, Tina. *Whose Antigone? The Tragic Marginalization of Slavery.* New York: SUNY Press, 2011.

Ellis, Mary Lynne. *Time in Practice: Analytical Perspectives on the Time of Our Lives.* London: Karnac, 2008.

———. "Shifting the Ego towards a Body Subject." In *Questioning Identities: Philosophy in Psychoanalytic Practice,* eds. Mary Lynne Ellis and Noreen O'Connor, 59–84. London: Karnac, 2010.

O'Connor, Noreen. "The An-Arche of Psychoanalysis." In *Questioning Identities: Philosophy in Psychoanalytic Practice,* eds. Mary Lynne Ellis and Noreen O'Connor, 47–58. London: Karnac, 2010.

——— and Ryan Joanna. *Wild Desires and Mistaken Identities, Lesbianism and Psychoanalysis.* London: Karnac 2003.

Roustang, François. *Il suffit d'un geste.* Paris: Odile Jacob, 2003.

25

Understanding Homophobia

Mark J. Blechner

Psychoanalysts and queer theorists both know that the questions we ask shape the kind of data we discover. Psychoanalysts since Sigmund Freud have asked often, "Why are some people homosexual? What causes this sexual attraction?" They have not asked so often, "Why do people hate and fear homosexuals? What causes this irrational emotional reaction? What causes the destructive and often delusional fear and hatred of gay men and lesbians?" This is odd, since homosexuality itself has harmed no one, whereas hatred and persecution of homosexuals has damaged many lives. It is also odd because the understanding of prejudice has been a fundamental aim of psychoanalysis throughout its history. *The Interpretation of Dreams* (Freud, 1900) was not only a landmark in the science of unconscious processes; it was also a relentless airing of and protest against the prejudice towards Jews in Freud's time. Psychoanalysis is the science of the irrational, and hence it is the field most suited to address the irrational fear and hatred of homosexuality that we call homophobia.

Jeremy Clarke (2011) tells the following anecdote:

At a recent conference held at the Institute of Psychoanalysis, in London, during lunch, a group of senior training analysts were chatting: "What does the Kleinian group think about teenage abortion these days?" Well, we don't assume the young woman is solely motivated by murderous and destructive instincts any longer, though that will come into it, of course... Ah... But now gay marriage—that really is against the facts of life.

What are the facts of life? Many psychoanalysts, sometimes not knowing much about the latest facts of sexology and other social sciences, rely on their common-sense notions of a healthy life. Often unconsciously, they amalgamate their upbringing, commonly held views of the culture, and religious beliefs into a view of how life should be lived and what constitutes mental health and psychopathology.

Is heterosexuality inherently pathological? Please read that sentence ten times without dismissing it. You may find eventually that it is no more sensible or ridiculous than the much more common question: Is homosexuality inherently pathological? I call this the test of "bias reversal" (Blechner 1993): taking a potentially prejudicial statement and turning it upside down, either by reversing genders or substituting the dominant group for the group that is the object of prejudice, thereby revealing unnoticed bigotry. Are white people inherently less intelligent than black people? Is terrorism against infidels inherently a characteristic of Christianity? Such questions highlight the essentially irrationality and bias of our "common-sense" prejudices. Both homosexuality and heterosexuality give pleasure, can be integrated into loving relationships, and harm no one. Why then do many people, psychoanalysts included, hate and fear homosexuals? What is the root of homophobia?

All of us are potentially prejudicial, and we are all better at observing the prejudice we experience as victims than the prejudice we perpetrate on others. People who have written authoritatively about the roots of prejudice against their own group nevertheless can express acute prejudice against other groups, employing the same psychic mechanisms that they have identified in others. For example, Janine Chasseguet-Smirgel (1996) decried the essential narcissism of homosexuality as a denial of difference. Yet Chasseguet-Smirgel, a Jewish, French psychoan-

alyst married Béla Grunberger, her Jewish, French psychoanalyst. This is an example of the "gender fetish" (Blechner 1998)
so prevalent in psychoanalysis — the obsessive and exaggerated
attention to the gender of someone's romantic partner, to the exclusion of so many other factors of equal or greater importance.
Therefore, I have proposed (1995) that we give prefixes to the
terms "heterosexuality" and "homosexuality." What we usually
call "homosexuality" should be called "gender homosexuality."
Many other significant factors can be concordant or different
in any couple, including age, social class, nationality, ethnicity,
religion, profession, sexual behavior preference and others. Any
one of them could be a prefix, such as "age heterosexuality or
age homosexuality." The prefixes "hetero" and "homo" could be
used to convey that you are attracted to people who either share
certain characteristics with you ("homo") or differ from you in
that way ("hetero"). Chasseguet-Smirgel, while a gender-heter-
osexual, was a religion-homosexual, a profession-homosexual,
and a nationality-homosexual. We have no reason to consider
any of those homosexualities to be inherently pathological, any
more than we should consider gender-homosexuality to be
pathological.[1]

Psychoanalysis has provided us the tools to identify the defensive process behind such gross pejorative generalizations:
they are projections of self-judgement onto a member of a
group perceived as outsiders, a psychic operation described viv-
idly in pre-psychoanalytic times by Jesus: "And why beholdest
thou the mote that is in thy brother's eye, but considerest not
the beam that is in thine own eye?" (Matthew 7:3). The psychoanalytic literature has many discussions of projection in relation to anti-Semitism, (e.g., Ackerman 1947; Grunberger 1964;
Chasseguet-Smirgel 1988) but relatively few discussions of projection in relation to homophobia (Corbett 2001). As a general
principle, if the object of hatred and prejudice is excluded from
a group's dialogue, then erroneous, even psychotic prejudices

---

1   See Kernberg (1975) and Segal (1990) for similar demonstrations of projec-
    tive mechanisms with respect to self- and other-prejudice.

can be sustained by the group. The shared projective defense be-hind much psychoanalytic homophobia could go unchallenged and unanalyzed only as long as the object of that projection was kept out of the psychoanalytic dialogue. Hence the importance of including gay men and lesbians in the scholarly and clini-cal community of psychoanalysts. By excluding open gays and lesbians from participation in the psychoanalytic community, psychoanalysts prevented their own cure from anti-homosexual prejudice.

Another unconscious source of homophobia is religion. The word "perversion" has its roots in religion. In the *Oxford English Dictionary,* "perversion" is defined as: "turning the wrong way; turning aside from truth or right; diversion to an improper use; corruption, distortion; specifically, change to error in religious belief." This definition highlights the trouble with the concept of perversion. In orthodox religion, there is a right way to do things, and if you do things differently, even if it makes you hap-py and you do not harm anyone, you are still wrong, perverted and sinful. Many clinicians have bought into such a translation from sin to psychopathology, even if the connection between pathology and sin is not fully conscious. This has caused a lot of clinical mischief and a good deal of suffering for patients. It may be that if the clinician thinks perversion, the clinician is also implicitly thinking, "I know the right way to behave." Not just the right way for me to behave, but *the* right way to behave.

There is an identifiable progression that has characterized much psychoanalytic and psychiatric thinking about the "psy-chopathology" of groups that suffer prejudice (White 2002; Blechner 2009). It starts with an acceptance of society's stand-ards and an identification of the distress and dysfunction of the individual as a problem inherent in the individual. Gradually (often too gradually), there is recognition that the individual may be suffering not from an inherent, intrapsychic neurosis, but from persistent perversion of living caused by unbearable requirements of surviving societal oppression. There is then a second, intermediate stage in which some theorists identify this maltreatment, and a growing recognition that the individual's problems can be cured not by intrapsychic change, but rather by changing the individual's relation to society. Finally, there is the third stage, in which there is recognition that for the ultimate removal of psychopathology, society itself must change.

In its early years, psychoanalysis was at the cutting edge of this progression. Freud bravely noted the damage done by sexual repression, sexual hypocrisy, sexually transmitted diseases and sexual abuse of minors. Freud (1905) was indeed a queer theorist as well as a psychoanalyst. He scandalized Vienna with his proposition that in our unconscious we are all quite queer ("polymorphously perverse" may be a more scientific term for "queer"). Freud's observations led to vast changes in society, a revolution that is still in progress (see Brill 1913). But over the years, especially in the mid-twentieth century, psychoanalysis as a whole abandoned its progressive role and became increasingly an enforcer of traditional values, valorizing the supposed normality of middle-class stereotypes. Women who wanted equal rights with men were told they had penis envy. Men who had sexual relations with other men were seen as pathological. Women who had as many sex partners as men were diagnosed as nymphomaniacs. It is possible that psychoanalysis could be rejuvenated today by becoming a more queer theory than academic queer theory, as it once was. In order to achieve this, psychoanalysis needs to apply its own tools to its own defenses.

Works Cited

Ackerman, N. "Antisemitic Motivation in a Psychopathic Personality: A Case Study." *Psychoanalytic Review* 34 (1947): 76–101.

Blechner, Mark J. *Sex Changes: Transformations in Society and Psychoanalysis.* New York: Routledge, 2009.

———. "Maleness and Masculinity." *Contemporary Psychoanalysis* 34 (1998): 597–613.

———. "The Shaping of Psychoanalytic Theory and Practice by Cultural and Personal Biases about Sexuality." In *Disori-*

enting Sexuality, ed. Thomas Domenici and Ronnie Lesser, 265–88. London: Routledge, 1995.

———. "Homophobia in Psychoanalytic Writing and Practice." *Psychoanalytic Dialogues* 3 (1993): 627–37.

Brill, A.A. "The Conception of Homosexuality." *Journal of the American Medical Association* 61 (1913): 335–40.

Chasseguet-Smirgel, J. *Creativity and Perversion.* London: Free Association Books, 1996.

———. "Review of Arnold Goldberg's The Problem of Perversion." *Journal of the American Psychoanalytic Association* 46 (1998): 610–19.

Clarke, J. "Interview with Dr. Mark Blechner." *Psychoanalytic Psychotherapy* 25 (2011): 361–79.

Corbett, Ken. "Faggot = Loser." *Studies in Gender and Sexuality* 2 (2001): 3–28.

Freud, Sigmund. "Three Essays on the Theory of Sexuality." (1905). In *The Standard Edition of the Complete Psychological Works of Sigmund Freud,* vol. 7, ed. and trans. James Strachey in collaboration with Anna Freud and assisted by Alix Strachey and Alan Tyson, 123–245. 1953; rpt. London: Hogarth Press, 2001.

———. *The Interpretation of Dreams* (1900). *The Standard Edition of the Complete Psychological Works of Sigmund Freud,* vols. 4 & 5, ed. and trans. James Strachey in collaboration with Anna Freud and assisted by Alix Strachey and Alan Tyson. 1953; rpt. London: Hogarth Press, 2001.

Grunberger, Béla. "The Anti-Semite and the Oedipal Conflict." *International Journal of Psycho-Analysis* 45 (1964): 380–85.

Kernberg, Otto. *Borderline Personality and Pathological Narcissism.* New York: Jason Aronson, 1975.

King James Bible. The Gospel According to Saint Matthew. 1611. See https://www.kingjamesbibleonline.org/Matthew-7-3/.

Segal, Hanna and Jacqueline Rose. "Hanna Segal Interviewed by Jacqueline Rose." *Women: A Cultural Review* 1 (2008): 198–214.

White, K. "Surviving Hating and Being Hated: Some Personal thoughts about Racism from a Psychoanalytic Perspective." *Contemporary Psychoanalysis* 38 (2002): 401–22.

26

Transgender, Queer Theory, and Psychoanalysis

Susan Stryker

The inclusion of trans*[1] material in this collection of essays on the encounter between psychoanalysis and queer theory necessarily raises the question of the relationship of trans* to queer, as well as trans* to psychoanalysis.

The five essays that deal explicitly with trans* issues — Gherovici, Corbett, Kaplan, Weatherill, and Geldhof and Verhaeghe — each approach these matters somewhat differently. Weatherill makes only passing, and transphobic, mention of transgender women when he approvingly quotes Germaine Greer's gratuitously vulgar dismissal of such individuals' claims to social existence: "just because you lop off your dick doesn't make you a fucking woman." For Geldhof and Verhaeghe, trans* positions are "extreme representatives" of a queer social movement that seems "to refuse the classical distinction between man and woman." For Kaplan, "trans" represents a benign albeit lim-

---

1 The asterisk after "trans" is an increasingly favored lexical strategy for indicating the variety of suffixed words and concepts to which trans might be prefixed: not only -gender, or -sexuality or -vestism, but also -species, -genic, -racial, or -national. It derives from the search-term symbol for a Boolean wildcard operator, i.e., a placeholder standing in for any string of search characters. It is gaining popularity precisely because it avoids, on the one hand, a welter of identitarian labels, and, on the other hand, opens up new affinities rooted in movements across categories. In subsequent usages of the term "trans" throughout this essay, the asterisk may be omitted but is always implied.

iting investment in fixed gender identities that is counterposed to the supposed fluidity, and desirability, of queer gender expression. Though he does not use the trans* nomenclature, Corbett's nuanced discussion of "queer childhood" is attuned to those moments "in which the social order of gender is challenged," and in which a "transforming nexus" of gender mallability is created that allows for gender's resignification through collective intersubjective fantasies between queer children and their significant others. For Gherovici, transness and homosexuality both address, in nonheteronormative ways, the imperative to assume a psychical position in relation to the question of sexual difference; they are divergent yet equally viable *sinthomes*, or answers to the unavoidable riddle of how the Real, Imaginary, and Symbolic registers might be knotted together.

Each author deals with the relation of transness to queer *theory*, rather than queer *identities*, somewhat differently as well. For Gherovici, queer theory is an expansive intellectual undertaking that includes trans* within its purview, and that enables a productive distinction between homosexual and transgender subjectivities. Corbett accords queer theory, along with feminism and social philosophy, a central role in contemporary psychoanalysis alongside its foundational Freudian tenets; he finds in this happy confluence of perspectives a set of insights into gender's contingency and variability that is eminently capable of positively recognizing and accommodating trans* gender non-conformities. Kaplan offers a less robust account of queer theory, equating it with a critique of gender binarism that points out the "blockiness" of such categories as man, woman, gay, straight and bisexual; transgender, which she equates with a greater investment in categorical fixity and a less flexible mode of inhabiting the categories through which social life is lived, therefore falls outside queer theory as she understands it. Geldhof and Verhaeghe, who consider queerness to be merely a defense against castration, expend no energy engaging with whatever critical-political-social correlates might follow from what they presume to be an inadequate (and ultimately indefensible) position. Weatherill uses transgender off-handedly, via Greer, merely to illustrate his point that the failure to acknowledge a Lacanian distinction between the Symbolic and the Real results in error: a point he deploys to critique Foucault (and thus by extension to critique queer theory) for acting as if the discourse of sexuality does not somehow inevitably falter against the opacity of the Real.

And yet, for all their differences, all these authors elide distinctions that might be drawn between queer theory and/or trans* theories — or even to acknowledge that such a trans* theoretical field might exist. Over the past quarter-century, trans* studies has become a thing in itself, and has positioned itself as a sometimes overlapping/sometimes separate, sometimes compatible/sometimes contestatory field vis-à-vis queer theory.[2] There is an explicitly psychoanalytic body of work within trans* studies — Jay Prosser, Patricia Elliot, Gayle Salamon, Sheila Cavanagh, and Shanna Carlson come to mind as salient examples[3] — that is referenced within the present collection only indirectly. Another "clinical encounter" between such scholarship and psychoanalysis would undoubtedly produce a different set of conversations, equally compelling as the queer ones collected here.[4]

Drawing a few pertinent distinctions between trans* and queer seems to be in order. To a significant extent, the concept of queerness has come to be associated primarily with homosexual feelings (however we might understand the relationship of these feelings to psychical dispositions towards masculinity

---

2 See, for example, on the formation of transgender studies as a distinct field, Stryker and Whittle (2005); Stryker and Aizura (2013).

3 For transgender studies work that explicitly addresses or makes use of psychoanalytic theory, see, first, Prosser (1998), as well as a spate of more recent work: Salamon (2010); Elliot (2010); Cavanagh (2010); and Carlson (2010).

4 The interdisciplinary academic journal *TSQ: Transgender Studies Quarterly* will publish a special issue on "Transgender and Psychoanalysis," currently scheduled as vol. 4, no. 4 (2017). Psychoanalytic clinicians and theorists who have written non-dismissively, or in non-psychopathologizing ways, about transgender psychical phenomena include Adrienne Harris, Virginia Goldner, and Oren Gozlan. See also Jacqueline Rose's (2016) excellent, psychoanalytically informed overview of transgender theorizing and literatures.

or femininity, or to the question of sexual difference). The exist-ence of homosexual feelings is rarely doubted. Transgender feel-ings, on the other hand — feelings that one's socially assigned gender is in some profound sense inappropriate or unsuitable for oneself, or that one's embodiment does not communicate the intelligibility of one's sense of self to others and must therefore be transformed — still often tend to be trivialized, ridiculed, explained away, or denied as such. Such feelings are really im-possible because there is no such thing as a "core" gender iden-tity (as critics of Stoller [1975] would have it), really a mistaken and politically suspect notion that can be corrected through a progressive pedagogy about sex-role stereotyping (as too many feminists to count are wont to say), really a fraudulent represen-tation based on conscious deception (as the "panic defense" of transphobic murders frames it), really (in some psychoanalytic interpretations) a narcissistic flaw, or really a psychotic error about the ontological givenness of biological sex dimorphism and the psychical necessity of assuming a symbolic position in relation to that dichotomy.

Trans* studies, as opposed to queer studies' focus on ho-mosexual desire, takes as some of its starting positions that "transgender feelings" are real, that agnosticism is an adequate stance regarding their origins, and that skepticism is the best stance regarding any monocausal etiology offered of them; that understanding the sources and implications of these feelings is a non-trivial pursuit that can offer substantive critiques of episte-mological and discursive frameworks that marginalize, deny, or dismiss such feelings and perceptions; and that psychopathol-ogy offers an extremely reductive and impoverished framework for addressing the questions of how these feelings emerge, how they are to be lived, or what is to be done about them at both the individual and societal levels.

The limitations and promises of psychoanalysis for address-ing transgender phenomena fall out along the lines sketched above. On the one hand, psychoanalysis has more often than not proven itself painfully maladept in dealing with the class of problems that transgender feelings present without resorting to pathologizing interpretations; it has not offered the same clarity or utility to trans* subjects, movements, or social projects that it has lent to feminism, gay liberation, or (homo)queer modes of life. On the other hand, as a supple analytical method for both intellectually comprehending and therapeutically intervening in the complex processes of psychical life, psychoanalytic theory and practice nevertheless harbor a potential for understanding transgender issues and apprehending their "truth" that has yet to be fully or routinely realized. Judith Butler's early work on "gender trouble" and "bodies that matter," so foundational for much contemporary trans* theorizing, is a feast that seems not to have been consumed by most psychoanalysts.

Taking the nonpathological reality of transgender subjectivity as a starting point, and reading out from there to more general conditions, puts pressure on, and demands the reworking of, such psychoanalytic concepts as sexual difference, masculinity, femininity, desire, castration, and lack. Trans* critique can thus perhaps revise currently orthodox psychoanalytic accounts of subjectivity, while also directing our attention toward the emerging technocultural contours of (post)human bodies and subjects yet to come, in which the psychical imperative to take up a position of sexual difference and *be* a sex might come to be understood as something other than a scene of compulsory heterosexuality. Why must the *hetero-* of sexuality be grounded only in naturalized and ontologized binary categories of "man" and "woman" that are conceived as incommensurable, and not in some more expansive notion of difference? As Deleuze and Guattari have proposed: not two sexes, but *n*-sexes.

Kaplan's clinical approach to working with trans* clients is a hopeful token of a psychoanalytic future capable of accounting for transness non-psychopathologically: she asks "how might the person concerned best live?" rather than attributing sickness to their difference; she avoids etiological questions and sectarian interpretations of symptoms, and establishes instead empathetic connections between analyst and analysand based on shared insights into non-heteronormativity. Corbett similarly "follows" the exploratory psychodynamic movements of his patients within the facilitative therapeutic environment he creates, witnessing and seeking to understand their potentially queer gender-transformative work, rather than prescriptively leading them toward hetero-gender-normative outcomes.

Geldhof and Verhaeghe, on the other hand, offer nothing of use for a prospective psychoanalysis premised on trans-depathologization. Their construction of a hierarchy of deviance along a trans/homo continuum reproduces and extends an interpretative lineage that can be traced at least as far back as Krafft-Ebing, who construed *sexualis metamorphosis paranoica* as the most extreme version of a psychosexual inversion whose milder forms included homosexual desire. In the transsexual case study Geldhof and Verhaeghe offer, that of Lacan's patient "Michel H," they interpret the analysand's demand for genital surgery as a "radical" refusal of difference which is "very pernicious for the subject," and to which the analyst "shall therefore never subscribe." It merits pointing out that Lacan himself, in his account of the "trans-sexualist *jouissance*" of the psychotic subject in the Schreber case, noted that the "Question Preliminary of Any Possible Treatment of Psychosis" (1958) was that of transference, which raises in turn the correlative question of counter-transference.[5] I, speaking as a transsexual subject who apparently functions non-psychotically in the Symbolic register, yet who has experienced precisely that surgical operation at the level of the "real body" that Geldhof and Verhaeghe say must be avoided at all cost, feel compelled to ask: who seems more likely than whom to be seeking shelter from the threat of castration? It is the denial of the psychical viability of post-operative transsexuality, and the analysts' motivated refusal to recognize the efficacy of a surgical solution, that can best be characterized as a defense.

---

5   "[T]his question that is preliminary to any possible treatment of the psychoses is a question that introduces, as we see, the conception to be formed of the handling, in this treatment, of the transference" (Lacan 2001[1958], 245).

As Gherovici demonstrates, however, Lacan can in fact be deployed in support of other analytical positions on transgender issues. In noting that any subject's assumption of a sexual identity is always symptomatic precisely because the phallus, in relation to which the subject must take a position, is "a defective tool to negotiate the Real that eludes us," Gherovici opens a space of possibility in which a transsexual desire for reworking and resignifying embodiment is of a kind with all other desire. Because all sex must be symbolized, and all gender embodied, the "problem" of transgender identification is no different than the "problem" of non-transgender identification: all subjectivity emerges into language precisely where identification fails. Transgender, in Gherovici's account, is just another technical art, one more creative solution among others, for tying the Borromean knot that holds the embodied subject together.

Works Cited

Butler, Judith. *Bodies that Matter: On the Discursive Limits of "Sex."* New York and London: Routledge, 1993.

———. "Imitation and Gender Insubordination." In *Inside/Out: Lesbian Theories, Gay Theories,* ed. Diana Fuss, 13–31. New York and London: Routledge, 1991.

Carlson, Shanna. "Transgender Subjectivity and the Logic of Sexual Difference." *differences: A Journal of Feminist Cultural Studies* 21, no. 2 (2010): 46–72.

Cavanagh, Sheila. *Queering Bathrooms: Gender, Sexuality, and the Hygienic Imagination.* Toronto: University of Toronto Press, 2010.

Elliot, Patricia. *Debates in Transgender, Queer, and Feminist Theory: Contested Sites.* Surrey: Ashgate, 2010.

Lacan, Jacques. "On a Question Preliminary to Any Possible Treatment of Psychosis" (1958). In *Écrits: A Selection,* trans. Alan Sheridan, 198–249. 1977; rpt. New York and London: Routledge, 2001.

Prosser, Jay. *Second Skins: The Body Narratives of Transsexuality.* New York: Columbia University Press, 1998.

Rose, Jacqueline. "Who Do You Think You Are?" *London Review of Books* 38, no. 9 (May 5, 2016): 3–13.

Salamon, Gayle. *Assuming a Body: Transgender and Rhetorics of Materiality.* New York: Columbia University Press, 2010.

Stoller, Robert. *Sex and Gender, Volume 2: The Transsexual Experiment.* London: Hogarth Press, 1975.

Styker, Susan, and Stephen Whittle, eds. *The Transgender Studies Reader.* New York: Routledge, 2005.

———— and Aren Aizura, eds. *The Transgender Studies Reader 2.* New York: Routledge, 2013.

27

The Psychoanalysis That Dare Not Speak Its Name

Ona Nierenberg[1]

In the opening essay of *Love In A Dark Time: Gay Lives from Wilde to Almodovar,* Colm Tóibin refers to Borges's essay "The Argentine Writer and Tradition" to describe the position of exile as a condition for creation, for the possibility of the emergence of the new. Tóibin situates gay literary figures alongside the Jewish, Argentine, and Irish artists that Borges refers to, underlining that the place of estrangement, of foreignness, is the *sine qua non* for speaking at the limits of the sayable. While certainly not sufficient, extra-territoriality is absolutely necessary to affect a break with the mortifications referred to by Freud (1926a) as "the compact majority" (274).

Psychoanalysis, Freud's creation, is born of exile, wanderings from the disciplines with which it shares borders (psychology, philosophy, anthropology, sociology, literature, poetry) while remaining entirely Other to them (Fuks 2008). As Freud conceived it, psychoanalysis shatters received notions of subjectivity, and by definition, *sexuality*, subverting the idolatry of common sense, pseudo-science and morality. Its originality was to bring into being a new realization of being human which marks a rupture from psychiatry and medicine. This break is not a social/historical contingency; it marks the specificity of the Freud-

1   Special thanks to Salvatore F. Guido, PhD for the conversations that led to this commentary.

ian field, where the truth of the divided subject undermines supposed knowledge and its limits. That is why encountering the pronounced antipathy towards psychoanalysis amongst so many of the queer theorists writing in this volume should give us pause. While surely it would be problematic to find an ideal of harmonious coupling, a complementary pair (i.e., "queer theory *and* psychoanalysis"), it is also unsettling to find such mistrust, disparagement and anger based on "the familiar psychoanalytic tropes" (Weatherill).

It is evident that many of the clinical psychoanalysts writing here who are oriented by a Freudian/Lacanian formation do not recognize their work in a theory and practice described as *normalizing, pathologizing,* and *denigrating* by queer theorists such as Downing, Snediker, Bond Stockton, Kuzniar, and Farina. How can we think about this *méconnaisance*, with psychoanalysis repeatedly identified with suspicion and hostility? Equally curious is the identification of Freudian or Lacanian ideas that would seem to be well-suited to the ideology of queer theory with other psychoanalytic thinkers. For example, Kuzniar's assiduous avoidance of acknowledging Freud as the discoverer of the unconscious and her misguided generosity in bestowing this honor upon Jean Laplanche. Furthermore, we should question what motivates her to identify Nancy Chodorow as the psychoanalytic source for the idea that heterosexuality should be analyzed as critically as homosexuality, when this is practically a verbatim quote from Freud's "Three Essays on the Theory of Sexuality" (1905). Of course, we must include in our query the occurrence of completely false identifications, for example, Farina's idea that the "Electra Complex" is part of the Freudian corpus and her assertion that, for Freud, the Oedipus complex is "solvable."

Here we find a series of "missed encounters" between Freudian psychoanalysis and queer theory, and such "misses" are most telling (and for a psychoanalyst there is no "telling" without the "missing"). What is revealed, among other things, is the enduring impact of the vexed history that marks the troubled relationship between institutionalized psychoanalysis and homosexuality. It is my proposition that this revenant haunts every effort by queer theorists to work with psychoanalysis, preventing queer theory from potentially finding a way through its impasses and logical contradictions with respect to identity.

Incalculable suffering to countless men and women took place in the name of psychoanalysis, and this must never be forgotten. However, what is equally essential to remember is that there is a distinction between the Freudian field and the institution of psychoanalysis, the latter being a construction made possible only by the rejection of the exilic essence of Freud's creation. It is *resistance* to psychoanalysis as Freud conceived it that led to petrifying and dogmatic psychoanalytic institutions, which is why Lacan cried for the necessity for a *return* to Freud. In my opinion, the future of any possible encounter between psychoanalysis and queer theory rests upon our rigor in upholding the differences between Freud's invention and the resistances through which the institution of psychoanalysis took place. This contrast has been kept in the foreground by some notable theorists who have done significant work on the question of the history of psychoanalysis and homosexuality, i.e., Henry Abelove (1986), Tim Dean and Christopher Lane (2001), Élisabeth Roudinesco (2002), Kenneth Lewes (1988). *Clinical Encounters in Sexuality* provides us with another valuable opportunity (never once and for all) to underline that the virulent homophobia that stains the history of psychoanalysis is a symptom of the *rejection* of Freud's strange invention. Ironically, by effacing the distinction between Freudian psychoanalysis and the institutionalization of psychoanalysis, queer theorists would situate themselves on the same side as those who pathologized homosexuality in the name of psychoanalysis by expelling what is most radical to Freud.

The reprobate discourse and practices that designated homosexuality a pathology cannot be separated from the effort to provide psychoanalysis with a home in the field of medicine, to suture the cut that constituted its birth. Freud observed the difficulty of those who called themselves psychoanalysts to remain stateless, on the side of uncertainty and the unknown:

"Sometimes I am amazed that analysts themselves should not be radically changed by their relation with analysis," he wrote in a letter to LaForge (Bourguingnon 1991, 27). As early as 1914, Freud expressed his great disappointment that the resistances to psychoanalysis that were once external became internal to its organization, and he recognized this as a far greater peril. Certainly, this reactionary direction was not the one Freud intended for the psychoanalytic movement.

Often characterized by his supposed pessimism, Freud was perhaps far too optimistic in calling his creation "the plague" during his one and only visit to America in 1909. The powerful immunological response that arose here took the form of suppressing psychoanalysis by domesticating it, insisting that it belonged to the land of medicine. While Freud (1926b) unwaveringly held that psychoanalysis is unequivocally Other to medicine and cannot be mapped on to a medical model of treatment, the Americans made clear that they fundamentally renounced the alterity of the Freudian thing by restricting the practice to medical doctors. Although the question of lay analysis appears to be about who can (or cannot) practice psychoanalysis, it is actually the kernel of truth that reveals what psychoanalysis is. "A profession of lay curers of souls who need not be doctors and should not be priests" was one of Freud's poetic descriptions of the odd path that refuses the illusory mastery of scientism or religion (Meng and Freud 1963, 126). The crisis over lay analysis, which reached a head in the 1920s had dire consequences for instutionalized psychoanalysis's relationship to homosexuality.

Among the many reasons Freud named medicalization as one of the greatest resistances to psychoanalysis was his awareness that his radically novel theory of human sexuality diverged completely from the medical conception (Nierenberg 2007). Whereas medicine considered human sexuality to be the fruit of an instinct, a sign of the continuity between human beings and nature, Freud discovered a peculiarly human foundation to sexuality that is characterized by a rupture with the "natural" order of things. The mythology of the drive allows for no human subject, no speaking subject, to escape the exigencies of "deviant" sexuality. All are subject to the drives' cacaphony, subverting any ideal of sexual harmony in human life. One of the four fundamental concepts of psychoanalysis, according to Lacan, the drive marks the impossibility of any biological real to function as a guarantee of desire, object, or sexuation. Where the *parlêtre,* the "speaking-being," is concerned, all aspects of sexuality are equally curious. The drive annuls any necessary link between homosexuality and psychopathology, as Freud's well-known position vis-à-vis homosexuality makes clear.

The borderline status of the drive, "lying at the frontier between the mental and the physical" (Freud 1905, 182), belonging neither to one side nor the other, proved nearly impossible to sustain after Freud's death. But without this concept, that founds the "out-of-sync-ness" between the human order and supposed "biological reality," there can be no psychoanalysis. Once the strangeness of the drive was replaced by ego-psychology's term "instinctual drive" (an oxymoron in Freudian terms), it opened the way for the return to the idealization/naturalization of reproductive heterosexuality and its complement: the pathologization of homosexuality. While Freud was able to leave behind the certainties of "normalcy and deviance," his followers retreated to this pernicious paradigm with all-too-well-known disastrous consequence.

While the chapters in *Clinical Encounters in Sexuality* reveal that psychoanalysis and queer theory have taken divergent paths, they share an inescapable and painful inheritance. However, any encounter between the two will prove difficult if the institutionalization of psychoanalysis is taken for the all of psychoanalysis. For the necessary mourning of the past to take place, this distinction must be made. It is by way of the "not-all" that we may reinvent the clinic of Otherness and the ethics of exile.

Works Cited

Abelove, Henry. "Freud, Male Homosexuality and the Americans." *Dissent* 5 (1986): 5–69.

Bourguingnon, André. *O conceito de renegaçao en Freud.* Rio de Janeiro: Jorge Zahar, 1991.

Dean, Tim and Christopher Lane. "Introduction." In *Homosexuality and Psychoanalysis,* eds. Tim Dean and Christopher Lane, 3–42. Chicago: University of Chicago Press, 2001.

Freud, Sigmund. "Address to the Society of B'nai Brith" (1926a). In *The Standard Edition of the Complete Psychological Works of Sigmund Freud,* vol. 20, trans. James Strachey in collaboration with Anna Freud and assisted by Alix Strachey and Alan Tyson, 271–76. 1959; rpt. London: Vintage, 1999.

———. "The Question of Lay Analysis — Conversations with an Impartial Person" (1926b). In *The Standard Edition of the Complete Psychological Works of Sigmund Freud,* vol. 20, trans. James Strachey in collaboration with Anna Freud and assisted by Alix Strachey and Alan Tyson, 183–258. 1959; rpt. London: Vintage, 1999.

———. "On the History of the Psychoanalytic Movement" (1914). In *The Standard Edition of the Complete Psychological Works of Sigmund Freud,* vol. 14, trans. James Strachey in collaboration with Anna Freud and assisted by Alix Strachey and Alan Tyson, 3–66. London: Vintage, 2001.

———. "Three Essays on the Theory of Sexuality" (1905). In *The Standard Edition of the Complete Psychological Works of Sigumund Freud,* vol. 7, trans. James Strachey in collaboration with Anna Freud and assisted by Alix Strachey and Alan Tyson, 1–162. 1953; rpt. London: Vintage, 2001.

Fuks, Betty. *Freud and the Invention of Jewishness.* New York: Sea Horse/Agincourt, 2008.

Lewes, Kenneth. *The Psychoanalytic Theory of Male Homosexuality,* New York: Simon & Schuster, 1988.

Meng, Heinrich, and Ernst Freud, eds. *Sigmund Freud: Psychoanalysis and Faith: Dialogues with Reverend Oscar Pfister.* New York: Basic Books, 1963.

Nierenberg, Ona. "The Lay and the Law: Legislating the 'Impossible Profession.'" *Journal for the Psychoanalysis of Culture and Society* 12, no. 1 (2007): 65–75.

Roudinesco, Elisabeth. "Psychoanalysis and Homosexuality: Reflections on the Perverse Desire, Insult, and the Paternal Function." Interview with François Pommier. *Journal of European Psychoanalysis* 15 (2002). http://www.psychomedia.it/jep/15/roudinesco.htm.

Tóibin, Colm. *Love in a Dark Time: Gay Lives from Wilde to Almodovar.* London: Picador, 2010.

COVER IMAGE

THERE CAN BE NO ARGUMENTS

On the Not-Meanings of Karla Black's There Can Be No Arguments

Medb Ruane

We expect to be able to recognize what we see in the visual field but visual experience occurs around a void, an emptiness, over which the artist places *semblants*. In *The Ethics of Psychoanalysis* (2008[1959–60]), Lacan likened this to a vase that puts a skin around a hole and veils the open sewer beneath. A "nothing" becomes a "something." An object is made to exist (148–49).

The marked and voided spaces around Karla Black's suspended piece *There Can Be No Arguments* play with fullness and emptiness, not only as background for the works in space she makes. The marks are written on the rim of the Real. They are not about metaphor or producing meaning. Strip meaning or the hope of it away and an encounter emerges. She dresses and addresses a void.

> This nothing in particular that characterises it in its signifying function is that which in its incarnated form characterises the vase as such. It creates the void and thereby introduces the possibility of filling it. Emptiness and fullness are introduced into a world that by itself knows not of them. It is on the basis of this fabricated signifier, this vase, that emptiness

and fullness as such enter the world, neither more nor less, and with the same sense. (Lacan 2008[1959–60], 148–49)[1]

Here, everyday materials with no monetary value or status transform into things of beauty. Polythene, powder paint, plaster and thread create billowing gossamer wings that gently float materials into air. Must we interpret it? No. Her title says that there can be no arguments and so we find ourselves also suspended between the will-to-language and the bodily events of looking, moving towards and around it, resisting the urge to touch it because there's a prohibition on a nearby sign.

Seen on this book's cover, the bodily aspect of our encounter with Black's work is mistranslated into a different genre and instead the work appears front-on as a two-dimensional image projected from a single-perspective geometral point. It is made to fit a master discourse with different rules.

The work still sings. You could be watching the draperies on an Empress' gown — or discarded plastic sheeting arranged by benevolent chance. Its curtain-like possibilities bring to mind the contrasting story of Zeuxis and Parhassios, first told by Pliny (*De Naturalis Historia*, Bk. 35, c. 36), who competed as masters of illusion to see whose painting looked most real. Birds actually tried to peck Zeuxis's painted grapes yet Parrhassios trumped him by painting a veil whose surface was so inviting that Zeuxis himself, according to Lacan (1998[1964]), "turned towards him [Parhassios] and said, *Well, and now show us what you have painted behind it.* By this," Lacan continues, "he showed that what was at issue was certainly deceiving the eye (*tromper l'œil*). A triumph of the gaze over the eye" (108; 111ff.).

Read clinically rather than aesthetically, the gaze is counterintuitive in that it functions not at the level of the visible but in terms of modes of satisfaction around which subjectivities emerge. Down in the clinic, the object *a*, the agent of discourse,

---

1   While Western culture rejects chipped or broken vases (fantasy of wholeness), Japanese culture practices the art of *kintsugi* as a way of valuing brokenness and imperfection by marking the chips/fractures.

acts on the divided subject whose relationship with the object of *jouissance* is completely veiled. The veil is drawn by the functioning of the master signifier (S1) and of knowledge relating to it (S2). In artworking, however, the relationship of the object *a* is to knowledge directly, not to a master signifier via a divided subject.

This distinction leads us to realize some key differences between the work of the artist and the work of the clinician. With a neurotic subject, repression teaches us that loss determines the object's mode of functioning such that the object functions as a lost object and precipitates desire. But in art generated through sublimation rather than by repression (whatever the artist's subjective structure), the object functions as having been recovered, not lost. Art, then, involves recoupment that is about regaining the object and getting rid of the loss by putting the loss in the Other.[2] By contrast, a neurotic subject puts the object in the Other and lives with the loss.

What both subjects share, notably, is the push-to-normalization coming from the Other — from contemporary life, culture and, especially, science. That mentality assumes that all human activity and behavior can be classified on a scale of one to ten and adjusted to better fit its norm. This psychologized model based on means, medians and modes recognizes no place, no point, outside its own scales. We, not it, must adjust.

Does any subjectivity wholly fit one of the (initially) fifty-one then fifty-eight (and increasing) so-called gender assignations set by Facebook? Does any assignation actually speak truthfully to our singular beings? The question for encounters like ours is

---

2 Black said: "[I]t's a bit of a Pyrrhic victory, in that perhaps too much is lost to consider it particularly worthwhile. I feel like the pure joy and/or beauty of the experience of the material world (in terms of color and light and actual stuff) that my work emerges out of, and also the joy and beauty of the human interaction with that (the raw creativity) gets more and more lost. This happens not only as it all gets closer to being formed into a physical object, but also as it goes through the mincer of language via explanation and instruction" (Hunter, May 2013).

of subjectivities and how they come to be one by one, one on one, not on a statistical scale.

Traditional art norms would not accommodate practices such as Black's. Within contemporary visual culture, she is confronted by historical canons that still persist, even when outdated and demonstrably untrue. In her revised introduction to *Women, Art and Society* (2007), Whitney Chadwick said that her own earlier (1990) questions had shifted and were now linked to issues of sexual orientation, race and ethnicity, as well as gender. She quoted Harmony Hammond, who identifies as lesbian and feminist:

> I see art-making, especially that which comes from the margins of the mainstream, as a site of resistance, a way of interrupting and intervening in those historical and cultural fields that continually exclude me. A sort of gathering of forces on the borders. For the dominant hegemonic stance that has worked to silence and subdue gender and ethnic difference has also worked to silence difference based on sexual preference. (13)

"Sexual preference" is about subjectivities, not about conscious choice or essentialist biologistic destiny. There are no universals. Bodies are sexuated one by one, each in their own way. Yet Black's interventions have been lampooned dismissively for what some call their "feminine" features, especially her colors (peaches, pistachios, pinks, paler pastels) and often fragile materials (chalk dust, eye-shadow, nail varnish, fake tan, body fragrances, even toothpaste). To spell it out, the clear implication is that color divides naturally into masculine and feminine (with gravitas attaching to the former) and that you can't use the same materials for "Art" as for your own body. If you do, it's not Art.

Black's retort at the 2011 Venice Biennale names the problem: "Why do people call it feminine? Because it is light, fragile, pale? Because it is weak, impermanent? When you start going to work on it you realize how ridiculous the description is. How can a work of art be feminine?" (Higgins 2011).

To be "feminine," a work of art would have to be governed by an Ideal, that is, a universal. Despite G.W.F. Hegel's (1975) long-ago warning that the Ideal of Art was on the wane, Ideals have governed previous historical moments with the object *a* veiled by a master signifier and works of art subjuncted to them. The Ideal functioned as a guarantee that the work was Art — and an implicit assurance that the void, abyss, Thing, was not only masked but did not pose a threat. This master signifier idealized oppositions such as man–woman, masculine–feminine, strong–weak, and more. Worse, such categories were considered natural, as part of the order of things, and were enforced by a series of segregations that either pathologized or exiled rogue signifiers or practices (Canguilhem 1989; Foucault 1989).

In Black's practice, as in other contemporary work, both are untied from the object. The object presents as Real without reference to a signifier or to images and shapes, that is, without necessary reference to symbolic-imaginary registers. This material writing emerges not from the place of the "private ego," as Hal Foster (2012) named it (771).[3] We can call it a transcription that de-psychologizes artworking by resubjectivating it through the mechanism of sublimation. It is a message from the unconscious that is not unconscious because it is formed.

Through her work, then, the artist reveals something about the relationship between an object of *jouissance* and knowledge in contemporary times. For in the contemporary clinic, the object *a* is now increasingly untethered from the master signifier, that is, from the guarantees of the ego-ideal and ideal ego and their imaginary negation of the abyss. The subject is left with no guarantee.

Dissenters — there are many to contemporary art — will say that art like this is "rubbish." This is manna for anyone who recalls Freud's work on infantile sexuality and how the body's waste is structured as objects of satisfaction. "Rubbish" here can stand for feces ("shit") and, as Freud (1908) remarked, "every-

---

3   See also Krauss (1994). On materiality, see Lacan (1987[1971]).

body is familiar with the figure of 'shitter of ducats'" (174). Some rubbish, then, strikes gold.

Works Cited

Canguilhem, Georges. *The Normal and the Pathological.* New York: Zone Books, 1989 (1966).

Chadwick, Whitney. *Women, Art and Society.* London: Thames and Hudson, 2007 (1990).

Foster, Hal. "The Predicament of Contemporary Art." In *Art since 1900: Modernism, Anti-Modernism, Post-Modernism,* eds. Hal Foster, Rosalind Krauss, Yves-Alain Bois, Benjamin H.D. Bucloch, and David Joselit, 767–82. London: Thames and Hudson, 2012.

Foucault, Michel. *The History of Sexuality. Volume 1: An Introduction,* trans. Robert Hurley. New York: Random House, 1989 (1976).

Freud, Sigmund. "Character and Anal Eroticism" (1908). In *The Standard Psychological Works of Sigmund Freud,* vol. 9, trans. James Strachey in collaboration with Anna Freud and assisted by Alix Strachey and Alan Tyson, 169–75. 953; rpt. London: Vintage, 2001.

Hegel, G.W.F. *Aesthetics: Lectures on Fine Art,* vols. 1 and 2, trans. T.M. Knox. 1818/1835; rpt. Oxford: Clarendon Press, 1975.

Higgins, Charlotte. "Karla Black at the Venice Biennale: 'Don't Call My Art Feminine.'" *The Guardian.* June 1, 2011. http://www.theguardian.com/artanddesign/2011/jun/01/karla-black-at-venice-biennale.

Huff Hunter, Becky. "More than Words: An Interview with Karla Black." *Art in America.* May 20, 2013. http://www.artinamericamagazine.com/news-features/interviews/more-than-words-an-interview-with-karla-black-/.

Krauss, Rosalind. *The Optical Unconscious.* Cambridge: MIT Press, 1994.

Lacan, Jacques. *Book VII: The Ethics of Psychoanalysis* (1959–60), ed. Jacques-Alain Miller, trans. Denis Porter. London: Routledge, 2008.

———. *Book XI: The Four Fundamental Concepts of Psycho-Analysis* (1964), ed. Jacques-Alain Miller, trans. Alan Sheridan. New York/London: Norton, 1998.

———. "Lituraterre." First published in the review *Litterature* (Larousse) 3 (1971). Republished in *Ornicar?* 41 (April–June, 1987): 5–13. Trans. Jack Stone, private circulation.

Pliny the Elder. *De Naturalis Historia.* http://masseiana.org/pliny.htm.

Reflections on the Encounters between Psychoanalysis and Queer Theory

Eve Watson[1]

Clinical Encounters in Sexuality brings together two altogether different disciplines that address the field of human sexuality: clinical psychoanalysis and queer theory. This encounter is underpinned by the centrality of sexuality to both disciplines and the crucial nature of psychoanalytic theory to queer theory's theorization of gender and sexuality. Beginning with Sigmund Freud, psychoanalysis has a long history of turning to other fields such as philosophy, art, literature, linguistics, science, mathematics, and religion to develop and differentiate its major themes. This collection adds the work of queer theory to this list of co-conspirators addressing the question of what it is to be uniquely human, especially important today in light of the homogenizing effects of globalization, marketization and digitalization. Queer theory proffers a breadth of critical thinking about contemporary sexuality, mechanisms of bio-power

1   I am deeply grateful to Noreen Giffney for her input into this Afterword via discussion, debate, and co-reflection together of the various themes.

    A version of this Afterword was discussed at the 14th Annual APW (Affiliated Psychoanalytic Workgroups) Conference, hosted by Lacan Salon, Vancouver which took place on August 27–29, 2016 in Vancouver, BC, Canada. I am grateful to the participants of the conference for their comments and questions, which helped me to extend and develop my ideas.

and regimes of normativization for psychoanalysts to address themselves to. Queer theory's use of psychoanalysis is critical to its Foucault-inspired project of critically exploring desire, pleasure, identity and the social fabric itself. Psychoanalysts, for their part, offer psychoanalytic theory, clinical practice and the extraordinary value of the clinical vignette, the psychoanalytic tool *par excellence.* In addition, theorists of psychoanalysis and sexuality bring their insights to bear on this "queer" marriage between psychoanalysis and queer theory for readers to add to their experience of the book.

As outlined in more detail below, the book shows that this "queer" marriage produces fascinating points of critical overlap and a fecundity of border significations between queer theory and psychoanalysis that inspire, provoke, disquiet and complicate contemporary thinking about sexuality. What emanates from the book's chapters is an uneasy relationship between queer theory and psychoanalysis. This unease is important, revelatory and open to analysis, which I frame in light of my own background in Lacanian psychoanalysis, as well as an interdisciplinary affiliation with queer theory. I propose that the sometimes uneasy encounters, which bring to the fore discord and friction as well as amity and congruity, can be framed as a series of problematics concerning the horizons of dichotomization relative to both fields, specifically how each field has approached what Patricia Elliot (2010) describes as the "two disabling dichotomies," that is, "between the biological and the social" and "between the normal and the pathological" (103).

The question of "disabling" or entrenching dichotomization refers to the reductionism of attributing difference in binaries of essentializing biological cause or oppressive social construction, and in terms of the normal or the pathological. For psychoanalysis, these binarizing dichotomizations fail to capture what it means to be human because psychic life involves unconscious dynamics that are not reducible to either the biological or the social but involve elements of both. Moreover, the normal/ pathological binary is sacrilegious to psychoanalysts (103) given the Freudian attribution that conflict, polymorphous perver-

sion, phantasy, and suffering and constitutive of human subjectivity. Deviations by psychoanalysis from the refusal of these
"disabling" dichotomizations underpin some of the complications and unease in the relationship between queer theory and
psychoanalysis. On the part of queer theory, the theorization
of social constructs in oppressive and immutable terms and the
elision of the role of the unconscious and the body in human experience has reinforced rather than loosened dichotomization,
which some queer theorists in the collection address variously
and with a commitment to dialogue and critical debate.

I have assembled these complications into a trio of organizing
currents. First, there is the importance for queer theory of differentiating between Lacanian psychoanalysis and "neo-Freudianism" and its influence on institutionalized psychoanalysis
during the inter-and post-World War Two decades. Neo-Freudianism is recognized by its adherence to, rather than its refusal
of, normal/pathological and biological/social dichotomizations.
Secondly, I explore the implications of this for understandings
of sexuality and clinical practice and for differentiating contemporary psychoanalysis from this painful history which is characterized by reprehensible practices of normativity and continues, in my opinion, to impact relations between psychoanalysis
and queer theory. In this, I invite queer theory to risk seriously
engaging with Lacanian psychoanalysis as one mode of interro-
gating tendencies towards reductive binarizations. Thirdly, the
book makes an intervention in acknowledging gay and lesbian
analysts and institutionalized homophobia that is a component
feature of the history of psychoanalysis. That psychoanalysis
became a co-conspirator and reflected society's persecution of
homosexuality throughout the middle and late decades of the
twentieth century demonstrates that psychoanalytic attitudes
and theories are not immune from the cultures in which they
are formulated (Drescher 2008, 454). This invokes the necessity for psychoanalytic clinicians to continue to engage with and
challenge the wide field of normalization that characterizes the
socio-cultural fabric, which psychoanalysis is inescapably part

of. I will return to each of these three points in more detail after briefly exploring each chapter's contribution.

The Encounters: Productions, Provocations and Remainders

In the book's first section, queer theorists employ the work of Freud, Lacan, Laplanche, Irigaray and Winnicott to put concepts such as identity, desire, *jouissance,* perversion, masculinity, femininity, gender, signifier, and drive under the microscope and trouble the category of "normal" and so-called "truths" of sex. Strongly evident throughout this section is the queer aim of deconstructing all binaries including masculine–feminine, desire–identity, heterosexual–homosexual, object choice–gender identity, and fixity–fluidity. What unfolds in these six chapters is a panoply of thinking that aims at subverting notions of progress, rationalism, essentialism, narrativization and scientism that predictably and inevitably telescope to a point of normativity.

Alice Kuzniar opens the queer theory chapters with a focus on the force and importance of *das Andere,* "an internal otherness" in human sexuality. Exploring the category of queer as non-identitarian within what Jacqueline Rose describes as the unconscious revelation of the "failure" of identity and with key references to Jean Laplanche, Kuzniar celebrates queer's "multiplicity, incoherence, transitoriness and impossibility." She critiques the Oedipal model for presuming a fixed and stable telos of gender identity and also contemporary consumerist culture in which "identity serves the purpose of controlling, commodifying, and marketizing the subject." For her, pet love demonstrates that it is a "quality" rather than object choice that draws us to the other. She argues that psychoanalysis must confront the failure of previous conceptual psychic models and develop new hypotheses to explain queer. For Lara Farina, the aim of queering the field of desire is a matter for her of "critical ethics" and her interrogation of Plato's *Symposium,* which decenters the ideal of complementarity and privileges desire as emanating from lack, is an ideal text for a theorization of same-sex desire that also holds out promise "for a queer injection of past narra-

tives into present ones." She interprets lack as "lack of a complimentary other" and assesses whether Lacan's interpretation of
lack and his theory of sexual difference ends up re-inscribing
the importance of gender complementarity in ascribing lack
to the feminine. She proposes that psychoanalysis "loosen up"
and become less sober on desire, in the manner of Plato's drink-
ing party. **Kathryn Bond Stockton** also seeks to disentangle the
ideal of sexual complementarity by extending the connection
between *jouissance* and sexual pleasure. Using the work of Irigaray, she critiques Lacan's assignation of *jouissance* as opaque and
mystical, preferring the term "bliss" against the "staid nature"
of its Lacanian psychoanalytic conception. She considers the
key role of Lacanian theory at the heart of much queer thought
especially in conceiving of desire and pleasure but nonetheless
critiques Lacan's "tragic tone" about desire's relation to lack, preferring the "subtleties and vibrancy" of bliss against pleasure.

    Lisa Downing takes psychoanalysis to task for its orthodoxy
about fixation in perversion and for "making a symptom out
of a pleasure," as well as queer theory for not harnessing better the energies and "athwartness" of perversion. She critiques
both the psychoanalytic category of perversion which she argues is narrowly defined by the Freudian notion of "fixity," and
also cautions against the dangers of normativity creeping into
the queer project by overinvesting in "fluidity" and de-specify-
ing all sexual identity labels. This could result in a tyranny of
prescribing fluidity, thus ironically making it ideological, tautological and normative and reducing its perverse possibilities.
Michael Snediker aims at a possible ethics "freed of normativity" and catalyzes Winnicott's ontological thought and aesthetic
practice alongside the queer theory of Eve Kosofsky Sedgwick
to opine on a queer pedagogy that would imbue psychoanalysis
with "an exegetical language as mutational as the unconscious's
own fitfulness." Preferring aesthetics to desire, he imputes an
ethical turn in Winnicott's work in allowing movement away
from sense towards "inhabiting a space of not-knowing" that
would have the effect of undoing closed spaces of ontology and
action. He proposes an aesthetic unconscious epitomized in

Winnicott's squiggle game that "imagines as ontological inde-terminancy." **Will Stockton** aligns himself with both Foucault's historicist approach to sexuality and Lacan's conception of sex as always falling outside of discourse insofar as there is a radical discontinuity between sex and sense in order to clarify a psy-choanalytic approach to sex and discourse that could be use-ful to historicizing sexuality. He criticizes Foucault's elision of the role of the unconscious in aligning everything to discourse but also favors Foucault's work for better illustrating symbolic inscription. In his reading of Shakespeare's Sonnet 20 and in deconstructing the "normative" narrative process and reading Shakespeare awry he puts the position of readers and their sex-ual positioning under scrutiny, and utilizing the work of Joan Copjec, implicates in sexual positioning the gap between dis-courses of sexuality and the real of sex.

In the book's second section, the psychoanalytic responses to the queer theory chapters demonstrate a breadth of psycho-analytic thinking, practices and responses to the provocations of the queer theorists. All of them bear witness to the enduring im-portance of sexuality in the psychoanalytic clinic and the inclu-sion of a wide variety of clinical vignettes reveals ways in which sexual conflict, disturbance and questioning are conveyed and symbolized between analysand and analyst. Some analysts in-terpret the implications of "queer" provoked in them and others consider those structures whereby certain subjects are rendered "normal" and "natural" through the production of perverse and different others by rigid thinking, certain narrative practices and by inattention to the workings of the unconscious in de-sire and identity. Some of the psychoanalytic responses express a commitment to the importance of the function of difference in human subjectivity and express concern about the impress of "fluidity" in eliminating all difference and categorization.

In the first of the psychoanalytic responses, **Bob Hinshel-wood** proposes that when it comes to our subjectivity, we re-quire something that keeps us together, holds the possibilities together. Whether we call this an identity, a non-identity, a core, a trait or a signifier is secondary to the requirement that as human beings, we require something that both differentiates us and singularizes us. Therefore to adopt a strategy of fluid sexual identity may be problematic "by undermining some more foundational sense of stability and inner security." He remarks on the judgmentalism of queer theory and proposes that it requires "a stronger theory of prejudice." For **Paul Verhaeghe** and **Abe Geldhof**, queer for them is located in "the silence of being" and the *jouissance* of the body insofar as the body is always *heteros,* that is, strange and antithetical to symbolization. They argue that as a discursive practice, a practice of naming that refuses the classical distinction between man and woman, queer in fact replaces the classical sexual dichotomy with a new one: queer/straight. Thus, queer is another name for *jouissance* and the refusal of castration. They take issue with the proclamatory nature of queer theory and argue, "if somebody wanted to be really queer, then he would have no reason to prove it." **Ann Murphy** welcomes the ethical imperative that queer theory proffers to psychoanalysis to question and interrogate the systems of power that suffuse all institutionalized bodies of knowledge and practice, including psychoanalysis with "institutionalized rigidity" and regimes of discipline, regulation and control. Against this, she emphasizes the enigmatic nature of desire, which is characterized by its intransigence to "agendas of improvement." Taking up Bion's assertion that certainty is the enemy of psychoanalysis, she argues that psychoanalytic ethics is cultivated by its inexorable emphasis on the singularity of the individual subject and the articulation of psychic pain and its attendant lack, limitation and conflict.

Ian Parker focuses on the history of the queer movement from its initial links to psychoanalysis and its move against traditional binary categories, to its current status as a verb connoting movement, a *doing,* restlessness. Employing a case study of Lacan's, he proposes that what is queer is the "subject" who does not correspond to and exceeds both the "individual" and the object of the case study. While the private and non-public nature of the psychoanalytic clinic is one thing, it is incumbent upon psychoanalysts to attend to queer discourse that circulates in the public sphere, to know the "affective communities" to which analysands attach themselves, but to avoid being ideologically mired in what **Carol Owens** describes as an ethically suspect "transformational ideology." Owens problematizes queer misuse and misunderstanding of fragments of Lacanian theory and also critiques the book's "staging" of the encounters. The "staging" destines the book to be an inevitable series of missed encounters that ultimately condemn psychoanalysis to an "ontological impasse" between a demand to reformulate old categories of sexual identity with the consequence of re-formulating psycho-social-developmental theories and grand narratives that queer theory deconstructs. In her chapter, **Claudette Kulkarni**, with a post-Jungian lens, questions the centrality of sexuality to the queer deconstruction of identity. For her, the value of queer theory lies in inspiring the therapist to resist cultural imperatives and keeping an open mind. For her, "fluidity and fixity need each other" and she worries that the queer tendency to resist all stability and fixity results in promoting another kind of normalization and rigidity. Through her work with sexual offenders, she is reluctant to reduce the specificity of the category of perversion when it comes to sexually-based offenses and is troubled by the queer reluctance to distinguish the "subversive" use of perversion from its other uses.

Aranye Fradenburg recognizes a gulf between the stakes of knowledge that motivate the clinic and those that motivate the academy, and notes that American analysts often abdicate their intellectual responsibilities and related social implications and don't pay enough attention to the urgent questions of our time. In her consideration of the problematics of categorization in the field of sexuality for psychoanalysis, she proposes that psychoanalysis must keep redefining perversion and critique all ontologies. For her, Oedipus continues to play a part in the prohibition of transgenerational sexuality and she also highlights the many interlinked versions of caring practice that families, the psychoanalytic clinic and queer theory investigate and transmit. **Olga Cox Cameron** reflects on the (hetero)normative telos of the Oedipus complex and Freud's "often contradictory think-

ing about sexuality and sexual identity" that Lacan reformu-
lated into his idea of the "nor-măle," which is a "master-ized"
discourse. Lacan's renewal of Freud's Oedipus complex was as
necessary as it was prescient. She explores the coercive ideologies and more closed narrative practices developed in the post-
Shakespearean era that informed Freud, and similar to Will
Stockton, implicates otherness and incoherence to the rendering of desire in Shakespearean tragedy.

For **Kathrine Zeuthen** and **Judy Gammelgaard**, a focus on
unconscious sexuality as "what remains non-understood" challenges the transgressive aptitude of queer theory due to its over-
emphasis on gender fluidity and non-Laplanchian equivocation
of gender and sexuality, which elides the enigmatic, plural, and
polymorph nature of sexuality. For both of these child analysts,
the enigmatic nature of sexuality leaves it prone to exceeding its
categorization. While they acknowledge that queer theory helps
them to question the categories of sexual identity by turning
to society and its effects and striations, they express concern at
the queer idealization of sexual queerness which does not correspond with their experience of the pain and suffering in their
patients caused by their "queerness." **Ken Corbett** also considers
the importance of the social critique of the normal, in particular
in considering how social orders and symbolic registers are "enigmatically transferred in idiomatic parent-child relations." His
relational approach highlights the clinical importance of reverie, space and fantasy and like Ann Murphy he prefers "the speculative to the declarative" when it comes to analytic practice.
His clinical vignette with a queer child shows the importance of
openness and non-judgment in analytic practice when it comes
to proffering up the field of symbolization in matters sexual.

Rob Weatherill makes the case that psychoanalysis takes a
middle position between biological essentialism and social constructionism in its gesture to both the body and the Symbolic's
role in subjectivity. Against queer efforts to "burst through difference and erase lack," psychoanalysis emphasizes division,
rupture and alterity and therefore goes beyond the queer ac-
claim of pleasure, Bersani's "correspondences of being" and the

vicissitudes of the sexual act. He insists that what is queer is not so much fluidity but life itself and specifically, life's disturbance, proximity and suffering. The tendency of queer theorists to reject suffering or lack by stigmatizing it "as part of some heterosexist plot" is to try to reduce everything sexual to representation that is for Weatherill, a narrow and "straight" enterprise. **Dany Nobus** takes the view that Lacan's later work is useful in approaching contemporary forms of sexuality. Taking Andre Green's assertion that "today's sexuality is not Freud's sexuality," he proposes dephallicizing and demasculinizing sexuality according to the terms of Lacan's formulae of sexuation, and argues that in its recognition of "choice" as a synonym for the "irreducible unpredictability of human development," a psychoanalytically-informed theory and practice of human sexuality may constitute a true "queer" alternative to every ideological effort at rigid categorization.

In her chapter, **Ami Kaplan** expresses both support for queer theory's interrogation of the category of "normal" and concern at its objective of moving beyond the gender binary, which she argues has had the unfortunate effect of tainting "binarism" as unacceptable even though it has an important meaning and use for her clients. She argues that transsexuality's reliance on gender identification challenges some tenets of queer theory's emphasis on fluidity. In her case study of a transsexual patient, she traces her non-pathologizing approach which incorporates insights from ego-psychology to support the patient's self-identification which allows her to navigate a place in the world. **Patricia Gherovici**, through a series of clinical vignettes, reflects on the contemporary clinic and the kinds of questions about sexuality raised by analysands. Stressing the importance of desire over identity and the dis-unifying nature of identity, she attests that neither biological essentialism nor social constructivism has been able to solve the problem of unconscious sexual difference. She questions whether contested notions like phallic attribution and castration are still valid tools in clinical practice and proposes Lacan's notion of the *sinthome* as a mode of creating and understanding a sexual identity.

The chapters in the book's third section offer an array of thoughtful and critical responses from writers and specialists in sexuality studies and psychoanalysis to the encounters between the psychoanalysts and queer theorists. This section includes provocations inspired by the book's encounters, reflections on the relationship between psychoanalysis and culture and problematics of psychoanalysis as *Weltanschauung,* the nature of homophobia, further considerations of transsexuality and the distinction between institutionalized psychoanalysis and Lacanian psychoanalysis.

Stephen Frosh reflects on elements of the incommensurability of psychoanalysis and queer theory and takes up the dilemma of psychoanalysis's cultural influence and its potential to become a worldview, against the concern that queer theory fails to care about what people actually say and fails to recognize the reality of sexuality in people's lives. His analysis of 'ego-psychology indicates the importance of locating it within its historical context and that it is indicative of the tendency within psychoanalysis for what is most radical to sometimes give way to "to a kind of conformist moralism," which psychoanalysis is tasked with contesting. Nonetheless he stakes a claim for bringing together psychoanalysis and queer theory to produce something new — "an enlivened psychoanalysis and a deeper and less simplistically celebratory queer theory." **Jacqueline Rose** queries the queerness of queer's relation to otherness, as well as the belief in the transformative power of psychoanalysis, which she states is mediated by its way of thinking that "is recalcitrant to the world of knowledge." Thus, psychoanalysis is positioned to provide a diagnosis of the resistance to acceding to political demands and why sexuality always exceeds what we do and what we want. For her, the question of "resistance" is one of the book's themes which she proposes functions to overwrite and appease "failure" which is also the psyche's strongest defense against any demand to transform itself. Like Frosh, she sees a value in queer's influence in psychoanalysis by engaging with the "darker places of the psyche" where our capacity for transformation is limited. **Tim Dean** critiques the scope of the psychoanalytic responses, which range from "the intrigued and engaged to the disturbingly phobic." He draws attention to the importance for psychoanalysis of considering how social normalization works and warns that all hermeneutic frameworks, including the Oedipus paradigm, make intelligible and normalize the opaque, enigmatic, alien and queer that is unconscious sexuality. For him, *Clinical Encounters in Sexuality* proffers more possibilities than not for creatively working with the differences that divide and connect psychoanalysis and queer theory.

In her meditative remarks, **Noreen O'Connor** principally addresses the psychoanalytic responses and the incitements inspired in her by them. She views the symptomatic relation between the sexes as the anti-normative meeting ground of psychoanalysis and queer theory. Psychoanalysis demonstrates that desire, love, hatred and fantasy are outside of conscious control and it also privileges "self-hood" which emanates "from imaginary identifications through fissures which insert us into the symbolic order of culture." She argues that psychoanalysis, with its emphasis on the dynamics of the unconscious/conscious, specifies the limits of freedom and choice available to us. For **Mark Blechner**, psychoanalysis as "the science of the irrational" and with the tools to identify the defensive process behind pejorative practices, is the field best suited to address homophobia. He interprets the exclusion of gays and lesbians from participation in the psychoanalytic community especially in the mid-twentieth century, which was counter to Freud's progressivism, as an exclusion from their own cure of "anti-homosexual prejudice." He calls for psychoanalysis to rejuvenate itself by applying its own tools to its own defenses. In her consideration of *Clinical Encounters in Sexuality* through the prism of transgender, **Susan Stryker** queries the elision by queer theory of transgender studies in its focus on homosexual desire, and also by psychoanalysis which has historically interpreted transgender psychopathologically as "narcissistic flaw" and "psychotic error." This has resulted in a poverty of thinking and practice, and a plethora of ignorance and politically suspect pedagogy. Stryker nonetheless asserts the potential for a psychoanalytically supple theory and practice that would better understand transgender issues and get closer to their truths. It is because all sex must be symbolized and all gender embodied for everyone that the supposed "problem" of transgender identification is ultimately no different from that of non-transgender identification, insofar as every subject is charged with assuming a psychical position in relation to the question of sexual difference. **Ona Nierenberg** considers the implications of the mistrust of queer theory towards psychoanalysis that emerge in the book and proposes that institutionalized psychoanalysis' troubled relationship to homosexuality "haunts every effort by queer theorists to work with psychoanalysis." She proposes that drawing out the distinctions between the institutionalization of psychoanalysis and *all* psychoanalysis, meaning the breadth of psychoanalysis as a theory and practice distinguished by different schools of thought, is critical for the necessary mourning of the past to take place and for the sake of future encounters.

Uneasy Encounters: Interpreting Differences in Coming Together

Underpinning the book's vigorous and fascinating dialogues, debates, tensions, disagreements and disjunctions is the question of the relationship between queer theory and psychoanalysis. This relationship is one that is challenged both by the weight of history and the difficulties of "interdisciplinarity," in other words, the problematic of finding common ground between two disciplines without each diluting the other. There is a further challenge in that both disciplines are oriented to the question of "otherness" and "queer" in humanity, but not in the same way. For queer theory, the question of otherness and queer is interrogated via political and socio-cultural regimes of dichotomization that cultivate modes of normativity and non-normativity. By contrast, psychoanalysis interrogates the question of otherness in terms of unconscious desire and its radically "other" status that emanates propitiously in parapraxes and in the linguistic figurations and (de)formations of speech acts. As Tim Dean (2000) puts it "from a psychoanalytic perspective, the queer is not opposed to the normal, but fissures it from within" (245). Yet in spite of these differences, the collection's encounters between two heterogeneous approaches that differently address the inalienable "other" and the "queer" in humanity show a commitment to discovery, confrontation and revelation. One revelation is a pervasive sense of unease between psychoanalysis and queer theory and parsing, contextualizing, and understanding this unease is an important step in enriching and extending the relationship between the two fields.

First, it is necessary to differentiate between Lacanian psychoanalysis and modes of "institutionalized psychoanalysis" and "neo-Freudianism" that deviated from the psychoanalytic "refusal" of dichotimization. "Neo-Freudianism" was comprised of followers of Freud who reinterpreted Freud's doctrine, particularly his theory of sexuality, and advocated a theory of adaptative neo-Freudianism. These theorists were persuaded that subjecthood was the product of the social environment as well as biology, and focused their attention on the importance for the ego of being conflict-free and adapting to the external world (see also Nierenberg 1999). They constituted what Elisabeth Roudinesco (1997) describes as "Freudianism's great shift to the west" in the inter- and post-War decades (195), comprising psychiatrists and psychologists who were almost all European in orgin and principally located in the United States. They founded the schools of self-psychology and ego-psychology with its links to followers of Anna Freud in the United Kingdom. Their establishment was supported by psychoanalysis becoming popular and a "mass ideology" in America and in Europe, especially France, and by the International Psychoanalytic Association's (IPA) facilitation of the establishment of neo-Freudianism (293).[2]

---

2   The rise of neo-Freudianism within institutional psychoanalysis can be linked to the election of the psychiatrist Leo Barteimer as president of the IPA in 1949, succeeding Ernest Jones who had been president since 1932 (Roudinesco 1997, 193). This was followed by the ego-psychologist, Heinz Hartmann, who headed the IPA Central Executive during the fifties (245) and the rise of other influential neo-Freudians such as Heinz Hartmann, Rudolf Loewenstein, Ernst Kris, and Irving Bieber in leading psychoana-

Within the neo-Freudian revisionist project, Freud's theory of the polymorphously perverse drive was supplanted by approaches focusing on the ego, such as Anna Freud's ego psychology, which emphasized the regulation of the unconcious by the ego, along with the addition of the notion of strong developmental lines and adaptational logic which added normative assumptions to psychoanalytic technique (Frosh 1999, 89). American ego-psychologists such as Heinz Hartmann and Erik Erikson sought "to convert psychoanalysis into a general psychology" (93) and focused on the "adaptive properties of the ego that sometimes seemed to make such 'adaptation' a biological imperative" (90). A plethora of psychoanalytic writings emerged that categorized homosexuality, lesbianism, and bisexuality in non-normative terms that psychoanalytic technique and treatment should intervene on (Bergler 1944, 1958; Bieber 1962; Greenson 1964; Hartmann 1961; Socarides 1962, 1988).

These approaches, along with the official psychiatric categorization of homosexuality as a mental illness in 1952 and 1968 (DSM-I, 98, 121; DSM-II, 44) resulted in an enshrining of heternormativity in theory and practice in Anglo-American and European psychoanalysis up until the early 1990s, when leading psychoanalytic organizations, due to fierce internal pressure from gay and lesbian members, agreed to incorporate anti-prejudicial policies in practice and training.[3] These heteronormative policies had disastrous effects on gay, lesbian and bisexual training candidates who were excluded from training unless they lied about or obfuscated their sexual orientation, and on

---

lytic institutions. The publication of a plethora of neo-Freudian writings in international psychoanalytic publications such as the *Psychoanalytic Study of the Child, American Journal of Psychoanalysis,* and *International Journal of Psychoanalysis* throughout the 1940s, 1950s, and 1960s also supported its rise in prominence. See Hartmann, Kris and Loewenstein, "Comments on the Formation of Psychic Structure" (1946) and "Notes on the Theory of Aggression" (1949); Bieber, "A Critique of Libido Theory" (1958); Socarides "The Function of Moral Masochism" (1958).

3   Homosexuality was not declassified as a mental disorder until 1973 and it was replaced by the term "ego-dystonic homosexuality" in the *DSM-III,* which was published in 1980 (*DSM-III,* 281).

analysands who were treated with normativizing methods. Real lives and living bodies were impacted and traumatized by the prescriptive ethos of these models (O'Connor and Ryan 1993; Roughton 2002; Frosh 2006). It is the unacknowledged effects of this trauma that imprint queer analysis of psychoanalytic discourse and practice with what Hinshelwood in his chapter calls "a prejudice against prejudice." Queer prejudice, judgmentalism and calls for psychoanalysis to be less conservative and rethink its theory are, in effect, indicative of a spectral return of the repression of Freud's (bi) and (homo)sexuality by this version of post-Freudian psychoanalysis. This repression symptomatically returns in the writings of queer theorists as a revenant of the past, haunting queer theory with remnants of the social abjection and historically prejudicial status of queers (see also Nierenberg).

The obliteration of the revolutionary potential of Freud's theory of sexuality by his revisionist successors can be traced across a twofold development: the misreading of his theory of the drive and the abandonment of his concept of bisexuality (Watson 2011, 58; Nierenberg 1999). The Freudian notion of bisexuality, which traces the drive's "freedom to range equally over male and female objects" (Freud 1905, 145–46, n. 1) and it represents the child's initial ignoring of sexual difference, is little short of revolutionary. Like the concept of the drive, it undermines the idea of an essentially deterministic link between biological sex and object and it explodes the possibility of any easy alignment of libidinal traits along genderized lines. But Freud's unwillingness to define bisexuality and his preference to leave it conceptually incomplete explains the almost total abandonment of the concept by his psychoanalytic successors. The misreading of the Freudian drive as "instinct" lent the new approaches support for the principle of the biological origins of the foundation of sexuality and from this was mapped the movement from child to adult along developmental or maturational models. In effect, the dividedness of the subject that Freud postulates at the centre of his theory of sexuality, revealed in its "bisexuality" and in the persistence of a non-adaptational perverse drive, was refused by the adaptive logic propounded by some of his revisionist successors (Watson 2011, 60, 69).

But perhaps the most significantly ambiguous element in Freud's work is his conception of the Oedipus complex and this is taken up by a number of writers in *Clinical Encounters in Sexuality* including Kuzniar, Farina, and Cox Cameron. On the one hand, there is the notion that the unconscious is neither rigid nor universally determined, i.e., the notion of the "plasticity" and diversity of all of the mental processes and their "wealth of determining factors" (Freud 1913, 123). On the other hand, a slippage occurs whereby culturally-determined standards of gendered desire filter into Freud's account so that a certain kind of identity produces a certain kind of desire, e.g., masculine identity produces a desire for the feminine (Freud 1900, 260–64). The child's desire for the mother, which Lacan reconceptualizes as the other way around, as the mother's desire for the child which is dangerous and necessitates a solution from a father figure to intervene on this duality, is strongly configured by Freud around the son and hardly ever about the daughter (Verhaeghe 2009, 18–19). Lacan (2007[1969–70]) went on to renew Freud's Oedipus with his linguistically-driven metaphor of the Name-of-the-Father and later, the *sinthome,* describing Freud's Oedipus complex as his "dream" (117). The Oedipus complex comprises the analysand's phantasmatic elaborations of the drives, often in dreams, which explains the ubiquity and importance of dreams. Freud's (1905) Oedipus complex is ultimately rooted in a struggle exemplified in the "Three Essays" where he expounds on the ubiquity of the drives and polymorphous perversion while also maddeningly asserting that "one of the tasks implicit in the object-choice is that it should find its way to the opposite sex" (229) (see also Cox Cameron). Yet for all of Freud's ambivalences, I argue that he was infinitely more radical than normative in his conceptualization of sexuality. There is for me both challenge and reward in reading Freud with critical openness as his theory of the drive ultimately refutes the traditional dichotomies of biological/social and normal/pathological by encompassing all of those spectra.

What is refused/repressed under certain conditions returns and this collection proffers a means for a "return" and a working-through of past traumas and pain by way of its encounters and dialogues. It is to be expected that this will be neither easy nor tranquil. I suggest that an acknowledgement akin to a mourning by queer theorists will help to work through the long-standing effects of normativizing approaches of twentieth-century psychoanalysis, notably those influenced by the neo-Freudian traditions. Symptoms, Freud (1905) wrote, "constitute the sexual activity of the patient" (163) and are understood as the return of repressed sexual impulses and ideas. Indications of this unmourned trauma emerge in the book's queer scholarship in which Lacanian psychoanalysis, which tended not to pervert Freud's ideas into normative sexual ideals and broke with the institutionalization of psychoanalysis, is construed identically to approaches that treated homosexuality on the basis of pathology. Other indications emerge in the queer calls for psychoanalysis to update its concepts, including the Lacanian concepts of desire and *jouissance*. Still other indicators are locatable in the curious fact of queer theorists failing to give Freud credit for his ideas and bestowing the honours on Jean Laplanche and Nancy Chodorow instead (see Nierenberg), and also in some queer theorists' unwonted reliance on interpretations of psychoanalytic texts rather than reading directly what psychoanalysts say themselves.

A mourning of this revisionist and normativizing legacy is also necessary for psychoanalysis. The leading worldwide institutions of psychoanalysis, the International Psychoanalytic Association (IPA) and the American Psychoanalytic Association (APsaA), have since the early 1990s introduced important changes and recommendations within their respective organizations to prohibit practices of heteronormativity.[4] But the

---

4 In 1991, in response to a potential discrimination lawsuit, the APsaA (American Psychoanalytic Association) adopted a sexual orientation non-discrimination policy regarding the selection of candidates. This was revised in 1992 to include the selection of faculty and training analysts as well. Committees were established to assess areas of antihomosexual bias and

mere fact of including gays and lesbians as training candidates, members and supervisors and prohibiting prejudice does not go far enough towards working-through its own exclusionary and painful history. As Roughton (2002) puts it in an assessment of Apsaa,

> We have overcome discrimination. That part is finished. We are now a gay-friendly organization that embraces lesbians and gay men as candidates, teachers, curriculum planners, supervisors, training analysts, committee chairs, editorial board members, researchers, authors, colleagues, and organizational leaders.
>
> Yet questions linger about how we could have been so wrong for so long and about where we go from here in re-thinking our concepts of sexuality. Some individual members retain their doubts about the appropriateness of it all, and more are still troubled about delinking homosexuality and psychopathology, at least in some patients. (13–14)

While homosexuality has become a topic for scientific programs and newsletters of the major psychoanalytic organizations, Roughton (2008) posits that full implementation of the policy will require an ongoing process of re-associating, which I argue is one that is also a mourning process. He further suggests that by remembering together, analysts can diminish their collective and individual dissociations of this unsavory element of psychoanalytic history. Until that happens, these dissociations will trouble psychoanalysis and the relative absence of gay and lesbian voices, which still characterizes psychoanalysis, will continue. Some of the responses in this book acknowledge and affirm this painful legacy.

---

work with institutes, as well as transform attitudes policies and curricula (Hoffman et al., 2000; Roughton 1995, cited in Drescher 2008, 452). The IPA did not address the issue of homosexuality until 1998 even though gays and lesbians were excluded from its institutes (Roughton, 1998). It instated a non-discrimination policy, approved in 1999. See https://www.ipa.world/IPA/en/IPA1/Procedural_Code/Non_Discrimination_Policy.aspx.

The wide representation of Lacanian psychoanalysis in the book is, in my opinion, indicative of Lacan's (2006[1958])non-alignment with neo-Freudian and revisionist models of psychoanalysis. He publically opposed all models that promulgated normativity as antithetical to the aims of psychoanalysis and his vociferous criticism of mid-20th century ego-psychology for promising to bring the "whole secret of sexuality to light" (612) is perhaps even clearer in his (2000[1955–56]) assertion that "the great secret of psychoanalysis is that there is no psychogenesis" (7)." The analyst's neutrality forbids him/her from taking sides with any norms and rather than defending or attacking these norms, it is the analyst's role to expose their incidence in the subject's history. He also took aim at the psychoanalytic field's increasing emphasis on biology in specifying sexual difference and in the application of a developmental telos in framing the subject, furiously writing that "if that is what psychoanalysis is, there is precisely nothing that could be further from psychoanalysis in its whole development, its entire inspiration and its mainspring, in everything it has contributed, everything it has been able to confirm for us in anything we have established" (7).

Lacan's theory of unconscious desire specifies the primacy of desire over the fundamentally secondary nature of sex acts, gender relations and sexual orientation. I propose that it is one of the strongest anti-normative psychoanalytic conceptual tools available to queer theorists (Watson 2009; Dean 2000). Desire is indicated by *objet a,* an expressly Lacanian concept circumscribing a radical lack that is constituted at the level of the body, a causal gap that is anterior to the advent of the symbolic chain of language. It falls outside of the field of representation and is literally what falls outside of the mirror-image during the first assumption by the child of the identity "I" in the mirror. This sex-less and non-gendered object cause of desire is ultimately ungraspable.[5] How subjects position themselves in relation to

---

5   The partial drive-ridden *objet a* is a nucleus or kernel of the Real that founds the gap in which desire is constituted. We come into being as desiring beings in the gap of what we lack. Lacan states that "this object ought to be

the object cause of desire and to *jouissance* entails a process of identification which Lacan (1999[1972–73])) calls "sexuation" (78–89). The positing of the existence of unconscious desire is the "queerest" of psychoanalytic concepts as Lacan's subject of desire, founded by the *objet a*, moves beyond Freud's notion of object-choice by leaving gender out of it. In this, Lacan effectively frees desire from normative heterosexuality — that is from the pervasive assumption that all desire, even same-sex desire is heterosexual in so far as it flows across both masculine and feminine positions (Watson 2009). That is what Lacan (1999[1972–73]) means by his assertion that "when one loves it has nothing to do with sex" (25). Thus, as Dean (2000) puts it, it is because the psychoanalytic alignment of sex with the unconscious makes sexuality refractive, non-adaptive and also perverse that it is likely to be of interest to queer theory (244).

Adding to this, sexuality for Lacan is of the order of the Real, which destines it to limits, impasses and dead ends in acceding to symbolic mediation.[6] The Symbolic is interposed on the Real which mediates the traumatic effects of sex and the Real of the drive, meaning that we emerge "languaged" but paying the price of separation from "being" and the Real of sex and the body which are destined thereafter to remain "extimate." This Real of sex, this sexual unconscious, is key to Lacan's (1999[1972–73]) axiomatic principle: "there is no such thing as a sexual relationship" (57) meaning there is no stable basis, no relation of oneness and rapport possible between men and women and the reason for this is the absence of any singular signifier of difference

---

conceived by us as the cause of desire […] and the object is *behind* desire" (*Book X: Anxiety,* Session 16 January 1963, 2).

6   In Lacanian psychoanalysis, the three orders of the Real, Imaginary, and Symbolic make up realm of human subjectivity. The Real is outside of representation, the Symbolic is the order of language and symbols, and the Imaginary is the order of the image. Symbolic mediation, which is speech and language, offers distance from the Real and mediates its effects in ways that the narcissistic image cannot. This traumatic Real, which is the part of the drive that cannot be represented, takes a leaf out of the Freudian unconscious by constantly undermining all sexual and social identities (see Lacan 1999[1972–73], 95).

between the sexes which would make gender identification stable. Thus the Real constantly undermines and resists adaptation and is stubbornly recalcitrant to all norms (Dean 2000, 244).

The absence of a sexual relation or "non-rapport" between men and women explains why culture does not function smoothly. Every culture has a strategy for managing sexual difference and providing self-identities and facilitating different ways of mutual interdependence with other subjects and the objects of their desire. Ultimately, the lack in the sexual relation calls for a social link with myriad denials and quests that encircle it (Ragland 2002, 252). Queer theory, none the least in its contributions to this collection, helps to reveal these denials and quests by refracting dominant socio-cultural ideological trends, points of impasse and knotty bifurcations in the big Other of contemporary sexuality that render certain subjects as "normal" and "natural." Queer theory, in its resistance to definition and in the ubiquity of its application, symptomatizes how sex and desire elude language. Lisa Duggan's (1992) description of queer captures this idea. She writes that rather than an identificatory position per se; queer seeks a positionality *vis-à-vis* the normative and attempts to offer "the promise of new meanings, new ways of thinking and acting politically — a promise sometimes realized, sometimes not" (11).

The impossible nature of sexuality's reducibility to language and writing emerges in *Clinical Encounters in Sexuality* not only in the uneasy relationship between clinical psychoanalysis and queer theory, but in the *lacunae* revealed in any encounter between sexuality and discourse. Our light-handed editorialization of the chapters leaves in unadulterated points of alignment as well as theoretical, conceptual and discursive discontinuities. This is designed to refract rather than disguise the points of non-encounter between the two disciplines, and between sexuality and its writing. This locates this project, to invoke Foucault (1981), in a practice that "understood like this does not reveal the universality of a meaning but brings to light the action of an imposed scarcity" (73). Throughout the book, sexuality is shown to be irreducible to a writing and something always slips away and remains ungraspable. To put this another way, "the sexual relationship doesn't stop not being written," (Lacan 1999[1972–73], 94). The fact that we are speaking-beings makes sexuality impossible to reduce to discourse, language and a sexual encounter between two people. It always remains outside (it "exists") which has the effect of causing us to talk and write about it *ad infinitum*. In figuring rather than configuring the gaps and oppositions that inevitably ensue when sex and writing come together, *Clinical Encounters in Sexuality* follows a logic of difference that aims at opening up rather than closing down.

Conclusion

Does this book succeed in opening up and "queering" the pitch of contemporary sexuality? I think it does. The queer theory chapters proffer a significant engagement with contemporary thinking on sexuality, notwithstanding that psychoanalysts have been turning to and resonating with queer theory since the 1990s (Drescher 2008, 452). In engaging with and challenging the wide field of normalization through a critical engagement with intersectionality, queer theory offers a frame for psychoanalysts to explore and critically assess the crucial facets of culture and society that impinge on the clinic, and by extension hold a spotlight to their own positions and assess biases and areas of unease in matters sexual. As Jack Drescher puts it, "the history of psychoanalytic attitudes towards homosexuality reinforces the impression that psychoanalytic theories cannot be divorced from the political, cultural, and personal contexts in which they are formulated" (452). Some of the psychoanalytic responses in this book show anxiety and apprehension about the queer provocations, indicating that homosexuality, "queerness" and the non-normative continue to provoke and cause unease.

In this collection, "queer" as a signifier rooted in prejudice is reworked to return the "gays/gaze" to psychoanalytic discourses with the aim of challenging and ultimately overturning prejudice. I suggest that this would benefit from more working-through and mourning on both sides. Some analysts take this up by reflecting on the fact that for all of its centralization of sexuality in human life, theory and practice, sexuality has fallen out of favor in the clinic. Hinshelwood, for example, decries that in Kleinian psychoanalysis "the psychoanalysis of sexuality has become secondary, or at least contingent on the analysis of narcissism, personal identity, and the relatedness to others." Nobus similarly asserts that contemporary (Lacanian) psychoanalysis "risks becoming sexually illiterate" if it doesn't become more wide-ranging and contemporary. A question of normativity is suggested in tendencies towards categorization in published material. Psychoanalytic approaches to transsexuality, for example, are characterized by a dearth of vignettes and those that appear tend to categorize it broadly in terms of psychosis and its intractability and untreatability (Limentani 1979; Safouan 1980; Millot 1990), which Gherovici, Kaplan and Stryker go some way to addressing. In this, queer theory's accusation of a nascent conservatism in psychoanalysis hits a mark and is a reminder of the necessity for psychoanalytic clinicians to continue to engage with and challenge the wide field of normalization.

In its most fundamental formulations, I agree with Tim Dean (2000) that "psychoanalysis is a queer theory" (268), even if its history has not always supported that. Psychoanalysis can proffer a theorization of models of normativity and challenge them to theorists, activists and clinicians who are interested in effecting social change. While social change is not the express aim of psychoanalysis, its interrogation of norms as a function of the organization and "civilization" of the drives, and as a mode of historically and socially organizing "difference," provides a tool for conceiving of norms as contingent, contestable and changeworthy. Thus I hope this collection functions as a reference and study text for analysts and clinical trainees, and as a teaching text for academics and students of queer theory and sexuality studies.

It is laudable that this collection is characterized by more than just conflict. There is enough common ground and shared history to dialogue and disagree and deepen the commitment to putting normativity under the microscope. Psychoanalysis and queer theory would agree that the Freudian Oedipal model is insufficient to explain the varieties of social relations today. The question of conflict is related to the question of the super-ego and is something to be alert to. Where, Jacqueline Rose asks in her chapter, is the superego in queer thinking? This is also broached by Bob Hinshelwood. In this book, it is projected into the "normal" other, the boring ordinary other who doesn't enjoy and doesn't take absolute pleasure, in some ways the pessimistic other of psychoanalysis. This queer projection ends up being tautological and categorizing of psychoanalysis, in the calls for psychoanalysis to "loosen up" and be less "sober." It may be helpful to reflect on the dissimilarity of the question of difference and the question of binarization. All binaries are the refusal of the non-rapport which is Lacan's idea that the oneness and harmony promised by sexual union is inherently impossible. Thus binaries are attempts to suture over uncertainty, inexistence and impossibility with a frame of dichotomization, not a frame of difference. Incorporating difference involves accepting the non-compatibility of the other. Queer theory also aims to overturn and discredit binaries but it must work hard not to reintroduce other binaries, the most entrenched binary being of course the normative and the queer. To be attentive to difference is to sub-scribe to the sexual "non-rapport," which is the impossibility of any binary to solve the problem of sex.

For readers of this collection, I hope that the book's encoun-ters, which reveal a diversity of thought and practice, as well as deep wounds, disagreement and unease, are provocative and critically engaging. For new practices and thought to emerge, a process of working-though traumas, conflicts and denials must occur, as well as a commitment to a ceaseless practice of inter-rogation of key tenets and formulations; this to be done with a spotlight on the role and effect of the contemporary zeitgeist in contemporary thought and practices. This is why an interdisci-plinary engagement is so important, because it gives perspective on the discourses underlying the thought and practices of single disciplines, thereby opening up the space for reflection. Without that, the ground for critical interrogation and the possibilities for the creative and new are precluded. An aim of this book, with the help of its readers, is to plough the furrow of possibility of what has yet to be thought and said in the complicated and contested field of human sexuality.

Works Cited

American Psychiatric Association. *Diagnostic and Statistical Manual of Mental Disorders (DSM-I)*. 1st ed. Washington, DC: American Psychiatric Publishing, 1952. http://www.turkpsikiyatri.org/arsiv/dsm-1952.pdf.

———. *Diagnostic and Statistical Manual of Mental Disorders (DSM-II)*. 2nd ed. Washington, DC: American Psychiatric Press, 1968. http://www.behaviorismandmentalhealth.com/wpcontent/uploads/2015/08/DSM-II.pdf.

———. *Diagnostic and Statistical Manual of Mental Disorders (DSM-III)*. 3rd ed. Washington, DC: American Psychiatric Press; 1980. https://onedrive.live.com/?authkey=%21ALHE Nu8RgKc%5Fsqc&cid=8115CF12F325A558&id=8115CF12F32 5A558%2135164&parId=8115CF12F325A558%2134949&o=O neUp.

Bergler, Edmund. *Counterfeit-Sex: Homosexuality, Impotence and Frigidity*. 2nd ed. New York: Grune and Stratton, 1958.

———. "Eight Prerequisites for the Psychoanalytic Treatment of Homosexuality." *Psychoanalytic Review* 31 (1944): 253–86.

Bieber, Irving, et al. *Homosexuality: A Scientific Study of Male Homosexuals*. New York: Basic Books, 1962.

———. "A Critique of the Libido Theory." *American Journal of Psychoanalysis* 18 (1958): 52–65.

Dean, Tim. *Beyond Sexuality*. Chicago: The University of Chicago Press, 2000.

Drescher, Jack. "A History of Homosexuality and Organized Psychoanalysis." *Journal of the American Academy of Psychoanalysis and Dynamic Psychiatry* 36, no. 3 (2008): 443–60.

Duggan, Lisa. "Making it Perfectly Queer?" *Socialist Review* 22, no. 1 (1992): 11–31.

Elliot, Patricia. *Debates in Transgender, Queer, and Feminist Theory.* Surrey & Burlington: Ashgate Press, 2010.

Foucault, Michel. "The Order of Discourse." In *Untying the Text: A Post-Structuralist Reader,* ed. Robert Young, 51–78. Boston: Routledge and Keegan Paul, 1981.

Freud, Sigmund. "On Beginning the Treatment" (1913). *The Standard Edition of the Complete Psychological Works of Sigmund Freud,* vol. 7, trans. James Strachey in collaboration with Anna Freud and assisted by Alix Strachey and Alan Tyson, 121–44. 1953; rpt. London: Vintage, 2001.

———. "Three Essays on the Theory of Sexuality" (1905). *The Standard Edition of the Complete Psychological Works of Sigmund Freud,* vol. 7, trans. James Strachey in collaboration with Anna Freud and assisted by Alix Strachey and Alan Tyson, 123–245. 1953; rpt. London: Vintage, 2001.

———. *The Interpretation of Dreams* (1900). *The Standard Edition of the Complete Psychological Works of Sigmund Freud,* vols. 4–5, trans. James Strachey in collaboration with Anna Freud and assisted by Alix Strachey and Alan Tyson. 1953; rpt. London: Vintage, 2001.

Frosh, Stephen. *For and Against Psychoanalysis.* 2nd ed. London and New York: Routledge, 2006.

———. *The Politics of Psychoanalysis: An Introduction to Freudian and Post-Freudian Theory.* London: Macmillian Press, 1999.

Gherovici, Patricia. *Please Select Your Gender: From the Invention of Hysteria to the Democratizing of Transgenderism.* New York and London: Routledge, 2010.

Greenson, Ralph. "On Homosexuality and Gender Identity." *International Journal of Psycho-Analysis* 45 (1964): 217–19.

Hartmann, Heinz. *Essays on Ego Psychology.* New York: International Universities Press, 1964.

———. *Ego Psychology and the Problem of Adaptation.* New York: International Universities Press, 1961.

Hartmann, Heinz, Ernst Kris, and Rudolf Loewenstein. "Notes on the Theory of Aggression." *The Psychoanalytic Study of the Child* 3/4, (1949): 9–36.

———. "Comments on the Formation of Psychic Structure." *The Psychoanalytic Study of the Child* 2 (1946): 11–38.

Lacan, Jacques. *Book XXIV: Love is the Failure of the Unconscious* (1976–77), private trans. Dan Collins, 2012.

———. *Book XX: Encore: On Feminine Sexuality. The Limits of Love and Knowledge* (1972–73), ed. Jacques-Alain Miller, trans. Bruce Fink. New York and London: Norton, 1999.

———. *Book XVII: The Other Side of Psychoanalysis* (1969–70), trans. Russell Grigg. W. W. Norton and Co.: London, 2007.

———. *Book III: The Psychoses* (1955–56), ed. Jacques-Alain Miller. London: Routledge, 2000.

———. "Guiding Remarks for a Convention on Female Sexuality" (1958). In *Écrits,* trans. Bruce Fink. London: W.W. Norton and Co., 2006.

———. *Book X: Anxiety* (1962–63), private trans. Cormac Gallagher.

Limentani, Adam. "The Significance of Transsexualism in Relation to Some Basic Psychoanalytic Concepts." *International Review of Psycho-Analysis* 6 (1979): 139–53.

Millot, Catherine. *Horsexe: Essays on Transsexuality.* Trans. K. Hylton. New York: Autonomedia, 1990.

Nierenberg, Ona. "A Hunger for Science: Psychoanalysis and the Gay Gene." *Gender and Psychoanalysis* 4, no. 2 (1999): 105–41.

O'Connor, Noreen and Joanna Ryan. *Wild Desires and Mistaken Identities.* London: Karnac Books, 1993.

Rado, Sandor. *Adaptational Psychodynamics.* 1969; rpt. New York: Jason Aronson, 1995.

Ragland, Ellie. "How the Fact That There is No Sexual Relation Gives Rise to Culture." In *The Subject of Lacan: A Lacanian Reader for Psychologists,* eds. Kareen R. Malone and Stephen Freidlander, 251–64. Albany: State University of New York Press, 2000.

Roudinesco, Elisabeth. *Jacques Lacan.* New York: Columbia University Press, 1997.

Roughton, Ralph. "The International Psychoanalytic Association and Homosexuality." *Journal of Gay and Lesbian Mental Health* 7, no. 1 (2008): 189–96.

———. "Rethinking Homosexuality: What it Teaches Us about Psychoanalysis." *Journal of the American Psychoanalytic Association* 50 (2002): 733–63.

Safouan, Moustapha. "Contribution to the Psychoanalysis of Transsexualism." In *Returning to Freud: Clinical Psychoanalysis in the School of Lacan,* ed. and trans. Stuart Schneiderman, 195–212. New Haven: Yale University Press, 1980.

Socarides, Charles. *The Preoedipal Origin and Psychoanalytic Therapy of Sexual Perversions.* Madison: International Universities Press, 1988.

———. "Advances in the Psychoanalytic Theory and Therapy of Male Homosexuality." In *Sexual Deviation,* 3rd ed., ed. I. Rosen, 252–78. 1964; rpt. Oxford: Oxford University Press, 2003.

———. "The Function of Moral Masochism: With Special Reference to the Defense Processes." *International Journal of Psychoanalysis* 39 (1958): 587–97.

Verhaeghe. Paul. *New Studies of Old Villians: A Radical Reconsideration of the Oedipus Complex.* New York: Other Press: 2009.

Watson, Eve. "Touching the Void: A Psychoanalytic Critique of the Encounter Between Psychoanalysis and Lesbian Sexuality." Doctoral Dissertation. University College Dublin, 2011.

———. "Queering Psychoanalysis/Psychoanalysing Queer." *Annual Review of Critical Psychology* 7 (2009). http://www.discourseunit.com/arcp/7.htm.

Mark J. Blechner is a psychologist and psychoanalyst in New York City. He has published three books: *Hope and Mortality* (1997); *The Dream Frontier* (2001); and *Sex Changes: Transformations in Society and Psychoanalysis* (2009). At the William Alanson White Institute, he is Training and Supervising Psychoanalyst. He is the former Editor-in-Chief of the journal *Contemporary Psychoanalysis*. As Founder and Director of the White Institute's HIV Clinical Service (1991–2001), he led the first psychoanalytic clinic devoted to working with people with AIDS, their relatives and caregivers. He has taught at Columbia University, Yale University and New York University.

Ken Corbett is Assistant Professor of Psychology at the New York University Postdoctoral Program in Psychotherapy and Psychoanalysis. He is the author of *Boyhoods: Rethinking Masculinities,* and *A Murder over a Girl.*

Olga Cox Cameron is a psychoanalyst in private practice in Dublin, Ireland for the past twenty-nine years. She lectured in psychoanalytic theory and also in psychoanalysis and literature at St Vincent's University Hospital and Trinity College Dublin from 1991 to 2013 and has published numerous articles on these topics in national and international journals. She is the founder of the Irish Psychoanalytic and Film Festival (annually since 2010). The theme for 2017 is "Psychoanalysing Documentary."

Tim Dean is Professor of English at the University of Illinois, Urbana–Champaign. He has published widely on psychoanalysis, sexuality, and queer theory. His most recent books are *Unlimited Intimacy: Reflections on the Subculture of Barebacking* (University of Chicago Press, 2009) and, as co-editor, *Porn Archives* (Duke University Press, 2014).

Lisa Downing is Professor of French Discourses of Sexuality at the University of Birmingham, UK. She is the author of numerous books, articles and chapters on sexuality and gender studies and critical theory. Her book-length publications include: *Desiring the Dead: Necrophilia and Nineteenth-Century French Literature* (Oxford European Humanities Research Centre, 2003); *Perversion: Psychoanalytic Perspectives/Perspectives on Psychoanalysis* (co-edited with Dany Nobus, Karnac, 2006); *The Cambridge Introduction to Michel Foucault* (Cambridge University Press, 2008); *Queer in Europe: Contemporary Case Studies* (co-edited with Robert Gillett, Ashgate, 2011); *The Subject of Murder: Gender, Exceptionality, and the Modern Killer* (University of Chicago Press, 2013); and *Fuckology: Critical Essays on John Money's Diagnostic Concepts* (co-authored with Iain Morland and Nikki Sulllivan, University of Chicago Press, 2015). She is currently editing a book on Foucault's afterlives for Cambridge University Press and writing a monograph on gender and selfishness.

Lara Farina is Associate Professor of English at West Virginia University and co-editor of *postmedieval: a journal of medieval cultural studies*. She is the author of *Erotic Discourse in Early English Religious Writing* (Palgrave Macmillan, 2006), as well as articles on medieval women's reading practices and queer approaches to the history of sexuality. Her recent research focuses on sensory histories, tactile experience, and bodily reconfiguration.

L.O. Aranye Fradenburg is Professor of English and Comparative Literature and the Founder of the Specialization in Literature and the Mind at the University of California, Santa Barbara. She is also a Faculty Member at the New Center for Psychoanalysis in Los Angeles, where she teaches classes on sexuality and infant observation, and is a Clinical Member of the THRIVE Infant-Family Program in Los Angeles. She has a private practice in Santa Barbara. Her latest book is *Staying Alive: A Sur-*

vival Manual for the Liberal Arts, published by punctum books in 2013.

Stephen Frosh is Pro-Vice-Master and Professor in the Department of Psychosocial Studies at Birkbeck College, University of London. He is the author of many books and papers on psychosocial studies and on psychoanalysis, including *Psychoanalysis outside the Clinic* (Palgrave, 2010); *Hate and the Jewish Science: Anti-Semitism, Nazism and Psychoanalysis* (Palgrave, 2005); *For and Against Psychoanalysis* (Routledge, 2006); *After Words* (Palgrave, 2002); and *The Politics of Psychoanalysis* (Palgrave, 1999). His most recent books are *Hauntings: Psychoanalysis and Ghostly Transmissions* (Palgrave, 2013) and *A Brief Introduction to Psychoanalytic Theory* (Palgrave, 2012).

Judy Gammelgaard is a Training Analyst and a member of the Danish Psychoanalytic Society and of the International Psychoanalytical Association. She is Professor and Head of the Centre of Psychoanalysis at the Department of Psychology, University of Copenhagen and lectures widely throughout Scandinavia. Her book, *Betweenity: A Discussion of the Concept of Borderline,* was published by Routledge in 2010.

Abe Geldhof is a Psychoanalyst and a Doctor of Clinical Psychology at Ghent University, Belgium. He wrote a PhD on Jacques Lacan's theory concerning the status of *jouissance* in psychosis.

Patricia Gherovici is a psychoanalyst and analytic supervisor, senior member and faculty at Apres-Coup Psychoanalytic Association, New York. She is co-founder and director of the Philadelphia Lacan Group and Associate Faculty, Psychoanalytic Studies Minor, University of Pennsylvania (PSYS). Her books include *The Puerto Rican Syndrome* (Other Press, 2003); *Please Select Your Gender: From the Invention of Hysteria to the Democratizing of Transgenderism* (Routledge, 2010); *Psychoanalysis Needs a Sex Change: Lacanian Approaches to Sexual and Social Difference* (Routledge, 2016); and (with Manya Steinkoler)

Lacan On Madness: Madness, Yes You Can't (Routledge, 2015). She co-edited with Manya Steinkoler, *Lacan, Psychoanalysis and Comedy* which is published by Cambridge University Press.

Noreen Giffney works as a psychoanalytic psychotherapist in private practice. She is Lecturer in Counselling in the School of Communication at the University of Ulster in Northern Ireland. She has published extensively on psychoanalysis, gender and sexuality studies and cultural studies, including the books: *Queering the Non/Human* (2008); *The Ashgate Research Companion to Queer Theory* (2009); *The Lesbian Premodern* (2011); *Theory on the Edge: Irish Studies and the Politics of Sexual Difference* (2013); and *Twenty-First Century Lesbian Studies* (2007). She is particularly interested in the writings of the psychoanalyst Wilfred Bion and has written a number of journal articles on the importance of his work for clinical practice. She is currently writing on the development of clinical insight using non-clinical case studies in psychoanalysis and psychotherapy. She convenes Psychoanalysis+, an interdisciplinary initiative that brings together clinical, artistic and academic approaches to, and applications of, psychoanalysis.

R.D. Hinshelwood is Professor Emeritus in the Centre for Psychoanalytic Studies, University of Essex, and previously Clinical Director, The Cassel Hospital, London. He is a Fellow of the British Psychoanalytical Society, and a Fellow of the Royal College of Psychiatrists. He spent many years working in therapeutic communities, and writing about them, including the book *What Happens in Groups* (1987), and he founded the *International Journal of Therapeutic Communities* in 1980. He has authored *A Dictionary of Kleinian Thought* (1989) and other books and articles on Kleinian psychoanalysis. *Observing Organisations* (2000) was edited with Wilhelm Skogstad and is among a number of texts on psychoanalytic applications to social science. In 2004, he published *Suffering Insanity,* a book on schizophrenia in psychiatric institutions. He founded *The British Journal of Psychotherapy* and *Psychoanalysis and History.* He recently published *Research on the Couch: Single Case Studies, Subjectivity and Psychoanalytic Knowledge* (2013); and a jointly edited book, with Nuno Torres, called *Bion's Sources: The Shaping of his Paradigms* (2013).

Ami Kaplan is a psychoanalyst in New York City. She received her MSW from New York University and her psychoanalytic training from the Psychoanalytic Psychotherapy Study Center. Her work has centered on gay, lesbian and transgender individuals. She has been active as a supervisor, lecturer, consultant and clinician with several New York City agencies involved in serving the LGBT community, particularly in those affected by HIV/AIDS. These agencies include "Body Positive," GMHC (Gay Men's Health Crisis), The Bedford Stuyvesant Community Mental Health Center HIV unit, PFLAG (Parents and Friends of Lesbians and Gays) and the New York City HIV Prevention Planning Group. Ami has been a Lecturer at the NYU School of Social Work. Her current clinical work focuses on transgender individuals. She is a member of the Policy and Procedures Committee of the World Professional Association for Transgender Health. She is involved in writing on resilience and transgender personality development.

Claudette Kulkarni is a retired Jungian psychotherapist. For the last nine years of her career, she worked in the Forensic Unit of Mercy Behavioral Health, Pittsburgh, PA, USA. Her previous experiences include nearly fifteen years, first as a Clinical Therapist and later as a Supervisor, at Persad Center, Pittsburgh (a community mental health center serving the LGBT community) where she had responsibility for the Transgender Team, as well as eleven years at the Women's Center of Beaver County, Beaver, PA (working with victims of domestic violence and adult survivors of childhood abuse). She was awarded her PhD in Depth Psychology from The Union Institute and the University, Cincinnati, Ohio. Among her publications are *Lesbians and Lesbianisms: A Post-Jungian Perspective* (Routledge, 1997); "Radicalizing Jungian Theory," a chapter in *Contemporary Perspectives* *on Psychotherapy and Homosexualities* (Free Association Press, 1998); and "The Whole Person: A Paradigm for Integrating the Mental & Physical Health of Trans Clients," co-authored with Sheila Kirk, MD, in *The Handbook of Lesbian, Gay, Bisexual, and Transgender Public Health: A Practitioner's Guide to Service* (ed. M. Shankle, Harrington Park, 2006).

Alice Kuzniar is Professor of German and English at the University of Waterloo, Canada. She taught at the University of North Carolina, Chapel Hill, USA for twenty-five years. For *Delayed Endings: Nonclosure in Novalis and Hölderlin* (University of Georgia Press, 1987) she won the South Atlantic Modern Language Association Award. She edited *Outing Goethe and His Age* (Stanford University Press, 1996) and authored *The Queer German Cinema* (Stanford University Press, 2000) as well as *Melancholia's Dog: Reflections on Our Animal Kinship* (University of Chicago Press, 2006). She has held invited guest professorships at Princeton University, Rutgers University and the University of Minnesota. *The Birth of Homeopathy Out Of the Spirit of Romanticism* will appear with the University of Toronto Press in 2017.

Ann Murphy is a clinical psychologist, psychoanalytic psychotherapist and visual artist. She is Clinical Lecturer in Psychiatry at Trinity College Dublin, where she was a founder and Director of the MSc in Psychoanalytic Psychotherapy. She lectures on psychoanalysis, particularly on the work of Melanie Klein and Wilfred Bion, on postgraduate courses at Trinity College Dublin and St Vincent's University Hospital Dublin, and is a training analyst and clinical supervisor. She has a private practice in Dublin. She recently published a piece on her solo exhibition, *Transitional/Transitive* (Dublin Castle, Ireland, 2012), in *The Winnicott Tradition,* eds. Margaret Boyle Spelman and Frances Thomson-Salo (Karnac, 2015).

Ona Nierenberg is a psychoanalyst in private practice in New York City and a Senior Psychologist at Bellevue Hospital Center, where she was Director of HIV Psychological Services for thirteen years. She is also a Clinical Instructor in the Department of Psychiatry at New York University Langone Medical Center, a member of Après-Coup Psychoanalytic Association, New York and an Overseas Member of APPI. She has published articles on psychoanalysis, sexuality and the discourse of science, as well as on licensing and the question of lay analysis. Among her current interests are the history of psychoanalysis, psychoanalytic institutionalization and transmission, and fate and chance.

Dany Nobus is Pro-Vice-Chancellor for External Relations and Professor of Psychology and Psychoanalysis at Brunel University London, where he also directs the MA Programme in Psychoanalysis and Contemporary Society. In addition, he is the Chair of the Freud Museum London. He is the author, most recently, of *Knowing Nothing, Staying Stupid: Elements for a Psychoanalytic Epistemology* (with Malcolm Quinn), and he has contributed numerous papers on the history, theory and practice of psychoanalysis to academic and professional journals.

Noreen O'Connor practices in North London (Perspectives Psychotherapy). She has served on the training committees of a number of psychoanalytic trainings. She has contributed as a lecturer, supervisor, and training analyst alongside her supervision of qualified analysts. She has lectured publicly and in universities in Britain and Ireland and publishes widely on psychoanalysis, philosophy, gender, and sexuality. She is co-author (with Joanna Ryan) of *Wild Desires and Mistaken Identities: Lesbianism and Psychoanalysis* (Karnac, 2003) and (with Mary Lynne Ellis) *Questioning Identities: Philosophy in Psychoanalytic Practice* (Karnac, 2010).

Carol Owens is a psychoanalyst and psychoanalytic supervisor in private practice in North Dublin. She has lectured on programmes in psychoanalytic studies at Trinity College Dublin, Dublin City University, and Independent College Dublin. She is a registered practitioner member of the Association for Psychoanalysis and Psychotherapy in Ireland and convener of the Dublin Lacan Study Group. She edited *The Letter: Lacanian Perspectives on Psychoanalysis* from 2003–2006, the *Annual Review of Critical Psychology* on Jacques Lacan and Critical Studies in 2009, and has served on the editorial board of *Teoria, critica y psicologia* since its inception. She has presented her work at numerous conferences, workshops and seminars and has published articles and book chapters on Lacanian practice, Lacan and subjectivity, Lacan and Žižek, and encounters between Lacanian theory, critical psychology and critical management theory. She is the editor (with Stephanie Farrelly Quinn) of *Lacanian Psychoanalysis with Babies, Children, and Teenagers: Further Notes on the Child* (Karnac, 2017). Her current project is a book on clinical and cultural treatments of ambivalence.

Ian Parker is Professor of Management in the School of Management at the University of Leicester, Co-Director of the Discourse Unit (www.discourseunit.com) and a practicing psychoanalyst in Manchester. His books include *Lacanian Psychoanalysis: Revolutions in Subjectivity* (Routledge 2011), and six books in the series "Psychology after Critique" (Routledge, 2015).

Jacqueline Rose is internationally known for her writing on feminism, psychoanalysis, literature, and the Israeli–Palestinian conflict. Her books include *Sexuality in the Field of Vision* (1986; Verso Radical Thinkers, 2006); *The Haunting of Sylvia Plath* (1991); *States of Fantasy* (1996); *The Question of Zion* (2005); *The Last Resistance* (2007); *Proust Among the Nations — from Dreyfus to the Middle East* (2012). She is also the author of the novel *Albertine* (2001). *Women in Dark Times* was published by Bloomsbury in 2014. *Conversations with Jacqueline Rose* came out in 2010, and *The Jacqueline Rose Reader* in 2011. A regular writer for *The London Review of Books,* she is a co-founder of *Independent Jewish Voices* in the UK and a Fellow of the British Academy. She is Professor of Humanities at Birkbeck Institute for the Humanities, University of London.

Medb Ruane is a writer and psychoanalytic practitioner based in Dublin who works with a range of clients. Her particular research interests are creativity, psychoses and sexuality. She has published and broadcast widely on culture, politics and psychoanalysis, edited various psychoanalytic publications including *Lacunae* and *The Review*, lectured in Dublin Business School, Independent Colleges and guest lectured at third-level and other institutions in Ireland and elsewhere. Her academic works and research have been funded by the Irish Research Council/University College Dublin/GREP, Dublin Business School and The Arts Council. Medb has also worked as a columnist for *The Sunday Times, The Irish Times,* and *The Irish Independent,* written essays and think pieces on visual and literary culture, and contributed to TV, radio, online, and print media.

Michael D. Snediker is Associate Professor of English at Queen's University, Canada. He is the author of *Queer Optimism: Lyric Personhood and other Felicitous Persuasions* (University of Minnesota Press, 2008). His book, *Contingent Figure: Aesthetic Duress from Nathaniel Hawthorne to Eve Kosofsky Sedgwick,* is under advance contract with the University of Minnesota Press.

Kathryn Bond Stockton is Distinguished Professor of English and Associate Vice President for Equity and Diversity at the University of Utah. Her most recent books, *Beautiful Bottom, Beautiful Shame: Where "Black" Meets "Queer"* and *The Queer Child, or Growing Sideways in the Twentieth Century,* are published by Duke University Press and both were finalists for the Lambda Literary Award in LGBT Studies. In 2011, she taught at the School of Criticism and Theory at Cornell University, where she led a seminar on "Sexuality and Childhood in a Global Frame: Queer Theory and Beyond." In 2013, she was awarded the Rosenblatt Prize for Excellence, the highest honor granted by the University of Utah.

Will Stockton is Associate Professor of English at Clemson University and the editor of *Early Modern Culture.* He is the author of *Playing Dirty: Sexuality and Waste in Early Modern Comedy* (University of Minnesota Press, 2011), and the co-editor of *Sex before Sex: Figuring the Act in Early Modern England* (University of Minnesota Press, 2012) and *Queer Renaissance Historiography: Backward Gaze* (Ashgate, 2009).

Susan Stryker is Associate Professor of Gender and Women's Studies at the University of Arizona. She has worked at the intersections of queer, feminist and trans studies since the early 1990s.

Paul Verhaeghe is a psychoanalyst and a Professor of Clinical Psychology at Ghent University, Belgium. His published books include *Does the Woman Exist?* (1999), a comprehensive study of hysteria based on Sigmund Freud and Jacques Lacan; *Love in a Time of Loneliness* (2000) which became an international bestseller and was published in eight different languages; *Beyond Gender: From Subject to Drive* (2001), which is a reconsideration of the role of sexuality; *On Being Normal and Other Disorders: A Manual for Clinical Psychodiagnostics* (2004), which received the Goethe Award for Psychoanalytic Scholarship (2007) and is considered to be a psychoanalytic answer to the failure of the DSM; and *New Studies of Old Villains* (2009), which is a radical reconsideration of the Oedipus complex. He published *What about Me?* in 2013 and *Authority* in 2016. His contemporary research focuses on the so-called "new" forms of psychopathology.

Eve Watson is a psychoanalytic practitioner working in Dublin, Ireland. She also teaches on graduate programmes at Dublin universities and was director of the clinical MA in Psychoanalytic Psychotherapy at Independent College Dublin (2008–2015). Trained in the Lacanian psychoanalytic tradition, areas of special interest include theories of sexuality and gender, critical theory, film and cultural studies. She has published in journals including *Lacunae* (2015, 2013, 2012, 2010); *Psychoanalytische Perspectieven* (2015); *(Re)-Turn* (2013); *Open Letter: Negotiating* *the Bond of Social Poetics* (2012); the *Annual Review of Critical Psychology* (2009); *The Letter: Perspectives on Psychoanalysis* (2004, 2005, 2006). She has book chapters in congress proceedings of the *Paris Ecole de Psychanalyse des Forums du Champ Lacanian* (2011, 2009). She is currently writing on the discourse of transsexuality, and on psychoanalysis and the feminine. She is a registered practitioner member of the Association for Psychoanalysis and Psychotherapy in Ireland (APPI) and is the editor of *Lacunae,* the APPI International Journal of Lacanian Psychoanalysis.

Rob Weatherill is a practicing and supervisory analyst in Dublin for more than three decades. He is a member of the two psychoanalytic organizations in Dublin and holds the European Certificate in Psychotherapy. He has taught psychoanalytic theory and practice at University College Dublin, Trinity College Dublin, and the Milltown Institute of Philosophy and Theology. He has written several books: *Cultural Collapse* (Free Association Books, 1994); *The Sovereignty of Death* (Rebus Press, 1998); *The Death Drive: New Life for a Dead Subject* (ed., Rebus Press, 1999); *Our Last Great Illusion* (Inprint Academic, 2004); *Forgetting Freud: Is Psychoanalysis in Retreat?* (Academica Press, 2011); *The Anti-Oedipus Complex: Lacan, Cultural Theory and Postmodernism* (Routledge, 2017). He contributed a chapter to *Living Together* (eds. David Kennard and Neil Small, Quartet Books, 1997). He has written over thirty papers and articles in journals and other media, in Ireland and abroad.

Katrine Zeuthen is Associate Professor and a member of the board of the Centre of Psychoanalysis in the Department of Psychology at the University of Copenhagen, Denmark. She is a practicing child psychotherapist and a candidate in the Danish Psychoanalytic Society. Her research focuses on infantile sexuality and sexual trauma. Her most recent publications in English are: K. Zeuthen and M. Hagelskjær Jensen: "The Body Locked by a Lack of Meaning" in *Representing the Un-Representable;* K. Zeuthen and M. Hagelskjær Jensen, "Prevention of Child

Sexual Abuse — Analysis and Discussion of the Field" in *Journal of Child Sex Abuse*; K. Zeuthen, and J. Gammelgaard, "Infantile Sexuality — The Concept, Its History and Position in Contemporary Psychoanalysis" in *The Scandinavian Psychoanalytic Review*; K. Zeuthen, S. Holm Pedersen, and J. Gammelgaard, "Attachment and the Driving Force of Development: A Critical Discussion of Empirical Infant Research" in *The International Forum of Psychoanalysis*.

Made in the USA
Lexington, KY
10 August 2018